Implementing
LDAP

Mark Wilcox

Wrox Press Ltd. ®

Implementing LDAP

Reprinted Febuary 2000

Published by Wrox Press Ltd., Arden House, 1102 Warwick Road, Acocks Green, Birmingham, B27 9BH, UK
Printed in USA
ISBN 1-861002-21-1

Trademark Acknowledgements

Wrox has endeavored to provide trademark information about all the companies and products mentioned in this book by the appropriate use of capitals. However, Wrox cannot guarantee the accuracy of this information.

Credits

Author
Mark Wilcox

Contributing Author
Simon Robinson

Development Editor
Anthea Elston

Editors
Victoria Hudgson
Adrian Young

Technical Reviewers
Stephan Osmont
Rory Winston
Pete Rowley
Rob Weltman
Simon Robinson
Jonathan Pinnock
Gavin Smyth

Cover
Andrew Guillaume

Design/Layout
Tony Berry
Frances Olesch

Index
Andrew Criddle

Photo Credits
Gary Dean Photography
The Picture Place Inc.

Author Biography

Mark Wilcox is the web Administrator for the University of North Texas in Denton, Texas where he oversees general web development, manages UNT's distributed learning web servers and web security services, and is the LDAP guru. He writes the "LDAP Heavyweight" column for Netscape's *ViewSource* magazine at http://developer.netscape.com/viewsource and serves as the Netscape Directory Developer Champion. Any free time has he spends with his wife, Jessica.

Acknowledgements

First I must thank God, if for nothing else, the Earth didn't explode in the middle of me writing this book!

Second I must thank my parents Steve and Judy Wilcox for everything they did for their wacky son. And I have to mention my sister, Molly, well, because she's my sister. I'm sure she was good for something.

Third I must thank my wife Jessica, because without you, life ain't worth living.

Finally I must thank a whole bunch of people:

My boss, Dr. Maurice Leatherbury, who first asked me to look into LDAP to build an electronic student phonebook. (Did he know he'd end up with an LDAP guru?) My staff, Sharon Marek and Kenn Moffitt, with whom I'll go into battle any day. Dr. Mark Rorvig, who first gave a first year master's student more control over his web server than any professor probably should have done! Every teacher I have ever had – each passed on something. Anthea Elston, at Wrox Press, who OK'd this book. Victoria Hudgson and Adrian Young, also at Wrox – you couldn't get any better editors. And last but not least: Tim Howes, Mark Smith, Rob Weltman, Simon Robinson, Mike McKee and the rest of my reviewers.

I'm sure I left someone out, but that's only out of forgetfulness.

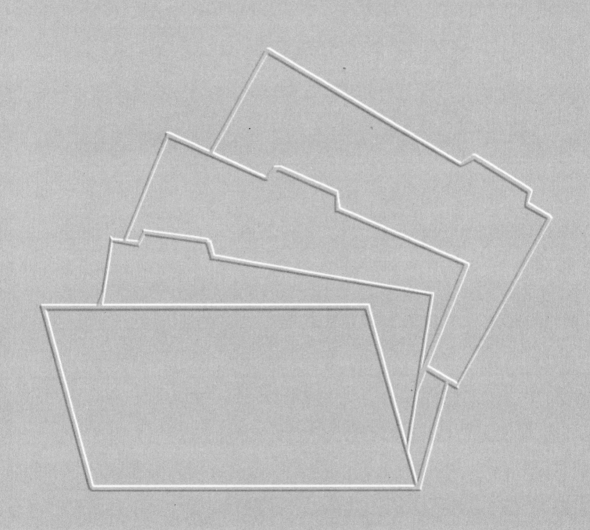

Table of Contents

Table of Contents

Table of Contents

Table of Contents

Table of Contents

Table of Contents

Introduction

Welcome to *Implementing LDAP*. In this book, we're going to cover many aspects of the Lightweight Directory Access Protocol (LDAP).

LDAP is the standard Internet directory access protocol. Directory services are vital to any organization. They are used to provide demographic data over the network – names, phone numbers, e-mail addresses and access control information. Most networks have at least one directory service, more likely two or three. LDAP is designed to replace all of those with a standard protocol that allows you to centrally manage your network assets. The major players – Microsoft, Novell, Sun and Netscape – all support LDAP in their core products.

In this book, you're going to learn exactly what LDAP is, how it came to be and why it is such an important cornerstone of the future of the Internet.

We'll discuss how to install an LDAP server, including details of two of the main servers currently available – Netscape's Directory Server version 4.0 and OpenLDAP. As part of this installation, we'll talk a bit about how to best build your Directory Information Tree, which is the database design of an LDAP server.

In the middle section of the book, we'll concentrate on building LDAP clients in a variety of languages. Whether if you're a C, Java or Perl programmer, we'll cover the variety of APIs for LDAP available in those languages. We'll also introduce the basics of Microsoft's ADSI. If you need to develop in a more esoteric language like PHP or Allaire's Cold Fusion, we also touch on how to implement LDAP with those languages. The final chapter of the book is a 'cookbook' of programs, which will illustrate the flexibility and versatility of LDAP.

The last section of the book has been designed to be a ready-reference for LDAP, including such things as a glossary, LDAP FAQ, references to the relevant RFCs and other such amenities, and a list of the main LDAP objects and attributes. This section ends with the presentation of an ongoing project demonstrating how you can use LDAP for tasks other than traditional directory services

If you've been interested in LDAP, but needed a guide to show you how to accomplish your LDAP dreams, then this is the book for you.

Who's This Book For?

This book is intended for programmers and system administrators who need to build LDAP clients and install LDAP servers. It likely will also appeal to that group of experienced web users who have heard about LDAP, but want a definitive reference on the subject. The book, like LDAP itself, has not been written with any specific programming language or operating system in mind, though it makes extensive use of one of the LDAP-enabled servers currently available – Netscape's Directory Server version 4.0.

What's Covered In This Book

- ❑ The reasoning behind a central, open standard directory access protocol and how LDAP meets the requirements
- ❑ The internals of LDAP, including the LDAP Data Interchange Format (LDIF)
- ❑ Detailed description of how to install and deploy an LDAP server
- ❑ Worked examples to browse and modify LDAP data in C, Perl, Java and Sun's JNDI
- ❑ An introduction to Microsoft's Active Directory Services Interface (ADSI)
- ❑ Brief overview of other available LDAP-enabled technologies such as PHP, Server-Side JavaScript and ColdFusion
- ❑ LDAP security and other advanced issues
- ❑ Real world applications demonstrating the flexibility and versatility of LDAP

What You Need To Use This Book

LDAP has been designed to be language-neutral and be accessible by all commonly used operating systems. However to get the most out of this book requires the installation of Netscape's Directory Server version 4.0. This application operates on the following platforms:

- ❑ Windows NT 4.0
- ❑ AIX 4.2, 4.2.1
- ❑ Digital Unix 4.0 (B, C, D, E)
- ❑ Reliant Unix 5.43
- ❑ HP-UX 11.0
- ❑ Solaris 2.5.1, 2.6
- ❑ Solaris 2.6

Note that Directory Server version 4.1 (in Beta at the time of writing) is also available for Linux (2.0.36).

You will also need:

- ❑ The Borland 5.x C compiler or Microsoft's Visual C++ 2.0 (or later) to run Netscape's C SDK and PerLDAP SDK. Note that a C compiler is NOT required for the alternative Perl LDAP SDK – Net::LDAP.
- ❑ Java Development Kit (JDK) version 1.1 (or later) to run Sun's JNDI and the Netscape Directory Java SDK.
- ❑ ADSI 2.5 can be downloaded from the Microsoft web site. To run the ADSI examples you need Visual Basic version 5 or later.

> Note: Since this book originally went to print, Microsoft has released Windows 2000, and with it Active Directory.

Conventions Used

We use a number of different styles of text and layout in the book to help differentiate between the different kinds of information. Here are examples of the styles we use and an explanation of what they mean:

> These boxes hold important, not-to-be forgotten, mission critical details which are directly relevant to the surrounding text.

Background information, asides and references appear in text like this.

❑ **Important Words** are in a bold type font.
❑ Words that appear on the screen, such as menu options, are in a similar font to the one used on screen, for example, the File menu.
❑ All filenames are in this style: Invoices.mdb.
❑ Function names look like this: OnUpdate().
❑ Code which is new, important or relevant to the current discussion, will be presented like this:

```
void main(String args[])
{
    System.out.println("Implementing LDAP");
}
```

❑ Whereas code you've seen before, or which has little to do with the matter at hand, looks like this:

```
void main(String args[])
{
    System.out.println("Implementing LDAP");
}
```

Tell Us What You Think

We have tried to make this book as accurate and enjoyable for you as possible, but what really matters is what the book actually does for you. Please let us know your views, whether positive or negative, either by returning the reply card in the back of the book or by contacting us at Wrox Press, using either of the following methods:

E-mail: feedback@wrox.com
Internet: http://www.wrox.com/

Source Code and Keeping Up-to-date

We try to keep the prices of our books reasonable and so to replace an accompanying disk, we make the source code for the book available on our web sites:

```
http://www.wrox.com/
```

The code is also available via FTP:

```
ftp://ftp.wrox.com
ftp://ftp.wrox.co.uk
```

If you don't have access to the Internet, then we can provide a disk for a nominal fee to cover postage and packing.

Errata & Updates

We've made every effort to make sure there are no errors in the text or the code. However, to err is human and as such we recognize the need to keep you informed of any mistakes as they're spotted and amended.

While you're visiting our web site, please make use of our *Errata* page that's dedicated to fixing any small errors in the book or, offering new ways around a problem and its solution. Errata sheets are available for all our books – please download them, or take part in the continuous improvement of our tutorials and upload a 'fix' or pointer.

For those without access to the Internet, call us on 1-800 USE WROX and we'll gladly send errata sheets to you. Alternatively, send a letter to:

Wrox Press Inc.,	Wrox Press Ltd,
1512 North Fremont,	1102 Warwick Road,
Suite 103	Acocks Green,
Chicago,	Birmingham,
Illinois 60622	B27 9BH
USA	UK

An Introduction to Directory Services

In this first chapter we will take a very general look at directory services – what they are and why we need them. We'll see how this works in practice, by taking an example of a typical organization, and finding out how things work with and without a centralized directory service. After that, we'll discover the importance of standards, and find out how proprietary standards compare with open ones.

In particular, this chapter will discuss:

- ❑ Directory Services in general
- ❑ Directory Services in a networked environment
- ❑ Problems relating to a lack of centralized directory management system
- ❑ Existing Directory Service implementations
- ❑ Standards and Directory Services

The Information Revolution

Ever since Roman times, when Caesar decreed that there should be a census of the land, people have been on a quest to gather and disseminate information about their fellow humans. The amount of data that has been gathered about people who live in the world today is somewhat scary. It's even more impressive (or scarier) to realize that the Information Revolution hasn't even reached its peak.

Of course, it is very difficult to run businesses without accumulating and managing information. The ability to ascertain meaningful information about a particular competitor, market or customer from a mound of data can be the difference between financial success and bankruptcy.

From Cavewalls to Science

When man first got the idea to start writing stuff down he did so on cave walls, clay tablets and papyrus. Eventually he got around to writing this stuff on paper. Once the printing press was invented, we got mass publication of books, magazines and newspapers. This information was gathered into collections that we call libraries (well libraries existed before the printing press, but not in great numbers). Since we have had the ability to create documents in electronic format, we have literally seen a data explosion, and we now augment this print media with audiovisual documents, as well like CDs and videotape. An entire educational discipline, Information Science, has sprouted up within the past 30 years to help manage access to this information on our computer systems. Information management has become big business in its own right.

We also live in the age of communication. The ability to communicate rapidly and reliably to many people (simultaneously if need be) is the nuclear reactor that powers the motors driving the information age. We would still be living in caves, hunting for saber-tooth tigers and foraging for berries if we couldn't communicate.

The Telephone, The Computer and The History of the 20th Century

Every major change in history has been the result of (or failure of) successful communication. This is not to say that every form of communication has to be the most advanced, but there is a correlation between the level of communication and the success of an operation. For instance, the Roman legions were able to conquer a large part of Europe and northern Africa using human messengers for communication – a primitive form of communication, but very useful for the Roman army nonetheless. The Muslim armies were able to take a large part of the known world in part because of their skill with the written word. The Chinese in the Middle Ages pioneered several discoveries that still amaze us today. Once again, a large part of their success was the ability to communicate effectively in print.

The success of the 20th Century has been shaped by its communications devices, the most successful of which is the telephone. Before the telephone, we had to communicate over long distances using very asynchronous means. There were smoke signals, mail services, telegraph, even tying messages to an arrow and shooting it into a distant tree. The beauty of the telephone is that it enables nearly synchronous communication, even over great distances, with a very simple, easy to use interface.

It's amazing to realize that the device I use to talk to my mom on every week is also the same device that helped prevent the Soviet Union and the United States from pushing the world into a nuclear holocaust, or that Roosevelt and Churchill used to help defeat Hitler in World War II. Don't forget that these same telephone lines also carry the majority of our data traffic from computers.

Computers are the second greatest marvel of the 20th century. Computers are very good at crunching numbers. This is no surprise when you think about it since the word "compute" really means "to figure out the answer to math problems." The original computers were large bulky machines that took up entire rooms and had the computational power of your average digital wrist watch. They used a system of vacuum tubes, punch cards and magnetic tape to run. In the 1960s we saw the creation of the transistor, which replaced the sizeable vacuum tubes with a much smaller, more reliable device.

Over the years, the computational and storage power of computers has gotten greater while they have become smaller. As computers progressed, both in terms of computing power and storage, they have taken on more complex (and peaceful) uses.

Without computers, it is difficult to imagine how we could have developed technologies such as communication satellites, supersonic flight and the rockets, which took man to the moon, not to mention microwave ovens, cellular phones and complex medical equipment. Modern civilization is dependent on computers.

Computers and the Information Age

Computers have also become very useful for storing information. They essentially store two types of information:

- ❏ Information about people – for example, address books, genealogical records and birthdays
- ❏ Information about things people do – for example, financial records, diaries of events and insurance records

Storing such information in a computer makes it easier to manage than traditional paper based systems and gives you more options on how you wish to display or disseminate the data.

Of course in today's computing world, nearly everyone who owns a computer also has a connection to the Internet. The primary purpose of getting online is not really to just look at the latest catchy web page, but to communicate with friends and work colleagues. All over the world, millions of e-mail messages are sent every day. Newsgroup postings are in the several tens of thousands. Chat rooms have blossomed like so many desert flowers after a summer storm. Marc Andreesen, the person who created Mosaic (the first graphical web browser) and later co-founded Netscape has been quoted as saying that the web is not the killer Internet application, but e-mail is.

The ability for people to quickly communicate to others, even thousands of miles away (heck, even in outer space), reliably, easily and cheaply has made the Internet that can be accessed by practically anyone. The fact that the phone companies went out of their way to try and wreck Internet telephone, even though Internet telephone wasn't even close to serviceable quality, is a sign that this communication device is revolutionary.

People are social creatures and as such they like to communicate. They like to communicate by talking with each other in person. They like to talk to each other over the telephone. People will write letters and send cards to each other. However, the important thing to remember is that people have a *need* to communicate. The *Information Age* is all about providing people with the means to communicate more effectively. The majority of countries in the world today conduct business in a market driven economy. They are trying to sell a product to a person or persons. Companies spend billions of dollars a year in trying to work out how to effectively encourage consumers to buy their products. One way companies try to market their wares is through direct marketing, where material is sent directly to the consumer usually in the form of a packet of mail. Examples of this type of junk mail are catalogs, brochures and letters. The people who receive this information have been selected because they meet a certain type of criteria.

Consumers or potential customers don't necessarily have to be someone living in a house. The potential market could also be other companies or organizations. As well as being in an active business market, people are also active in political and social organizations where they need to communicate with one another to get their agendas across.

What I am trying to get across is that there is a lot of communicating going along and this wouldn't be possible if people couldn't find other people to communicate with. The tools people use to find other people to communicate with are referred to as **directories**.

Introducing Directories

Let's start with a simple working definition of what a directory is:

> **Directories are specialized databases (both in print and electronic formats) that are designed to make it quick and easy to look up information.**

Directories can range from a stack of Post-It notes on the refrigerator to large volumes that list members of organizations. The most common example of a directory is the everyday telephone book. Essentially, a directory is just an item that provides essential contact information and is indexed, either by the name of a person or an organization. In today's world, the most basic information listed in a directory would be a telephone number. Often these directories will also include mailing addresses, fax numbers, leadership contact information for organizations, and now e-mail and web site addresses.

> *An index is a system that matches a particular item with its location in a database. This database can be electronic or physical. You find indexes just about everywhere. You will find one at the end of this book. You look up a topic and then you see the page numbers where that topic is discussed. This sure beats flipping through the entire book each time you want to find out something, doesn't it?*

Directories are a big business in the age of mass communication. As we have seen, computers play a big part in improving the means of communication. That is because computers now have the power to consume more data than any human being can enter. Sure you might fill up a hard-drive or two, but hard-drives are cheap, so you could say that computers contain an insatiable capacity for accumulating information.

Sometimes the information that is gathered and entered into our computers is for purposes that are useful for demographics or marketing reasons (that is, it has an immediate use). However, other data is stored without having any known use for it. Data like this needs to be organized in such a fashion that allows it can to be quickly accessed when it is finally needed. Organizing this personal information for later retrieval is the basis for developing electronic **directory services**.

Directory Services

Directory services provide access to data, much like a typical database does, but they do so in a manner that relies on the **attributes** of specific information that is organized. An organized collection of attributes that forms a single record of information is called a **directory entry**, often just referred to as simply an **entry**.

> **A directory service is a service (provided by a person or electronically) that allows you to access a database of information very quickly. This database is called a directory and the service describes how you interface to the directory.**

Attributes are the bits of a directory entry that describe the entry. They are like fields in a traditional database. For example, if you have an entry for a person, one of the attributes would be the last name.

A directory entry is akin to a record in a database. In fact, electronic directory services are just specialized databases. Attributes are used to help describe an entry in the directory by providing portions of information that complete the whole. Just like a molecule is made up by a collection of atoms, a directory entry is made up of a collection attributes. By themselves attributes have no real value, but as a whole in the context of a directory entry, they provide the necessary information to describe that entry.

Talking to a Directory Service

Any request that is asked of a directory service is based upon matching that request with a particular attribute or attributes in the entries contained within that directory. For example, if you wanted to find my telephone number, you'd ask the directory service, "Give me Mark Wilcox's telephone number". Now if you wanted to find out my mailing address you would say "Give me Mark Wilcox's mailing address". Finally if you wanted to see everything the directory service had on me, you would say "Give me everything on Mark Wilcox".

Obviously, in practice it won't be quite as easy as this, because most directory services we'll use are electronic based and don't understand natural human language. Instead, we'll use a **syntax** and a **protocol** to talk to the directory service. The syntax defines the language we should use to talk to the directory service and the protocol defines the rules we should follow when we talk to this service.

The name Mark Wilcox may have some value outside of the directory service, but the telephone number, 940-555-1234 would be meaningless without placing into the context of a directory entry for me. Thus `"name=Mark Wilcox"` and `"telephone number=940-555-1234"` becomes a useful way of answering the question "What's Mark Wilcox's phone number?".

Clients that access an electronic directory service are much more likely to read the information, than write to the server, so access is highly optimized for data lookup, rather than for data input. This means that directories will not usually contain sophisticated transaction controls and rollback features as you might find in a conventional database. Directory services are structured such that new information is either entered all at once or not at all. If you enter bad data, the only way to fix it will be either to correct the entry later or to delete it.

Ubiquitious Directory Services

Thanks to the telephone company, government regulation and an open publishing industry, directories in print have become very commonplace. They have even become ubiquitous enough that most of us take them for granted. Printed directory services are a common part of life and are fairly standardized, at least the most common ones, such as the phone books. Even directories that are not published by the telephone company, like church phone books, follow the same layout and setup of the common telephone book This has put the directory services tool in the hands of the average person and made the telephone the ubiquitous instrument that it is today.

Directory services work so well, we get pretty upset when we can't use them. However, despite the fact that we enjoy a standard directory service that contains the names, telephone numbers and addresses of everyone who owns a phone, there is not a common directory service for electronic communication.

One reason for this is the fact that the common business model in the computer industry is to avoid cross-compatibility, so that you can force people to buy copies of your software to be able to access data. It also has a lot to do with the difficulty of using a computer. Most software programs are not intuitive to the power user, much less the common user, so there's a lot of "dirty" data that has been stored which is nearly impossible to index.

Another reason why a common electronic directory service hasn't existed is that computers change so rapidly. The massive behemoths that comprised the early computer industry are now over-matched by the microchip in your common toaster. (Why you need a microchip in your toaster is a topic for another book.) Today's systems are so fast and powerful they are able to crunch data in ways that just encourages more data to be entered. The fact that improper planning probably means that the data is unmanageable always seems to fall by the wayside. Data entry that is unplanned and unmanaged is often useless for indexing (which is one of the reasons why searching the World Wide Web is really a fruitless endeavor from an information retrieval point of view).

A final contributing reason as to why we don't have a standardized common electronic directory services (in particular a common store for e-mail addresses and personal homepages) is that there is no central clearing house for the records.

The advent of the Internet and personal computers has led to a great deal of decentralized computing. Very little of the Internet is centrally managed and the same thing is true of personal computers. Anyone can get an e-mail address (actually addresses) very quickly and change them at will without having to call the 'e-mail company' first. If you want a standard telephone number, you get it through a central telephone company who then manages that number for you. Sometimes individual networks that have e-mail accounts provide directories for them in house, but often these directories are developed *ad hoc* and are often very kludgy. Thus there is no central repository of e-mail addresses from which to start, and there is not even a standard way of creating an e-mail address.

This is not say that there are not any public or commonly available electronic directory systems. On the web today, you can visit many sites that do provide the ability to search for people and businesses. Most of these services, however, are just providing a gateway service to a very large telephone book that they have purchased access to. These services are becoming a standard clearing house for e-mail addresses, where people can register their own addresses. Yet we still yearn for a more comprehensive system that is easily shared by all of our electronic systems.

The ability to look up personal information that directory services provide is often referred to as 'white pages' information (named after the white pages in the telephone book that lists similar information). However, electronic directory services can also provide a way to look up resources besides personal information. We live in a networked world that is made up of servers, personal workstations, printers, scanners, plotters, routers, modems, even distributed networked code. To successfully communicate in this bustling environment, we must be able to access all of these devices, and thus we need a directory of not just people, but things too.

Now, building directory services is not the kind of job that makes programmers or project managers drool in anticipation, yet this is exactly the kind of service that we need in our day-to-day lives – more than ever now that the Internet has opened up our 'virtual selves' to the world at large. Providing easy reliable electronic access to common directory information is going to transform the way we work and live in the next advancement of the communication age, the Networked Age.

Directory Services in Our Daily Lives

Directory services don't sound like a big deal until you think about how you could not function without them. In this section we are going to look at three common directory services used most in our daily lives. They are:

❑   Telephone Directory Service
❑   Television Show Listings Services
❑   Domain Naming Service for the Internet

The Telephone Directory Service

I have my mom's telephone number, my work number, my home number and few others scattered about in my brain. I can call any of these numbers from memory. However, there are many others that I cannot recall, such as my wife's work number, which provides no end to her grief! This is not that surprising because there are hundreds of thousands of phone numbers.

But there are solutions to this problem. I can look up the number in either the telephone book or by dialing a special phone number to the telephone company where I can ask for the number. Usually within minutes I can find the number to call. The layout of the phonebook and the database that stores this information is common to all locations throughout the world. This means two things. First, I don't have to learn a new 'interface' or page layout if I happen to be in a new city when I need to find a number. Secondly, it also means that I know what information I'll be required to provide when I switch phone companies.

The White Pages information in telephone books is collected and published at no cost to the telephone 'consumer', but to get listed in the Yellow Pages requires paying an extra fee. This is because they provide a different type of listing – whereas the white pages are simply listed by name, the Yellow Pages are listed by the service provided by a company or organization. Thus if you were new to a city and wanted to find a listing of all the Chinese take-out places in town, you would pick up the telephone book and head for the Yellow Pages. You would look for restaurants and then more specifically, Chinese take-out restaurants.

Both the white and yellow pages have a common indexing system to allow quick searches of people or services. This easy indexing system also makes it easy to load into a database so that telephone operators that work at the central phone company can provide the ability to look up phone numbers to any telephone that the phone company services.

Another reason why the telephone book is so popular is because each book is broken down for a particular region, generally by city. In the cases of large cities, the phonebook might even break down by sections of that particular city. What this does is make each telephone book manageable for the area that a particular customer is likely to use. Sure we know that we could call anyone in the world that has a telephone. Someday I might need to call someone who lives a 1000 miles away from me, but for that I'd rather call an operator, even if it cost me a small fee, than to be saddled with a telephone book that was the size of a small encyclopedia set. That's because most of the numbers that I'm going to call are going to someone in my local area. If I want Chinese take-out, I'm going to call the restaurant in my local city, not the Chinese restaurant 500 miles away.

The lowly telephone book is the gold standard because it is ubiquitous, easy to use and it provides the answers to our common questions. The fact that we have managed to have access to the thousands of phone numbers in the world in an organized fashion that anyone can use has not been lost on network professionals. In many ways, what we are looking to achieve with electronic directory services is to recreate the success of the common telephone directory.

Television Show Listings Services

The two most common forms of entertainment today are television and motion pictures. Thanks to satellites and cable, we now have several hundred possible television channels we can watch, each with their own lineup of the television shows. We would be hopelessly lost if we didn't have some sort of directory that we could consult to see what was on.

Television directories usually provide multiple points of access to help the potential viewer out. You can look up a show by time, channel, day of the week and title of the show. Because each channel will specialize in a particular format of content, this makes it easier for you to narrow your search.

For example, you might want to look for something on cable. You would focus your search by saying 'See what's on NBC?' and if the person who's looking up the information knows which channel is affiliated with the NBC network, they can lookup that channel and see what TV show is on. By specifying 'NBC' as a search parameter, you have substantially reduced the amount of data to be searched and hence the time taken to find what show you want.

Some TV listing services, like the magazine *TV Guide*, give the user the ability to not only see the name of the show, but also a synopsis of what the particular show is about. Perhaps TV listings services are not as essential or as vast as the telephone directory service, but they do constitute another examples of directory services.

Domain Name Service for the Internet

The Internet is the most popular phenomenon of the 1990s. Nothing else has changed the world in such a rapid fashion except for maybe the telephone in the early 1900s. One of the popular misconceptions is that the Internet has a physical existence, as if a building stood in New York City, right next to the United Nations, where a large computer sat beeping away, called THE INTERNET. Of course this is wrong.

The Internet is comprised up of thousands of networked computers and other hardware including personal computers, servers, mainframes, routers, cell phones, televisions, printers, heck, maybe even a toaster or two. To be on the Internet means that you are able to carry binary traffic to or from a central backbone network using the **Internet Protocol** (**IP**). Primarily, the **Transmission Control Protocol** (**TCP**) is the protocol we use to send much of what we use on the Internet. Common services like e-mail, web and news all use protocols that are based on TCP, which in turn uses IP to get back and forth. Thus, we usually just refer to TCP/IP as the Internet protocols. Another protocol, called **User Datagram Protocol** (**UDP**) is also used for applications like chat and streaming media. The difference between TCP and UDP is that TCP guarantees notification of delivery and order, while UDP does neither.

The Internet is made up of clients and servers. For example, a client makes a request to a web server for a web page. The web server receives the request and sends back the web page. The TCP part actually ensures that the messages passed back and forth are received intact. The Internet Protocol takes care of making sure that each computer can find every other. The way this is accomplished by making sure that each computer has a unique identification number called an **IP address**. This number is similar to a Social Security Number or a telephone number. An IP address is a number (up to, but not always 12 digits) that is divided up into four sets of three digits ranging from 0 to 255. Actually only a subset of these numbers are used so that there is a range that a network can use for testing.

Of course, most web users don't even know about IP addresses. Those who do hardly ever refer to their machines by them. Most people refer to a particular computer by a unique name, called a **fully qualified domain name** or **FQDN**. However, most people don't know these names either – they just refer to computers by particular names. An example of an FQDN is www.whitehouse.gov. As humans, if we want to access a service, like the US President's Homepage, we could attempt to reach the web server running on www.whitehouse.gov. Through some Internet magic, the computers would know how to reach others by doing what's called a **domain name lookup**. This lookup returns the IP address of the other machine.

In the early days of the Internet, the 'cyberworld' was small and everyone knew each other. The domain names were kept in a simple text file that was stored on each computer that was on the Internet. The name of this file was called hosts because each computer on the Internet was called a host. It was a called a host because it could potentially host several different services, such as e-mail, ftp and remote login. A centralized hosts file was maintained and computers who were on the Internet downloaded a copy of this file on a regular basis. In the *ad hoc* early days of the Internet this system worked without trouble.

However, within a short time, the hosts file contained several thousand entries and it was becoming too large for the entire list of hosts on the Internet to be contained in a simple text file. So, a replacement was developed called the **Domain Naming Service** or **DNS**, which was implemented as a database. However, it was soon found that a single database copied on to DNS servers everywhere did not solve the problem, so the DNS was developed as a caching, distributed database system.

How DNS Works

First lets look at the relation of an FQDN to an IP address. Every FQDN is made up of at least a domain and a host name. Between the host name and the domain, can be one or more sub-domains. A domain is the root name of an organizational type, such as government, company or non-profit organization. To be entered into a domain, you must register with the Internet Network Information Center (InterNIC) that manages the domain for a country. The domain part is the last two (possibly three) sections of a FQDN. For the FQDN, www.whitehouse.gov, the domain name is whitehouse.gov.

The .gov ending is of particular importance. This is referred to as a top level domain, which means that nothing can follow it. In the United States there are currently 6 top level domain names. They are:

Top level Domain Name	Refers to
.gov	US Government site
.com	US Commercial site
.org	US Non-profit organization
.net	US Network (like an Internet Service Provider)
.edu	US Educational site
.mil	US Military site

An FQDN can also include a top level country code. These country codes are two letters and the abbreviations are determined by the International Standards Organization (ISO). For sites that are located in the United States, the country code is assumed. Here are some common country abbreviations:

Country Code	Refers to
.au	Australia
.uk	United Kingdom
.de	Germany
.ca	Canada
.mx	Mexico

The host in www.whitehouse.gov is www. The www simply refers to the name of a machine that will answer requests to host www inside the whitehouse.gov domain. The host name could be anything – it does not have a relationship to the services it provides, though network managers usually give some sort of mnemonic name to the machine that refers to its central purpose. For example, we typically name our central web servers www, our central mail servers mail or mailhost, and our FTP servers, ftp.

The network can be further segregated into sub-domains, which gives network managers flexibility to organize their systems into smaller, more manageable, pieces. For example, if you were a network manager for a university, you may want to set up a web server for each college that is separate from your central Web server. Let's say that for your College of Education, you allot a sub-domain name of coe. If your root domain is acme.edu, then the FQDN for the College of Education would be www.coe.acme.edu.

The use of top level domains and domain names allows for several thousand possible combinations of names. This is called a **namespace**, and refers to the possible names available to any host on the Internet. Without this division, we would quickly run out of names for machines on the Internet. There can only be one www domain name, or one mail etc. So the ability to segregate the network into multiple domains and sub-domains is very important.

The top level (.edu, .com, .gov, .au etc) provides the namespace. The sub-domain (acme.edu, yahoo.com, gov.au) provides the namespace for any further sub-domains (for example, coe.acme.edu). The result of this naming convention is nearly a limitless number of names for machines on the Internet. For example, the host www.coe.acme.edu is different from www.coe.acme.org and mail.teachers.coe.acme.com is a different machine than mail.financial.yahoo.com.

Large organizations would be provided a domain name, such as acmewidgets.com for the *Acme Widgets Corporation.* They will also obtain a section of the IP addresses possible on the Internet. The largest section an organization can obtain is called a class C address. In IP addresses, the order from domain to host name is reversed. For example, for an IP address 198.137.240.92, the host number is 92 and the class C address is 198.137.240. This means that all of the addresses in the range of 198.137.240.000 to 198.137.240.255 are reserved for acmewidgets.com. How Acme Widgets decides to divide up its class C addresses is up to the company's network manager.

Name Server Lookup

Across the Internet, there are several special servers that are set up to handle DNS requests and they are called **name servers**. A name server is responsible for maintaining a database of the names and IP addresses of the hosts it provides lookups for. It can also host pointers to other name servers that might manage a sub-section of a particular domain. It will also contain pointers to servers that manage the entries "up-stream", for requests that are not found in the particular name server. Suppose a user on the acme.com network needed to find the address for www.yahoo.com. First the lookup will go to the acme.com name server and discover that yahoo.com addresses are not maintained there. To complete the request, it will pass the request to the .com root server, which will then point to the yahoo.com name server, which in turn will come back with the address to www.yahoo.com. (Whew!)

To get a domain name like whitehouse.gov or acmewidgets.com, you not only must you register with a NIC, you must also make sure that two name servers agree to be the name servers for your domain. A name server or series of name servers will be maintained by any network provider such an Internet Service Provider, a university, or a large company, etc. These name servers will be responsible for the hosts inside their networks. This means that for hosts inside your domain, lookups occur very quickly because you only have to go across your local area network to do name to address translation (for example, www.whitehouse.gov to its IP address, 129.100.11.55). From the outside, a request from a far away network will travel the Internet pathways until it reaches your name server and asks to look up a particular host name. To help speed these lookups, searches for hosts that are not local are cached for a fixed period of time to minimize the number of lookups that need to be performed across the Internet.

A Typical DNS Request

Here is how a typical DNS request works.

1. A client inside the acmewidgets.com network makes a request for a particular host, e.g. www.yahoo.com.

2. The client asks its local name server for the IP address of www.yahoo.com.

3. If the local name server doesn't contain it in either its standard tables or its cache, it passes the request to the .com name server that is managed by the InterNIC.

4. The root .com server looks up the name server for yahoo.com and passes the request to that name server for yahoo.com.

5. The name server for yahoo.com looks up www.yahoo.com and returns its IP address back to the acmewidgets.com name server.

6. The acmewidgets.com name server passes the IP address back to the client. The name server places the www.yahoo.com and IP address in its cache. The cached entry (consisting of an FQDN and an IP address) will expire in a few seconds (eons in Internet time).

7. The client can continue on with its transaction.

This process is illustrated in the diagram below:

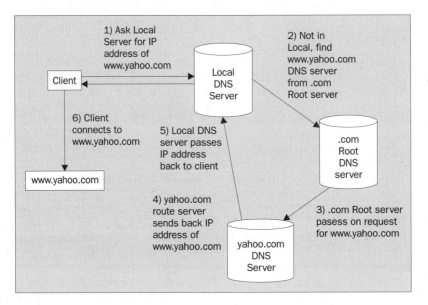

This mechanism insures that any client on the Internet can find any host on the Internet with an FQDN. Each network is responsible for adding, deleting or changing hosts on its network and maintaining its own DNS entries. This enables for very quick lookup, because often people will be contacting servers that are on their network, rather then sites that are located off the network. For those sites that are not on the network, the lookups are cached locally so the price of a 'long-distance' lookup is only paid once.

As long as the root servers, i.e. those that manage the top level domains, contain pointers to the correct name servers for each domain, everything works great. However the system is not infallible. A couple of years ago, an error occurred during a server upgrade at the root level and for a couple of days several sites were not accessible up via DNS. There was nothing any of the lower networks could do because the error occurred at the root level.

Why Do We Need Directory Services?

Without DNS, the Internet could not function very well, if at all, in its current configuration. It's hard to imagine how we would even use the telephone effectively without a common directory service like the telephone book, or how we could manage to keep up with the many different television show listings.

Yet this is exactly what we do with e-mail. Not only is there not a single e-mail directory, our own private e-mail address books that we store in our e-mail programs are not easily portable or shareable between different e-mail programs. Similarly, we don't have an easy way to manage all the different network resources that a modern organization needs to function. These include workstations, file and print servers, application servers, user accounts and other peripherals. If you put all of the personnel information a company needs to have on hand, to run and keep together on a variety of systems, you begin to wonder how they function at all. Somehow, in some way, they always do, but in this era of Internet time and multinational, multi-organizational partnerships, they can't for long.

The management of people's phone numbers and e-mail addresses has proven to be out of most organization's grasp – and this doesn't even take into account room changes, inventory and user account management. The solution to this problem is centralized directory system in a similar manner to a telephone directory, but optimized for a networked world like DNS.

To illustrate how important directory services are in today's world of computer networks and information overload, let's take a look at a fictional (yet typical) company, Acme Widgets, and see what kind of problems it runs into managing its day to day business. We'll then go on to see how the same company functions with a central directory service in place.

Life Without a Central Directory Service

The Acme Widget Corporation has hired Sam Carter as a systems administrator. Acme Widgets is one of the largest makers of widgets in the world. They have offices in three different cities – their headquarters are located in Dallas, Texas, where Sam is based, and they also run an office in Chicago, Illinois, and a small branch in London, England.

Each office is a separate entity when it comes to computer resources. Each has its own local area network (LAN), its own administrative mainframe and assorted network peripherals like printers. The offices are linked on a wide area network (WAN) via dedicated phone lines. While the offices in Chicago and London can access the Internet, the central servers are located in Dallas.

On the first day of work Sam reports to the human resources department. The human resources staff has him fill out some paperwork that they will later transfer to their database applications located on the Company's central mainframe.

- ❑ In the first application a clerk will enter his full name, social security number, job code, birth date, department, physical home address, home telephone number, and his supervisor's name for payroll purposes.
- ❑ In a second separate application, the operator will enter his name, social security number, birth date, physical home address, home telephone number, his wife's name and his wife's social security number for benefits purposes.

Both of these programs are on the administrative mainframe that is accessed through a standard terminal emulation program. Neither program can share data with the other, so all data has to be entered manually. This means that his name, social security number, etc. have to be entered twice, by the same person, at the same terminal. This doubles the chance that a mistake might be made in data entry and also means double the work if a change has to be made.

Next Sam walks down the hallway to the security office, where the security office staff member enters his name, social security number, his supervisor, his supervisor's supervisor, his room number, the make of his car, his car's license plates and his car's VIN number into the office's DBase IV database that is running on an ancient 386. The security office goes on to issue him a photo-ID badge, keys and a parking permit. Again this system contains similar data to human resources, but there is no data sharing. Since the data had to be entered manually into a different system, the odds of making a mistake continue to increase. Indeed, unknown to Sam, the clerk transposed the last two digits of his social security number.

The only data that is shared between these offices in terms of paperwork, is that the mainframes do a daily dump of payroll and benefits that can be looked at in the central office in Dallas. No other system in the entire company has the ability to share information.

Sam then makes for the office where he will work in the Information Systems (IS) division of the Acme Widgets Corporation. The first thing that he notices is that his phone number is different to that provided by human resources. He is told not to worry about it because 'everyone knows that you can't trust the data in the mainframes'. To keep things straight, the administrative assistants for the IS department keep a Microsoft Excel spreadsheet that has everyone's correct numbers on it. They print and distribute these once a month.

> *Keep in mind that the mainframe data that everyone says that you can't trust, is the only information that is centrally managed and synchronized between all three offices of Acme Widgets!*

The diagram below shows the trips Sam has to make on his first day at the office, including the relationship of departments to their databases.

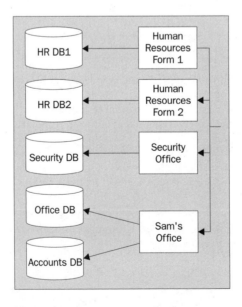

Sam finally settles in and is briefed on the systems he will have to manage. Acme Widgets supports a number of different types of computers for the Company's many departments. The majority of the computers in the company for personnel outside of marketing are Pentium 100s running Microsoft Windows 95. The marketing division has a significant number of Apple Macs. Novell's NetWare is used as the Networking Operating System (NOS) to connect both the Windows 95 and Macintosh machines together, so that they can share file and print servers. This requires one particular user ID and password to connect to the Novell networks. Novell's GroupWise is used as the e-mail package for these users.

Within the past year, IS has begun to install Microsoft Windows NT machines as application servers to reduce the amount of disk space is required on each of their Windows 95 machines. Because Novell's NDS for NT (which synchronizes Novell and Windows NT user IDs and passwords) had not come out when the rollout started, users who are using applications from the NT machines were required to have a separate user ID and password.

In the Engineering department, the staff also have access to a number of Sun Microsystems workstations that run the Solaris 2.6 operating system. Many of these users also use Windows 95 boxes, so that they can get access to some of the common Microsoft applications they use, like Word and Excel. These users are required to have separate user ID and password system. Consequently, some people in Engineering have at least three separate user IDs and passwords!

Finally, Lotus Notes is being used as a workflow application to guide materials from marketing to engineering and to the printing office. The people who are on the Lotus system also must have a Lotus user ID and password.

What this means is that there is a significant user population that has three or more user IDs and passwords. Sam learns there is also a new project that has popped up to allow users to communicate between the three offices using the Internet as a Virtual Private Network or VPN. The VPN will require that all traffic will be encrypted and secured using user IDs and passwords and client-side certificates.

> *A client-side certificate is an electronic document, which acts like a name badge signifying that a user is a particular individual, because a trusted third party, who issued the certificate, has verified this to be true. They are used in secure electronic settings to verify a person's identity.*

Sam has learned that a major stumbling block has arisen, because to get everyone access to the VPN will require all system administrators to issue user IDs and passwords to the "jerks in the other locations" and that they themselves will have to manage the certificate database somehow. The administration of the networking systems is a nightmare. There are three separate operating systems to manage, each with their own user ID and password database, without a common interface to manage them centrally. Each one has its own quirks and bugs plus every administration interface is different. Nobody has an idea how to manage the certificates yet.

Sam's job is one of continuous hassle. Users constantly complain to Sam and to the rest of the IS department about how they have to remember so many different user IDs and passwords. In addition, Sam is under pressure from upper management, who have decided that they want a central directory of the company's web services, including both internal users (the Intranet) and the external members of the VPN (called an Extranet). This way they can look up user's names, phone numbers, his or her department and supervisor's name. Finally, a significant portion of Sam's time is spent changing forgotten passwords, fixing broken permissions to systems and trying to figure out how to turn off access to all machines when users leave the company.

Over time, Acme Widgets has collected a huge store of information on their mainframe computer. While mainframe reliability has never been questioned (it's still the standard we compare all other reliability too), they are about as user friendly as an angry gorilla. At Acme Widgets, this has lead to problems of keeping the data it stores up-to-date. Because the people have utilized PCs and networking systems, they have created extra data stores that have allowed for the multiplication of the same data between systems, each of which have a different manner of access. All in all, it's one big headache for both end users and system administrators like Sam.

The final outcome of Acme Widgets not having a centralized directory service is illustrated below:

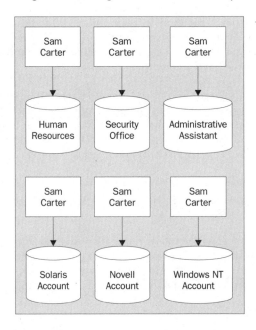

While this type of software production might make for good business sense in the old business school of thinking, it has made it very tough for end users to use networked computers. This setup has also given more than a few system administrators ulcers, sleep deprivation, and burnout.

Life With a Central Directory Service

Now we will take a look at how Sam's job might be different if Acme Widget employed the use of a centralized directory service.

On the first day of work, Sam reports to the human resources department. They enter his information into the central directory application. This includes his name, address, home telephone number, his wife's name, both of their social security numbers, his supervisor, his office room and office telephone number. They also enter the codes for his benefit options. At the bottom of the screen is a series of checkboxes that will be used later on by the security officer. The one that says Employee is checked. The other options besides employee are Visitor, Client, or Vendor.

Sam verifies the data and then the information is distributed to the mainframe applications, one for benefits and the other for payroll.

Next he visits the security office. Here the clerk asks for his social security number, which is entered into the office's directory server client, which retrieves his base information from the directory service. The security office only gets to see Sam's social security number, name, office contact information, supervisor and employee status. The only other information needed is his car's license plate and VIN number, and a photograph which is digitally transferred into the system. The security office then hands him his parking tag and his identification badge with the appropriate security information. This badge is about the size of a credit card and has his name and photograph on it. On the back of the card is a magnetic strip, upon which is written a code that is the key to look up his employee client-certificate for electronic transactions.

Finally Sam reports to his office. There, one of the administrative assistants notices that his room and phone number are blank. The assistant logs into the system and updates his office information. The assistant can only see Sam's home phone, his SSN, name and office contact information.

Here is a new diagram that shows Sam's first day's travels again. Note the relationship of the departments and the central directory service. This time they all update a central database but each department has a different application interface to the system:

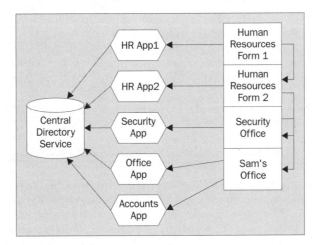

Network access is also greatly simplified. Sam swipes his name badge through a card reader and a user ID and password are generated for him. The Novell, Lotus, Sun and Microsoft systems all draw their user IDs and passwords from the central directory service. He has separate rights on each system, but the base authentication scheme is centralized.

The directory server also manages his client-certificate, so that when he must work on the VPN to the offices in Chicago or London, he is able to do so. The sessions are encrypted and trusted.

Users are impressed and no longer complain about having too many user IDs and passwords. Some system administrators are even getting to go home at 5 o'clock like the rest of the staff! Management is pleased, because their staff can look up anyone's contact information and even their appointment calendar through a web-based gateway that accesses the central directory server on the backend.

Each office maintains its own directory servers. These servers are replicated between the branches for redundancy and to improve efficiency. The servers take care of passing changes between them on an hourly basis through encrypted, secure transactions.

The new system at Acme Widgets might be viewed thus:

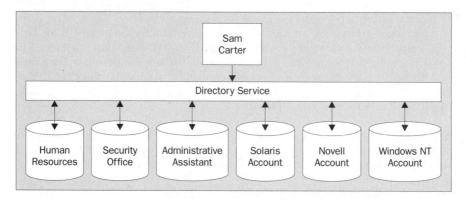

The Benefits of a Centralized Directory Service

A centralized directory service is able to make the second example possible because it improves several key areas of management in the organization.

❑ Entry and management of personal data, such as name, phone number and supervisor, is centralized.

This information is entered and stored in one place. If some of the information is entered wrongly or subsequently needs to be changed, it is easy to fix.

❑ Information on user ID and password locations for computer systems is centralized.

Instead of having user IDs and passwords scattered over several systems, they are managed from the central directory service. This way, security is improved because users only have to worry about one set of user IDs and passwords. This makes it easier for users to create a strong password (one that is harder to guess), because they only need remember the one. An additional factor is that it is now easier to remove dead or disabled accounts thus reducing the number of doors open to a would-be hacker.

❑ The procedure for determining the status and role of an individual in the organization is standardized.

In a large organization, there will be a number of people that will come and go. It is important to determine the exact status or relationship to the company they represent. This is important for business and security purposes, because employees and guests are not likely to have the same access rights to all areas of the organization.

❑ Lookup of names, addresses, phone numbers and other "white pages" information is standardized.

Employees need to contact each other for a variety of reasons. In a large organization, the numbers can be in the thousands. The means of contacting an individual are numerous too – telephone, fax, e-mail and standard mail. This information will change over time, so centralizing the management of it makes it easier to find people in the organization. Effective communication is still one of the most efficient ways to run a company.

❑ Lookup of network resources like printers, servers, certificates and other "yellow pages" information is standardized.

Network resources are multiplying faster than people in an organization. It is imperative that you have a way to manage all of your network resources in a standardized fashion. Making it easier for users to find the resources will make them more productive and reduces the workload of network administrators. It also increases security and reliability, because you can keep tabs on the status of all of your devices.

❑ Management of the system is distributed.

Centralizing the management of the system will increase reliability and make it easier to keep it up to date. However, the type of information a directory system keeps is very fluid, that is, it changes constantly. To help keep the information current, it is important that the people who are closest to the source of information be given the ability to keep it up to date. By having all systems draw their information from a centralized resource will make it easier to encourage people to use the system, instead of trying to maintain their own separate systems. So, the data itself is centralized, but that management of that data can be distributed.

For better or worse, people want access to directory services and they will build one if one is not provided for them. People have kept Rolodexes for years. These Rolodexes contain personal contact information such as name, phone and fax numbers. Personal Information Managers (PIMs) have always been perennial computer software sellers and are designed to provide similar functions that Rolodexes have. One of the reasons that there is a physical standard like Rolodex is because it is easy to use, and it provides access to all of the relevant information needed. It is very easy to add, modify or remove information from a Rolodex. Often it as easy as either adding or removing a business card. PIMs are a dime a dozen in computers because no-one has figured out how to make one that is as easy to use as a Rolodex.

There is nothing resembling a true standardized service, like a telephone directory for network resources, that is scalable to cover an entire organization, much less something grander, like the entire Internet. This is not to say there are not products that attempt to provide such a service, but there just isn't one that has vanquished all competitors or eliminated the need for something better. A central directory service sounds simple enough, but to implement one requires more effort than you would think. For a system to succeed it must be easy to use, able to draw its data from many different resources and it must be modifiable, for use in a variety of circumstances. The system must be secure and it must be reliable. If its not secure, network security professionals won't place their critical systems on it out of fear that their network or organization will be compromised. If it's not reliable, users won't want to depend on it because they will think that it will fail when they need it.

Many companies have tried to provide such solutions and their efforts have failed, or at least only partially succeeded. What is needed is a standardized solution that can be used by all units of an organization. This includes the ability of the system to be utilized and customized by many different systems through the use of a standard application programming interface (API).

Standardized Directory Services to the Rescue

We have identified that the best possible solution to our current information problems is through a centralized directory service. We have also identified that the best way to provide such a directory service is through a standardized mechanism. If such a mechanism can be found, then it will be easy to implement the solution for everybody in an organization, and even beyond that organization by connecting other companies like clients and partners.

With a centralized directory service, you can provide for a mechanism, which can reliably provide a rich data environment that can satisfy your organization's needs, ranging from phone numbers to synchronizing user IDs. By using a standards based directory service and by following some simple guidelines, you can even prepare your organization to participate in a global directory service initiative.

It is possible to build your own directory service using a database of some sort. This database could be constructed using Microsoft Access or be a series of flat-files – in practice both kinds of system are found. However, for many organizations, their current directory services are those *ad hoc* solutions that are only good for that particular organization. They are generally not very scalable or dependable.

A better solution for your organization would be to use a standard service of some kind, and develop in-house applications to utilize it. You would thus rely on vendor support so that if something goes wrong with the service, someone else will help fix it. This makes our job a bit easier and makes it more likely that future applications will be able to be interconnected out of the box. After all, it's easier to comply with a single open standard than a multitude of proprietary ones.

Our standardized solution should meet some basic goals before we decide upon implementing one in particular:

❑   Multi-Platform – Most organizations have multiple-platforms in use. The platforms we would want to reach would include all versions of Windows, Apple Macintosh, Linux/Unix and IBM mainframes.

❑   Multi-Vendor support – Multi-vendor support is important because it can help keep prices low and also lessens the blow if a vendor should go out of business.

❑   Common standard – The standard we choose should be a known standard and recognized by many others as a standard (i.e. ANSI/ISO recognition).

Vendor-Derived vs Open Standards

When you are talking about standards, it is important to realize that there are a variety of ways a standard can be generated. It is also important to make sure that the standards being used are true standards and not just standards in a company's 'marketing eyes' only. Essentially there are two types of standard:

❑   Vendor-derived

❑   Open

Vendor-Derived Standards

Vendor-derived standards are often proprietary, but if the vendor gains a large enough market share, the standard may become so prevalent that it becomes the primary way we operate in a certain area. Often vendors will let their 'standard' way of providing a service be ported from a particular vendor's system to another, but for a price. If another vendor pays the price to develop the standard on a different platform (called a port), they must sign a license agreement to make the port. This agreement states that the porter will abide by the stipulations that the original vendor makes.

An example of such a standard would be the Java programming language. The Java language was originally developed by Sun Microsystems to run on networkable consumer devices. This was before the Internet and the World Wide Web had become mainstream media. Once this happened Java was repositioned to become *the* Internet programming language.

Java programs are designed to be written on one machine and then have the ability to run any other machine, regardless of platform (e.g. operating system). The only requirement needed for a Java program to run is a Java Virtual Machine (JVM). The JVM is actually a native program for a particular operating system, providing an architecturally neutral platform for Java programs. This ability has made Java into one of the hottest programming languages in the last 15 years or so. It has also opened up some interesting debates – for example, do people really want a cross-platform language if that means giving up the look of their favorite system?

Traditionally, a programming language is just a syntax. The standard syntax is determined by a standards group and then anyone can write compilers for these languages free of charge. However, the Java language actually consists of three parts:

❑ Java language **syntax** – This defines the keywords and concepts that make up a Java program. This part is open for anyone to use.

❑ The **standard libraries** – Java provides a standard set of libraries that contain standard functionality for writing cross-platform network and GUI applications. These libraries are also open for anyone to develop to. In fact Sun gives away the source code of the standard libraries for free so that other developers can see how to write well formed Java code.

❑ The **Java Virtual Machine** – The JVM is the key to making the language cross-platform. Without a JVM, Java is just another programming language. To develop a JVM, you are required to sign a licensing agreement with Sun and in some cases you must pay a fee.

Microsoft and Hewlett-Packard have run afoul with this third section. (Indeed Microsoft has violated the libraries requirement also.) They have written their own JVMs that are not compliant with Sun's (i.e. hey don't abide by Sun's standard). Microsoft's JVM is more well known because of their dominance in the operating system market.

Standard Java has been ported to several different operating systems – Windows, Apple Macintosh and all of the common Unix variations, including Linux. And it is possible to write programs that run on all of these systems with very little porting necessary. (Though, occasionally bugs do crop up among JVMs that must be dealt with.) There is a large base of Java code and libraries out there. There are tens, if not hundreds of thousands of Java developers now and perhaps over a million Java users. Java is being improved quickly and it is now on a standards track through the International Standards Organization (ISO).

However, Sun still maintains the standard, even if ISO sticks a rubber stamp on it. The only people who can help Sun with their development of Java are those who Sun invites to help. Sun now has the Java Community Process, which makes it easier for third parties to propose and implement new APIs in a manner similar to the traditional open standards process that we will discuss in the next section.

The conclusion to draw from this is that one company can become a standard through successful business operations. However, if you develop to a company's proprietary standard, you are dependent upon that company for any changes.

Open Standards

Open standards are those standards that are developed by standards committees and organizations, made up by many members who are from competing organizations and corporations. They can be national or international in scope. These standards are published in an open, free forum where people who want to build on what the standards committee has defined can get their information.

For computer programs this means that Company A can develop to a particular standard, as can Company B, and neither has to pay anyone for that right.

An example of this is the Internet. The Internet is built upon several layers of protocols (primarily the TCP/IP protocols) that have been agreed upon by the **Internet Engineering Task Force** (**IETF**). The Internet's open standards have enabled developers everywhere to port the TCP/IP protocols to nearly every conceivable computing device. From mainframes to cell phones, the Internet is everywhere. In a large part, this is due to these free, open standards.

Of course not every developer implements the standard the same way or as completely as another, but every service has to meet some basic functionality.

This book is about helping you along the path using a particular open standards solution: the **Lightweight Directory Access Protocol** (**LDAP**), which is the TCP/IP (e.g. Internet based) directory service solution. We will have more to say about LDAP later (and indeed, throughout the book), but first we must briefly look into other solutions, both vendor-specific and open standards.

Vendor-specific Directory Service Solutions

Sun Microsystems NIS+

Sun Microsystems claims to be *the* company that built the Internet. According to nearly any marketing survey, their machines are the ones that run the critical systems at nearly all of the major Internet sites. Sun has always been the leader when it has come to networking computers. Products that they have developed inside of their walls have become the market leader and now form the standard with which all Unix networks must be compliant.

One of these systems is the **Networking File System** or **NFS**. NFS enables client computers to import directories (called a mount) from one machine across the network onto their own and treat that drive as if it was a local drive. Of course, Novell's NetWare and Microsoft's networking technologies enable Windows PCs to do the same, but Sun's NFS was the first. Sun has continued to develop NFS and today NFS clients ship on all major versions of Unix.

They have even created a new version called WebNFS which uses the HyperText Transfer Protocol (HTTP) as its network communications system. WebNFS is designed to allow you to gain all of the benefits of NFS access from a web browser. Unfortunately, none of the major browser vendors have added WebNFS support yet, though this may change, because Sun is making the source for WebNFS available and is sending the protocol to the W3C for inclusion as a recommended web standard. Sun is also working on a Java API for WebNFS so Java developers can add WebNFS support to their applications.

Sun also has created two other systems for managing computers and users on a network. The first version was called NIS. (Originally, it was to be called YP, for 'yellow pages', but the name was changed after a trademark lawsuit with British Telecom.) NIS was rewritten and replaced with today's version which is called **NIS+**. NIS+ stands for **Network Information Service Plus**.

NIS+ has been implemented on a wide variety of machines and most modern versions of Unix operating systems ship with clients that can communicate with NIS+ servers.

What does NIS+ do?

NIS+ is an object-oriented database system that allows you to manage user account information, so that you can log into any machine on the network with a single account, not just your local machine. It also manages host information by mapping IP addresses to host names in a section of the domain. A client can connect to any computer on the Internet if properly configured. NIS+ is able to this because it manages to keep unique namespaces through the use of hierarchical domains, in a similar way to DNS. Whereas DNS is used only to look up information about other computers however, NIS+ can be used to lookup information about any type of network related information.

The management of NIS+ is achieved through the use of tables. Tables can also be linked to other tables or to actual directories in the network. This gives the system administrator a great deal of flexibility in return for more administrative overhead. An incorrect NIS+ setup can lead to a breach of security, but NIS+ in itself should be much more secure than the older NIS.

NIS+ is not an open standard, that is, no-one can develop it for any system without first paying a fee. Also it has only been ported to Unix systems, so it is not a *de facto* standard either for PC/Mac-based networks.

Starting with release of Solaris 7 (which you might also see referred to as Solaris 2.7), Sun's directory strategy became clearer. They have released a product called Sun Directory Services (SDS) which is based on LDAP. SDS allows for the central management of user and host information in a central LDAP server. This includes the ability to grant user access to any host in the network, as with NIS+, including Remote Authentication Services (RAS) which are used to authenticate dial-up user accounts. In the current release of SDS, the back-end LDAP server is Sun's implementation. At the time of writing, Netscape, AOL and Sun have entered into a partnership. One of the rumors is that Netscape's Directory Server will become the back-end LDAP server for Sun Directory Services. Solaris 8 is supposed to take SDS even farther by adding native LDAP support to the Solaris operating system.

Novell's NetWare Directory Service

The Novell name and the word 'network' go hand in hand. They were the ones who brought networking to the world of PCs during the late 80s and early 90s, primarily through the use a product called **Netware**.

NetWare was designed to run over IPX (Internetwork Packet Exchange). IPX is similar to TCP/IP but specifically was built to work over Ethernet. In version 5 of NetWare, administrators all of Novell's traffic can be carried over TCP/IP, the "Internet" protocols.

> *Ethernet is the common name for the most popular form of Local Area Network cable. Ethernet uses its own protocol, Carrier Sense Multiple Access / Collision Detection (CMA/CD) to carry traffic. Ethernet can carry a number of different networking protocols including IPX, TCP/IP and Appletalk.*

To help manage user accounts in a NetWare environment, Novell created the **NetWare Directory Services** system, or **NDS**. NDS allows network administrators to manage users, machines and printers in the network in a rather sophisticated manner. In the mid-90s, Novell released GroupWise, an e-mail and groupware product, and has since become a major player in the directory services market.

NDS is designed to provide access to directory objects available to a user primarily in a Novell NetWare environment. NDS has been licensed to several Unix vendors, and according to Novell, 80% of all Unix machines shipped already have NDS installed. Novell has also released NDS for Windows NT, which enables Microsoft NT servers to access NDS services. Caldera, one of the Linux corporate providers, has also made NDS available for the Linux platform and there is talk about porting NDS to IBM mainframes. You can also access NDS services from Apple Macintosh systems.

Novell has also formed a partnership with Netscape to port Netscape's server line to Novell NetWare, which will enable Netscape users to communicate with NDS.

What does NDS do?

NDS is an object-oriented database protocol that is designed to provide an enterprise wide management system of network resources. These include items like user information, such as names, user IDs and groups. They also include items like printers and file systems. Its data model was derived from a protocol called **X.500**, which we will be talking about toward the end of this chapter. X.500 defines the **Directory Application Protocol** (**DAP**) and is also the parent protocol for LDAP.

NDS allows you to manage each record in the system as an object and each object will have particular attributes like first name, printer name, description, password, etc. These objects are also divided into a tree, where each branch can be managed by a different manager.

If you have any experience with NDS, then you are already several steps ahead when it comes to understanding an enterprise-wide, open directory service solution like LDAP.

The Problems with NDS

By now, NDS should have solved the problem of a general Internet-wide directory service, but has been unable to for several reasons.

- ❑ *Novell's corporate strategy became unknown.* They tried to compete with Microsoft on the desktop OS and application front in the early 90s. The development of NetWare was stalled as they wandered around looking for a center.
- ❑ *Lack of application support.* NetWare is great for file and print sharing, but historically, it does not run applications very well. Windows NT has gained ground, because you can run Windows applications from an NT server. Since NT can also be a file, print and web server, it's just a directory services solution away from being a replacement for NetWare. If Microsoft's Active Directory, which will appear in Windows 2000, is a success, then it will make NDS redundant.

❏ *Lack of cross-platform support.* Since NDS is a protocol, in theory it does not need Novell's NetWare to exist. Novell has partnered with many Unix vendors to have NDS ported to their systems and have a version of NDS to handle the administration of Windows NT machines through NDS. Even with this support, NDS is primarily found only on NetWare networks.

❏ *A 'brick wall' in terms of objects.* Due to the way versions before NDS 5 were implemented, there is a size limitation in the total number objects in the system. NDS 5 is going to use the POET Object Database Management System as a back-end and is said to be able to handle up to a million objects. NDS 5 has yet to be deployed widely, so that is still an unknown.

NDS suffers from many of the same problems that prevented NIS+ from obtaining preferred status. Like NIS+, NDS is not an open standard (though it is derived from one − X.500). It does provide many of the services you would want in a centralized directory service, but is severely limited in only being portable to PC-based machines.

Also, Novell was late to the TCP/IP game. GroupWise used to require a gateway server to send Internet mail, which meant it was not taken up by developers as a system to use in an Internet world. However, Novell has been quick to catch up and NetWare 5 should be its strongest showing yet. All of NDS and NetWare are now available through the standard Internet protocols in NetWare 5. (This includes making NDS available as a LDAP v3 compliant directory server.)

Novell is also working with the IETF (the Internet's governing body) on designing new extensions to the LDAP protocol that would enable LDAP to better manage replication (exact copies of the master database on other machines) and redundancy (make it harder to kill the server by duplicating many of the internal structures) which would lead to greater reliability. Because Novell has committed to providing open-standards interfaces to its proprietary systems, it still begs us to look to another open standard solution like LDAP to give us the widest range of possibilities.

Microsoft's Active Directory

Microsoft is the 500 pound gorilla of the current computer world. Where Microsoft goes, it is sure to be heard and followed. In the past 20 or so years, Microsoft has switched its primary business − operating systems and programming tools for those operating systems − from the creaky old DOS to the heavy duty Windows NT. Where DOS could only be networked by accident and sheer will, Windows NT was designed for a networked world.

Microsoft is attempting to make Windows NT *the* network operating system, hoping to replace both Unix and Novell as the primary networking operating system. They realize that one of the requirements that will need to be met for this to happen is to have an enterprise wide directory service.

Microsoft's directory service is called **Active Directory** and its core protocol is going to be LDAP, the Internet directory services protocol. Not much is known about how Active Directory will actually work as of yet, because it is part of Windows 2000, which is slated for release sometime in 1999.

Active Directory Promises

What this does mean is that we can only talk in terms of promises. If Active Directory does support the core LDAP functionality and is accessible from the standard LDAP APIs then there is a good hope that this could be the solution we are all looking for.

Active Directory would be able to handle user authentication, user preferences and network resources in a standard fashion with a common interface. The common interface is designed to be programmatically available from:

❑ Microsoft's COM

❑ An SDK called the **Active Directory Services Interfaces** (**ADSI**) that is available for Windows 95/98/NT and Novell NetWare 4.x+

❑ Any API capable of accessing an LDAP server

The fact that you can access Active Directory from COM makes it available to programmers who are used to working in the Microsoft Windows environment – the hundreds of thousands of Visual Basic and Visual C++ programmers. It also makes it easier for Microsoft to connect the existing Microsoft Office and BackOffice applications to the Active Directory.

ADSI is designed to work with any directory service like NIS, X.500, LDAP, Novell NDS (or the older Bindery) and of course the Windows NT directory services. Of course they will work best in a Microsoft dominated environment. However, this does mean that ADSI makes it easier for other third party applications to add in support as they see fit. Because it will provide access from Novell NetWare, Microsoft is attempting to make a bridge between Novell NetWare and Microsoft Windows NT.

As Active Directory is an LDAP server, it opens up the possibility of linking applications on Unix based systems and those that run standard Java.

Microsoft has the momentum now. They control the desktop and are making significant gains in the server environment. Active Directory holds a lot of promise for end-users, developers and system administrators alike. Unfortunately Windows 2000 is still in beta. There are rumors that Active Directory may not even ship with the first version of Windows 2000, as it was first announced.

Until Active Directory hits the streets and some real world experience is gained with the product we won't know how it really works. Also, because it will only ship with Windows 2000, and likely only work with Microsoft operating systems (and maybe Macintoshes), it still might be a viable solution for us. However, it would still be a vendor specific solution, though if it is actually available via LDAP, that would be a definite bonus.

Our quest continues for a cross-platform solution that is not dependent upon a single vendor.

Open Standards Directory Service Solutions

An Open Solution: X.500

The idea behind an open standards based directory service is not new. The first attempt was called **X.500**, the **Directory Access Protocol** (**DAP**). This technology was proposed by the International Telecommunications Union, which is another international group like the IETF. The ITU prefers to use the OSI communications stack (also known as the OSI model) as opposed to the TCP/IP communications stack that the Internet runs on. (The OSI communications stack is just another suite of network protocols similar to TCP/IP.)

DAP is divided into 5 basic functions:

❑ The data model
❑ The namespace

❑   The modes of operation
❑   Authentication framework
❑   Distributed access methods

The **data model** is one made up of records called **entries** that have data fields called **attributes**. Each attribute in an entry is of a particular type and can contain one or more values. Each attribute has a particular syntax for data entry, in either text or binary format.

The **namespace** is the mechanism used to access the data contained in an X.500 server. The namespace allows us to import data into an X.500 system so that each entry is unique. The key to this strategy is the concept of the **Distinguished Name (DN)**, which is made up of attributes of the entry. What this means that everything that is in the DN will be found in the individual attributes of the entry. The namespace is divided up into a hierarchy, so that the relationships of one entry can be compared to another.

The **modes of operation** define what actions we can perform against an X.500 server. These operations would be in the form of a bind (which is like authenticating to the server), a search, a comparison of entries, modification of an entry, the addition of an entry and the removal of an entry.

The **authentication framework** helps define how clients should be able to identify themselves to the server, which helps determine what kind of access the client has. For obvious reasons, you would not allow just any client to modify the server – only privileged ones. However, you would want to allow anyone to search the directory.

From the start, X.500 was designed to live in a networked environment. The idea was not to put all of your entry 'eggs' in one basket, but to allow the records to be divided up between multiple servers. These separate servers are called **Directory Server Agents (DSA)**. If a search request to one DSA was not found, then that search could be passed on to other DSAs, either in the form of a referral or by chaining several servers together (thus you could search several servers at once in a single search). DSAs were also designed to be part of a global environment, where they would all be connected together in a similar form to DNS. The X.500 namespace, as part of its standard, allowed for a country attribute to help define where in the world a particular entry existed.

At the top of the X.500 hierarchy would be the root domain and from there it would break down by country. Each country (c) would then have one or more root X.500 servers. These servers break down further based on organization (o). The organization further breaks down into departments (or organizational units, ou), sections within a department and finally to individual people (denoted by a common name, cn). Thus you would be able to find any user in the world from any other place in the world by placing a single request and having it search through the X.500 hierarchies.

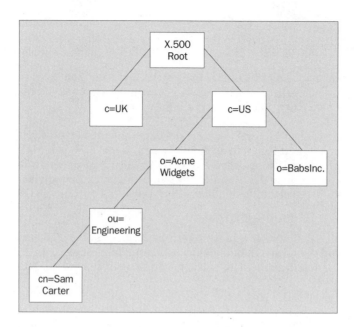

This was a very ambitious idea. You might even consider it a bit too much like 'Big Brother'. Yet the idea of a centralized open standard for personal information in an organization was widely regarded as a good thing, if it could only be built.

The biggest problem was that it was so hard to implement. One of the biggest drawbacks to X.500 was that it had to use the OSI protocol stack. This protocol stack is very difficult to implement in the first place. It's impossible to implement on very small machines, which means "big iron" mainframes are required to run OSI networks.

As we discovered earlier, TCP/IP runs on just about anything, which is why the Internet is everywhere. Also the necessary technical expertise for managing OSI networks was not that widely distributed (in particular in the US, where much of this development work was taking place) because OSI was found mostly in Europe and the US government (except for the military which used TCP/IP). In contrast, TCP/IP networks were very common in academic institutions. In addition, building directory services is a difficult job, even if you do have a standard network to build on.

The X.500 protocol has now been implemented in TCP/IP, but LDAP has more momentum. However, it does go a long way to fixing our central directory service problem.

The Lightweight Directory Access Protocol (LDAP) was designed to provide an easy to build interface gateway to X.500 servers. The rest of this book will discuss how LDAP can provide such a gateway service, and furthermore, how it can eliminate the need for X.500 altogether.

An Open Gateway Service

Another option we could have is that instead of trying to shoehorn a particular service to fit an entire organization, we can overlay something between the user (or client) and a fully fledged service. The particular service that was overlaid could be proprietary or it could be an open standard.

An overlay service is referred to as a **gateway**. Gateways in a sense are like the network version of human translators. The World Wide Web and the CGI specification have enabled many gateways to appear. An example of a WWW gateway is database connectivity. In a typical client-database server environment, the client must have a special program called a database driver to communicate with a database that lives on a computer somewhere. Database vendors make a good chunk of their money by selling these database drivers. The drivers themselves are platform specific and require a manual installation on each client. Obviously this doesn't work well in the Internet environment. So this is where the WWW and CGI step in. CGI stands for **Common Gateway Interface**.

Let's look at an example to see how this works. The client is a simple web browser. The browser visits a particular web site and makes a request. This request can be a standard GET or could be form submission. The web server then passes this request to a third program via the CGI specification. The CGI program is language independent. This program could be written in Perl, C/C++, Java or a specialized package like Allaire's ColdFusion. The important part to remember is that this program is what actually makes the database connection. The CGI program connects to the database, submits the query, parses the results and sends those results back to the client. The client views those results as a standard web page. The client only needs to understand HTML and HTTP (the basic web protocols). The web server itself doesn't even understand the database connection, it just passes the request to the CGI program. The CGI program understands HTTP, HTML and the special tools it needs to talk to the database. The database doesn't have a clue about HTTP or the WWW. The database just understands that it has been passed a query and it responds as it would do to a client not running on the web. In this instance, the CGI program is the gateway service.

After the difficulty of implementing X.500 was realized, some people at the University of Michigan (UofM) looked into ways of improving the situation. This came at a time, when the Internet was beginning to make its transformation from academia to the world at large. They came up with an intermediary protocol – the **Lightweight Directory Access Protocol**, or **LDAP**.

LDAP was not originally designed to be the directory service itself, but rather to act as a gateway protocol to a directory service underneath. The first directory service chosen was X.500, because that was the most common directory service for the worldwide network community. Because X.500 servers did got gain that large of a foothold even with the invention of LDAP, the UofM developers decided to put a database back-end with LDAP so that a LDAP server itself could act as a directory service.

Thus LDAP is what we will discuss as the solution to the directory services problem.

LDAP — the Directory Services Solution

The reason we will are going to spend the rest of this book looking at LDAP is that it answers all of our issues. In this section, we'll see how.

❑ Centralizes the entry and management of personal data like name, phone number, and supervisor.

Originally LDAP was designed to be a gateway service to X.500. Later, it was found that it was feasible to build an independent directory service using LDAP.

❑ Centralizes the location of user ID and passwords for computer systems.

Centralized user management was one of the key roles LDAP was designed to provide. It can support the synchronization of user ID and passwords. LDAP allows you to use a number of secure authentication mechanisms such as the Kerberos protocol through the use of the standard **Simple Authentication and Security Layer** (**SASL**) providers and **Secure Socket Layer** (**SSL**) support.

❑ Provides the Simple Authentication and Security Layer (SASL) providers, and the Secure Socket Layer (SSL) protocol.

This gives the system administrator several options in user management.

❑ Centralizes the procedure for determining the status and role of an individual in the organization.

LDAP provides several possible mechanisms for helping to manage the roles of a user in the organization. You can arrange your department through the use of organizational units and groups. You can even manage multiple organizations with a single LDAP server.

❑ Centralizes the lookup of names, addresses, phone numbers and other 'white pages' information.

LDAP has been optimized for reading from the data store as opposed to writing to it. This is done through the use of attribute indexing. LDAP also gives the administrator options as to what types of data can be stored in the form of text or binary data. You have the option of including a photo of an individual that can be retrieved during a search. In version 3 of the protocol, you can search LDAP servers via a standard URL syntax.

❑ Centralizes the lookup of network resources like printers, servers, certificates and other "yellow pages" information.

An administrator is not limited to just storing information about people in an LDAP server. You can store any information you like information on printers, file/application servers and remote machines is already supported. It is possible to store other data types, including distributed software agents. Already Sun has a proposal in about how to make an LDAP object to store Java class files for storage. There is also talk that eventually CORBA (Common Object Request Broker Agent) will be supported in the future. This ability gives the administrator a lot of flexibility in what can be stored in their LDAP servers.

❑ Management of the system is distributed.

While LDAP helps centralize management of directory service information, you can help spread the support of the server around. The security model available now in LDAP allows for very granular support. You can enable it so users can change only their password or home contact information, but nothing else. You can grant access to administrative assistants so that they can change office management information, such as who the person's manager is or the office phone number, but nothing else. This model helps ensure that the data in the server stays up-to-date, while still providing a common interface making it easier to manage overall.

LDAP also meets our three criteria we want from a standard interface.

❑ Multi-Platform.

LDAP servers have already been made available on a variety of platforms, including all of the major Unix variants, Windows NT, OS2 and IBM mainframes. LDAP interfaces are becoming available for Windows NT, Sun's NIS+ and Novell's NDS. LDAP clients are available for all forms of Unix, Macintosh, Windows 3.1/95/98/NT and even for the venerable Microsoft DOS. No other service has such cross-platform support.

    ❑   Multi-Vendor support

LDAP is an open recognized protocol so anyone can support it. In 1996, over 40 major vendors including Microsoft, Netscape, Sun and Novell announced they would provide support for it in their products. Microsoft has made LDAP one of the key protocols behind their new Active Directory services. Netscape has made LDAP the central protocol that forms the hub of its new server strategy. This type of support means that LDAP is not a flash in the pan, but a working, viable strategy. There are already many APIs available for developers to use to create LDAP clients or LDAP-enabled legacy applications.

    ❑   Common standard

At the time of writing, LDAP is a proposed standard to the IETF and is on the official standards track. However, this will likely take many years to go through (if it even does). This is not something new – many of the protocols have this status on the Internet. Thus, there is the chance that there will be many directory service protocols for the Internet, just as there are a number of protocols for sending mail over the Internet. Yet LDAP is likely going to remain *the directory service protocol* for many years to come. Support for LDAP is now viewed as a top-tier requirement from many different vendors. It is now the recognized standard for providing directory services.

Summary

In this chapter, we looked at the things a directory service needs to do and how it can help in the day to day running of an organization. It can be used to provide access to personal information like names, user IDs, e-mail addresses, and telephone numbers, to help locate networked resources like printers, and also help with security by managing a centralized resource of user IDs and passwords.

Potential solutions for a centralized directory server were discussed based on vendor-specific and open standards. We learned that potential vendor solutions were robust, but relied on one particular vendor and were not cross-platform to any great degree. We discussed the X.500 Directory Access Protocol and its basic functions, and saw why it was difficult to implement. Finally, we looked briefly at LDAP, which was originally designed to be a simple gateway to X.500, and later became a directory service in its own right.

The important points to note from this chapter are:

    ❑   Directory services are essential to daily life in a networked world
    ❑   Personal information that is needed for the running of any organization is being kept in many disparate systems
    ❑   Centralized directory services can improve productivity and increase security while reducing management overhead
    ❑   A system based on open standards is the best possible solution

Introducing the Lightweight Directory Access Protocol

In the last chapter, we learned what directory services are and why they are so important. We saw how directory information in a typical organization can be scattered through a variety of departments and systems leading to huge management headaches, and how directory services present an excellent solution to this problem. We briefly previewed Sun's NIS+, Novell's NDS, Microsoft's Active Directory and the X.500 protocol.

At the end of the last chapter, the **Lightweight Directory Access Protocol** (or **LDAP**) was introduced. This is a directory access protocol which can either act as a gateway to other directory services or provide the service itself. This chapter will be dedicated to discussing LDAP in general terms. The remainder of the book will include in depth coverage of LDAP and how to use LDAP services.

In this chapter, we will cover the following:

- ❑ How LDAP came about
- ❑ Why it is important
- ❑ LDAP terminology – the protocol, the data format and the API

Why LDAP?

As we saw in the previous chapter, there is a need for a standardized way of managing directory information. We discussed the various vendor-derived solutions and one of the strongest open standards solutions: X.500.

The Problem with X.500

X.500 showed a lot of promise. It gave us a global namespace, a platform and data-independent way of describing our directory information. This is very important, as the computing world we live in is not a homogeneous one. We have computers of every shape and size connected via various cables to a global network referred to as the Internet.

Also, there is no such thing as a typical user, a typical organization or a typical organizational structure. Textbooks, pundits and marketing representatives like to talk about how things are 'typically' set up. While there are common elements to any organization or group of people, in the end, no two things are ever exactly alike.

To have the freedom we require to manage our directory information, we must have flexibility in dealing with this varied information, with the minimum performance overhead. In the end, we need to spend more of our time worrying about how to grow our business and less time worrying about how we manage it. In order to maintain this flexibility, we cannot run the risk of being forced into a solution that will lock us into a fixed, proprietary standard.

While waiting on committees to formulate decisions can sometimes drive people nuts, its often the best way in the long run. After all, the U.S. Constitution – the world's best known 'open standards' document – has managed to run the United States with minimum amount of change for the past 200 or so years. You'd be hard pressed to argue that the United States has not had a successful run.

X.500 is also an open based standard, agreed upon by many companies and countries in the world, and has been proven to work over the past decade, so X.500 has had a good run. Unfortunately, it runs on the OSI communications stack, which is hard to implement, especially on standard PCs and Macintoshes that make up the majority of the networking infrastructure. However, OSI is not the most widespread communication model.

Since 1994, access to the Internet has been on a meteoric rise. In less than six years, it has gone from an academic's playground to become the only medium to come close to challenging TV as the world's most dominant communication technology. In addition, the protocols that run the Internet, that is TCP/IP, are more easily implemented on an ever-increasing range of computer equipment.

The upshot of this is that because of the difficulty in implementation and because it is based on OSI rather than the Internet protocols, X.500 is not that flexible or indeed that useful to many modern computer users. Thus, a system needed to be developed that has all the benefits of X.500, but which is easy to implement and runs on the widespread TCP/IP protocols. This is where LDAP comes in.

OSI Versus the Internet Model

Before we go on, lets compare the OSI and Internet communication models, as shown in the figure on the next page:

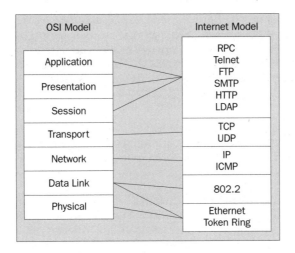

The OSI model is a very simple layer model that describes the technologies needed for communication between computers. The idea is that when a piece of the network puzzle is added to a system, whether it is a network interface card, a cable or a piece of software, the "puzzle piece" fits one of the OSI layers. For example, a network interface card or a modem would fit into the Physical layer. The network cable or telephone line is part of the Data Link layer. The various communications protocols used to transmit data back and forth over the network cable/telephone line are part of the Network and Transport layers. The protocols used to open communications between computers on the network fit into the Session layer. The software needed to translate data from the network to the computer and back again is the Presentation layer. The software the end-user needs to communicate with, for example an e-mail program, is the Application layer.

In contrast, the Internet model is a world of straight protocols, essentially leaving the hardware out of the discussion. (Under OSI, there are strict rules on how devices must physically connect, even down to the wire. Under the Internet, it's just assumed the computer has a connection, leaving the "how" up to the user.) Instead, you have protocols for the communication of the Local Area Network – the Ethernet and Token Ring. This is then built upon by a couple of basic protocols for communicating over distance (802.2, IP, ICMP). Building on top of these are more protocols (UDP, TCP) that make it easier to use the distance protocols. Finally, the top layer consists of the application protocols that most of you are probably acquainted with, such as HTTP (the World Wide Web protocol) and SMTP (the standard protocol for transporting e-mail). In the Internet model, this topmost layer determines how the computers should talk to each other. All the other layers, starting with TCP and going on down, just make sure that communication can take place.

The Development of LDAP

The developers of LDAP removed some of the confusing and more clunky parts of the X.500 protocol, as well as moving the underlying network communications protocol from OSI to TCP/IP, and revealed the Lightweight Directory Access Protocol. The first version to be widely used was LDAP version 2, which was specified in RFC 1777 in 1995.

RFC stands for 'Request For Comment'. RFCs provide a way towards the standardization of Internet protocols. Standardization is achieved only after rigorous reviewing and multiple interoperable implementations. However, some widely used protocols are only detailed in RFCs and yet are they are not official standards. In fact, there are relatively few protocols that have made it right the way through the standards process. An RFC can be viewed as a de facto standard of sorts

In 1996, LDAP leapt from being this unknown protocol, to the 'Cool Protocol of the Month' when companies like Netscape, Microsoft, and Sun announced they were going to support it in their core products. Netscape went further, hiring two of the primary developers of LDAP: Tim Howes and Mark Smith.

The original version of LDAP was created at the University of Michigan, whose LDAP server is still considered to be the defining server, with development continuing despite the loss of the primary developers. It has continued to succeed in a similar fashion to the Apache web server, which, curiously enough, was launched when the core developers of the NCSA web server left for Netscape.

LDAP has continued to develop and mature. In December of 1997, RFC 2252, which specified version 3 of the LDAP protocol, was ratified. Members participating included Sun, Netscape, Microsoft, Novell and Critical Angle (now Innsoft). The members of this group comprise the largest providers of networking operating systems, and employ all of the key members of the original LDAP implementation team.

To say that RFC 2252 was a watershed moment in the development of open-standards based directory services would be a major understatement. LDAP version 3 (**LDAPv3**) has now made it possible to give us the power we need to finally synchronize all of our networking and directory information into a manageable system.

LDAP was originally designed to be just a gateway between X.500 directory server agents, which was where the actual 'directory serving' took place, and a client. This is illustrated in the diagram below:

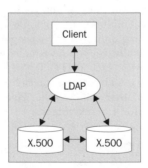

However, it became quickly apparent that X.500 was tough to implement, even on large, non-PC computers. Hence LDAP was given it's own database, enabling it to act as a directory service itself and not just a gateway.

A standard 'C' API was also developed to make writing LDAP clients easier. The API shipped with a set of standard command line tools that made it easy to test out LDAP servers. At first, Unix-based systems were the most common hosts. These command line tools, together with the standard API, made it easy to implement LDAP via shell scripts and also the Perl programming language. Because LDAP servers can provide access to their own data stores or those of existing X.500 servers, LDAP became the primary protocol for implementing directory services from other clients.

The success of the World Wide Web and its already standard ability to 'stand-upon' all of the other standard Internet protocols led to the development of the LDAP URL syntax, which is now fully defined in LDAPv3. Most modern browsers now implement this LDAP URL format for accessing LDAP servers. The reason why this is important is because web browsers are everywhere. They are on a large, growing percentage of desktop computers and are appearing in everything from television sets to cell phones. By enabling LDAP access from a URL in a web browser, that now means that electronic directory services can be quickly and easily accessed easily by millions of people.

The question you are probably now asking yourself is 'Does LDAP answer my needs?' More specifically, does it meet the questions we posed in Chapter 1? Remember in Chapter 1, we said that we wanted an open-standards based directory service that could run over the Internet protocols (TCP/IP). LDAP fits that need because it is an open-standards based directory service standard that has been agreed upon by the largest and most influential computer companies and organizations. It also runs on top of TCP/IP, has the largest momentum of any other competing directory service protocol (such as X.500 over TCP/IP or NetWare Directory Services) and can now be directly access from a web browser.

Just in case that is not enough for you, here are five more reasons why LDAP is the right choice as a directory services solution.

Five Reasons why LDAP is the Right Choice

Open Solution

The first reason why we would like to use LDAP is that it is an open standard. Anyone is allowed to develop LDAP servers or clients, or provide suggestions for future enhancements of existing implementations, without paying any fee.

The fact that LDAP runs on top of TCP/IP means that its underlying transport mechanism is well known, tested and still being improved. A TCP/IP stack is available for use on every computer, from a Palm Pilot to a mainframe, thus guaranteeing wide availability.

Netscape, Sun, IBM, Novell and many others have already developed LDAP enabled applications and servers. Some applications, such as Netscape's Directory Server use LDAP natively. The tools are already there – they are just waiting to be used.

A Secure, Extensible Format

LDAP uses the same object data format as X.500, where each object is made up of attributes that are indexed and referenced by a distinguished name. The name of each object is unique to fit into a global namespace that helps determine the relationship of the object and allows for the object to be referenced uniquely. What this means is that in a directory, no object stands alone. Each object has a relationship to every other object in the directory service. For example an object that describes Sam Carter would have a relationship inside the Acme Widgets directory service. These relationships include all of the objects that belong to certain organizational groups inside Acme Widgets, like the Accounting Department, or all of the printers on the Acme Widgets Network. Other relationships can include organization by data type, e.g. all of the people, all of the computers, all of the routers etc. This data format also allows for maximum flexibility. We will be looking in more detail at the LDAP data format later on in this chapter.

Furthermore, the data format is designed to handle a wide range of data, including text and binary. There are now recognized formats for entries, that is records within a directory service, to include everything from personal details to the storage of Java objects.

Finally, the data format facilitates the use of security, which can be applied to each entry if necessary, or on a branch level in the directory tree, though this is to be strongly discouraged in all but the most unusual of cases.

Programmable from Standard APIs

An API (Application Programming Interface) is a standard interface that programmers use to write their applications. This relieves the programmer from having to worry about the implementation of LDAP itself because the APIs will work against any LDAP compliant directory server. Instead they can invest their time and effort in making sure their overall application works. APIs allow programmers to build better 'cars' instead of having to re-invent the wheel each time they write an application.

The University of Michigan, who led the development of LDAP, created their own C API that has even been referenced in RFC 1823, not as a standard but as an informational document. Due to its widespread distribution and the fact that it is free, it is now the *de facto* standard API. The University of Michigan API has now been ported to DOS, Windows 95/NT, all versions of Unix and IBM mainframes. It is a solid and ubiquitous API.

In addition, Netscape has released their own C, Java and Perl LDAP Software Development Kits (SDKs), all of which are released as open-source projects. These SDKs include LDAP APIs for the particular language (C and Java) as well as documentation and examples. The Netscape Java LDAP API class files now ship with all versions of the Netscape Communicator web browser suite or can be downloaded from Netscape's web site. The C and Perl SDKs can be downloaded from Netscape's web site as well. The Netscape C and Java APIs share many similarities making it easy to transfer programming knowledge to and from each language, which extends development power.

Also, Sun have developed the **Java Naming and Directory Interfaces** (**JNDI**) as part of their Java Enterprise Beans program. They designed JNDI to be to directory services programming what Java Database Connectivity (JDBC) is to database programming in Java, that is to say, it will provide a common interface to programmers, regardless of the directory service which is being accessed on the back-end.

The idea behind this is that code you write today to access an NIS+ server can be kept intact if you switch over to LDAP later. This is achieved through the use of **providers**, which are special libraries that you load when you run a JNDI application to access directory services. Each different directory service protocol has a provider that implements a common interface. There can be multiple vendor versions for each type of provider – for example, both Sun and IBM have released a provider for LDAP using JNDI. There are also existing providers for NIS+ and NDS.

Microsoft has released their own development kits in the form of the Active Directory Services Interfaces (ADSI). The Microsoft development kits are available in both C++ and Microsoft Java versions. ADSI has been developed to allow programmers to interact with Microsoft's up and coming Active Directory, which is going to be their enterprise directory service. ADSI should also be able to access any LDAP compliant server, but will likely work best with Microsoft's LDAP implementation.

Perl, a popular programming language for system administrators and web programming, has two LDAP APIs. One is the Netscape PerLDAP SDK, which we briefly mentioned earlier. This API is a Perl "wrapper" around the Netscape C API. The other Perl API, called Net::LDAP, is a pure Perl implementation. By the time you read this, both APIs should share fairly similar feature sets. PerLDAP and Net::LDAP are both free and open source.

Gateway Services

It is very easy to make gateways to LDAP from other services, like the web, and have LDAP provide a gateway to other directory services. One example of using LDAP as a gateway service is in accessing Novell's NDS. Such a gateway has existed for a couple of years now. What this allows you to do is to search the proprietary NDS directory service via the open standard LDAP directory service protocol.

Another common gateway service is a web-based gateway. By providing a gateway like this, you make it very simple to use a 'thin' client to access directory information. Modern web browsers allow the use of languages like Dynamic HTML (DHTML) or client-side Java to create fairly sophisticated user interfaces with a minimal amount of development effort. In the future, XML (eXtensible Markup Language) should make this even easier, since it should provide for a common format to keep LDAP data in transit in a web environment. If you are not familiar with XML, a good web site is can be found at `http://www.xml.com`.

Native LDAP clients are now a part of both Netscape and Microsoft's web browsers, which means that the ability to access any LDAP server is now widely available.

It's also easy to distribute web-based clients – you just set up a server and give people a URL to look up. LDAP servers can supply a gateway to other services such as X.500 servers, existing legacy databases or even to other proprietary services like NDS or NIS+. Thus LDAP directories can become like *meta-directories*, providing access to potentially millions of records through a simple standard interface.

LDAP gateways make it easier on users to search, because they only have to learn the proper search technique for one type of service. They also make life easier for programmers, who only have to program to one type of service. They are easier to manage, because you only have to worry about managing one 'super-server', as opposed to a hundred different servers that each speaks a different language.

Our first diagram here shows how LDAP is likely to be used. An LDAP client queries against an LDAP compliant server which gets its data from a data source, which most likely will be a traditional database technology, but it could be a non-traditional source like an X.500 server or Novell NDS server.

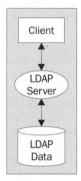

Our next example demonstrates how LDAP can be used as a gateway service. Here our client is a web browser that makes a request on a web server, most likely through a traditional HTML form. The web server then processes this request through a server-side process which could be either a traditional Common Gateway Interface program or something more advanced like a Java servlet. This server-side program then queries an LDAP server, which again gets its data from a database, an X.500 server or any other source. The results of this query are then passed back to the web server process and in turn returned to the client in the form of HTML.

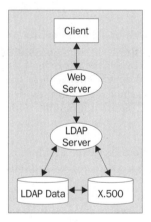

Vendor Support

While it might be possible for a company's own application programmers to write an LDAP server, it usually makes more sense to obtain one from a supplier.

The University of Michigan's LDAP server is still popular – and it's free. This utilizes the open source movement, much like the Apache web server or the Linux operating system. This gives several thousand developers access to a wide support group, and the opportunity to improve the server.

Also the major players within the Internet and networking worlds have all released their own LDAP servers, including:

- ❑ Netscape
- ❑ Novell
- ❑ Sun
- ❑ Microsoft

Netscape has made LDAP the key part of its entire overall product strategy. All Netscape products – from organization-wide browser management, and central server management (which include web, mail and newsgroup servers) through to certificate management for secure transactions – are all managed by their LDAP server, the **Netscape Directory Server**. Netscape has even licensed the Directory Server to other vendors to be included in other products.

Novell's NetWare 5 includes an LDAP interface to provide LDAP access to the NDS tree including the GroupWise address book. This means that NDS networks can now be exposed through a public interface, enabling a wide range of Internet applications.

Sun is working on a similar product for NIS+. For now, the focus is on improving LDAP for use in storing network data, including Java objects and using LDAP to manage their mail servers. There is an open source program, called **ypldap**, which facilitates the use of an LDAP server to manage NIS+ systems without replacing all the NIS+ clients. (The ypldap program is an open source client and not officially supported by Sun.)

Microsoft's Active Directory, which is going to be an integral part of Windows 2000, will have LDAP as its central protocol. Once this happens, all of the major networking vendors will have LDAP accessible directories in place.

You can see from the above discussion that LDAP use is widespread and has a great deal of vendor support. With several common APIs, it is now very straightforward to write LDAP applications and with Netscape and Microsoft's visible commitment to LDAP clients, LDAP is definitely here to stay.

What is LDAP Made Of?

The way to break into LDAP is to realize that the term 'LDAP' means many different things, which are summarized in the table below:

Parts of LDAP	Description
The Data Format	Defines how the directory information is stored and recalled
The Protocol	Defines how clients and servers interact with each other
The API	Defines how to programs that can interact with an LDAP server

In the rest of this section, we'll be looking at each of these different aspects of LDAP in greater detail.

Definition of LDAP Terminology

One of the hardest parts about dealing with the LDAP data format is the terminology. One of the terms you'll hear and read about is an **entry**. An entry is what we call a record in the LDAP server. It is akin to a record in a traditional database. An LDAP entry can also be called an object or an object entry.

A LDAP entry is made up of **attributes**. Attributes are divided into name/value(s) pairs. These attributes are similar to fields in a traditional database. An attribute will only have one name, but it can have more than one value. The values of an attribute can be either text or binary, depending upon the definition of the attribute.

Each entry is uniquely identified by it's **distinguished name (DN)**. The DN is made up of components, each of which is called a **relative distinguished name (RDN)**. The components that make up the RDN are taken from attributes in the entry. We'll see an example of a DN later in this chapter.

Object classes determine what attributes are available to an entry. They are akin to tables in traditional databases. However, object classes differ from traditional database tables in that they are extensible. What this means that if you can have an object class that allows a set of attributes (such as last name, e-mail address, etc.) and you want to add extra attributes to this object class, you can declare a new object class that extends from the earlier one. This new object class would have the ability to recognize the older object class's attributes as well as the new ones you added.

Each server will have a **schema**. The schema is the blueprint of the server and it specifies all of the object classes and attributes that are available to be searched and stored in an LDAP server.

The directory service is accessed like a tree and is referred to as a **Directory Information Tree (DIT)**. The directory server itself is called a **Directory Service Agent (DSA)**. For the rest of the book consider the terms "directory server" and "LDAP server" to be interchangeable.

Object classes, attributes and schemas are covered in more detail in Chapter 3.

LDAP: The Data Format

The key component of LDAP – and its most difficult part – is the data format. The data format is designed to be not only cross-platform but also cross-cultural. It is designed so that each entry can participate in a global naming scheme, called a **namespace**.

It is important to remember that people already have their own personal directory service. To get them to use a centralized service, it must be easy to use, answer the questions they want answered and the information must be correct. In other words if you want users to switch from their decentralized directory services to a standardized central directory service it must be easy to use, contain correct information and it must be useful to the end user. Remember, if directory services were easy, you probably wouldn't be reading this book.

The data in an LDAP server is organized in a hierarchical/relational format. (I know this sounds contradictory, but bear with me!) It is hierarchical because every entry in the server, apart from the root entry, is below another entry. It is relational because you can group entries together. This type of format maybe confusing at first, but it is how we generally try to categorize information.

For example, take life on this planet. (I'm not a biologist, so I'm going to keep things pretty basic.) Let's make 'Life' the root entry. Next, we further classify life as plants, animals, fungi, protists and bacteria.

Since we are animals, we'll follow the tree down the animal 'branch'. Animals can be defined as either vertebrates or invertebrates. Keeping things simple, let's just follow down the vertebrate line. The next line would be mammals, reptiles, fish and birds, and under mammals, the next entry could be me, Mark Wilcox. (Well OK, it should be People, and then me, but hey let's not get too detailed here.)

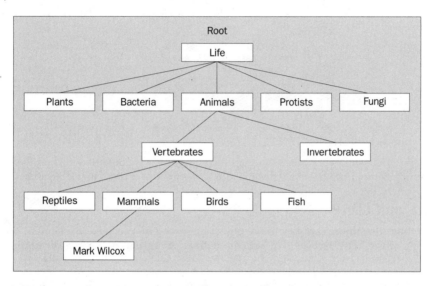

An example of a life group would be my family members. We will call it the Wilcox family, with Mom, Dad, sister and wife:

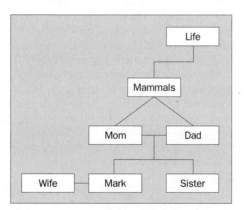

The LDAP hierarchy is similar to that of the above 'Life' example, except that it contains entries which refer to organizations and the objects those organizations deal with.

In LDAP, the top level is called the **domain**. There can be several domains in an LDAP implementation. This is because, like X.500, LDAP is designed to help provide a global directory service. Typically, the top-level domain will just be the root of the organization or organizations that a particular company manages.

The branches are in the form of **organizational units**, which are usually departments in an organization, but can be any convenient sub-division of that organization. Each entry that is not a domain and not an organizational unit is called a **leaf**. It is wise to have people in an organization as entries in both an organizational unit called `People`, as well as under their department related organizational unit, since this can speed up searches.

A very basic LDAP hierarchy is illustrated in the diagram below:

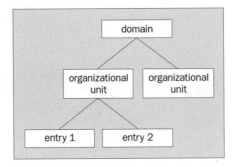

Domains, organizational units and every other type of information that is contained in the LDAP server must have a unique entry, and these entries must be a member of a particular object class.

Schemas, Objects and LDAP

Each LDAP server defines the object classes and the object hierarchy in a schema. Remember the schema is the blueprint of the LDAP server. The schema defines the format of the records in the database.

The entries in LDAP are in the form of objects. The object paradigm was chosen because it allows any form of data to be stored in an LDAP server. Also, objects can be extended without having to be completely redefined. To illustrate what I mean, let's consider a database. In traditional database design which uses the familiar table/field model, you are fixed to a particular design once the database has been created. If you have a table of some kind and you want to add some fields to it, you would normally have to redesign and recreate the table from scratch. Under the object paradigm, however, if you have an Object A and you want to use it to create Object B, you can just declare that you want to use all of the attributes available under Object A and then add some new attributes to make Object B. Another neat off-shoot of this is that now all objects that are of type B are also objects of type A because Object B is derived from Object A.

By using objects, it is possible to store a wide variety of data, including for instance:

❑   The organization itself, such as where it is located
❑   People, like their names and passwords
❑   Particular machine attributes, including password management information, such as how many times a user can re-try to authenticate and how old the password can be before it expires
❑   Other computers on the Internet, similar to DNS

Starting with X.500 and carrying onto LDAP, one of the goals of these protocols was to define schemas containing the maximum number of possible attributes that might appear in an object, so that, while users might need to define their own objects, the likelihood of them needing to define extra attributes would be minimized. There are provisions for defining your own attributes, and most of the commercial LDAP server vendors have done so.

The majority of values in an LDAP record are normally text based, but you can also include binary data. Often the binary data is in the form of photographs stored in the JPEG format, pictures of employees for example. However, you should never put a large amount of binary data into a LDAP server, as LDAP was not designed to help provide access to large binary objects. Often it is better to keep binary data in a separate spot like an FTP or WWW server and provide a reference URL in the LDAP record.

Object Types

There are four LDAP object types that are in common used:

❑ Person objects
❑ Organizational Unit objects
❑ Group objects
❑ Domain objects

Person Objects

Person objects are records that are used to describe people in an organization. They can take the form of `organizationalPerson` or `InetOrgPerson`.

The following attributes are typically required in a person object:

❑ Full name (called common name or `cn`)
❑ Last name (called surname or `sn`)
❑ First name (called `givenname`)

They often include extra attributes like:

❑ User ID
❑ Telephone number
❑ Fax number
❑ Location
❑ City

Organizational Unit Objects

Organizational units are object types that allow you to branch your directory information tree. You can identify an organizational unit by form such as "Accounting" or "Printers" or by function such "People" and "Groups". Organizational units are defined by the object class `organizationalUnit` and by the attribute name of `ou`. The attribute `ou` is often included in object classes outside of `organizationalUnit` such as the `inetOrgPerson` class.

Group Objects

Group objects are objects which contain an attribute called `uniquemember`. This attribute contains one or more values that are distinguished names of member entries. Normally groups will be group of people like "the Accounting Group" but you can group any type of entry together, including other groups. The group object class is called `groupOfUniqueMembers`.

Domain Objects

Domain objects are what I call the root level objects. These include the object class `domainObject`. They are called root level objects because they form the root of a Directory Information Tree and are the base of all DNs for entries contained in the server. These include the attributes of `organization`, `country`, `location` and `domain`.

Attributes and Distinguished Names

An entry can have an attribute with more than one possible value. For example, an employee can have more than one telephone number (one for work, one for home). Or an employee might go by a nickname, so you could have more than one first name (one for Richard and one for Dick).

When building a distinguished name (DN) for a `person` object, you want to make the lead entry in the DN the user ID, because this entry is probably unique for the entire server. If you don't have a user ID field, you may have to combine entries to make a unique entry. A possible combination would be one of common name and employee number.

Here is an example DN for a person object:

```
dn: uid=mewilcox,o=airius.com,c=us
```

Don't worry about the meaning of all of the attributes, as these will be explained later. They are defined as mnemonics, but until you learn them, they will be stumbling blocks to you. It is helpful to keep a short list of the common attributes handy until you learn them.

Here is a sample entry for `person` object:

```
dn: uid=scarter, ou=People, o=airius.com
cn: Sam Carter
sn: Carter
givenname: Sam
objectclass: top
objectclass: person
objectclass: organizationalPerson
objectclass: inetOrgPerson
ou: Accounting
ou: People
l: Sunnyvale
uid: scarter
mail: scarter@airius.com
telephonenumber: +1 408 555 4798
facsimiletelephonenumber: +1 408 555 9751
roomnumber: 4612
userpassword: scarter
manager: uid=husted, ou=People, o=airius.com
```

Here is a breakdown of the example record:

Record Entry	Record Meaning
dn: uid=scarter, ou=People, o=airius.com	Distinguished Name
cn: Sam Carter	Common Name
sn: Carter	Surname (last name)
givenname: Sam	Givenname (first name)
objectclass: top	Object class of type top
objectclass: person	Object class of type person
objectclass: organizationalPerson	Object class of type organizationalPerson
objectclass: inetOrgPerson	Object class of type inetOrgPerson
ou: Accounting	Organizational unit value of Accounting
ou: People	Organizational unit value of People
l: Sunnyvale	Location
uid: scarter	User ID
mail: scarter@airius.com	E-mail address
telephonenumber: +1 408 555 4798	Telephone number
facsimiletelephonenumber: +1 408 555 9751	Fax number
roomnumber: 4612	Room number
userpassword: scarter	Password
manager: uid=husted, ou=People, o=airius.com	This person's manager

This record is very simple, but it should be clear as to how this is useful. In this one record, we have stored Sam Carter's name, his department (Accounting), his location (useful if your organization spans multiple sites, or if the entry is in a global directory), his e-mail address and phone number. An important business information item is included here in the form of the manager field. By including the manager and accounting value, an ou field, we have now helped link Sam into his organization's structure.

LDAP: The Protocol

The extract shown below from RFC 2251 (the LDAPv3 standards track) explains the LDAP protocol model:

> *The general model adopted by this protocol is one of clients performing protocol operations against servers. In this model, a client transmits a protocol request describing the operation to be performed to a server. The server is then responsible for performing the necessary operation(s) in the directory. Upon completion of the operation(s), the server returns a response containing any results or errors to the requesting client.*
>
> *In keeping with the goal of easing the costs associated with use of the directory, it is an objective of this protocol to minimize the complexity of clients so as to facilitate widespread deployment of applications capable of using the directory.*

What this says in "protocolese" is that the protocol is designed to put most of the work on the server. This makes it easier both to write less complex clients and to deal with the results.

As we will find out starting in Chapter 6, developing LDAP applications is actually a straightforward endeavor. The difficulty lies in the design of the schema and the management of the data itself.

When a client interacts with an LDAP server it goes through three basic steps:

1. Connects to the server

2. Performs a series of operations with the server

3. Disconnects from the server

The connection and disconnection are standard TCP/IP connections.

Conserving TCP/IP Connections

LDAP uses the TCP/IP protocols for its basic network communications. TCP is CPU and memory intensive for creating connections between computers on the network. This is because TCP was designed for lengthy conversations and goes to great lengths to make sure that those conversations are able to occur. This requires a lot of overhead to make that sure that each message gets through successfully. This overhead includes finding multiple routes to each computer, breaking up the messages into packets, reassembling packets into complete messages and making sure that all of the packets were received and in order. Data correction (which is correcting data sent between computers so that the message received by a computer is the same as the one sent) is so critical that often a congested network is overfilled with packets that are flying back and forth to say they didn't get the last message that was sent.

The greatest 'hit' in terms of initial performance in any TCP connection (including those protocols like HTTP and LDAP which rely on TCP) is the initial startup and shutdown of those connections. If you can limit these hits to just one per application, performance levels will improve.

LDAP is an efficient protocol and can be used in limited bandwidth environments, and multiple operations can share a single connection. Also LDAP data is primarily text based and text does not take up a great deal of space and is easily compressed. Each operation is considered to be unique – they just happen to use the single shared TCP connection.

Because LDAP is a directory access protocol, it does not define how the directory entries are stored for later retrieval. This gives directory server developers a great deal of freedom in the design of their LDAP servers. It is possible to store the entries in a database, a flat-file or a proprietary back-end service like NDS. All that matters is that the server is able to speak LDAP to an LDAP client.

LDAP Operations

LDAP defines six possible operations that can be performed:

- ❑ Binding to the server
- ❑ Searching the server
- ❑ Compare entries
- ❑ Adding an entry to the server
- ❑ Modifying existing entries
- ❑ Removing an entry from the server

Binding to the Server

Binding to the server is akin to authenticating to the server. It is not the same as connecting to the server. A bind must match a given entry in the server, in most cases this entry will be a personal entry. When you bind to the server, you are telling the server that all operations that occur over this connection will be performed as that particular user. You do have the option to not bind a specific user, at which point the server will bind your connection as an anonymous user. All access rights to LDAP data is based upon how the connection is bound.

Many of the **access controls** to the data are based upon how a client is bound to the server. Access controls are special attributes that define how users can interact with LDAP data including searching, reading and modifying the data contained in a directory server. During a single connection, a client can bind and rebind several different times, while still maintaining a single open connection to the server. You might rebind if you need extra privileges (e.g. you might initially search as an anonymous user, but rebind to gain rights to modify or add a new entry). However, a client often binds once for a particular session and then disconnects.

Most services providing directory lookup as their only option often bind as anonymous users. As with anonymous operations in many services, the options open to these clients are often severely limited because an anonymous user has fewer privileges.

Most servers provide for some form of anonymous searching, but modification of the server requires that a client be bound as a non-anonymous entry in the database. In the current version of the protocol, you can specify granular control over the entries stored in the LDAP server, and so can cover access on a global or by entry status.

For example, you can enable the directory server so that individuals can modify their passwords, but that only their department's administrative assistants can change their managers and phone numbers. You can then say that human resources are the only people who can change the person's name or social security number. This gives a fine control of the data. We'll go into detail about how to bind to a server in the chapters on the various LDAP APIs (Chapters 6 – 10). We will also discuss security in more detail in Chapter 12.

Searching Entries

A key function of any directory service is the ability to look up information. LDAP provides a very sophisticated lookup operation in the form of its search functions and search filters.

Entries in the database are objects and objects have attributes with particular values. In order to search for a particular object, you can specify a value for one or more particular attributes. The search string we send to the server is called a **search filter**.

Shown below is an example filter where we are looking for all of the entries that are named Sam Carter:

```
(cn=Sam Carter)
```

The cn stands for **common name**, which is basically an entry's identity tag. A common name, always prefixed by 'cn=', can be a unique name such as 'cn=Big Boss' or it can consist of combining attributes together: 'cn=Sam Carter' is the same as linking 'givenname=Sam' and 'sn=Carter' with a space in between.

If you wanted to search for, say, any Sam Carter that worked in Engineering, you could use a more sophisticated filter:

```
(&(cn=Sam Carter)(ou=Engineering))
```

Here, the & means AND, and ou is the attribute label for **organizational unit**.

Suppose we wanted to look for all of the Carter's that worked in Engineering or Accounting. Well, to achieve this we could use the following:

```
(&(cn=*Carter)(|(ou=Engineering)(ou=Accounting)))
```

In the above line, the | means OR. The * is the wildcard character.

If you wanted to look for all entries and *not* include a particular series, you would use something like:

```
(&(!(cn=Sam Carter))(cn=*Carter))
```

Here, you would be looking for anyone with the name of Carter, except Sam Carter. Note that the ! means NOT.

All searches will return the **distinguished name** (DN) of the entry plus a series of attributes. A distinguished name, is the unique name of the entry in the LDAP server, and corresponds to the primary key in a relational database.

In the above section, we have looked briefly at filters, but there are also other possible ways of handling the results of a search. These will be covered in more detail later when we talk about using the LDAP APIs starting in Chapter 6.

Comparing Entries and Attrributes

A compare tests to see if an attribute value specified in a search matched that of an attribute contained within a particular entry on the LDAP server. The compare succeeds if there is such a match and fails if there is not one.

Modifying Entries

Modification of a LDAP database is usually straightforward.

All modifications are one of two types:

- ❏ Adding a new entry
- ❏ Modifying an existing entry

When you add a new entry, you must tell the server what type of entry it will be by specifying its object class. These object classes have two kinds of attributes: required attributes, which must be present, and optional 'allowed' attributes. Any new entry must have all of the required attributes filled with values before the entry can be added.

When you make modifications to an existing entry, you have the option of adding an extra value to an attribute or replacing an existing value. To complete a modification, you supply the DN of the entry to the server along with all of the new or changed attributes. The server then carries out the operation (e.g. adds the new value, changes a value for an attribute or deletes an a value).

Modifications are dependent upon the current binding of the client having the requisite permissions to write to the server in a particular part of the server's data tree. For example, the server administrator has the ability to make the server read-only, in which case it will not accept *any* writes. The server can be set up so that only particular user has rights to modify certain entries. All servers have an entry called `cn=Directory Manager`, and if a client is bound as this entry, then it can modify any record in the database. Similarly, you could have an Engineering Manager entry, an Accounting Manager entry, and so on, which can modify their respective members of their departments.

Modifications are also covered in more detail with the LDAP APIs in the later part of this book.

Removing Entries

Removing an entry is similar to modifying the database.

Removing an entry is as simple as supplying the server with the DN of the entry you want to remove and having the necessary rights to do so. The rights to remove of an entry should only be granted to a few unique entries, Directory Administrators for example, in order to prevent accidental or malicious deletes.

Other Protocol Services

There are three other services that version 3 of the LDAP protocol defines:

- ❏ Referral
- ❏ Replication
- ❏ Encryption/Security

Referral Service

The referral service is designed to allow LDAP servers to link to each other. This service allows you to implement a directory service between multiple organizations, or for the Internet.

You specifically set up the server to handle referrals and where to pass the referrals. Let's look at an example to see how this might work.

Suppose you have successfully deployed a series of LDAP servers across your organization and you have successfully entered data into each server. One server is located in Dallas, Texas and another is in the other corporate office in San Jose, California. In your server administration files, you tell your Dallas server to handle any search requests specifying the location of San Jose by informing the client that it needs to refer to the server in San Jose. Similarly, you would tell the San Jose server to do the same for any searches that include the location of Dallas. The result of this is that whenever a client performs a search in Dallas looking for someone in San Jose, the server responds by saying that the request needs to be referred to San Jose, and at this point, the client has the option to continue or to stop. This interaction will most likely occur without the user being aware, in much the same way DNS works for host name lookups on the Internet.

Replication Service

A directory server needs to provide a high availability service. It needs to be up around the clock and have the ability to respond quickly. One way to improve on both of these factors is by having multiple servers.

Multiple servers improve reliability, because if one server goes down, then at least one more is still running. You can improve speed with multiple servers in several ways:

❑   Load balancing requests between servers
❑   Removing the distance between clients

If you have a company that spans the country, it makes sense to have an LDAP server at all of your sites. Having multiple servers reduces requests to one particular server and can decrease overall network traffic – if you only have only one server, you can quickly overwhelm its network connection. It can also lessen the distance or the number of hops the data needs to travel.

In some cases, you may even want to have replicated servers that do nothing but talk to machines. For example, if you are using LDAP for authentication, you may want to have LDAP servers that are separate from your public 'address books', which do nothing but service authentication requests. This can dramatically increase speed, and means that if your public servers go down, you can still conduct business because your internal servers live on.

Security Service

Since LDAP servers can contain personal information, they can contain some of the most sensitive data in your organization. LDAP servers can reduce the network management overhead and improve the overall efficiency of your machines on the network, through the management of user IDs, passwords and certificates. In fact you would want to use LDAP to manage your network and computer systems to help guard against illicit access to the actual LDAP data store.

The latest versions of LDAP servers support a wide range of security/encryption protocols such as the Simple Authentication and Security Layer (SASL) and Secure Socket Layer (SSL) encryption. With Kerberos and SSL in conjunction with user certificates, it is possible to encrypt all transactions with an LDAP server, while ensuring that the client is bound as who they say they are.

By reducing the number user IDs and passwords an individual has to remember, it is easier to enforce policies that make stronger passwords and reliable password changes. It is also easier for the system administrators to keep track of who is using the network and who has access to the network.

The data in the server is protected through the use of Access Control Lists and client binding, regardless of server vendor. By default, all of the data in the server is protected from any action. The administrator of the LDAP server must specifically grant read, write, search, compare and delete access to the user before anyone can access the data.

Miscellaneous Protocols

One other area that LDAP version 3 has tackled is that of obtaining information about the LDAP server itself. It is now possible to query the server and find out about its schema. You can now even modify the schema from a client (rather than manually changing the configuration files). This gives you a great deal of flexibility in deploying your LDAP server.

LDAP: The APIs

One major factor that makes LDAP so exciting and has lead to its quick development is the ease of development of LDAP clients. Since the summer of 1998, there are now at least four major development efforts to make it even easier to develop LDAP clients. If you prefer to program in C, C++, Java or Perl there is now at least one API for you. In most cases you have a choice of SDKs to choose from in any of the listed languages. We will cover a wide variety of APIs in this book starting in Chapter 6.

University of Michigan API

The University of Michigan as part of their reference work provided the original LDAP API with their LDAP server. It was also used to help build the first LDAP clients and is still widely used. This API is written in C and was designed originally for the Unix/Linux platform.

Since its initial release, the API and the example clients have been ported to DOS, Windows and Macintosh systems. The first book on LDAP, *LDAP: Programming Directory-Enabled Applications with Lightweight Directory Access Protocol* by Howes and Smith (ISBN 1578700000) covered this API as well as the initial release of the Netscape C API.

The development of this API has continued to remain strong, but recent events and developments from Netscape may change this. This is because both Netscape and the Michigan code bases are now open source. This means that no single entity owns the code and that potentially the development is open to the thousands of Internet programmers. Michigan's code has been open since its initial release, but Netscape's didn't come until May of 1998.

Also in 1998 we saw the development of the OpenLDAP initiative. The OpenLDAP group has taken the University of Michigan server and C APIs for further development under an open source development environment like the Netscape SDKs and Apache web server.

Netscape SDKs

Netscape Communications Corporation is the company that only exists because of the Internet. The people who built the Mosaic web browser founded Netscape and continue to play a big part in Netscape's development. Mosaic was the first graphical browser that found widespread acceptance across multiple platforms.

What most people don't realize is that many of the other people who have helped build the Internet into what it is today are also a part of the Netscape core team. For example, Rob McCool, who wrote the NCSA web server while working with Marc Andreesen, who led the Mosaic development at NCSA in Illinois, heads Netscape's server division. NCSA was very popular in its time, but development on it stopped when Rob left for Netscape.

People who were using NCSA decided to continue development on the server themselves because the server was free, they had the source code and it worked pretty well anyway. They decided to call that server "a patchy version of NCSA" and thus they named it Apache. The Apache web server is now the most popular web server.

In a notion of great foresight – my words not theirs – Netscape saw the importance of a standardized directory service in the new era of the Internet and electronic commerce. They also had good reason to believe that LDAP was going to be the standard protocol to provide this unifying directory service. So, Netscape brought in Tim Howes and Mark Smith from the University of Michigan to run their Directory Server division. Howes and Smith are two of the people that pioneered the development of LDAP and still serve in the IETF to help further development of the LDAP protocol.

Since this has happened three things have occurred:

- ❑ Netscape launched its LDAP server, the Directory Server and made this server central to the Netscape server/management services line
- ❑ Netscape has developed SDKs for LDAP written in C, Java and Perl
- ❑ Netscape released the source code for their LDAP APIs

This has helped raise the consciousness of LDAP in the minds of system administrators and programmers everywhere.

The C and Java SDKs are near duplicates of each other. They both provide the same functionality and operate in a similar fashion. The C SDK is essentially a clean rewrite of the Michigan API to make it easier to fit into the extensions Netscape has added. The Perl SDK was developed with Clayton Donley, a Perl developer. This SDK actually interfaces with the C SDK using Perl's ability to easily interface with C.

During the summer of 1998, Netscape made available the source code to all of their SDKs in a similar fashion to what they had already done with their browser code. These developments have not resulted in the attention that the opening up of the browser has, but could pay bigger dividends in the long run. To make LDAP the unifying mechanism that it should be, it will need to be easy to make applications interface with LDAP servers. The two best ways of making this happen are to give developers a wide range of languages to choose from and to make sure that the APIs are not cornered by a single vendor.

By developing these three SDKs in Perl, C and Java, they have given developers many choices. The C SDK is already familiar to many existing LDAP developers and C/C++ is the most common language for development today. By opening the source, it gives developers the ability to port the programs to many different platforms including non-traditional devices like cell-phones. Developers now have the ability to provide support for many different languages that could otherwise not have occurred.

The Java programming language is definitely the hottest development language today. Java by default enjoys cross-platform deployment and localization with minimal effort on the programmer. Since Netscape's Java SDK is similar to the C SDK, they have made it easy to transfer skills and port programs from one programming language to another. This speeds up development and also helps leverage the growing popularity of the Java language/platform.

Perl is a very popular programming/scripting language. Larry Wall developed Perl to help him administrate Unix systems. Since he had already developed two other open development packages (including Patch, perhaps the smartest utility ever), he allowed Perl to be worked on by many others. Since a great deal of the work of managing Unix systems involves manipulating text files, Perl excels at parsing text strings. This ability has lent itself to the task Perl is probably best known for – CGI programming.

CGI programming, which enables the web to become a two-way street, requires the processing of the information passed from a web browser back to a program running on the web server. The information that is transferred back and forth is in the form of text streams. Since CGI requires a great deal of parsing of text, Perl is seen as being the best tool for the job. Another requirement of most CGI programs is that they are fairly simple, and don't really need the extra overhead of everything that writing programs in something like C or Java requires.

Perl is an interpreted language, so there is no need for a compiler – you just write your program and run it. It also doesn't require you to declare your variables, so it reduces the stress of the variable management that many a programmer suffers from. However, one of the unique things about Perl is that you can extend it, hence you can create Perl programs that do more complex tasks, requiring you to declare variables for example.

Perl programming is very widespread and there are hundreds if not thousands of programmers out there who like it a lot – some would say that their enthusiasm borders on religious zeal. There are Perl libraries (called modules) that can do nearly any task you can think of. By providing a Perl SDK to LDAP, Netscape has given another option to programmers and leveraged yet another popular development platform.

By providing these three SDKs Netscape has done an excellent job of making tools available to make LDAP the unifying directory mechanism its developers sought it out to be. Just like you can't build a house with just a hammer, you can't implement a major new protocol with only one language.

The popularity of the Netscape C SDK has now surpassed that of the University of Michigan API, when used with Unix and the Microsoft Windows (95/NT) platforms. The Java SDK is now included with every release of the Netscape Communicator suite which has helped increase its popularity. Also, the Perl SDK is in the process of linking with the first Perl LDAP SDK.

Netscape C, Java and Perl SDK Internals

You'll notice that often I'll switch between API and SDK. While you can split hairs over their differences (an API is just some code, an SDK gives you documentation and examples), in reality they mean the same thing to a developer.

To help gain a better understanding of how LDAP works, and perhaps to help you choose which SDK you may want to use for your own LDAP client development, let's spend some time discussing the Netscape C, Perl and Java SDKs. As we have already said, Netscape's C API is very similar to that of the University of Michigan but significantly different from how Sun and Microsoft implement their SDKs. We cover the Netscape C and Java SDKs in Chapters 6 and 8 respectively. We cover the Netscape Perl SDK, also called PerLDAP, in Chapter 7.

"Conversations" that occur during LDAP transactions all occur in a text based format. This means that all the information that is transferred – whether it's e-mail addresses, image files, or digital certificates – must all be converted into text, if they do not currently exist in that format. The conversion format that they follow is called the **Basic Encoding Rules** (BER) and is defined by the IETF. BER is a standard format for the transmission of data across the Internet, so this is not something new.

Also, because LDAP has the possibility of being used anywhere in the world, there must be support for languages that are not English and related languages. These common languages use an 8-bit (1 byte) encoding format called Latin-1. Unfortunately, Latin-1 does not support the basic characters for many other European languages (like Finnish), much less pictogram-based languages such as Japanese. To support these languages, a different character encoding format must be used, called **UTF-8**, which allows for the display of the standard (16-bit, 2 byte) Unicode format. UTF-8 is a binary encoding format of the Unicode character set.

Unicode supports all the most common modern languages. Like the common ASCII format, it uses a series of numbers to represent each character. To make it easy to switch from ASCII to Unicode, and to also support legacy applications, the Latin-1 character format numbers are the same for ASCII as they are for Unicode.

The UTF-8 encoding format is a variable width encoding format and it works like this: all Latin-1 characters are represented by their ASCII equivalent, so they are all 1 byte in length. If a character needs to be represented which is not in the Latin-1 character set then the most significant bit is flipped, which indicates that this character is longer than a byte. This is how UTF-8 is able to support many more characters than Latin-1 offers. The C API requires some work to make it support UTF-8, and there is little or no support for it in Perl. In Java, however, UTF-8 is the natural format for any application. The Java virtual machine takes care of translating between any encoding differences based on the locale the JVM is setup for.

Many of these details are hidden from the programmer. The SDKs help provide abstraction so that the programmer can concentrate on developing applications, and not how the data is going to be sent or delivered.

Essentially all three APIs are similar. The C, Java and Perl SDKs all share three common elements:

- ❏ LDAP Connection
- ❏ LDAP Operations
- ❏ LDAP Entry

The Netscape SDKs are designed to separate LDAP programming into three layers. Shown below is a diagram illustrating Netscape's LDAP SDK model:

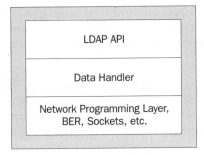

The top level layer is the LDAP API and provides the public interface to the programmer. At this layer, a programmer will make all of the calls to connect to an LDAP server, perform a query, etc. The middle layer, the Data Handlers layer, is where the necessary conversion is done for transfer from the client to server and vice versa. For example this is where binary data would be converted to Base-64 (a special encoding protocol for distributing binary data within text) or where the UTF-8 encoding for localization would be performed. Even though UTF-8 has been a standard for many years, many computing systems can't handle the full level of detail UTF-8 provides, so there is a need to convert some non-Western characters to Base-64 for display.

LDAP Connection

The functions/methods and variables that make up this area are concerned with the actual TCP/IP connection to the server. LDAP connections are a bit different from your typical HTTP connection. Remember that you can perform multiple operations over a single LDAP connection and each operation can be considered unique. Some of the values you could set in the connection might be the user your client is bound as, the maximum number of results you can accept, and basic tests such as establishing whether or not a connection has been made.

LDAP Operations

The functions and variables within the area of LDAP operations include everything needed to interact with the server. This where you set up the methods which search for entries contained in the LDAP server. This is also where you can add, modify or remove entries, and you can carry out more complex tasks such as backing up LDAP servers if a primary LDAP server should go down.

LDAP Entry

Each SDK contains a data structure that represents an entry in an LDAP server. In the C SDK, this is a structure, in Perl it's a Perl module, and in Java it's a class. This enables the programmer to get information about the entry. Some of this information is the DN of the entry, the class of which the entry is a part, and each of the attributes that make up the entry.

Multi-tasking

In the C SDK, you have the option to perform operations that are either synchronous or asynchronous. In a synchronous operation, your application is blocked until the operation returns a result. If you choose to do asynchronous operations, on the other hand, your application continues execution without blocking and you must continue to poll the connection for the results of the operation. In the time between the request and the reply, your application may be doing other useful work.

Having the option of asynchronous operations gives the programmer the ability to add multitasking to LDAP programs. This means that you can write a client which can continue to perform other operations while waiting for the results of a search. (At the time of writing, this is not possible in the Perl SDK.)

Java, however, has threading built in. Threading is how programmers take care of modern multitasking operations. There are no synchronous/asynchronous operations in the Java SDK, because if you want to do other things while a search is being performed, say, you can just create a new thread and then have that thread do the search. This is one of the benefits of Java.

The Netscape SDKs all benefit from three things:

❑ They are cross platform and cross-language
❑ Their source code is open for inspection, modification and use
❑ Netscape's strong commitment to LDAP

Because the SDKs are available in C, Perl and Java, and they are able to interact with any LDAP compliant server, the majority of the examples in this book will focus on these languages. This is because they are designed only to interact with LDAP servers. The idea behind this is that you only have to communicate with only one protocol: LDAP. This is different from the Sun and Microsoft SDK model where they offer the ability to communicate with many different directory protocols.

Sun and Microsoft's LDAP SDKs

It might strike you as ironic that we would discuss Microsoft and Sun under the same heading, given that they are often viewed as being such wide opposites. In terms of LDAP SDKs, however, they are very much cut from the same cloth. Where the Netscape SDKs view the world only through LDAP-colored eyes, Sun and Microsoft come from a 'service providers' point of view.

Sun's Java Naming and Directory Interface (JNDI) and Microsoft's Active Directory Service Interfaces (ADSI) enable the programmer to connect with a variety of network and directory services. The other services include Sun's NIS/NIS+, Novell's NDS and Microsoft's original networking technologies like Windows NT domains. The goal is to enable the programmer to connect to any directory-like service from either JNDI or ADSI from a protocol neutral API/SDK.

The reasoning for this is simple. Sun and Microsoft both have existing directory service infrastructures that they know are not going to be available as LDAP compatible services for a long time, if ever. (Or that is how it seems at the time of writing!) They are both also trying to compete with the other for platform dominance, and are both attempting to replace Novell's NDS. To help achieve this, they want programmers to be able to contact other directory systems, but mainly, they want to be able to connect with their own existing services, as well as LDAP.

The best way to think about how this works is to compare the way these companies are opening their directory services to the developers in recent years in the area of database communication. Sun's Java Database Connectivity (JDBC) and Microsoft's Open Database Connectivity (ODBC) have both made it easier to communicate with a wide variety of database systems via a common API.

Some of the differences between the two LDAP SDKs is that Sun's is only available in Java, whereas Microsoft ADSI is based on COM and is therefore programmable from several languages. We will cover Sun's JNDI in Chapter 9 and Microsoft's ADSI in Chapter 10.

The next two diagrams help demonstrate the difference between the Netscape LDAP SDKs view of directory services and the Sun JNDI/ Microsoft ADSI point of view.

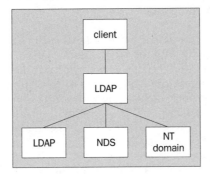

With the Netscape SDKs, the developer only needs to learn how to communicate via the LDAP API and an LDAP compliant server. It is up to the server vendor to worry about how to handle the communication from LDAP server to its back-end such as NDS or to a Windows NT domain.

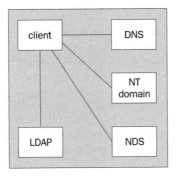

When using JNDI and ADSI, it is the programmer's task to decide which protocol to access. However he or she does have the advantage of a common API to access these various protocols.

Other SDKS

Net::LDAP

While Netscape has released PerLDAP as a supported SDK, it still requires the user to have a C SDK to interface with. This has lead to the development of another Perl LDAP module – Graham Barr's Net::LDAP library. This allows you to develop LDAP applications in straight Perl without requiring any extra libraries, which means you can port between any platforms, the only cost being speed of access. (Note that speed is a problem Java shares too.) Of course, now that 300-400 MHz desktop machines are becoming commonplace, speed has become a relative issue.

IBM's LDAP Provider for JNDI

Sun has made the JNDI open source so that anyone interested can write a service provider to use with it, just like anyone can write a database driver for JDBC. This is in the interest of making the most directory services available to the programmer.

As part of its AlphaWorks project, IBM developed a fully LDAP compliant provider for JNDI. However, an LDAP provider already ships with the JNDI, and AlphaWorks projects are, well, Alpha – meaning that they not usually as robust or portable as non-AlphaWorks software. IBM has begun to "graduate" some AlphaWorks technologies from AlphaWorks to "real" products, and this provider may be graduated at some point. Remember to check the AlphaWorks site at http://alphaworks.ibm.com for details.

We will cover these extra SDKs in more detail in Chapter 11.

Bear in mind the fact that none of the API's listed here are designed specifically for a particular LDAP server and it should be possible to use them to query any LDAP complaint server.

Summary

In this chapter, we have covered the basics of LDAP and the three fundamental parts that it comprises. We have seen that it was designed to be a simple client to X.500 servers, but is now used as both server and client. LDAP also retains most of the X.500 server's data format and namespace. We learned the wide support it has received among the Internet community and industry means that LDAP is a viable protocol that can be implemented today.

During the discussions in this chapter, we have learned about the data hierarchy and relationships of LDAP. This included a look at how the object hierarchy data structure is a natural data structure. We also discussed how security is built into the protocol and how the security functions give the server administrator a great deal of flexibility in building a directory service. Finally, we looked at the various APIs and their pros and cons.

The important points to remember from this chapter are summarized below:

- ❑ LDAP is derived from X.500
- ❑ LDAP is comprised of the data format, the protocol and the API
- ❑ LDAP servers can provide data from their own data store or act as a gateway service
- ❑ LDAP has vendor support
- ❑ LDAP has several APIs to develop clients

3

Object Classes, Schemas and LDIF

In this chapter, we start to dig into the details of LDAP. As you may have figured out already, LDAP is, roughly speaking, a type of specialized database application. A database application is basically a facility that allows a user to ask the database for some information (called a query) and returns all the data that matches that query in the form of records. LDAP is a protocol that defines how a particular type of data – directory data – should be structured for easy retrieval in a global scope using the Internet protocols, TCP/IP.

The primary focus of LDAP is to define directory data records in a standard format so that any user can access and store information locally on his or her machine. The way LDAP achieves this is through **object classes**, which are made up of **attributes**. Every **entry** in an LDAP server is made up of one or more object classes. Every LDAP server defines the object classes it accepts, and the way it handles requests to those object classes through a **schema** or **data definition**.

In this chapter, we're going to go into some depth about object classes and everything that makes up the core of the LDAP data format. We'll also cover the **LDAP Data Interchange Format**, usually referred to as **LDIF**, which is how we deal with LDAP data in real terms. We will thus lay the technical foundations upon which we will build our LDAP applications.

By the end of this chapter, you will have learned:

- ❑ What an object class is
- ❑ Why object classes are important
- ❑ The types of attributes
- ❑ Object class definitions
- ❑ The importance of schemas
- ❑ The basics of LDIF

LDAP, as an Internet based protocol, is designed to run on any hardware, operating system and language that can run the basic Internet protocols, TCP/IP, as described in Chapter 1. It doesn't really care how its operations are carried out or by whom. However, it does define how the computers involved in an LDAP transaction – the client and the server – should speak to each other.

A protocol defines how two or more entities should converse.

Databases vs. Directory Services

While the term *Directory Services* brings to mind something like a phone book, a true directory service should contain much more varied data than simple telephone numbers. While most directory service projects seek to provide an easily accessible mechanism for getting e-mail addresses and phone numbers, you never really know what you might want to include into your LDAP server. This is because we live in a networked world where we routinely interact with remote computers, remote printers, remote users, as well as engage in secure electronic transactions.

To be able to use a remote printer, your computer must know where it is. How will the computer manage this? (Hint: It's what this book is about!). This will be through an LDAP server.

Since an LDAP entry could conceivably contain any form of data, we need the most abstract form of data structure we can find. This data structure also needs to be designed so that it provides **metadata** about its entry. Metadata is a way of describing data, generally providing the minimum amount of information needed to locate a complete data source. A library catalog card is an example of metadata – containing just enough details for the client to easily find the required book: author, ISBN number, library catalog number.

We want a system which combines flexibility and speed, but we also want a consistent method of accessing and retrieving data stored in directories. The LDAP data model meets these requirements. Databases have provided this kind of mechanism in the past (and in fact they still make up the back-end of most LDAP servers). LDAP allows us to store information for later access.

Drawbacks of Traditional Database Applications

Traditional databases, however, are not as flexible as we would like. The massive databases like those created by Oracle or Microsoft's SQL Server are designed to provide their clients with a robust user environment which reduces the risk of data being lost or corrupted in this flaky computer world we operate in. These large database management systems are extremely complex to manage and have been optimized for reads and writes to be averaged out. Compare this with an LDAP server like Netscape's Directory Server, which has been optimized for read access because LDAP servers will be read more often than written to. Traditionally, LDAP servers are also easier to manage than say an Oracle server, because an Oracle (or any other large RDBMS) is meant to be able handle a larger set of problems than a LDAP server must. This is why traditional database design and administration is a very difficult task (which is why database administrators make the big bucks).

On the opposite end of the scale from Oracle and SQL Server are flat-file and MS Access databases. **Flat-file databases** are so called because they don't have any relationships defined in them and are generally contained in a single file. Flat-file databases can be accessed very quickly, but they do not scale very well, and it is very hard or impossible to define any relationships between the data.

One of the most popular databases in use today is the Microsoft Access database application. Access has a very nice GUI and wizards built in that make it very easy to make a relational database. Unfortunately, Access has problems because it doesn't fully support **Structured Query Language** (SQL) which is a standard for querying databases. Also Access is not designed for multiple simultaneous user access, which really limits its usefulness in a network application.

Relational Database Management Systems

The most common databases today, the **Relational Database Management Systems** (**RDBMS**), are designed for reliable service and transaction management. Because they deal with how data is interrelated, a lot of code is committed to making sure that any changes made to the data (that is, insertions, updates and deletions) are carefully monitored, so that if anything goes wrong, the integrity of the database is maintained. Today's powerful RDBMSs like Microsoft's SQL Server and Oracle have done a very good job at protecting their data in this way.

However, the upshot of this drive toward data integrity is an increased difficulty of use. It takes a lot of work to create and manage RDBMS data sources. You constantly have to redesign and build new databases to handle migrations, and a lot of hard work is needed to determine the best way to retrieve data and display it in a meaningful fashion.

For example, you can store just about any type of data in these systems, but you had better get your database format right from the start. If you design a table, the simplest form of a database, and later on you decide to modify that table, you are in for a battle. You must create a brand new table with the new format. Only then can you move your data from the old table to the new one. If you are talking about just one table, this might not be so bad, but considering that some databases can have several hundred tables all linked together, this can become a nightmarish transition. Imagine the problem of a company's central database with gigabytes of data that has to be restructured and the company depends on that data for its livelihood – there would also be plenty of sleepless nights and black coffee.

As you can see, database design is not a trivial task. Because of the cost involved in modifying a database structure in terms of time and risk, database administrators earn every penny of those $80,000 salaries. Yet, considering the value of many of these databases to companies, DBAs are still, of course, heavily underpaid!

However, there are other ways (such as LDAP) of constructing a database system without having to struggle with the complexity of an RDBMS. LDAP servers can contain a variety of information, which requires a variety of attributes to properly describe it. Examples of such information include descriptions people, store application configuration information, or persistent objects (for example, you can store the state of a Java class between invocations).

We have learned that the LDAP service is going to be constructed as a unique, hierarchical data structure. Experience has shown that directory services are more often read (or searched) rather than written to. This means that if they are out of synch (perhaps someone's phone number changes and it's not updated in the server) for a short period of time that is not generally a problem, so long as they are updated on a regular basis.

Introduction to LDAP Objects

LDAP entries are like records in a traditional database. An entry is treated as an object. In the programming world, we refer to objects as having data and methods (or functions) that act on the data. For LDAP however, we are only concerned with the data. Each object has one or more attributes, which are in the form of name and value. Each attribute can have one or more values.

When we need to reference one object from another, we must *name* the object. We name an object because we must have a way to refer to that object when we are talking about it. One of the characteristics of us humans that separates us from the animals is that we must name everything. Each object will have a unique name called a **Distinguished Name** (**DN**), which will be different from any other name in the entire LDAP tree (which could span the entire world).

> An LDAP object is an entity that is described with attributes and has a unique name, by which it is referred to when used along with other objects.

Why Objects?

Learning to deal with objects is one of the hardest concepts people have to grasp. Because we live in the physical world, we deal with physical tasks. While we know everything is made up of atoms and molecules, we often don't really grasp the concept of millions of atoms that are spinning around that make up the world around us, including ourselves.

We refer to everything in terms of what we can see, hear, smell and so on. So, instead of saying that we have a 'gathering of water molecules, high up in the air', we say we have 'clouds'. We even give names to that what we can't normally see, like air – heck, we even give name to that which is made up of mostly nothing – outer space.

In the past ten to fifteen years, programmers have tried to grasp object-oriented programming (OOP) languages like C++ and Java. The hardest part about these languages is generally not the syntax of the language, but 'thinking in objects'. This is hard because programming is really how we tell the computer to do something. When you tell a person how to do something, you tell them in steps. This is no different in computer programming, where we call these steps 'procedures' or functions. In OOP, we hide these steps inside of objects. Traditionally, objects are only discussed in a large-scale manner is in the context of object-oriented programming, where objects have properties or attributes and methods that modify those attributes. The aim of OOP was to improve programming by making it easier to 'share the wheel', e.g. reuse code.

So, instead of talking about objects in the abstract, perhaps an example would help us understand what we mean.

An Object Example

Objects are all around us. People are objects. Computers are objects. Trees, insects, flowers, atoms and *Guns 'n' Roses* CDs are all objects.

But what makes an 'object' an object?

That question is difficult to answer in a simple but complete way, but for the purpose of our discussion, we will define an object in very simple terms as *something we can reference*.

To help us grasp what is meant by an object, let's briefly discuss how me might describe a *Guns 'n' Roses* CD. We will describe the CD using a series of related types of objects, which we call object classes. An object class describes the type of object, and the object itself is the individual instance of that type, which comprises the LDAP entry. The term object is simply how we refer to entries when 'talking LDAP'. Remember also that an object has attributes that describe it. An attribute will have a name, such as 'musictype' and one or more values like 'Rock and Roll' and 'Heavy Metal'.

To classify a particular CD, we at least need the following attributes:

- ❑ Album name
- ❑ Singer or Group Name
- ❑ Song
- ❑ Year Produced
- ❑ Record Company

So an example of a CD object could be (in psuedo-LDIF):

```
DN: Album name=Appetite For Destruction,Singer or Group Name=Guns 'n' Roses,
    Year Produced=1987
Object class: CD
Album name: Appetite For Destruction
Singer or Group Name: Guns 'n' Roses
Year Produced: 1987
Song: Welcome to the Jungle
Song: It's So Easy
Song: NightTrain
Song: Mr. Brownstone
Song: Paradise City
Song: My Michelle
Song: Think About You
Song: Sweet Child O' Mine
Song: You're Crazy
Song: Anything Goes
Song: Rocket Queen
Record Company: Geffen
Record Company: Uzi Suicide
```

Metadata

You can think of a directory entry as being a type of **metadata**, that is, it helps provide a reference to an item by providing a small subset of information about the item. A library catalog card is a form of metadata about a book. The record is not the book itself, but rather it provides just a small subset of information that can be used to describe the book. A would-be reader or purchaser of the book could use that record to find out more about the book. The information on the card would typically include the title, the author, the subject, the edition of the book, maybe even a synopsis of the book, and of course the catalog number. This gives you basic details about the book, while also helping you locate the book on the shelf, but nothing more.

Card catalog records are typically organized into three areas:

```
Author
Title
Subject
```

However, since many catalogs are now computerized, this distinction is somewhat blurred, but it still pretty much works this way.

Suppose you want to find all of the books by Stephen King – you would look through the *author index* until you found Stephen King. Or you might decide that you want to find all of the books on LDAP. So you would go look under the *subject index*. If you find the subject areas, you could safely assume that all of the books found there are about the Lightweight Directory Access Protocol. And then there are times when you know the title of the book you are looking for, but not the author. The *title index* helps you locate the entry. Of course, if you don't know what the book is about, you can get an idea by reading the *synopsis* on the card, if it has one. The *catalog number* is helpful, not only for locating where the book is in the library, but also for providing extra information about the book.

Most lay-people think that the classification systems exist only as a means to shelve books. But in fact, because each classification scheme organizes by subject area, a person who understands the basics of the classification system can usually tell something about the books in a particular area, just by the catalog number (also known as their call number). For example in libraries that use the Dewey Decimal system, call numbers that start with 500 are in the Science section.

Thus, metadata is very important in the real world.

LDAP servers deal in metadata because they don't usually serve up the object described (unless we soon figure out transporter technology and then perhaps we can indeed be stored in a computer!), but instead they provide information that is useful for locating the object the entry describes. It not only can help you find the object, but sometimes it can even tell you extra things about the object.

LDAP Objects Defined

So far, we have discussed various means of how to store our data for later retrieval. We have learned why entries containing attribute lists (called objects in LDAP) are the most flexible data model to use, because they don't really define anything in stone, while still providing a common reference point.

Another facet of objects in LDAP is that some attributes are required and some are optional. Generally, attributes that are required are the ones that are used to uniquely identify that particular object. The optional attributes are ones that just help to describe that particular object in detail. To determine what attributes are required and optional we use object classes to define them.

All entries are uniquely identified through the use of a **Distinguished Name** (**DN**) that is made up of existing attributes in the entry. Each part of a DN is called a **Relative Distinguished Name**, or RDN.

LDAP entries are ordered in a hierarchical fashion, as inherited from the X.500 Directory Access Protocol. The hierarchy is defined by a particular object class.

LDAP RFC Objects

Objects need to have a common format so that they can be shared between different vendor implementations of LDAP servers. To ensure this, the object classes themselves and their possible attributes are defined in an RFC – RFC 2256. This is designed to help standardize the LDAP data definitions, in particular how they relate to the earlier X.500 Directory Access Protocol. One of the areas where the X.500 legacy is maintained in LDAP is in the data format. This is helpful, because the X.500 data model was well designed and makes it easier for LDAP to be a gateway service between a user and an X.500 server.

Data formats take the following form:

```
( 2.5.4.5 NAME 'serialNumber' EQUALITY caseIgnoreMatch
       SUBSTR caseIgnoreSubstringsMatch
       SYNTAX 1.3.6.1.4.1.1466.115.121.1.44{{64} )
```

`2.5.4.5` is an **object identifier**, referred to as an **OID**. OIDs are used to help identify object classes and their attributes in a unique fashion. They are broken into groups and if you know how to read the OID syntax, you can figure out where the particular object or attribute originated. Any organization that wishes to create their own object classes or attributes should define them in their own OID namespace. The `2.5.4` in the OID above refers to the IETF defined objects and attributes. You can get your own OID by visiting the Internet Assigned Numbers Authority (IANA) at `http://www.iana.org/`.

The `NAME` label means that the name of the attribute or object class follows directly after. In the example above, it is `serialNumber`.

`EQUALITY` refers to how a comparison should be made between two `serialNumber` attributes. In the above example, the `caseIgnoreMatch` means that, when comparing the values of two `serialNumber` attributes containing alphabetic data, the case does not matter. For example, `ab1292de` is equal to `AB1292DE`. Other example values for `EQUALITY` could be `distinguishedNameMatch`, which means that the value must be a distinguished name, or `telephoneNumberMatch`, which ignores parts of text that are usually parts of a telephone number like `"-"` and `"()"`.

`SUBSTR` means that a match is successful if the search term is equal to part of the value of a `serialNumber` attribute. Because the `SUBSTR` label has the value `caseIgnoreSubstringsMatch`, the match is made regardless of case. `ab129` is considered to be equal to `AB129`.

The `SYNTAX` field is used to describe which particular object syntax definition you can use. The `{64}` means that the suggested upper limit for the value of this attribute is 64 characters. Since this is only a suggestion, it could be more, or it could be less, depending upon the particular LDAP server. This is like a field limit in a more traditional database. A syntax definition defines what type of data you can stick into an attribute value. The majority of attribute's syntax will be text. Other value types could be Distinguished Name and binary. The syntaxes are given as OIDs and are defined in the X.500 standards. Luckily, most servers and APIs tell you what the syntax of an attribute is, in humanly understandable terms.

In summary, the above data definition means the following: the attribute's name is `serialNumber` and when we compare two `serialNumber` attributes containing alphabetic data, the case does not matter. Finally, the entry can be up to 64 characters in length.

Whew! Aren't you glad you don't have to mess with these definitions everyday?

The next section covers a few common definitions of LDAP object classes and attributes. All of these definitions can be found in RFC 2256 on any of the many Internet RFC depositories.

Object Class and Attribute Definitions

Object Classes

The values of the `objectclass` attribute of an entry define what type of object the LDAP entry is. The `objectclass` attributes are handled a bit differently from other attributes. This is because an `objectclass` attribute defines what other attributes can appear in an entry. The best analogy I can give for an `objectclass` attribute is to say that it is similar to a table in a traditional database. In traditional databases, a table defines the fields for a record in the database. In LDAP, an `objectclass` defines what attributes are in an LDAP entry. The relationship of an `objectclass` value and its attributes are kept in the server's schema.

The following code extract defines what an `objectclass` attribute is:

```
(2.5.4.0 NAME 'objectclass' EQUALITY objectIdentifierMatch
        SYNTAX 1.3.6.1.4.1.1466.115.121.1.38 )
```

The next definition is slightly different:

```
( 2.5.4.1 NAME 'aliasedObjectName' EQUALITY distinguishedNameMatch
        SYNTAX 1.3.6.1.4.1.1466.115.121.1.12 SINGLE-VALUE )
```

Note that in the above definition, the `aliasedObjectName` attribute has an extra label that says `SINGLE-VALUE`. This means that this particular attribute can only have one value. If this label is missing then the attribute can have one or more values. The above extract defines how to handle an aliased object class. An aliased object class is one that does not contain any actual attributes, but instead points to another object class that holds the 'real' information. This is useful if you have migrated data or if you provide a different name to a different entry.

Attributes

Now we come to defining attributes:

```
( 2.5.4.41 NAME 'name' EQUALITY caseIgnoreMatch
      SUBSTR caseIgnoreSubstringsMatch
      SYNTAX 1.3.6.1.4.1.1466.115.121.1.15{32768} )
```

This is the definition of the `name` attribute, which as you can probably guess, is the attribute to define how fields that name an entry are used. Attributes that use `name` include:

❑ cn (common name)
❑ sn (surname or last name)
❑ givenname (first name)

The definition for the common name attribute is:

```
( 2.5.4.3 NAME 'cn' SUP name )
```

We define the common name attribute's values to be the names by which the entry is often referred. For example, my full name is *Mark Edward Wilcox*, but most people just know me as *Mark Wilcox*. So, to make it easier for people to look me up in an LDAP server, I'd have two cn values, Mark Edward Wilcox and Mark Wilcox, because these are the two names by which I'm commonly known. If the entry was to describe a printer, we might give it a cn value such as Marquis Hall Printer. This would help people locate this printer because they are more likely to know *Marquis Hall Printer* than, say, the printer's IP address. The SUP element of the above definition means that the common name attribute follows the data entry restrictions and the matching rules of the name entry, outlined earlier.

The next type of definition is for user certificates, which are special files used for encryption over a network:

```
( 2.5.4.36 NAME 'userCertificate'
      SYNTAX 1.3.6.1.4.1.1466.115.121.1.8 )
```

User certificates can also provide 'digital signatures' for automated logon or e-commerce. It should be noted that the SYNTAX value is different and is for entry information that should be stored in a binary format.

The following four attributes *must* be present in all subschema entries:

❑ cn – this attribute must be used to form the RDN of the subschema entry
❑ objectclass – this attribute must have at least the values top and subschema
❑ objectclasses – each value of this attribute specifies an object class known to the server
❑ attributeTypes – each value of this attribute specifies an attribute type known to the server

A **subschema** entry is the entry that all LDAP v3 compliant databases have that contains all of the relationships between object classes and their attributes. It also contains all the definitions of attributes.

Operational Attributes

The following definition is taken from RFC 2251, which defines the LDAP version 3 protocol:

Entries may contain, among others, the following operational attributes. These attributes are maintained automatically by the server and are not modifiable by clients:

❑ *creatorsName* – the distinguished name of the user who added this entry to the directory
❑ *createTimestamp* – the time this entry was added to the directory
❑ *modifiersName* – the distinguished name of the user who last modified this entry

❑ *modifyTimestamp* – the time this entry was last modified

❑ *subschemaSubentry* – the distinguished name of the subschema entry (or subentry) which controls the schema for this entry

An **operational attribute** is an attribute that is defined for use by the server. These attributes are used by the server to perform special actions, on either the attribute or entire entry. For example, an operational attribute might let the server know that it should encode all userpassword attributes using the SHA-1 algorithm. Another example of an operational attribute is the modifytimestamp used by the Netscape Directory server to show the time when the entry was last updated.

Certain object class attributes can be used to help define the hierarchy of the Directory Information Tree (DIT). For example, if we had an LDAP server that contained many different organizations' directories for a given country, then the result might look like this:

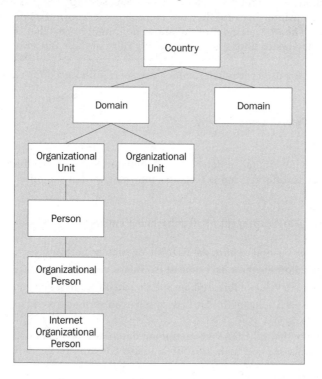

The top of the DIT is defined by the attributes of the country object class (e.g. US). The branches in the next level are defined by the Internet domain name of the organization (represented with the domainclass object class), for example, unt.edu and airius.com. The level below the domain contains the first branches inside the organization, which are the organizational units in this example (the organizationalUnit object class). The leaf of the tree in this figure is the person, which is made up of person, organizational person and Internet organizational person, represented by the Person, organizationalPerson and inetOrgPerson object class attributes respectively. The reason why there are 3 object class attributes for a particular person is because organizationalPerson extends person and inetOrgPerson extends organizationalPerson.

What is meant by 'extend' in this context is that each new object class inherits all of the attributes of the earlier object class and then adds its own attributes.

Schemas

The term **schema** literally means 'outline'. In the database world, schemas are used to define the structure of the database – that is, the outline of the database. In LDAP, schemas provide a similar function. Every LDAP server must use a particular schema, which defines what attributes can be stored in what types of object. There is even kind of a 'super-schema' that the RFCs define by describing what the basic LDAP object classes are and how they should be used. Every LDAP server supports this 'super-schema'.

A basic LDAP schema defines:

- ❑ The server's name
- ❑ The port(s) it operates on
- ❑ The Directory Manager of the server
- ❑ The root domain of the object tree that the server will reference.

The Directory Manager is a special account created in LDAP servers that is the 'super-user' for the server. It can modify or read any attributes or entries contained in the server. It is wise to only use the Directory Manager account to set up your server and then use a different account to manage your server after it has been set up.

LDAP servers are designed to enforce strict schema checking, which should make sure that every LDAP server supports the basic LDAP functionality – that Company A's inetOrgPerson object class is the same as Company B's inetOrgPerson object class.

Example Schema

Shown below is an extract from the basic schema definition that the Netscape Directory Server uses (one of the most common LDAP servers that is available today). It's found in the slapd.at.conf file and comes with every version of the Netscape Directory server:

```
#   slapd.at.conf for Netscape Directory Server 3.1
#
#   DO NOT MODIFY!
#
#   The attributes listed in this file are Standard Attributes and are
#   expected to present in Directory Server 3.1. Editing this file could
#   cause interoperability problems.
#
#   User Defined Attributes should be added by selecting
#   Schema | Edit or View Attributes from the Admin Server.
#
#   User Defined Attributes are placed in slapd.user_at.conf.
#
#   All attributes are viewable over LDAP in the cn=schema entry under
#   attributetypes.
```

```
#
#  The format of this file is:
#
#   attribute attribute-name [attribute-aliases] [attribute-oid] syntax
#
#   If no OID is specified, <attribute-name>-oid will be used as the OID
#

#######################################################################
# X.500(93) User Schema for use with LDAP
# Taken from <draft-ietf-asid-ldapv3schema-x500-00.txt>
#######################################################################

attribute objectClass                      2.5.4.0              cis
attribute aliasedObjectName                2.5.4.1              dn
attribute knowledgeInformation             2.5.4.2              cis
attribute cn            commonName         2.5.4.3              cis
attribute sn            surName            2.5.4.4              cis
attribute serialNumber                     2.5.4.5              cis
attribute c             countryName        2.5.4.6              cis
    .
    .
    .

#######################################################################
# LDAP Attributes                                                     #
# Taken from <draft-ietf-asid-ldapv3-attributes-07.txt>              #
#######################################################################

attribute createTimestamp                  2.5.18.1             cis
attribute modifyTimestamp                  2.5.18.2             cis
attribute creatorsName                     2.5.18.3             dn
attribute modifiersName                    2.5.18.4             dn
attribute subschemaSubentry                2.5.18.10            dn
```

The full version of this file (which is too long to show in its entirety here!) contains a very complete list of attributes, and you would be hard-pressed to think of any that have been left out. The labels you see in the far right-hand side define how each attribute should be enforced.

Here are a few of the more common ones:

- ❑ cis – *case-ignore string* which means that the strings abc and ABC are equivalent
- ❑ ces – *case-enforce string* meaning that the strings abc and ABC are not equivalent
- ❑ tel – means that the data must be entered in a recognized telephone format
- ❑ bin – means that attribute must be entered as binary data.
- ❑ dn – refers to the attribute's distinguished name, which is unique for every entry in an LDAP server

Without this basic schema, the Netscape Directory Server will not work. (In appendix D, you can find out how to extend the existing schema.)

An Example LDAP Directory

To help bring the information presented in this chapter together, we will briefly take a look at how we might build an LDAP directory. Since we will neither get into the details of the various LDAP servers until the next chapter, nor begin to really talk about building LDAP clients until Chapter 6, this discussion will be kept very basic.

Let's assume we have an organization named *Airius, Inc.* Airius is a regional aviation carrier with locations in Dallas, Texas and Denver, Colorado. They have several different organizational departments, such as Aviation Crew, Accounting, Marketing, Human Resources and so on. Each organizational department has a set of managers, who are in charge of their departments. Airius's domain name is `airius.com`.

Deciding on a Naming Scheme

There is no formal or required way for building an LDAP directory or building the distinguished names that form the unique key for each LDAP entry. The way we build the DN (and in turn describe our directory structure) is called a **naming scheme**.

Problems with the X.500 Naming Scheme

Originally, the concept was to follow the X.500 scheme. This scheme would base the root of the tree at the country level (`c=US`), and then the first branch was the organization's name (`o=Airius, Inc`). Unfortunately, there is no mechanism to insure that every organization has a distinct name in the entire country, much less the world. This means that there is a good possibility you could have a multi-organizational LDAP server that could have two organizations with the same name, but are two totally different organizations. For example you could have an Airius, Inc. that was an aviation company and an Airius, Inc. that made vacuum cleaners. To help provide an extra level of uniqueness, X.500 practices recommend adding in extra location information, such as the city. This is referred to as locality (`l`) in LDAP and X.500, and state (`st`). The process, however, leads to the creation a very long DN, before we even begin to discuss the structure of the internal organizational tree. If you are wondering why this is, it's because a DN is required to have all of the parts that make up the directory in it. That is, a DN must not only have an attribute from the entry, such as the user ID, but in X.500 it also has the organization's name, the city, state and country where the organization is located, even if the organization only existed in a single city. While I don't know of any restrictions on the absolute size of a DN, in practical terms, the shorter they are, while still maintaining uniqueness, the better. This is because people may have to type in the DN, and the more characters there are to type, the greater the likelihood of a mistake occurring. Another reason why this system has problems is that if your organization moves or merges, it can be very difficult on the directory administrators to migrate the data and restructure the directory.

An example DN using the X.500 scheme might look like this:

```
dn: cn=Mark Wilcox, ou=Air Crew, o=Airius, Inc, l=Dallas, st=Texas, c=US
```

Success with Internet Domains

Already a standardized naming scheme exists that is very popular. This is the Internet domain naming scheme. The domain naming scheme is how we provide unique names to every host on the Internet, such as `www.yahoo.com`. As you might remember from Chapter 1, the domain name for `www.yahoo.com` is `yahoo.com`.

There are two ways we can use this scheme in LDAP. One way is to set the organization attribute (o) to equal the full domain name, such as o=airius.com. An example of a DN built with this use of Internet domain names might look like this:

```
dn: cn=Mark Wilcox, ou=Air Crew, o=airius.com
```

Another way is to use the domain component attribute (dc). Each dc is set to part of the domain name, such as dc=airius,dc=com. The domain component model is recommended in a draft specification from the Internet Engineering Task Force (IETF) in RFC 2377.

An example DN built in this manner might look like this:

```
dn: cn=Mark Wilcox, ou=Air Crew, dc=airius,dc=com
```

As you encounter LDAP in your day to day work, you are likely going to see both ways of using Internet domains (and even the X.500 model, which some directories still use).

Further Considerations

You might be tempted to organize entries in the tree by the departments people work in. (Remember that one function the DN provides to help provide uniqueness in the directory.) Fight this temptation, because not only do people change departments, but also the organizations are likely to go through reorganization, at least once in their lifetime. However, if you go with a design based more on function – that is, you group entries by what type of object they are, such as People or Applications – your directory will be easier to manage. You won't have to keep moving people's entries around, even if your organization reorganizes itself every 6 weeks like in some kind of Dilbert cartoon. You can still put the department a person works in as a standard attribute in their entry, just don't include it in an entry's DN.

Another consideration is that when you add a person entry, you should include the uid (user ID) attribute in the DN, instead of the person's cn (common name) attribute. This is because it is likely that you will have two or more people in your organization that will share the same name, but you shouldn't have any duplicate user IDs.

Building the Airius, Inc Directory

We will root the Airius, Inc. LDAP directory at the organization level. For this example, we are going to keep it simple, so we will use the organizational attribute (o). The value for this will be o=airius.com. We will add two people entries and an entry for a group of users.

To layout the directory data we will use the **LDAP Data Interchange Format** (LDIF) to describe the directory. Don't worry about the details of LDIF just yet – we'll be discussing these in the next section.

Here's how to build the root entry of the directory and this uses the organization object class:

```
dn: o=airius.com
objectclass: top
objectclass: organization
o: airius.com
```

Shown below is the addition of two new entries, which will form the branches of our tree, using the `organizationalUnit` object class:

```
dn: ou=Groups, o=airius.com
objectclass: top
objectclass: organizationalUnit
ou: Groups

dn: ou=People, o=airius.com
objectclass: top
objectclass: organizationalUnit
ou: People
```

Next, we'll add our people entries, one for Sam Carter, who's in the Denver office and works in Accounting. The other entry will be for Mark Wilcox, who's located in the Dallas office and works in the Air Crew department:

```
dn: uid=scarter, ou=People, o=airius.com
cn: Sam Carter
sn: Carter
givenname: Sam
objectclass: top
objectclass: person
objectclass: organizationalPerson
objectclass: inetOrgPerson
ou: Accounting
ou: People
l: Denver
uid: scarter
mail: scarter@airius.com
telephonenumber: +1 303 555 4798
facsimiletelephonenumber: +1 303 555 9751
roomnumber: 4612
userpassword: sprain

dn: uid=mwilcox, ou=People, o=airius.com
cn: Mark Wilcox
sn: Wilcox
givenname: Mark
objectclass: top
objectclass: person
objectclass: organizationalPerson
objectclass: inetOrgPerson
ou: Air Crew
ou: People
l: Dallas
uid: mwilcox
mail: mwilcox@airius.com
telephonenumber: +1 214 555 9187
facsimiletelephonenumber: +1 214 555 8473
roomnumber: 4117
userpassword: irrefutable
```

Finally, we will add an entry that is a group of Accounting Managers:

```
dn: cn=Accounting Managers,ou=groups,o=airius.com
objectclass: top
objectclass: groupOfUniqueNames
```

```
cn: Accounting Managers
ou: groups
uniquemember: uid=scarter, ou=People, o=airius.com
uniquemember: uid=tmorris, ou=People, o=airius.com
description: People who can manage accounting entries
```

Notice that the `uniquemember` attribute of the last entry is a DN that points to the group's member entry. You probably noticed that each entry shares a common `objectclass` attribute with a value of `top`. This object class is the parent of all `objectclass` attributes.

Shown below is a visual illustration of our simple directory:

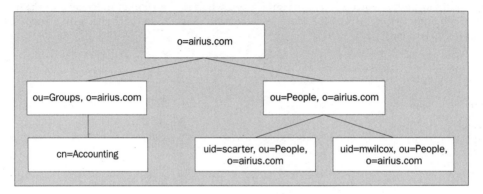

What is LDIF?

Essentially, what we need is a format that we can use to work on LDAP data in a consistent manner with both our applications and our end-users. The name of this consistent user format is called the **LDAP Data Interchange Format** or **LDIF**. LDIF is a text-based format that displays entry information by using mnemonic named attributes and text values.

LDIF is where we do most of our work. We use LDIF to display to our users and to load data into our servers. In fact, a number of utilities exist that just manipulate LDIF files. Shown below is a text version of an LDIF entry for Sam Carter from the `Airius.ldif` file that ships with Netscape Directory Server:

```
dn: uid=scarter, ou=People, o=airius.com
cn: Sam Carter
sn: Carter
givenname: Sam
objectclass: top
objectclass: person
objectclass: organizationalPerson
objectclass: inetOrgPerson
ou: Accounting
ou: People
l: Sunnyvale
uid: scarter
```

```
mail: scarter@airius.com
telephonenumber: +1 408 555 4798
facsimiletelephonenumber: +1 408 555 9751
roomnumber: 4612
userpassword: sprain
```

Note that this is the same entry that we looked at in the previous section – let's take a moment now to think a bit more about what it actually means. You should recognize some parts of this entry. However some of the attribute names will probably not make sense to you at first, but they will come in time.

The first attribute for each entry is the dn attribute, which is the distinguished name of the entry. Remember that the distinguished name for each entry must be unique in the LDAP server, and that the parts that make up the distinguished name are known as relative distinguished names (RDNs). The distinguished name in the above example is:

```
dn: uid=scarter, ou=People, o=airius.com
```

Notice that this DN breaks down into three essential parts, each separated by a comma. The first part is the name of this entry. We use the uid attribute, as recommended by Netscape in their deployment guide (http://developer.netscape.com/docs/manuals/directory.html), because a user ID is more likely to be unique for the organization, while still maintaining an easily understood relationship to the entry.

The second section of the distinguished name is marked with the ou attribute, the letters ou standing for Organizational Unit, which defines the branch that this entry falls under. You should group all of your person objects that you want searched under the ou=People branch. This is because if you use a DIT structure that represents the actual layout of the organization, directory administrators will discover that there is a lot more work for them to do just in the day to day running of the organization. This is due to the fact that people change jobs and organizations reorganize. Note that each entry can have one or more ou attributes in their entry.

The final section, the one marked by the o attribute is the organization attribute. When we first built LDAP servers, the o attribute was often filled with the name of the organization. Now that DNS is stable and domain names are very widely available, it is wise to put your organization's domain name as the organization value. This is because your domain name will be unique within a global namespace that your LDAP server may become a part of.

You should also note that all of the parts of the DN, except for the organization name, are each represented in the entry. This is a requirement of LDAP.

The table below summarizes the different parts that make up the entry for Sam Carter:

English Name	LDIF Value
Distinguished Name	dn: uid=scarter, ou=People, o=airius.com
Common Name	cn: Sam Carter
Surname	sn: Carter

Table Continued on Following Page

English Name	LDIF Value
First Name (i.e. Given name)	givenname: Sam
Object Class	objectclass: top
Object Class	objectclass: person
Object Class	objectclass: organizationalPerson
Object Class	objectclass: inetOrgPerson
Organizational Unit	ou: Accounting
Organizational Unit	ou: People
Location	l: Sunnyvale
User ID	uid: scarter
E-mail	mail: scarter@airius.com
Telephone Number	telephonenumber: +1 408 555 4798
Fax Number	facsimiletelephonenumber: +1 408 555 9751
Room Number	roomnumber: 4612
Password	userpassword: sprain

The following screenshot is from Netscape Communicator and shows the full LDIF output of an LDAP entry inside the Navigator web browser. The LDAP client in Netscape Communicator is in the Address Book component (discussed in Chapter 5) and if you look at the Location box, you'll notice the LDAP URL (which will be covered in more detail in Chapter 6).

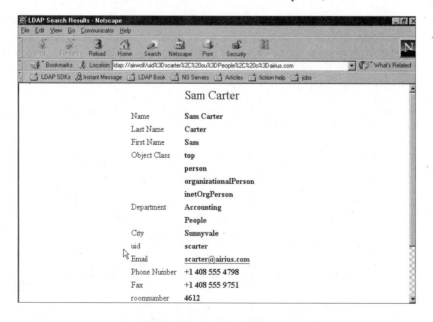

LDIF Examples

One of the benefits of working with a plain text format is that it is trivial to write simple tools to process or create LDIF files. This includes situations where we must take existing legacy data and then make it fit into our LDAP server.

In this section, we'll look at two simple examples that take example legacy data and then output an LDIF file based on that data. Our examples will be written in Perl and Java respectively. We'll concentrate primarily on the LDAP clients inside Netscape Communicator and Microsoft Internet Explorer because they provide a simple, common, standard environment that mimics working with LDAP servers. This way you can get some experience working with LDAP data without the overhead of setting up an LDAP server.

Perl and LDIF

Larry Wall created the Perl programming language to simplify the administration of Unix workstations and servers. Unix uses many text files to build a Unix system, so text management takes up a great deal of a Unix manager's time. Perl excels at text management, is quick to develop in and it is usually fast enough in operation that you don't need to rewrite the program in C for production. Perl can interface with C, so that where you need some extra 'boost' or access legacy APIs, you can easily do so without having to rewrite the APIs from scratch in Perl. Perl's simplicity and its ability to deftly handle text has made it *the* CGI development language of choice.

> *Common Gateway Interface (CGI) programming is the original way of developing interactive programs over the World Wide Web. CGI applications run on the web server and are called from the web browser, usually through the use of HTML forms.*

Perl has even been ported to all versions of Unix, VMS, and the Windows 95/NT environment. You can easily port any Perl program from one environment to another. Thus Perl is also a good language when developing or deploying an LDAP server, because you will be dealing with a lot of text files. Often you will use a program written in another language to feed your LDAP database, but you will likely want Perl around to clean up your data before giving it to the LDAP 'feed' program.

Our Perl example here will take a simple comma-delimited file and parse it out to an LDIF file. The PerLDAP SDK by Netscape has a module just for dealing with LDIF files, but we're just using a simple example here so we won't bother with the SDK just yet. This example should work with any version of Perl 5.004 or later.

> *We'll be looking at the PerLDAP SDK from Netscape in detail in Chapter 7. Note that you can download the files for the examples in this chapter, and in the rest of the book, from the Wrox Press web site at* `http://www.wrox.com`*. You can download a version of Perl for Windows NT from* `http://www.perl.com/ports/win32/Standard/x86`*.*

Let's use a simple text file as our example that has one record (entry) per line, with a comma separating each attribute in the record. The entry takes the following form:

```
Last Name, First Name, User-ID, Email Address, Division, Phone Number, Location,
Fax Number
```

Here's an example line of input that is stored in the `acmewidgets.txt` file:

```
Perlstein,Karla T,Kperlstein,KPerlstein@acmewidgets.com,QA,(415) 703-
2452,Waco,(804) 551-5412
```

This is a very simple record and it will be very easy to create the output. The comments in the program should explain most of the Perl parts if you are not familiar with the language. You can put whatever values you want in those fields, just as long as they look like 'real data'. You don't need many lines, just a handful will do fine for this example.

We do need to set three variables in the program before we can build our record:

- ❑ The organizational attribute (`$org_root`)
- ❑ The base organizational unit (`$base_org_unit`)
- ❑ The object classes (`@object_classes`)

In LDAP, you must list all of the object classes that your entry is a part of. The first object will always be `top`. In our entry, the final object class will be `inetOrgPerson`, which is derived from `person` and `organizationalPerson`. So, we populate the array `@object_classes` with this.

We pass the name of the text file and the output file on the command line. On both Unix and Windows boxes, the command to execute this program (named `txt2ldif.pl`) is like this:

```
perl text2ldif.pl acmewidgets.txt acmewidgets.ldif
```

```perl
#!/usr/local/bin/perl -w
#This first line should be set to the correct
#path to the Perl binary if you are using it on a UNIX box

#This is a comment
#The next line loads in the 'strict' library. This library helps
#prevent careless mistakes, in particular when we use other libraries

use strict;

#text2ldif.pl
#Mark Wilcox mewilcox@hotmail.com
#This Perl script will parse an TEXT text file that contains 1 LDAP entry per
#line. The elements of the entry (e.g. the LDAP attribute data) must be seperated
#by a delimiter of some sort (e.g. by a ',' or a '|')

#usage: text2ldif.pl input_file output_file

#Let's declare some variables

my $input_file;
my $output_file;
my $line;
my $class;

######LDAP Schema Base Attributes Here######

#organizational root
my $org_root = "o=acmewidgets.com";
```

```perl
#my base organizational unit
my $base_org_unit = "People";

my @object_classes = ("top","person", "organizationalPerson", "inetOrgPerson");

############################################################

#get command line parameters
$input_file = shift;
$output_file = shift;

#if user gave both an input file and a output file, proceed
if ((defined($input_file)) && (defined($output_file)))
{

   #open input_file to read
   open(IFILE,"$input_file") || die("Failed to open input file: $input_file.
                                                      Reason:$!\n");

   #now open output_file to write
   open(OFILE,">$output_file") || die("Failed to open output file: $output_file.
                                                      Reason:$!\n");

   #now read in the file, 1 line at a time
   while (<IFILE>)
   {
      #remove the trailing hard-return
      chomp();

      #default line variable is $_
      #make code more readable, set it to $line
      $line = $_;

      #now we break the line up into individual parts
      my($last_name,$first_name,$uid,$mail,$division,$phone,$city,$fax) =
                                                      split(/\,/,$line);

      #now we will print the record to the output file
      #print distinguished name
      print OFILE "dn: uid=$uid, ou=$base_org_unit, $org_root\n";

      #print out object classes
      foreach $class(@object_classes)
      {
         print OFILE "objectclass: $class\n";
      }

      #print rest of the record
      print OFILE "sn: $last_name\n";
      print OFILE "givenname: $first_name\n";
      print OFILE "cn: $first_name $last_name\n";
      print OFILE "ou: $base_org_unit\n";
      print OFILE "ou: $division\n";
      print OFILE "uid: $uid\n";
      print OFILE "mail: $mail\n";
      print OFILE "userpassword: $mail\n";
      print OFILE "telephonenumber: $phone\n";
      print OFILE "l: $city\n";
      print OFILE "facsimiletelephonenumber: $fax\n\n";
   }
```

```
close(IFILE);
close(OFILE);
}
else
{
    print "usage text2ldif infile outfile\n";
}
```

When this code is run, the output would look like this:

```
dn: uid=KPerlstein, ou=People, o=airius.com
objectclass: top
objectclass: person
objectclass: organizationalPerson
objectclass: inetOrgPerson
sn: Perlstein
givenname: Karla T
cn: Karla T  Perlstein
ou: People
ou: QA
uid: KPerlstein
mail: KPerlstein@acmewidgets.com
userpassword: KPerlstein@acmewidgets.com
telephonenumber: (415) 703-2452
l: Waco
facsimiletelephonenumber: (804) 551-5412
```

Java and LDIF

Java has become one of the hottest programming languages in computing for the last few years, in particular for Internet programming. One reason is that it has been designed to be a platform-neutral language (as Perl is). This means that we can develop a Java program on a Windows NT machine and then move it to a Unix server for production work without recompiling, like we would have to do in a language like C++.

Another reason why Java has enjoyed a great deal of popularity is because it has built-in networking and database connectivity. We will explore Java's networking abilities in later chapters, but here we will explore Java's ability to connect to databases in an easy fashion, using a very simple case.

Our Perl example showed one way we could convert existing data into a LDIF file ready to be loaded into an LDAP server. Our Java example will show another way to handle existing directory data, which this time is from a database. Since JDK 1.1 has included database connectivity in the form of the Java DataBase Connectivity package (JDBC), we are able to connect to databases not only in a platform-independent manner, but also in a database-independent manner. All that is required to switch from one database to another (say from Oracle to Microsoft SQL Server) is to switch drivers. Sun's standard JDK also includes an JDBC-ODBC bridge which enables us to communicate with databases that use Microsoft's ODBC (Open DataBase Connectivity), a common database access protocol that widely available in the Windows world, but is also available on many Unix platforms.

The diagram below shows the steps a Java program needs to go through to connect to an MS Access database:

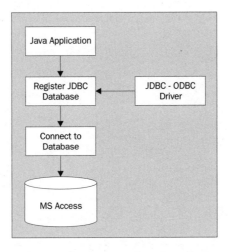

We won't discuss JDBC in detail here because this topic requires its own book. And don't worry too much if this is all very confusing to you, I'm just putting this example here to show you a way to get data from a traditional database into a format we can then import into a LDAP server. I happen to like Java, but you could use C/C++ or Visual Basic (or even Perl) if you prefer.

In our example here, I have built a Microsoft Access database with a single table called `Acmewidgets.mdb`. It has the following fields:

- ❑ `LNAME` – last name
- ❑ `FNAME` – first name
- ❑ `UID` – user ID
- ❑ `EMAIL` – e-mail address
- ❑ `DIVISION` – company division
- ❑ `PHONE` – telephone number
- ❑ `LOCATION` – location of office
- ❑ `FAX` – fax number

Feel free to populate the database with whatever values you want. You don't need many records, a handful will do for this example. After you have created the database, you will need to create an ODBC connection for the database.

Consult your documentation for help in creating your database and setting up an ODBC connection if you want to try out this example. Alternatively, you can use the AcmeWidgets.mdb file that is available along with the source code that accompanies this book.

You will also need a copy of Sun's standard Java Development Kit version 1.1 or later, which includes the JDBC package. After you compile the program, you run it with the following command at the command line:

```
java db2ldif
```

This program will produce a file named `acmewidgets_Java.ldif`. The entries should look similar to the results produced by the Perl program in the earlier example.

```java
/**
db2ldif
A Java program to take a database and convert into a LDIF file.
*/

import java.io.*;
import java.sql.*;

public class db2ldif
{
public static void main(String args[]){
    String filename = "acmewidgets_Java.ldif";
    String url = "jdbc:odbc:acmewidgets";
    Connection con ;
    Statement stmt;
    String query = "SELECT Acmewidgets.LNAME, Acmewidgets.FNAME, Acmewidgets.UID,";
    query += "Acmewidgets.EMAIL, Acmewidgets.DIVISION, Acmewidgets.PHONE,";
    query += "Acmewidgets.LOCATION, Acmewidgets.FAX FROM Acmewidgets;";
    String [] objectclasses = {"top","person","organizationalPerson",
                                                    "inetOrgPerson"};
    String root = "o=airius.com";
    String base = "People";

    try {
        Class.forName("sun.jdbc.odbc.JdbcOdbcDriver");
    } catch(ClassNotFoundException e){
                System.err.print("ClassNotFoundException: ");
                System.err.println(e.getMessage());
    }

    try {
        con = DriverManager.getConnection(url,"","");
        stmt = con.createStatement();
        PrintWriter out = new PrintWriter(new FileWriter(filename));
        ResultSet rs = stmt.executeQuery(query);
        System.out.println("executing query...");
        out.flush();
        while (rs.next()) {
            String lname = rs.getString("LNAME");
            String fname = rs.getString("FNAME");
            String uid = rs.getString("UID");
            String email = rs.getString("EMAIL");
            String division = rs.getString("DIVISION");
            String phone = rs.getString("PHONE");
            String location = rs.getString("LOCATION");
            String fax = rs.getString("FAX");

            out.println("dn: uid=" + uid +", ou="+ base + ", " + root);

            for (int i = 0; i < objectclasses.length; i++) {
                out.println("objectclass: " + objectclasses[i]);
            }

            out.println("sn: " + lname);
            out.println("cn: " + fname + " " + lname);
            out.println("givenname: " + fname);
            out.println("uid: " + uid);
```

```
        out.println("mail: " + email);
        out.println("ou: People");
        out.println("ou: " + division);
        out.println("userpassword: "+email);
        out.println("telephonenumber: " + phone);
        out.println("l: " + location);
        out.println("facsimiletelephonenumber: " + fax);
        out.println();
    }

    out.close();
    stmt.close();
    con.close();
} catch (SQLException ex) {
    System.err.println("SQLException: " + ex.getMessage());
} catch (IOException iox) {
    System.err.println("IOException: " + iox.getMessage());
    }
    }
}
```

An important item to note is that LDIF is plain text. LDAP servers that support the version 3 of the protocol will actually process all text internally in the UTF-8 format, which is also called Unicode. This 16-bit character set supports all of the characters of major modern languages. It also encompasses the earlier TEXT standard, so legacy code is still preserved. Java supports UTF-8 natively (and without developer intervention). All of the Netscape SDKs support Unicode natively, unfortunately Unicode support on most of our operating systems is poor.

Also, since LDIF is plain text, you may wonder how it supports binary data. This is through the use of something called Base-64 encoding, which enables us to represent binary data as plain text. This is the same mechanism we use to send e-mail attachments and is specified in an Internet standard called the **Basic Encoding Rules** (**BER**). Most current LDAP servers are not configured to support large quantities of binary data. Instead, it is better to put the binary data on a web server or FTP server and provide a URL from the LDAP server to the location of the binary file.

Summary

This chapter has covered the LDAP data model and why it exists the way it does. We have learned that records in an LDAP server are called entries, and that entries can also be called objects, with attributes that describe each entry. The attributes are in the form of name/value pairs, although each attribute can have one or more values. In each entry there is a special attribute called `objectclass`, which defines what other attributes the entry may have. We also looked at schemas that define the relationship of object classes and their attributes.

Finally, we examined how we can exchange data between LDAP servers and clients with LDIF, including two programs that help change existing data into LDIF.

Choosing and Installing an LDAP Server

In the first few chapters we have concentrated on what LDAP is and what potential it has for use in an organization. We studied its organizational format and saw that there are numerous SDKs out there for us to develop our own LDAP applications if we so choose.

Now it is time to settle down and actually put something together. After all, we are programmers, not students. While we many of us can enjoy a good book, you are not likely reading this for summer fun. You want to know how LDAP can help you and your organization.

The only way for this to happen is to start working with LDAP, and the first step is to obtain an LDAP server. In this chapter we will discuss a few of the many available servers and focus on one in particular, the Netscape Directory Server.

We will focus on the following:

- ❑ The availability of LDAP servers
- ❑ Choosing an LDAP server
- ❑ Obtaining the OpenLDAP server
- ❑ Installing the OpenLDAP server
- ❑ Overview of the OpenLDAP server
- ❑ Obtaining the Netscape Directory Server
- ❑ Installing the Netscape Directory Server
- ❑ Overview of the features of the Netscape Directory Server

LDAP: Server or Access Protocol?

When Tim Howes, the person who's the closest to being the 'Father of LDAP', was first given the assignment to improving directory services at the University of Michigan, he realized that developing clients to access X.500 servers was too difficult using the PCs of the time (that is the late 80s, early 90s). As a result he first started the process of creating a standard protocol to interact with X.500 over TCP/IP. This standard protocol became LDAP. However, as his team began to work on making X.500 accessible through LDAP he realized that X.500 had problems in implementation even on the server level. So, they decided to extend LDAP itself so that it could become a server.

The original LDAP server was released from the University of Michigan and it used the freely available Berkley databases that were common on Unix platforms. The Berkley databases were not relational databases like Access but instead used a single key to index a record, essentially a very effective hash table management system. This is pretty much what the LDAP/X.500 data model is. You have attributes (e.g. keys) that provide access to a record (an LDAP entry). There is always a primary key – the distinguished name. The Michigan server has enjoyed a great deal of popularity because it is free, open source, and it works.

As LDAP has matured, our options for LDAP capable servers have grown. There is now even a new open source LDAP project, called OpenLDAP, which is similar in flavor to the Linux or Apache movement. Note that this is different from the University of Michigan server, because the Michigan server is dependent upon NSF grants.

LDAP Server Types

Your LDAP server choices now available are numerous. However, they basically come down to one of two types – either they are 'native' LDAP which means that they were designed from the ground-up to be LDAP servers, or LDAP is provided as an extra way to access the server. The latter is most common for vendors who already have existing directory services like Sun or Novell. Native LDAP servers are really servers that provide LDAP access to a database, you can even do this to provide LDAP access to existing database data.

LDAP Vendors

In this section, we'll look at a comparison of some of the existing LDAP servers.

Novell

To say that Novell is one of the leaders of networking computers is like calling Bill Gates one of the richest men in the world. It's an understatement. Novell enjoys an installation base that numbers in the millions and even when they faced some recent dark times, they still had a billion dollars in the bank as cash reserves.

The Internet and a management rebirth has given rise to a new Novell, which is much more focused on their past successes and is poised to make them a company to be reckoned with for years to come. Novell's primary mechanism for managing computers, printers and users is through the use of Novell Directory Services (NDS), which is also derived from X.500 – yes, the same X.500 that LDAP is derived from. Novell felt that the object model provided a good basis for deploying directory services. Novell, of course, deployed it over a different protocol, IPX, which they felt was kind of an enhanced TCP/IP connection. At the time, they probably were right – it was an age where proprietary protocols ruled and no network connection was really the master of anything.

That time has now passed and today companies live and die by how well their products adhere (or at least appear to adhere) to open standards. In a very short period of time, Novell has made all their key products use native TCP/IP as their communications protocol. This includes NDS and GroupWise – their mail/workflow application. It also should be noted that Novell shipped NetWare (the name for its networking system), ahead of schedule and before Windows 2000.

The latest release of NetWare allows you to search NDS via LDAP. Since NDS already derives from X.500, this makes it a very logical and successful implementation. If you are already using Novell and have experience with their system, you may want to investigate this solution.

Microsoft

Microsoft is the 500 pound gorilla of the computing industry. Indeed, it's almost an industry unto its self. Microsoft has long been a player in the networking market, starting with its NetBEUI protocol that dates back to DOS. When Microsoft released its flagship line of operating system for business, Windows NT, it created a new networking model – the domain model. A domain is like a collection of computers that share access rights for resources and for the early versions of Windows NT it worked. Until the Internet came up and made TCP/IP the dominant networking protocol, the domain model served Microsoft well. However, the domain model is not unsatisfactory because the NT domains are not adequately directory-based.

Microsoft wants everyone to use Windows NT as their corporate operating system, and they realize that if they wish to replace Novell and Unix, they need a networking model that incorporates directory support. This is why Microsoft created the Active Directory system. This uses LDAP and dynamic DNS as its core protocols while supporting many other protocols to help make it co-exist for migration purposes. Unfortunately, at the time of writing, Active Directory has not shipped. It is slated to come out with Windows 2000.

In the mean time, though, Microsoft does enable users to interact with its Exchange mail server's address book through LDAP.

Sun Microsystems

Sun is one of the industry leaders when it comes to the Internet. With their Sun Solaris product, they are the largest provider of the Unix operating system. They are no strangers to LDAP, as they even ship a X.500 server for organizations and they included LDAP in their Java Naming and Directory Interfaces (JNDI) package.

Sun's foray into LDAP comes in the form of the Sun Directory Services (SDS). SDS consists of a set of applications that are centered around LDAP, and is actually an LDAP server written by Sun. SDS has the ability to replace NIS/NIS+ in Solaris machines, providing native LDAP authentication. Alternatively you can set SDS up as an NIS server (but not an NIS+ server), which uses LDAP as its database. This NIS server capability is important because you can still use NIS but gain the benefits of LDAP (i.e. centralized management, open standards) until you can migrate entirely to LDAP. Not only can you authenticate NIS clients against SDS, but if you support the RADIUS protocols for your remote users over a telephone connection, SDS allows you to authenticate RADIUS users against LDAP as well.

As I am writing this, Netscape, America Online and Sun have entered into a partnership. This could have future consequences on the product development of SDS. I don't expect SDS to fade away, but I personally expect Sun to eventually integrate Netscape's Directory server into SDS in the future. I don't know that for a fact, but it's a strong hunch. I expect it because Netscape's Directory Server is the leading LDAP server and Netscape has the architects behind LDAP working for them.

University of Michigan

The University of Michigan was the lead research center in the initial development of LDAP. Their server has continued to be the reference implementation, in much the same way as NCSA web server was the benchmark web server when the World Wide Web was first born (at least after the release of Mosaic).

The University of Michigan server runs primarily on Unix machines and is configured through a series of command line configuration files and command line utilities. This is the standard configuration for most Unix programs and for Unix administrators – this is how they like it.

The University of Michigan server is still available for use and is free. It still is a popular server that is undergoing development. It has gained a new lease on life through the OpenLDAP program, which is discussed next.

OpenLDAP

OpenLDAP hopes to do for the University of Michigan LDAP server what the Apache server did for the NCSA server – provide a free open server that is rock solid and, hopefully, the best of breed.

Currently the OpenLDAP server only runs on Unix, but the client tools work on Unix or Windows NT. They state that they do hope to support the Berkley 2 DB API, SSL/SASL encryption, full LDAP v3 support and Windows NT server by the end of 1999.

OpenLDAP is also supporting the open development of several client tools as well as LDAP servers. If you are interested in an open source LDAP server, then you should check this server suite out.

Innosoft

Innosoft is a provider of directory and messaging software. They are notable because in the spring of 1998 they purchased Critical Angle, whose director, Mark Wahl was also one of the key players in the development of LDAP. They have LDAP servers and LDAP administrative tools available that conform to the LDAP v3 spec.

Netscape

Netscape will always be remembered the company that brought the World Wide Web to the masses. In the future, they may also be known as the company that made LDAP a household (or at least an IS department) acronym. They were the first major company to announce support for LDAP with their Directory Server product. With the release of their version 4 browser (i.e. Communicator) and version 3 of their server line (SuiteSpot), they made LDAP the hub around which they built their product line.

With the Netscape Directory Server you can manage all your Netscape SuiteSpot server line utilities from a single administration screen and you can manage user profiles/preferences in Directory Server. These preferences can include such things as the server names, user IDs, program configuration and so on for any of the Netscape Server products, like their Messenger mail or Calendar mail server or the preferences for user's Netscape Communicator profiles.

Netscape even ship a version of Directory Server that can be embedded within Independent Software Vendors (ISV) software.

Considering that Tim Howes, the man who pioneered LDAP, is one of their Vice-presidents, then it seems likely that Netscape will remain a major player in the LDAP arena for the foreseeable future.

General OS Support

We have spent the better part of this section talking about particular LDAP implementation choices, but things are rapidly changing. One major item of change is the way the Sun Microsystems partnership with the new AOL/Netscape alliance plays out in terms of LDAP server development.

Just about every major OS vendor – Sun, HP, IBM and Microsoft – intend to make native LDAP authentication available as part of their OS within the next few years. Indeed, at the time of writing, HP have publicly announced that they are going to release a version of Directory Server for HPUX. We really are on just the tip of the iceberg of LDAP development.

Finally if you use Unix and NIS, you might want to check out Padl Software who makes a commercial product called ypldap. The ypldap product enables you to use LDAP for NIS authentication even if you don't have access to Sun's Directory Services. Padl Software also has available free, open source tools you can use to add LDAP support to other services besides NIS, such as Pluggable Authentication Modules (PAM). PAM is an industry standard that allows administrators to plug in different authentication mechanisms into their systems without having to rewrite any of the authentication code. Before PAM, if you wanted to change authentication mechanisms (e.g. instead of using standard passwords, you wanted to use "single use only" passwords), you had to rewrite all of your applications that required authentication – e.g. standard login, FTP – before you could use the new system. Now with PAM, you can change authentication systems, by simply adding in a module, which is simply a piece of compiled code, into your authentication system. It sounds complicated, but in practice it's very simple. For more information look up `http://www.padl.com`.

LDAP Server examples

To get an understanding of what LDAP is and how to write clients for it, we first need an LDAP server to work with. In this section, we are going to look at a couple of different LDAP implementations to see how LDAP servers are different and we will focus on using the leading LDAP server – Netscape Directory Server.

OpenLDAP Project

One of the great traditions of the Internet has been the open development and free distribution of software. In fact, much of the Internet would not exist as it does, or be as widely distributed as it is, if it were not for this open forum – now widely known as the **open source movement**. Richard Stallman has been given the credit for starting it with the development of the Emacs editor and the Free Software Foundation's GNU project. Larry Wall, the creator of Perl, and Linus Torvalds, who wrote the original Linux kernel, have also made the open source movement very popular. Eric Raymond wrote a watershed paper called *The Cathedral and the Bazaar* (`http://www.tuxedo.org/~esr/writings/cathedral-bazaar/index.html`) that helped to define the development of open source based software (the Bazaar) on the Internet, as compared to the development of software by large corporations (the Cathedral).

This paper helped make open source more respectable, at least in the eyes of managers, system administrators having for a long time known the benefits of open source. Many people think that open source is popular because it's often distributed for free, but this is not the case. Often the reason open source is chosen is because it works better than commercial grade software, there isn't a commercial grade software option available and the quality of support for popular open source software.

In a very short time, open source went from being something teenage hackers did, to a level of respectability which is making the computing establishment take notice. Long standing companies like IBM and Intel have started to invest in open source products like the Apache web server and the Linux operating system. Netscape opened the source of its web browser (Navigator) and that of its LDAP libraries. They also invested in other open source projects. All of this has made the open source movement a very hot topic now and has encouraged the developers of such products to continue on with their endeavors.

As most Internet protocol projects, the original reference for LDAP implementations were given away for free along with the source code from the University of Michigan. The source code is important because it allows developers to see how the designers of the particular protocol intended to see servers developed. It also allowed new developers to take the source code and fix it, or add new features as they were needed. In a way, it's like going to the hardware store and buying a kit to build something. Most people are going to take the kit and just put it together following the instructions booklet. Some people, however, are going to see how to improve the kit and add their own features. Others might even see problems in the kit and look at ways to fix them. The difference between hardware and the Internet is that these improvements and modifications can be shared by everyone within minutes.

The OpenLDAP group wants to build upon this tradition so that LDAP can be made accessible to everyone. Their goal is to provide full LDAP v3 support including SSL/SASL functionality that can use any database technology as the back-end and will run on Unix or Windows NT.

The version we will be looking at is OpenLDAP 1.2. There might be a new version out by the time you read this, because open source developments release more often than traditional commercial software companies.

Installing OpenLDAP

The first thing you need to do is download the OpenLDAP source from http://www.OpenLDAP.org. For this section, we will be covering the installation of the Unix version because, at the time of the writing, this was the only one available. By the time you read this, a Windows NT version, most likely with precompiled binaries, will be available. Most of the administration/usage issues should be the same for both the Unix and Windows NT versions.

Note that the instructions included in this section may vary depending on your particular OS. I primarily used Caldera OpenLinux-Lite 1.1 but I have also used it on Solaris 2.6.

Like nearly every Unix program on the Internet, the software comes zipped in a GNU `gzip` archive and tarred. You must first unzip the file with a command like this:

```
%gunzip OpenLDAP-dist.tgz
```

Then you must untar the newly unzipped file. It will probably work like this:

```
%tar xvf OpenLDAP-dist.tar
```

This will make a directory called `ldap`. To proceed with the install, you will need to `cd` into that directory. A directory listing will show you that there are quite a few files and directories included in this distribution. The standard distribution includes:

❑ The code for the server/server utilities
❑ An LDAP SDK
❑ Example clients
❑ Some test programs

Building OpenLDAP can be an adventure, which is not a knock against OpenLDAP, that's just the best way I can describe how any installation of any application from source can go. Because OpenLDAP is designed to compile on so many different systems and it comes in source code form, there is a bit more work involved than if you purchase a product off the shelf. (However I don't think it's that much more work to install OpenLDAP than say the Apache web server.)

Now there is a simple thing you can do to reduce the number of headaches you can have in building OpenLDAP or any other open source application. The simple thing to do is to make sure your system is up to date. What I mean by this is that make sure that your operating system has all of the required patches, you have the latest stable release of your C compiler and programming libraries. If you use one of the open source Unix-like systems such as Linux, make sure you have a current release. This is because Linux is maturing rapidly, and many problems can be avoided if you have the latest release. Keeping up with the latest patches and releases doesn't just make it easier to compile software, these updates usually fix security holes as well.

The OpenLDAP installation uses the GNU Autoconfig utility to help make building OpenLDAP a bit easier. GNU (which stands for 'GNU is Not Unix') is name of the utilities that come from the Free Software Foundation and are very popular on Unix systems. (For your information, many of the GNU utilities have been ported to Windows NT.) The `Autoconfig` utility is able to provide information about the system to applications that wish to use it .

You run the `Autoconfig` utility by typing `./configure` at the command line.

The `configure` script runs `Autoconfig`. This script has options you can specify that allow you to "personalize" the installation. You might wish to do this, if you want to install the server and its utilities in a separate partition to protect the rest of your system during development.

Probably the item you will most likely customize is the use of threads which, as we have said before, allow applications to do more than one task at a time. Most modern operating systems support this. However, getting the necessary libraries together and set up correctly has brought more than one capable system administrator to their knees (me included!). If you have trouble getting the `configure` script to run all the way through, try turning thread support off by typing the following at the command line:

```
./configure -without-threads
```

After `Autoconfig` is finished, you should be ready to compile the system. This will configure the installation of the LDAP clients that come with OpenLDAP and the `slapd`, which is the LDAP server. If you want to see all of the options `configure` has, type `./configure -help` at the command prompt. The next step is to type the following at the command line:

```
make depend
```

This will run the make utility, which is a special program designed to make it easier to compile large projects. It is used on both Unix and PC systems (though the version for Microsoft Visual C++ is called nmake). When you run make, it looks for a "makefile" in the directory. This file contains instructions for make on how to build the application. Makefiles can be broken into sections called targets that are like subroutines in a programming language. When we type "make depend" what we are saying is to follow the instructions for the "depend" target in the makefile. You didn't have to create the makefile for OpenLDAP – it was created for you by Autoconfig when you ran the configure script. If you are interested more in make, there are plenty of resources on the Internet about this utility (not to mention the "man" pages on it that come with any Unix installation). If you want a book on the subject, there is one. It's called *Managing Projects with make* and is published by O'Reilly & Associates.

This particular target will compile all of the programming libraries that are needed by the LDAP clients and servers.

After you have run "make depend" just type make at the command line. This will now compile all of the clients and servers. (By default you will only build the LDAP server slapd, unless you specify another server such as the slurpd, which is the LDAP replication server.)

When the previous step is finished, you can then test things out by going into the tests directory. Type make at the command prompt. This will build any utilities that didn't get built in the first time around and then run the scripts in the test directory. These scripts import data into the built server and then run some sample queries against it.

Here is an example of some of the test script output:

```
Cleaning up in ./test-db...
Running ldif2ldbm to build slapd database...
Starting slapd on TCP/IP port 9009...
Using ldapsearch to retrieve all the entries...
Waiting 5 seconds for slapd to start...
Comparing retrieved entries to LDIF file used to create database
>>>>> Test succeeded
>>>>> ./scripts/test001-ldif2ldbm completed OK.
>>>>> waiting 5 seconds for things to exit
```

Tests? What Kind of Tests?

The tests that are run are designed to give the compiled OpenLDAP installation a test drive. Here is a brief rundown of what's happening during the tests.

Test 1: The ldif2ldbm Test

This test starts up the LDAP server and loads it with the ldif2ldbm utility. The ldif2ldbm utility is the one that is used to load the initial LDAP data from an LDIF file. After the database is loaded, the ldapsearch command line utility is then run and dumps the entire LDAP data that was just loaded. The data is then compared with the original data. If both sets of data are identical, the test is assumed to have passed.

This test is designed to show that LDAP server is able to achieve basic functionality. If Test 1 fails, it's probably a safe assumption that the rest of the tests will fail also because this test, out of all of the tests, really examines the core LDAP server's installation.

Test 2: The Populate Test

This test is exactly like Test 1 except that it uses the `ldapmodify` command line utility to populate the server. This simulates adding entries from an external LDAP program. We'll talk more about how to populate LDAP servers with external clients starting in Chapter 6.

Test 3: The Search Test

This test makes sure that the server is responding as expected to all types of searches including: AND, OR, NOT, exact and regular expression based searches. This test uses the `ldapsearch` command line utility.

Test 4: The Modify Test

This tests the LDAP server's ability to successfully handle the modification of LDAP entries. This test uses the `ldapmodify` command line utility and performs the tasks of adding a new entry, modifying an entry and deleting an entry.

Test 5: The modrdn Test

As of OpenLDAP version 1.2, this test had not been written yet. However, here's what I expect it to do. This test will demonstrate that the OpenLDAP server can handle modification of relative distinguished names. RDNs are the left most part of a DN and this test will demonstrate if the server can handle modifying the RDN including in all of the places where it might be stored, such as `uniquemember` values in group memberships.

For example if we have a DN of:

```
cn=Sam Carter, ou=People, o=airius.com
```

The RDN would be "cn=Sam Carter". An example `modrdn` operation would change the "cn=Sam Carter" to "uid=scarter". Thus the DN would then become:

```
uid=scarter,ou=People,o=airius.com
```

Test 6: The ACLs Test

This test checks out the Access Control Lists (ACL) mechanisms for the OpenLDAP server. ACLs are how we manage security in LDAP.

Test 7: The Replication Test

This final test is designed to see if the `slurpd` server, which is the LDAP replication server, is working properly. This test will only run if you opted to compile the `slurpd` server during configuration. The compilation of the `slurpd` server requires you to be able to compile with thread support. Server replication is the ability to copy (replicate) parts of the LDAP server's data to other LDAP servers. You might want to do this to improve performance by spreading operations out among servers or to improve reliability because if your data is replicated, you can still perform LDAP operations if an LDAP server goes down.

Example OpenLDAP Operation

Here is an example of the OpenLDAP server and tools in action after we have run the `configure` script and run the tests to make sure it's working as the OpenLDAP developers expect it to.

To start up the OpenLDAP server, first go into the `servers/slapd` directory. Type the following at the command prompt:

```
./slapd -f /<path to your OpenLDAP root>/tests/data/slapd-master.conf -p 9009 >
log &
```

If you don't see any error messages, you can assume that it's running. The command line switch "-p 9009" instructs the server to run on a different port than the standard LDAP port which is 389. The reason why we do that for testing purposes is that you don't have to worry about interfering with any existing LDAP servers and also because you don't need administrative privileges to run services on any port greater than 1024.

To try an example search, you can go to the `clients/tools` directory. There you will find the OpenLDAP version of the `ldapsearch` command line tool.

Try typing the following at the command line:

```
./ldapsearch -h localhost -p 9009 -b "o=University of Michigan, c=US" "sn=Jensen"
```

This tells the `ldapsearch` tool to search a LDAP server located on our local machine on port 9009 and start the search at a base of `o=University of Michigan, c=US` with a query (which in LDAP is called a filter) of `sn=Jensen`. This will return all entries that have attribute named `sn` and a value of `Jensen`.

An example returned entry might look like this:

```
cn=Barbara Jensen, ou=Information Technology Division, ou=People, o=University of
Michigan, c=US
objectclass=top
objectclass=person
objectclass=organizationalPerson
objectclass=newPilotPerson
objectclass=umichPerson
cn=Barbara Jensen
cn=Babs Jensen
sn=Jensen
title=Mythical Manager, Research Systems
postaladdress=ITD Prod Dev & Deployment $ 535 W. William St. Room 4212 $ Ann
Arbor, MI 48103-4943
seealso=cn=All Staff, ou=Groups, o=University of Michigan, c=US
uid=bjensen
userpassword=bjensen
mail=bjensen@mailgw.umich.edu
homepostaladdress=123 Wesley $ Ann Arbor, MI 48103
krbname=bjensen@umich.edu
multilinedescription=Mythical manager of the rsdd unix project
nobatchupdates=TRUE
notice=Off sailing this month.
onvacation=FALSE
labeledurl=http://www.umich.edu/ U-M Home Page
drink=water
lastmodifiedtime=960404035839Z
lastmodifiedby=cn=Barbara Jensen, ou=Information Technology Division, ou=People,
o=University of Michigan, c=US
```

```
modifytimestamp=960404171405Z
modifiersname=cn=Manager, o=University of Michigan, c=US
homephone=+1 313 555 2333
pager=+1 313 555 3233
facsimiletelephonenumber=+1 313 555 2274
telephonenumber=+1 313 555 9022
```

Benefits of OpenLDAP

The OpenLDAP project is based on the assumption that people will want an open source alternative to commercial LDAP servers. The future of OpenLDAP looks promising, particularly if they deliver on their promises of security (SSL/SASL) support, as well as RDBMS and multi-platform support. As the web server market has already shown, there is not only room but also demand for both types of servers (open source and commercial/closed source).

I'd also like to add that OpenLDAP does appear to be growing in support. In the LDAP circles I hang out in, essentially all I hear is either OpenLDAP or Netscape Directory Server when people talk about their LDAP server of choice.

Netscape Directory Server

LDAP and Netscape go hand in hand. Netscape have been in the LDAP business for a long time, in Internet terms, and bring a great deal of experience to the table. Netscape's name for the integration of the Directory Server into organization management is called Mission Control. This was originally developed to enable organizations to modify Netscape Communicator for their own internal versions, but Netscape now hopes to make it into the essential tool for managing organizational infrastructures through LDAP.

Installing Netscape Directory Server

In this section, we are going to go through the installation a Netscape Directory Server, step by step.

The first thing you need to do is obtain the software for your particular platform. You can either download version 4.0 from Netscape's web site for a 60 day trial or order it on CD-ROM from Netscape. There are versions for most common versions of Unix and Windows NT (a beta of version 4.1 is available for Linux). In this chapter, we'll be concentrating on version 4.0 of the Netscape Directory Server.

On both Unix and NT, the installation of Directory server is a wizard-like process. This is important for two reasons. One is that it makes it easier for novices to install a fairly complicated system. Second, from Netscape Suitespot 4.0 onwards, all of the server configuration is stored inside an LDAP server – Netscape Directory Server itself.

The wizard installation is easier on the novice, than say the OpenLDAP installation. Under OpenLDAP the most help you get during installation is from the GNU `Autoconfig` utility as part of the `configure` script. There is very little help during the initial setup of OpenLDAP to help you configure your LDAP server and the Directory Information Tree (DIT). With the Netscape Directory Server installation, help is available during every step in the process of building your DIT. It will even install test data for you.

The benefits of storing the configuration information in an LDAP server may not be readily apparent at first. It is stored in a special DIT whose base is `o=NetscapeRoot`. This administration server data is managed inside a standard LDAP server, but because the root is different, this data is separate from the rest of the directory information. The benefit of storing this data there is to centralize management of configuration information. Many organizations run what we call "server farms", that is groups of computers that are replicas of each other whose roles are to split up the task of serving data. You can have a server farm of web servers, database servers, etc. One of the hardest tasks of managing server farms is that the data is managed in configuration files that are stored individually on each machine. This means that if you need to change a parameter in one file, for example to add a redirect for a web site, you have to manually change the same file on each machine. Doing this takes time and is risky because each time you open the configuration file, you risk making a typo and suddenly one or more of your machines is serving up incorrect data. Storing configuration information in LDAP gives you the ability of only having to perform an update in one place – on the LDAP server. To reduce the likelihood of losing your entire operation, should something happen to that LDAP server, you can replicate the data between other LDAP servers, the benefit being that if you lose your master server, then you can switch to one of the backup servers that contain the same information.

The Installation Wizard

When you start the wizard, the first screen that comes up invites you to choose which Netscape Directory Server package you wish to install:

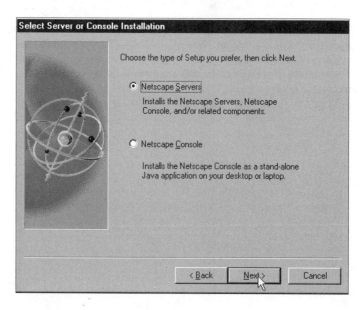

Netscape Directory Server 4.0 includes a Java application called the **Netscape Console**. The Netscape Console is the tool through which you manage all of your Netscape servers. You can choose to install the Directory Server and the Console, or the Console separately. You might, for example, want to install the Console on multiple machines to provide a superior, consistent management interface to your servers. The Console does not store any configuration information itself. Instead it queries against an LDAP configuration server for all of its server management. The configuration server is a standard LDAP server, except that it manages information under a special tree that starts at `o=NetscapeRoot`. There shouldn't be any public directory information in the `o=NetscapeRoot` tree, only entries that are for the configuration of Netscape servers should be stored there.

The Netscape Console application constitutes slight break in tradition for Netscape. In the past, the management of Netscape's servers was done via a web-based interface. While this was certainly an improvement over the kind of configuration that involves messing around with text files, common in servers like Apache, it did lead to some clunky interface designs at times, because of the limitations of HTML. Netscape Console, on the other hand, acts very much like a traditional GUI, providing a consistent cross-platform look and feel. Not only does it provide a rich interface to the server management, it also offers a hint at the promise of Java-based GUIs.

Choose the default installation, indicated above which gives you all the Netscape Servers plus Netscape Console.

> Note that you also need to choose the **Custom** option when that particular screen is presented.

The next screen shows you the first information you get about this new way of managing your server configuration information:

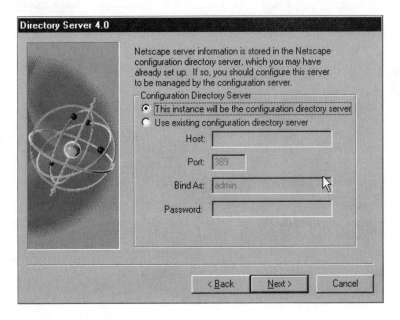

Most likely you will go with the default, but if you already have an LDAP server setup for handling Netscape server configuration information, you can enter the details here.

The next step in the installation wizard allows you set the initial root of the Directory Information Tree for your Directory Server:

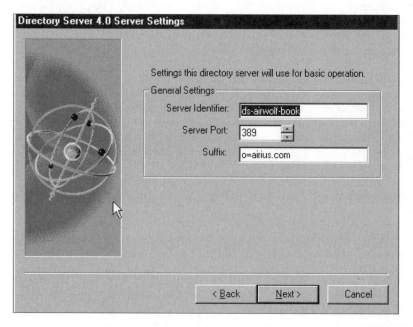

I put `o=airius.com` here because I know that I'm going to be playing with the example data that comes with Directory Server which has a root of `o=airius.com`. If you wish to follow the examples in the book, you should put `o=airius.com` here as well. Now if this were a real server intending to go into production, I would put my organization's domain name here in the form of either `o=domain.com` or `dc=domain,dc=com`.

Note that the Directory Server is capable of managing multiple roots. This means that you can have more than one DIT on your server. One benefit of this is that you have the ability to store your own administrative configuration on the same server, maybe in a separate tree. Secondly, this ability allows you to provide directory services to multiple organizations. An example of this can be found on sites like `http://www.switchboard.com` which allows you to search telephone directories over the Internet. The majority of servers such as these now support LDAP queries and they must be able to store multiple organizations to support telephone directory services.

Each configuration directory server is responsible for a particular domain. This is similar in concept to Primary Domain Controllers in Windows NT but follows the domain model of the Internet. Here, you can set the domain for your Administration Server:

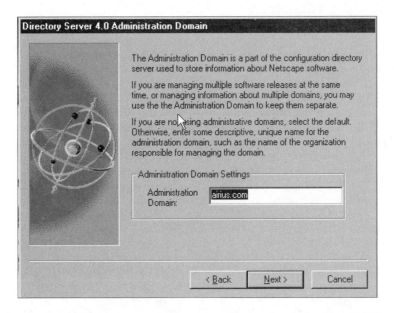

For example, this server is set up to manage servers in the `airius.com` domain. We might also set up a configuration server for other areas like `hr.airius.com` or `engineering.airius.com`. The reason why you might wish, or need, to add extra servers is to split up management tasks. This could be done because you have so many entries, and it is easier to manage users by splitting them up. Another reason might be because you work in a distributed computing environment where each department manages its own user data. A final reason is that while you may serve up a "people" directory server in a central location, you might find it easier to let departments manage configuration information within their own domains to keep that information separate or to reduce network traffic/congestion. You can add extra domains from Netscape Console.

The final step you can perform for the initial setup is to do an initial population of the server database with information:

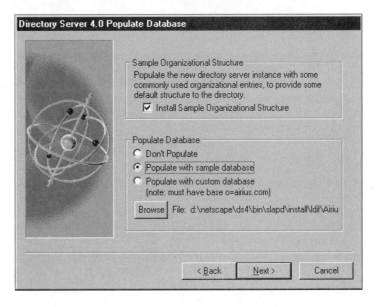

Note: You will only get this screen if you chose the Custom option.

I would recommend the creation of the Sample Organizational Structure if you have not done an LDAP installation before. This will create some basic standard entries like an organizational unit for People and Groups. It will also create a group for directory administrators. Also, I would highly recommend that you go with the installation of a sample database, the data for which is contained in the `airius.ldif` file. This means that you can test out interacting with an LDAP server without having to come up with your own data. This data contained within `airius.ldif` is what we will be using throughout the rest of the book. If you already have existing data in LDIF format, you can populate the database at this point also by choosing that option.

The installation wizard will then install the Server and Netscape Console for you. After finished you can start up the Netscape Console:

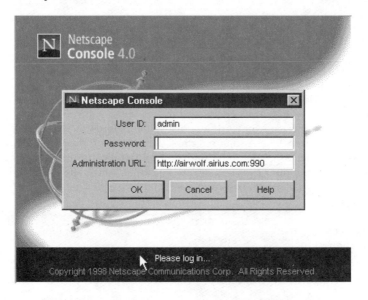

The login screen will contain the default administrator user ID (`admin`) when you installed the system. You will have chosen a password during the install procedure as well.

Netscape Directory Server Gateway

Notice that the URL entered above is an HTTP URL and not an LDAP one. This URL actually performs two functions – if you use Netscape Console, it allows you to manage the LDAP servers, but if you go to that same URL from a browser, then you get a web page served up by the Administration Server that contains one or more links to the Directory Server gateway:

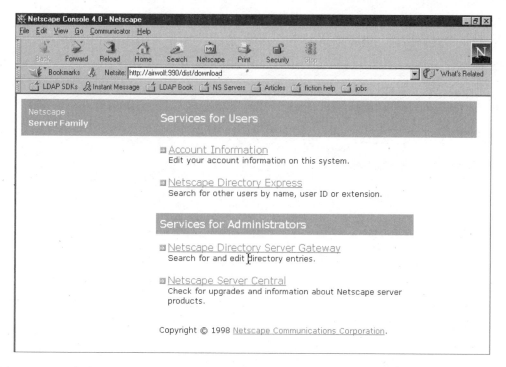

This web page uses the Directory Server Gateway, which has shipped with every version of the Netscape Directory Server. It is a set of CGI programs that are capable of interacting with LDAP servers along with some HTML template files that you can customize to build the user interface. In fact, you are not limited to just using this HTML page for your editing purposes, you can enable the gateway for use with any web server. Of course, you can also build your own gateway if you so wish.

The first option shown above, Account Information, allows a user to log in and change some basic information about themselves in the LDAP server. This option will prompt the user for a user ID and password before proceeding.

Searching

The second option, Netscape Directory Express, is really the meaty LDAP gateway of this service. In fact, Netscape Directory Express is a highly customized version of Netscape Directory Server Gateway. You might want to look at it as an example of what you can do with the Directory Server Gateway. You can customize Directory Express further to take more advantage of the other capabilities of the Directory Server Gateway. Choose this and you can search for entries based on their name, user ID or e-mail address:

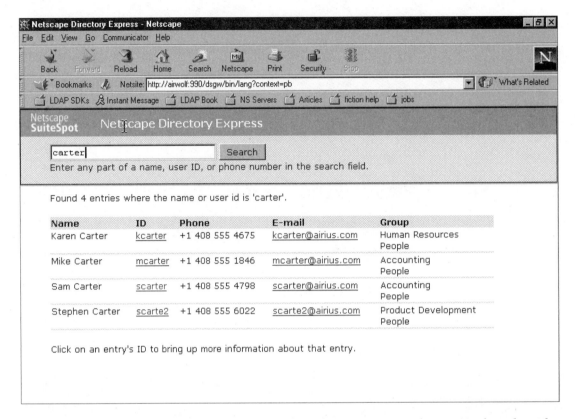

As you can see from the above screenshot, a search on the name Carter has returned results with some basic information, such as the user's full name, their user ID, telephone number, e-mail address and the groups they are a member of. All of this display information is customizable.

If you click on one of the ID hyperlinks, you can see the user's full entry:

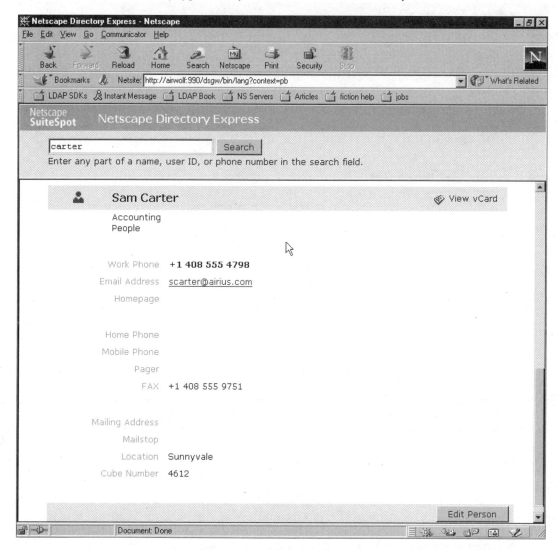

This screen shows a bit more information about the user, such as their home telephone number. You can even import their vCard, which is the *de facto* standard for digital business cards.

If you scroll down the window you will see a Edit Person button, which will allow you to edit the entry, if you can authenticate to the server as a user that has access rights for that entry. The rights are managed via Access Control Lists (ACLs) which are stored in the LDAP server. We will cover more about ACLs in Chapter 12. Usually a user will have the ability to edit certain attributes in their own entry such as their password and home telephone number.

Suppose a user logs on to edit their personal entry, they would see a screen something like this:

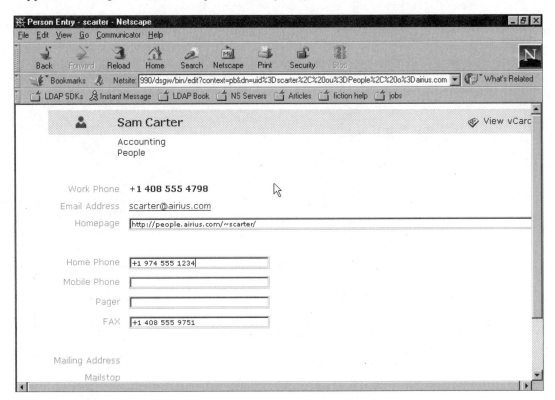

You cannot get to this screen unless you have authenticated as a non-anonymous user, that is, you have bound to the LDAP server as a user with an ID and password. In the above screenshot, the fields with text entry boxes are those that can be modified. On the other hand, fields without edit boxes, such as **Mailing Address**, can only be modified by users with the appropriate rights. This gateway has actually queried the Access Control Information (ACI) for this particular entry to determine whether or not the current user has the rights to modify this attribute. ACLs can be set up to manage access based on a set of entries, for a single entry or down to attribute level.

Directory Administrators have many more rights than the average user and the Directory Manager account has full access to the entire database – it is the administrator account to the LDAP server. In fact its DN and password are stored separately from the rest of the system, so that the Directory Manager can still get access even if you lose all of your user accounts.

Because of the special privileges Directory Administrators have, the default gateway is set up differently for them, allowing more functionality than is allowed for other users, such as the ability to add new entries.

Shown below is the screen for the Directory Administrator:

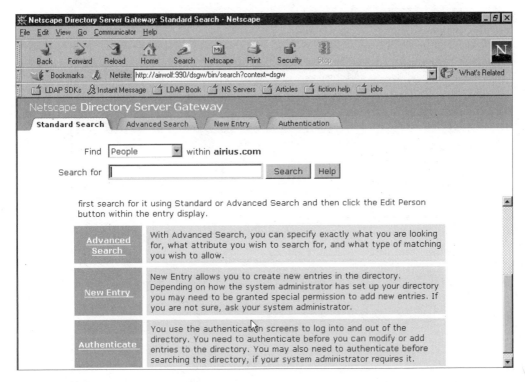

The two new screens that you can go to from here are:

- ❑ Advanced Search
- ❑ New Entry

The **Advanced Search** screen allows you to have more control over your searches. This screen is presented here because the Directory Administrator would often need to carry out much more specific searches than the average user. In fact, the latter would hardly ever never need to access an entry with a view to reading it or modifying it. More likely he would get just one piece of information and then exit.

Shown below is an example of an advanced search:

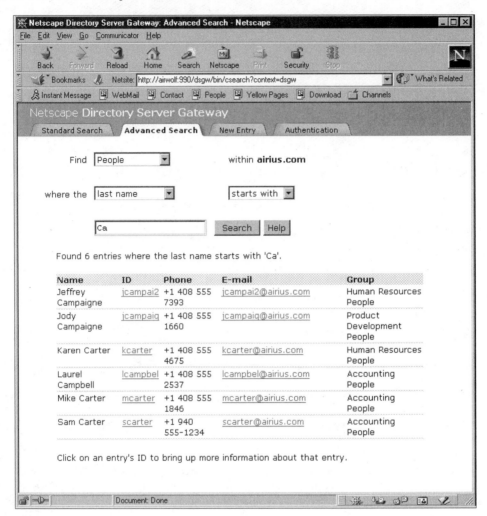

Adding New Entries

The Directory Manager account allows Directory Administrators to can add new entries, and here is one such example:

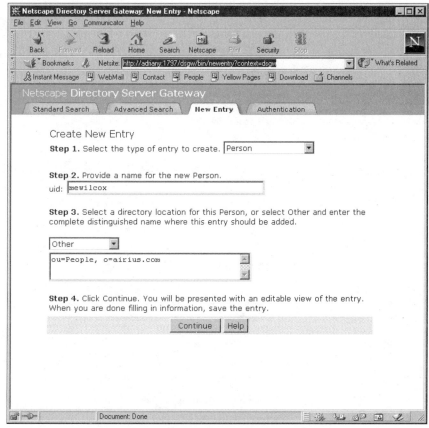

This screen is defining two important attributes in the entry: the object class and the distinguished name of the entry. Let's take a look at what's going on in the screen above:

Step 1

This step allows you to determine what type of entry you want to have. This could be a person, a Windows NT person or group (only available on Directory servers running on Windows NT), a group, an organizational unit or an organization. These are not the only entry types (i.e. object class values) that the server supports, just the ones that the gateway supports by default.

Step 2

Here you to choose the relative distinguished name (RDN) of the entry. The attribute type will depend upon the entry type. For example, for a person the attribute might be uid. If it's an organizational unit the attribute would be ou.

Step 3

This is where we define the location in the tree where we want the entry stored. For example, we will store all of our people into the ou=People, branch. You do have the option of specifying the exact DN of the entry if you wish.

Step 4

You click on Continue and you get the next screen:

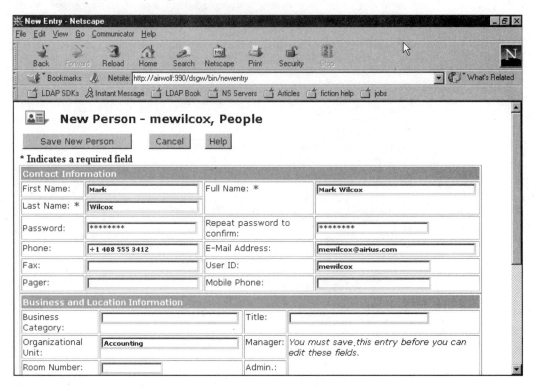

Here you can fill in all of the details you wish about a particular entry such as a person's name, their e-mail address, their phone number, etc.

After you are done filling in the fields and you wish to complete, click the Save New Person button to add the new entry to the server.

You can add new users shown in the screenshots above, as long as you authenticate as a user who has rights to do the job. This "gateway out of the box" does limit you to the types of entries you can create, although you can modify this.

Once you have added the entry, you can confirm its presence on the server by doing a standard search:

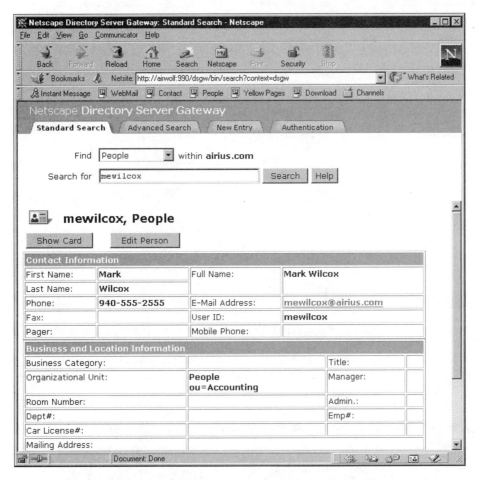

The Gateway provides a mechanism to deliver LDAP search and modification access to your users in a very simple way without any concerns about client deployment. (If they have a web browser, they have access to the Directory Server Gateway.)

Now that you have seen the Gateway, you'll get to experience Netscape Console, which provides a richer interface to the LDAP server and is designed for Directory Server administrators.

Managing Netscape Console

From Netscape Console, you can manage any of the servers in the Netscape server line, including the older version 3 server. The version 3 servers use a web based GUI, so when you actually need to manage one of these servers, the Console will start up Netscape Communicator to access the administration web site for that server.

You can centrally manage your servers whether you have local access to the server or remote access – all you need is a live Internet connection.

This is what the Netscape Console main management screen looks like:

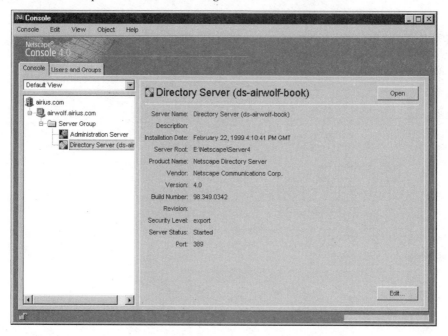

The central management screen will show all of the Netscape servers you have under your control with this tool including all of the administrative domains you may have. In our screen above, we only have one administrative domain with one Administration Server and one Directory Server. You can however, add more using the Console menu options at this screen.

You also can search an LDAP server from this screen by clicking on the Users and Groups tab:

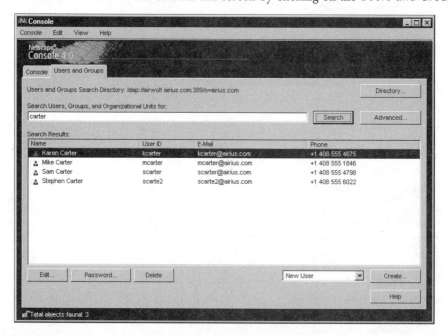

From this screen, you can perform a general search, edit an entry or create a new entry.

The **Advanced** button gives you more control over the searching of the LDAP server and the **Directory** button enables you to specify which server you want to search.

If you double click on an entry you can also see more of the entry, and you can edit the entry if you so choose (and are able to). You'll also notice that you can manage Netscape server licenses for the user with this interface. Some of the Netscape Suitespot server software is managed on a per user basis – with this screen you can see what software a particular user has been granted a license for:

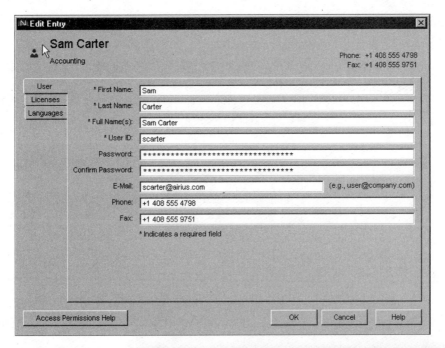

If you choose the **Open** button at the top right of the main Netscape Console window (also called the Server Topology), you will get the screen shown here:

The main purposes of this first screen are to allow starting, stopping or restarting the server and certificate management. Certificate management is for using Directory Server to manage your PKI (Public Key Infrastructure) which is necessary in a secure, encrypted, e-commerce environment. You can use Netscape Directory Server to manage both server certificates and personal certificates for improved user authentication. This is covered in more detail in Chapter 12.

The Configuration tab enables you to manage the basics of your LDAP server database. At its core, LDAP is a database access protocol. Calling it a 'directory' is just some fancy terminology for a type of database application.

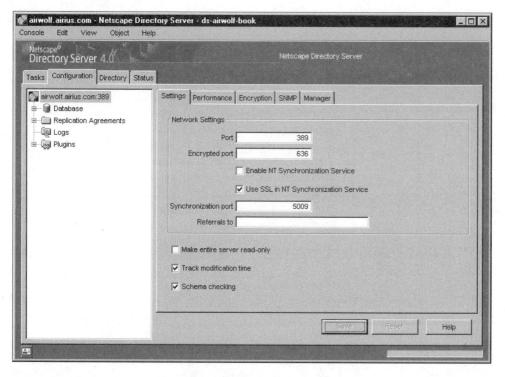

The screenshot above also enables you to:

- ❑ Back up your server
- ❑ Manage the schema (e.g. database design)
- ❑ Import/export data
- ❑ Replicate LDAP data between servers

The Directory tab is used to manage the data in the server:

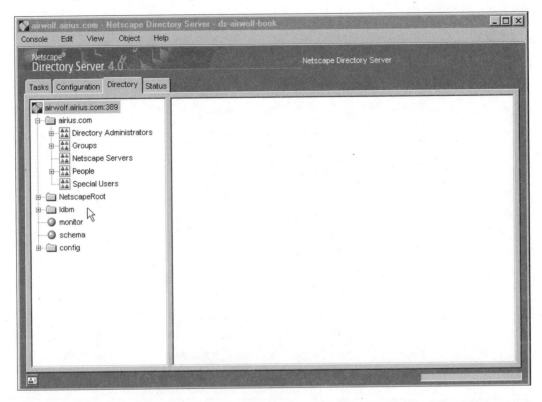

This screen allows you to browse through the server tree and add a new entry. The difference between adding an entry here in this screen and the Directory Server Gateway is that we can add any entry allowed by the schema. To add entries via the Gateway that are not one of the standard ones available "out of the box", you'd have to re-customize the Gateway. Using the screen above, we can also move the entry in the tree or delete an entry.

A nifty feature that Directory Server 4.0 supports, which no other LDAP server yet supports is the LDAPv3 Virtual List View control. The VLV control allows you to display all of the entries in the server without limits – the server controls the number to display at a time to prevent a search from overloading it. Normally you are limited to the number of entries you can see during a particular search, unless you are the Directory Manager.

Directory Server 4.0 also supports the ability to create groups of entries dynamically – that is, to create a new group whose membership is based upon the results of a LDAP search query. This is useful because sometimes you need to group items or members on an *ad hoc* basis. Perhaps you might want to create a group of all users who live in Houston, Texas, or create a group that is made up of all the printers located in the Engineering building.

The final tab in this window is labeled Status. This enables us to see the different performance metrics of our servers:

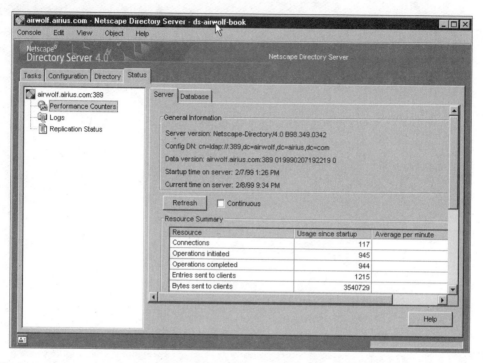

The Performance Counters can help show you how your server is actually performing. For example this will tell you the last time the server was started as well as other parameters that can help determine how the server is performing: the number of connections, the number of operations started and the number completed. These metrics (that is performance measurements) are given to you as a total since startup, and the average per minute. To get an accurate gauge of performance, you'd have to pay attention to these numbers over a period of time. Unfortunately I don't know of a way to store these numbers outside of the server, nor how to build a graph that could show performance characteristics over time. Besides server metrics, it also provides metrics on the actual underlying database. These metrics include measurements of the number of direct accesses made on the database and the number of search queries satisfied by the results delivered from the database cache. Besides metrics, you can also get access to the log files from here. You can reconstruct most of the metrics of your server from the log data. You can also see any error messages that might have been delivered to your system during operation.

Benefits of Netscape Directory Server

Netscape Directory Server is the current leader in the LDAP server market and its search/read performance is quite remarkable – it is the fastest directory server in the world, by an astonishing margin. You can also use the Directory Server to synchronize with multiple Windows NT domains, users and groups, which gives you a quick way to provide single login capabilities through LDAP.

The Directory Server 4.0 brings you an improved management interface and performance improvements. It supplies internal transaction management – the ability to recover the system in catastrophic failure, or if the need arises, a master server can be rebuilt with data from a slave.

There is also a good deal of support available for you if you decide to use the Netscape Directory Server. Netscape maintains a sizable documentation site at `http://developer.netscape.com/directory/`. They also maintain two developers' newsgroups, one of which is open to the public and the other is restricted to developers who are members of the Netscape's Developers program.

You can also occasionally find support for the Directory Server on the Directory newsgroup at `http://www.mozilla.org/directory/`. However, this newsgroup is really devoted to the open source development of the Netscape Directory (LDAP) SDKs and tools. This URL should *only* be used to post development-related material. Other comments will not be taken seriously, or most likely will be ignored – it will only increase the frustration level of developers.

OpenLDAP vs Netscape Directory Server

Shown below is a summary of the different operations and options that the OpenLDAP and Netscape Directory server support to help you keep track of their features.:

Option	OpenLDAP	Netscape Directory Server
LDAP v3	not yet	Yes
SSL/SASL	not yet	Yes
Multi-Platform	Multi-Unix	Yes
Multi-DBS	Yes	Yes with Server API
Open source	Yes	No
Public Help forum	Yes	Yes
Commercial Support	No	Yes

Summary

There are a variety of LDAP compliant servers on the market and in this chapter we have looked in depth at two of them. Each LDAP server from the major vendors offers its own particular pros and cons. You have to decide what functionality and requirements your organization needs before you decide which server is most suitable for you.

Make sure that when you decide to purchase or develop applications that require user management that they are LDAP compliant. By choosing a reliable, supported LDAP servers and LDAP compliant applications you will be able to make it easier to manage user access while reducing the overall cost of ownership.

In this chapter we learned about a variety of LDAP servers and taken a more in depth look at how to install and use the Netscape Directory Server. In the next chapter we'll move on to learn how to implement an LDAP server in an organization.

5

Deploying a Netscape Directory Server

In this chapter we will discuss how to deploy a Netscape Directory Server, and in the process will delve deeper into LDAP and LDIF. The reason why we focus on Netscape Directory Server as our preferred LDAP server is because Netscape is the market leader in LDAP servers. They have one of the most complete LDAP version 3 implementations on the market.

In particular, we will cover:

- ❑ A review of LDIF
- ❑ Installing a default LDIF file using Netscape Directory Server
- ❑ Testing the LDAP server
- ❑ Designing your own LDAP data
- ❑ Implementing an upload mechanism
- ❑ Advanced issues

LDIF Revisted

As we have seen, LDAP Data Interchange Format, or LDIF, is the way we express LDAP data in human readable terms. Let's review quickly what exactly LDIF is:

- ❑ UTF-8 (Unicode) text format
- ❑ Contains attributes and values for an LDAP database entry
- ❑ Will always contain the DN of the entry
- ❑ Binary data is encoded in Base-64

Whenever you deal with LDAP data outside of an LDAP server, you will use LDIF. Learning how to interact with LDIF is an important part of learning how to use LDAP. In the first part of this chapter, will learn how to create and use LDIF outside an LDAP server. This will help reduce the learning curve a bit, while still providing a useful set of examples.

Netscape's Communicator web browser suite contains an address book that allows you to search an LDAP server to get addresses and contact information. It also allows you to maintain your own local address book:

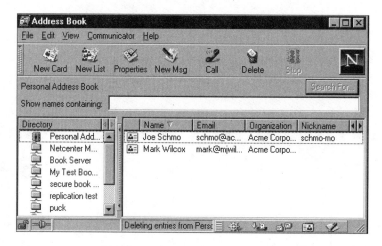

An e-mail package's address book is nothing new — in fact, every e-mail package that I know has an address book. Unfortunately, it's not very easy to transport an address book from one package to another. Netscape hopes to help eliminate this technological gap by allowing the export of its address book as an LDIF file. Now, if you are thinking, 'big deal', keep this in mind — Microsoft Internet Explorer 4.0 web browser's address book can import LDIF files. This is most impressive, because sharing address book information is something most of us need, and LDIF has enabled this to happen. Of course, you might think that a comma-delimited text file could do the same thing, but these files can be quite limiting, in particular considering the type of data a LDIF file might contain.

For example, in a comma-delimited text (sometimes referred to as comma separated values) address book 'database', you are forced to have the same number of fields in every record, even if these fields are empty. And if you need to add extra fields to certain records, but not all of them — well, you're out of luck. If you really need those fields in certain records, you have to add them to every record. You're also out of luck if certain fields have more than one value, because there is not a way to handle multiple field values in a comma-delimited text 'database'.

With LDIF, since it's LDAP, each entry (i.e. a record) in your address book 'database' only needs to have the attributes that actually contain values. If some entries need extra attributes, no problem, you can simply add them to the LDAP server. (In the example in this section, the Netscape Communicator and Internet Explorer address books are acting like LDAP servers in relation to the importing/exporting of LDIF data).

Exporting Netscape's Address Book

Let's now see how easy it can be to export address book data from Netscape Communicator (my version is 4.5) into Microsoft's Internet Explorer 4.0 (MSIE 4.0). The screenshot above shows the basic address book client, and in the next one, you can now see an example of an empty record waiting for input. (Netscape calls it a "New Card", following the Rolodex business card manager paradigm):

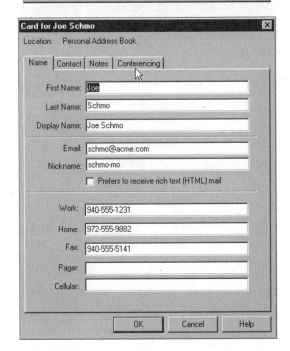

The following two screenshots show a completed entry. First the Name tab:

And now, Joe Schmo's entry under the Contact tab:

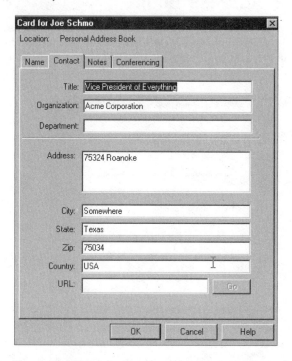

As you can see, the Netscape address book is pretty much just your ordinary address book GUI. Now say your colleague decides to use Microsoft Internet Explorer and would like to have a copy of your address book, because you share many of the same contacts. In the stone-age days before networking and the Internet, this would have been a nightmarish possibility at best. There just wasn't an easy way to swap address books around – you would probably have had to copy them out by hand. But things are changing. Just as HTML has helped render proprietary word-processing formats a thing of the past, LDIF will replace proprietary address books.

Here is what a blank MSIE 4.0 address book looks like:

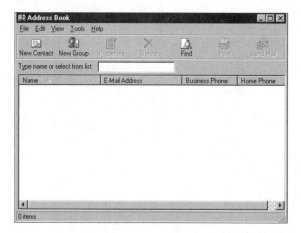

Now we will start the process of adding the records from our Netscape address book to our empty MSIE 4.0 address book. First we will need to prepare the Netscape address book for export by choosing File | Export in the Address Book menu:

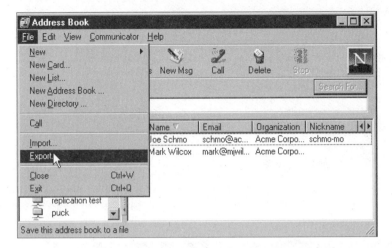

Save it as an LDIF file. Netscape will add the .ldif extension for you. Just remember where you saved it so that you can import it into MSIE 4.0. Now, importing the file is just as easy in the MSIE 4.0 address book. Run the application and Choose File | Import | Address Book:

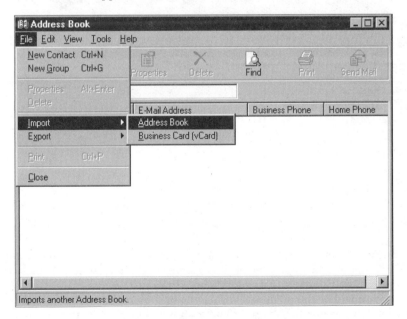

This will bring up a popup window that allows you to choose several different input formats:

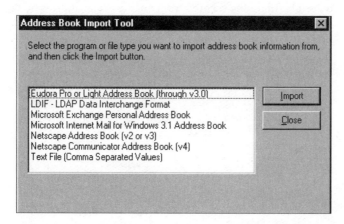

To import an LDIF file, you just need to choose the LDIF–LDAP Data Interchange Format option. Then just browse to where you saved your earlier file, select that file and click Open. You should see something like this:

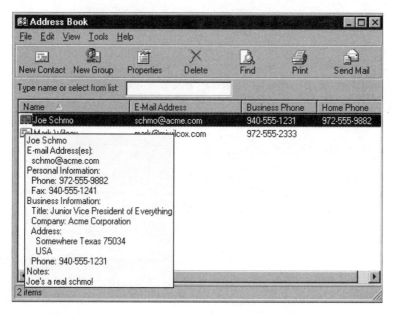

You might be wondering why I'm going through all of these steps when the Netscape Communicator Address Book (v4) option is on the import menu. Well, there are three reasons. The main reason is that this option only works on Communicator address books prior to version 4.5. Secondly, this is a book on LDAP, so what would be the point in showing you how to import a Communicator address book? Third, if you have access to a LDAP server and want to dump some entries for your personal address book for your laptop to compose messages while your off-line, well now you know how.

You will notice that the yellow box that provides a complete snapshot is a tool tip. This only shows up if you pause your mouse over an entry.

While MSIE 4.0 can import a Netscape address book without the first conversion, this is still a relevant exercise – Netscape may change their address book format in the future, but they will always export it out as LDIF. Also, LDIF files are a means for you to export your existing directories into people's own personal directories, in particular if they will be working off-line.

Export Microsoft Internet Explorer's Address Book

Now that we have seen how easy it is to import Netscape's address book into MSIE, what about the other way around? The problem we will discover is that while MSIE imports an LDIF file, it cannot export an LDIF file. (If someone knows the reason why it imports but doesn't export LDIF, would they let me know.)

To export MSIE 4.0's address book you choose File | Export from the menu, in a similar fashion to Netscape's mechanism. Choose Address Book, to export the entire Address Book. It is similar to Netscape's except this time you will notice that you have more than one choice, but none of them are LDIF. The only options are Microsoft Exchange Personal Address Book and Text File (Comma Separated Values). For our purposes, choose Text File:

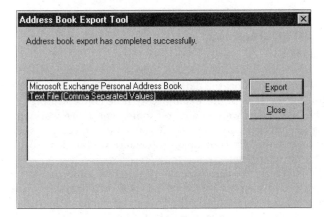

Click on Export and you will be asked to choose the location to save your file. Once you have done this, then click on Next.

Now you will see a screen that will allow you to choose which fields you wish to export. Keep all of the defaults and make sure that all of the 'Name' attributes are checked. The rest are optional:

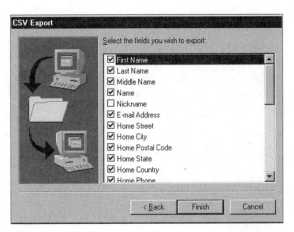

Here is an example of the output from this operation:

```
First Name,Last Name,Name,E-mail Address,Home Street,Home City,Home Postal
Code,...
Joe,Schmo,Joe Schmo,schmo@acme.com,,,,,,972-555-
9882,,Somewhere,75034,Texas,USA,...
Mark,Wilcox,Mark Wilcox,mark@mjwilcox.com,,,,,,,,,,,,972-555-2333,...
```

The " . . . " represents that there is more text, but carried across the screen. Microsoft exports data in comma-delimited format like this so you can import the data into a Microsoft Excel spreadsheet or MS Access database. The alternative is to have them saved in a plain text format that is readable by Notepad.

In versions of Netscape Communicator earlier than 4.5, the only option you had for importing files was the LDIF format. Now it is possible to import data from:

- ❏ LDIF
- ❏ Eudora
- ❏ Outlook
- ❏ Outlook Express (MSIE address book)
- ❏ Comma-delimited files

So, although we can now directly import the data from an address book from Internet Explorer to Netscape Communicator, for the sake of this example, we'll be concentrating on the LDIF option. Since this book is about LDAP, and I want you to get some experience working with some LDAP like data, let's just play along like this is really needed. (If you want you can just skim this chapter and concentrate on the next section that starts in Chapter 6 where we build "real" LDAP clients.)

So, for earlier versions of Netscape, we can solve the problem of importing addresses into Netscape using a simple Perl script. Such a script, `csv2ldif.pl`, is shown below. (This is quite similar to the Perl example from Chapter 3 that you may recall.) This script changes the comma-delimited text file exported from MSIE 4.0's Address Book and converts it into a LDIF file to ready to import into Netscape Communicator's address book:

```perl
#!/usr/local/bin/perl
#csv2ldif.pl
#A Perl script to change MSIE 4.0's Address Book into a LDIF file
#usage csv2ldif.pl some_csv_file.csv
#will output a file named some_csv_file.ldif

#match up as many csv field names to standard LDAP attributes as possible,
#otherwise (for fields without standard LDAP equivalents) just take name,
#take out any spaces, turn text into lowercase and make that field name.

my %csvHash = ();
my %ldifHash = ();
my @csvArray;

$csvHash{"First Name"}= "givenname";
$csvHash{"Last Name"}= "sn";
$csvHash{"Name"} = "cn";
$csvHash{"E-mail Address"} = "mail";
```

```perl
$csvHash{"Business City"} = "locality";
$csvHash{"Business Phone"} = "telephonenumber";
$csvHash{"Business Fax"} = "facsimiletelephonenumber";
$csvHash{"Notes"} = "description";
$csvHash{"Business State"} = "st";
$csvHash{"Business Street"} = "streetaddress";
$csvHash{"Business Country"} = "countryname";
$csvHash{"Business Postal Code"} = "postalcode";
$csvHash{"Company"} = "o";
$csvHash{"Nickname"} = "xmozillanickname";

my $csv_file = shift(); #get filename from command line

open(CSV,"$csv_file") II die ("Failed to open $csv_file.$!\n");

my ($ldif_file,$foo) = split(/\./,$csv_file);


open(LDIF,">$ldif_file.ldif") II die ("Failed to open $csv_file.ldif.$!\n");

#load CSV file into an array
while (<CSV>) {
    chomp();
    push (@csvArray,$_);
}

#get field names
my @csvFields = split(/,/,$csvArray[0]);

my $csv_fields_length = @csvFields;
#now convert those csvFields to LDAP fields
my @ldifFields;

for ($z=0;$z<$csv_fields_length;$z++)
{
    $ldifFields[$z] = $csvHash{$csvFields[$z]};

    if (! defined($ldifFields[$z]))
    {
        $ldifFields[$z] = $csvFields[$z];
        $ldifFields[$z] =~ s/ //g;
        $ldifFields[$z] =~ tr/A-Z/a-z/;
    }
}

my $csv_length = @csvArray;

for ($i=1;$i<$csv_length;$i++)
{
    @csvRecord = split(/,/,$csvArray[$i]);
    for ($x = 0; $x < $csv_fields_length;$x++)
        {
        $ldifHash{$ldifFields[$x]} = $csvRecord[$x];
    }

    #each record must have a dn field
    print LDIF "dn: cn=".$ldifHash{"cn"}.",mail=".$ldifHash{"mail"}."\n";

    #each record must have these 2 object classes
    print LDIF "objectclass: top\nobjectclass: person\n";
```

```
    while (($key,$value) = each %ldifHash)
    {
        print LDIF "$key: $value\n";
    }

    print LDIF "\n";
}

close(CSV);
close(LDIF);
```

Note that this program has two limitations that can affect the LDIF output – the data that you want in the address book must not contain any commas or any carriage returns. These could occur in any **Notes** fields or in **Address** fields where you would want to write complete sentences or write more than one line. The commas are inserted in between the data entries by MSIE 4.0 prior to exporting, and are parsed by the Perl split() function. If a note or address contains one comma, split() will create two entries and the result would be that the record's data does not match the field names from that point on.

On the other hand, the end of a record is determined when chomp() finds a carriage return (¶). If you have an **Address** field like this:

```
Floor 13¶
West House¶
24 West Street
```

chomp() will assume that Floor 13 is the last entry of the first record, West House would be a record all on its own and the next record would begin with 24 West Street.

To run the script on a Windows 95/98/NT machine you would type a command line statement like this one:

```
perl csv2ldif.pl my_address_export_file.csv
```

This will create a new file called my_address_export_file.ldif. Of course, if you named your .csv file differently you would type that name in!

Here is an example LDIF file would be produced:

```
dn: cn=Joe Schmo,mail=schmo@acme.com
objectclass: top
objectclass: person
homestreet:
locality: Somewhere
sn: Schmo
homecity:
homephone: 972-555-9882
mail: schmo@acme.com
st: Texas
homestate:
telephonenumber: 940-555-1231
postalcode: 75034
```

```
o: Acme Corporation
cn: Joe Schmo
countryname: USA
homepostalcode:
givenname: Joe
jobtitle: Junior Vice President of Everything
homecountry:
streetaddress:
```

You can now import the resulting file into your Netscape Address Book by choosing File | Import. Remember that LDIF is represented in `attribute: value` syntax. The attributes are usually represented as a mnemonic that is designed to save space, while still giving you an understanding of what that value is supposed to represent.

Also remember that because this is LDAP data, the entry must have a distinguished name (represented by the attribute dn) which is the unique key to the entry. It also must include one or more object classes. This entry includes the object classes `top` and `person`. You should also note that this entry is most likely not directly importable to any LDAP server, because it contains attributes which are not defined in the LDAP RFC as being a part of the person object class, such as the `xmozilla*` variants. The `xmozilla*` attributes are special attributes used by Communicator for determining things like whether a particular person prefers HTML mail or not.

In fact, you could import it if you were to turn schema checking off, but this is not recommended, because you can easily corrupt your LDAP data in this way.

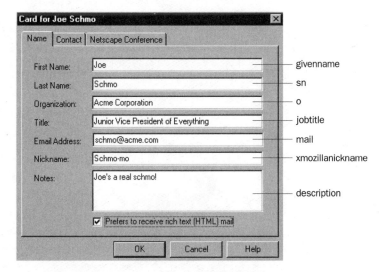

LDIF: It's not just for Address Books!

The LDIF format is not just for passing information between address books. It's also the primary way the majority of us will interact with the LDAP server. We get an LDIF file back when we perform a search on an LDAP server and we can use LDIF to perform updates or changes to the data in the LDAP server. We also use LDIF to perform the initial design of our LDAP database, called **schema building**.

Installing the Netscape Directory Sample Data

As we begin a further exploration of the LDIF format and LDAP deployment, we should begin working with a functional LDAP server with some functional data. We will use Netscape Directory Server, because it offers the majority of the LDAP version 3 features and is fairly easy to work with. The Netscape Directory Server ships with a number of extras that make it easier to work with LDAP. This includes a ready-to-deploy web to LDAP gateway, command-line tools to perform simple operations, and some sample LDAP data, which makes it fairly trivial to get a test server up and running.

During the installation of Netscape Directory Server 4 (covered in the previous chapter) you had the ability to import the sample LDIF file, `airius.ldif`. If you installed that sample data at that point, then you can skip the rest of this section if you want and move onto the section entitled *Testing the LDAP Server*.

If you didn't import the file, the first step is to start up the Netscape Console. From here, you can choose the Directory Server to which you wish to add the LDIF file. Click on the Configuration tab and then choose File | Import from the menu. This will bring up a screen similar to this:

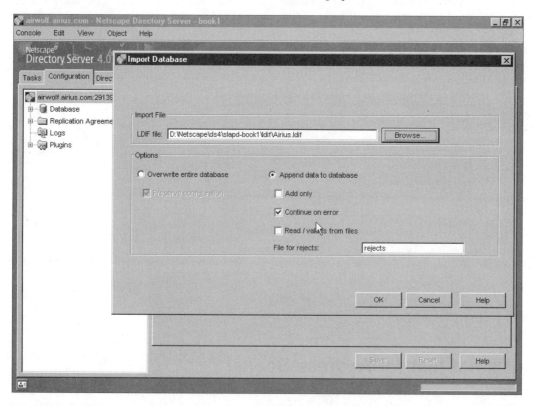

Click on the Browse button. This will present a File Chooser dialog, similar to the one you see when you open a file from your favorite word processor. There should be a few LDIF files in there, make sure that you choose the `airius.ldif` file if you wish to follow the examples throughout this book. Then click OK. This will stop the server and install the file. After the file is installed, it will restart the server.

Testing the LDAP server

Now that we have loaded the sample LDIF file that is supplied with Netscape Directory Server, we need to see if it responds. The easiest way to test this out is by using the LDAP client built into Netscape Communicator.

The first step is to open up the address book by selecting Address Book from the Communicator menu option. Then choose File | New Directory from the Address Book menu. You should see something like this:

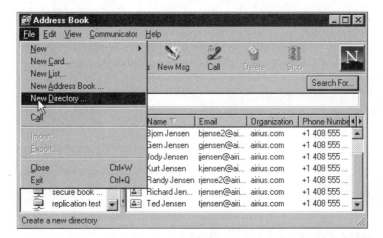

Choose New Directory and this will bring up a dialog asking for the Directory Server preferences (actually these are the preferences for any LDAP capable server). The Description is what will show up in the Communicator's Address Book's server selection. The LDAP Server is the host name of the machine that your Directory Server is on and the Search Root for this example is o=airius.com. Unless you set your Server on a different port than the standard port, you can leave the rest of the defaults as they are:

Click OK on this window, and OK on the Preferences window and you are now set. Next, open the Netscape address book. From the list of servers, choose the description that refers to the new Directory Server that we just added to the list. In the Show names containing: box type *Jensen, and then click on the Search button. It should come back with a window full of names.

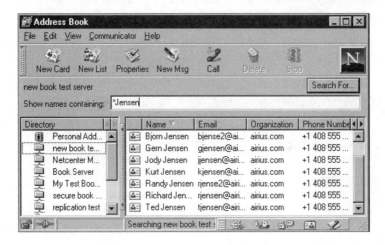

You can feel free to pat yourself on your back now. You have successfully completed the first stage of Netscape Directory server deployment!

Designing your own LDAP data

So far, we have explored the very basics of LDIF and have learned some of the basics of what LDAP is or can be. We are now ready to begin our progression to full implementation. If you have been reading non-stop for a while, now would be a good time to put this book down, go for a walk and then come back. You want your head clear as we start to dive into this subject. I promise I'll wait for you.

Had a good walk? OK then.

Hopefully you have an idea of what you want your LDAP server to do for you and perhaps you now have some ideas of what else LDAP might do for you. Write these ideas down. Make them as simple as possible and keep them flexible. We want to make our mistakes now in the design phase and not after we have actually put the production server in place. Like any database system, the hardest work is not in the initial implementation, but fixing the mistakes we made when we built it. The more you think things through up front, the better you will be. However, don't get to worked up about it, because we are after all human and we will make mistakes. LDAP is also still a fairly new technology, so some of the kinks are still being worked out.

How you build your own server will greatly depend upon how you see it being used. The most likely purposes for which it will be used are:

❑ As an employee contact database
❑ User authentication

You might have more esoteric uses in mind, such as a central application configuration database or as a place to store your distributed Java class files. For now, though, we will concentrate on the basics of employee contact and user authentication, as they are often tied together.

'Basic' LDAP

The most basic uses of LDAP are for providing a central resource that contains information about people inside an organization. The reasons why people generally look to LDAP tend to be for the same reasons why they generally look to any other directory type service – to make their lives easier. People want to have a central resource they can check for information about the members of their organization.

In general there are three basic types of questions they are trying to answer with this resource:

- ❑ Contact information (phone, email, postal, fax, etc.)
- ❑ Organizational role (e.g. vice-president, engineer, web committee members, organizational hierarchy)
- ❑ Organizational status (e.g. with the organization, left organization, visitor of the organization)

This type of information also helps determine what types of access a particular user has in the organization, in particular what types of access users have to computer/information systems.

Generally speaking, before LDAP, this type of information was kept in other systems. When people start to go about building directory services, they usually think that they should either stick with their legacy systems for everything or stick everything in LDAP. This is not the case; there are places where both types of systems are appropriate.

Many organizations have spent a great deal of time building complex relational databases with packages like Oracle or Microsoft SQL Server. These packages contain several business rules (database queries and stored procedures that are specific to how you run your business) and rewriting them from scratch would make the Year 2000 bug look like a typical day at the park. This is OK, because an RDBMS can do things that LDAP is not designed for.

On the other hand, LDAP can do some things better than an RDBMS. Each of these systems is a tool and each tool has a range of jobs it is good at. Remember the saying, 'If all you have is a hammer, everything looks like a nail.' Pick the right tool for the job, don't stick with one tool just because it's comfortable.

Relational databases provide great transactional security, which helps to protect the data integrity of the system. What this means that when you update the database, the RDBMS will only allow for the update to occur if all the intermediate steps succeed. You might be updating several fields and tables at once, so the update only happens if all of these fields/tables are updated without incident. Most LDAP servers do not provide this functionality because it is not usually needed from a directory service. However, there is a process underway to add standardized transaction support to LDAP for those servers who want it.

LDAP servers are optimized for very quick read access (much faster than from any RDBMS system), which usually means that it takes longer to add an entry to the system. This is not a problem or bug in LDAP – it's one of those laws of life – it just takes longer to put something in its place so that you can find it later than it does to just put it down anywhere. This is an acceptable compromise because LDAP data doesn't change very often. It can generally exist with some degree of allowed inconsistency, just so long as the errors are fixed in a short time.

For example, suppose Bob and Dave switch offices. During the switch an LDAP update occurs, but only Dave's office information is changed through human error. This means that when someone looks up Bob or Dave, they will see the same office information. This is probably manageable for a short period of time, because if someone calls the phone number, they will likely be directed to the right number. Also, it is known that this information will be updated in the morning, so that within 24 hours, the office information will be correct. Of course, there are systems where this inconsistency will not be acceptable. One area would be a monitor for crucial medical instrumentation – you would not want an inconsistent data store for such an item. In this case you would preferentially use an RDBMS.

You can also mix the tools. A common example of this usage is print servers. Print servers contain print queues, which of course are constantly updated. The constant update would take forever in a LDAP server, because it is optimized for lookup and not for updating. However, the print server's basic information like it's location, name, address, manager, etc. are pretty much fixed, so LDAP would be a good storage place for that. The process would then be to look up the location of the print server first and then print. You could then check the print server's print queue (contained in the print server's database) to see when your print operation is done. The diagram below helps demonstrates this process:

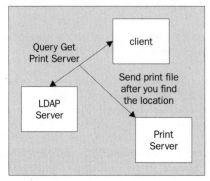

LDAP for Authentication

Besides providing directory lookup information, another common use of LDAP is for user authentication. As you will see, this can range from simple user IDs and passwords to encrypted personal certificates. An authentication example is shown in Chapter 6 and in Chapter 13, we learn how to provide authentication in a Java servlet.

A Brief History of User Authentication

We generally control access using devices like user IDs and passwords. The basis of using these dates back to the beginnings of multi-user machines. As more users started to use the same machines, a more sophisticated mechanism was needed in the forms of **access rights** (normally read, write and execute), and then came the concept of users and groups.

In this scheme, there is an **owner** of a particular object on the machine (e.g. a file or a directory or software) and there are **groups** that contain a list of users with a particular set of rights on an object. You can then specify the following rights, for example: the owner can read, write or execute the object and the group can only read or execute it, thus protecting that object from being altered by other users. In many cases, there is also a third global level of access, known as 'world' rights, where you can specify what level of access a user has, who is neither the owner nor a member of the group. In Unix, we refer to owner, group and world read/write/execute rights as **file permissions**.

These file permissions are represented by a series of 9 bits (actually 10, but the 10th one denotes whether it is a directory or a regular file). The 9 bits are broken into 3 groups of 3. The first group represents the owner, the second group represents the group permissions and the final group represents the 'world' permissions. Each bit in each 3 bit grouping represents a particular type of access. The first bit (r) denotes whether that particular section (user, group, world) has *read* access or not. The second bit denotes *write* access (w) and the final bit denotes *execute* access (x). If access is turned off (the bit is set to zero), then it is represented by a -.

Here is an example of Unix file permissions:

```
-rwxr-xr-- webuser webgroup 1000 10:15 Jul 19 myfile.txt
```

This would denote that the file myfile.txt has the following permissions.

- ❑   owner: read, write, execute
- ❑   group: read, execute
- ❑   world: read

As time went on, it soon became clear that this method of restricting and allowing access was far too simplistic, especially for very large and complex systems. You might only want certain groups to have access to the files, but some groups should have more rights than others. For example, you might have a file that lists your company's current financial plans. You would then allow the sales, marketing and financial services groups to have access to that file, but nobody else. You would include an additional specification: the sales and marketing groups should only be able to read the file, whereas the financial services group should be able to modify it as well.

The way this kind of granular control was implemented was through the use of **access control lists** (**ACLs**). These provide similar functionality to file permissions, but you can specify them in a file that lists the actual permissions. Often, permissions are allowed to cascade down so that you can have better control over your system, while not managing your files to death. Both Unix and the Windows NT file system (NTFS) provide this functionality.

Though ACLs have helped provide finer control over access, a bigger problem has arisen that has yet to be solved – the granting of access once a user is on the system. Normally, the granting of access to computer systems is based on user IDs and passwords. Unfortunately this system has one weakness – us humans. Users often pick bad passwords, such as their wife's or child's name. Sometimes they manage to pick good ones that aren't easily guessed, and they end up writing them down somewhere. Or they give out their IDs and passwords to the first person who calls up and asks for them. What this leads to is people who shouldn't have access to these accounts obtaining access.

One of the reasons that users generally write their passwords down or pick passwords that are easy to guess is because they have to remember so many of them – it's not uncommon for users to have to remember 6 or 7 different ones. Because people have so many things to memorize (and to computer users, passwords are more hassle than necessary!) they fall into bad habits.

There are ways to get users choosing better passwords, such as putting in rules that force them to enter a certain number of characters, requiring that passwords have at least one non-alphanumeric symbol, have mixed case, and so on. These ways of improving passwords only work if you can make it easier on the user. However, the best possible way is to reduce the number of different login IDs a user has to remember.

Smart Cards and Biometric Systems

To be honest, even typing user IDs and passwords is still fraught with error. Actually, the best system is to not use user IDs and passwords, but something like a smart card that the user swipes like an ATM card on the keyboard. The smart card might contain tools like single use passwords that make it harder for someone to copy and get into the system illegally. The cards might also contain digital certificates, which can become the electronic equivalent of a photo ID to verify a user's identity.

In the future, biometric systems like finger-print readers will become common. This will make it even easier for users to get into systems, while making it harder to gain access illicitly.

Regardless of whether we use passwords, digital certificates or fingerprints, if the information can be stored digitally, it can be stored using LDAP. We'll talk more about security in Chapter 12.

Designing Your LDAP Directory Service

Unless you are launching an entirely new organization or your organization has just suddenly gone through a large growth spurt, the chances are you already have some sort of directory service in place. This is most likely in the form of NIS/NIS+, NDS or Windows NT Domains. You may also have data contained in other resources, such as mainframes or database systems. Because of the enormous popularity LDAP has experienced within the past couple of years (and hopefully increasing as a result of this book), you have seen some of the things that LDAP is capable of.

What we need to discuss now is exactly how we might want to implement LDAP. While there are many tasks that LDAP could indeed perform, you need to make sure you pick LDAP for the right tasks and use other available tools for their intended purposes. Too often, we let our technology and know-how define our solutions and requirements, rather than the other way around. The technology does not have to control you – you control the technology.

And before we go any farther, let me tell you that the next section is quite a bit of reading. If you have your Netscape Directory server (or any other LDAP server) up and you want to go play with the client programming SDKs, go ahead. You can always come back to this section when you want to read more about LDAP.

Why Choose LDAP?

The reasons for choosing LDAP are fourfold:

- ❏   The current Directory Service is not manageable or reached its limit
- ❏   Need a distributed database application
- ❏   Central, open access to directory information for mail clients
- ❏   Implement an X.509 digital certificate/encryption solution

Let's briefly discuss each of these options and how LDAP might help.

Current Directory Service Unmanageable

Some directory services, in particular Windows NT's domains, are only scalable to a certain level. At this upper limit, they cannot handle the usage or they become impossible to manage (Sun's NIS breaks at about 50,000 entries). They take up too much bandwidth because of the data they need to copy back and forth and they do not allow for incremental updates.

In addition, many of these original directory systems do not contain any sophisticated management tools and use network bandwidth inefficiently (for example, they send their entire database across the network just to do a simple user lookup). Often, they are held together through a system of vaguely understood of scripts and handwritten notes. While they may work, they do require a great deal of management. If you have a system like this, you will have to decide at some point whether to replace it with LDAP outright – that is, provide an LDAP interface to the system for mail/address book clients – or migrate into the system.

Probably the best tactic to employ is to phase in LDAP. However, since LDAP is still a new technology, there are several systems out there that won't be able to access it for a while. For this reason, you will need to setup some LDAP gateway systems. One such system is `ypldap`, developed by *Padl Software* (`http://www.padl.com`), which responds to NIS queries but actually uses an LDAP server to service those queries. Sun Directory Services by Sun Microsystems also provides a similar service, but only on Solaris based machines. The `ypldap` system runs on many different flavors of Unix.

> *If you are interested in a theory on how to provide a single login for a heterogeneous NIS and Windows NT network you should read* A System Administrator's View of LDAP *by Bruce Markey, at*
> `http://developer1.netscape.com:80/viewsource/markey_ldap.html`*.*

It's interesting to note that there are already several locations where LDAP servers are delivering requests against more than a million entries – much larger than any other current directory service.

Need a Distributed Database Application

As networks have grown, so have the need for databases. Sometimes it is neither efficient nor feasible for the database to be centrally located or managed. This might because of the size of the organization or location. So you may decide to split the database up, but you still need to synchronize the data. LDAP would be useful for this because it is very easy to set up a system where different people manage different parts of the LDAP database, whilst at the same time allowing them to replicate and synchronize data with each other.

Central, Open Access to Directory Information for E-mail Clients

As we have seen already, while telephone books are aplenty, we don't have a truly central email directory. LDAP can provide this functionality for use with clients that can query an LDAP server as an 'address book' server. This is preferable over a standard RDBMS, because LDAP lookups are much quicker.

Digital Certificates

As more transactions are being done electronically, we have lost some of the security we have in the physical world. This is solved through the use of encryption and digital signatures. Encryption protects your data so that it is only seen by those who should see it. Indeed, we do this with our daily mail by putting it in envelopes. Electronically, we don't have an easy way to verify an individual's identity. One mechanism to do this that is safer than user IDs and passwords is through the use of digital certificates or signatures. These certificates are pieces of text that have been cryptographically branded so they are hard to duplicate through brute force computations. The point here is that it's easy to decrypt the message and only the correct original author of the message has the proper key to encrypt the data in the first place. Generally, these certificates are given out by organizations (called Certificate Authorities) who verify the owner of the certificate. This helps build a chain of trust which is important in securing a system and very important in any kind of economic transaction.

A problem with digital certificates is that while they are strong and have enormous potential in securing systems, they are very difficult to manage. With LDAP, we can easily manage certificates by matching digital certificates with entries in the LDAP server. Once we have this management system in place and a set of Certificate Authorities that we trust to issue these certificates, then we can begin to use digital certificates for granting access to our systems. In a digital certificate authentication system, a user would provide their certificate (through either their web browser, or even better through the use of a smart card) and the system would check the certificate contained in the LDAP server. If both certificate's matched, then the user is allowed in.

LDAP also provides an easy mechanism to remove certificates and maintain a list of those that have been removed. This helps prevent people from getting access after their access privileges have been denied, either because of termination or because of an expired certificate. (To prevent the amount of damage that can occur because of a stolen certificate, certificates are only good for a certain amount of time.)

The system of Certificate Authorities, digital certificates and certificate management is called a Public Key Infrastructure (PKI). The common standard for digital certificates is X.509.

If you were wondering, X.500 and X.509 are related – well they did come from the same standards body.

LDAP Implementation

In the majority of applications, an LDAP database will contain information about people. Even the other common entry types in an LDAP server generally serve the purpose of making it easier to manage information about people (for example, groups, organizational units and so on). After this common purpose is fulfilled, we begin to look to LDAP to provide other facilities.

The first step is to decide what technologies besides LDAP you are going to use for your directory service. You may still need an RDBMS to provide access to legacy applications which don't support LDAP, or you might have a database set up with business rules that you just can't get rid of overnight. If you have to, you can use both an RDBMS and LDAP, but you will need to decide which system will be the 'master'. You will also have to work out how you will synchronize between the two disparate systems. Most likely, this will be in the form of some middleware tool or script that you will run on a regular basis. Your system should be able to tolerate some delay in updates in both systems. If there is data that can not tolerate such a delay (for example a bank balance), then one system should be proclaimed the master and only that system should contain that data. When determining which system should be the master, you should consider the one that is accessible by the greatest number of clients.

Even if you don't need an RDBMS for any of your directory needs, you may still need one as you initially build your system, because it is probable that much of your existing data is in a database format. Also, because LDAP tools are still evolving, you maybe more familiar with using RDBMS facilities to build queries, the results of which can then be imported into LDAP.

The next step is to define exactly what data you have or will need for your directory service. You will need to bring as many people in on this process as possible. This will help make sure that you don't forget anything, but also help empower the people who will need to buy into the central directory. The toughest part of any directory system is not in the building, but the selling of such a system.

Developing your Directory Information Tree

Directory data is represented as a **Directory Information Tree** or **DIT**. As we saw in Chapter 2, LDAP data is represented in such a fashion.

Naming the Root

Since LDAP was originally intended to be a front-end for the X.500 Directory Access Protocol, much of the X.500 data model was kept. We have since learned that X.500 is just too complicated for many reasons, one of which is its naming model.

The original idea behind X.500 was that the base of your tree would be in the form of something like:

```
o=Acme Corporation, c=US
```

The intention was that there would be a mechanism to help with the naming of such a system. In many European countries this worked fine, because there was a national system in place to allow the naming of organizations on a national basis. In the United States, there is no such system. You can have an Acme Corporation in Dallas, Texas and one in Chicago, Illinois. Yet these companies can be totally separate entities. Following this pattern of naming the base roots of organizations, you could end up with something like this:

```
o=Acme Corporation,l=Dallas,st=Texas,c=US
```

As you can imagine, this can lead to extremely long and unwieldy DNs.

While the X.500 community was trying to develop a standard mechanism for developing unique organizational names, the Internet domain system grew. This latter system allows for a unique name that represents a unique entity in a global context. Because of the commercialization of the Internet, a system has been worked out to deliver unique names for any organization in the world, including a mechanism to deal with trademark disputes.

So the powers that be in the world of LDAP realized that while we would need to keep some sort of legacy access to X.500, it was time to throw off the vestiges of that protocol (such as the inflexible naming scheme), lest LDAP become forgotten as well. It was decided by the LDAP founders that Internet domain names should be used to simplify the naming scheme for DNs.

There are two ways to achieve this:

Put your domain name in the organization (o) attribute like this:

```
o=airius.com
```

The other way is to use the system as defined in RFC 2377, which utilizes the Domain Component (dc) attribute like:

```
dc=airius,dc=com
```

There are two main benefits of using this system:

- ❑ The naming authorities (such as the InterNIC in the US) are already accepted as being the final authorities on giving domains. The domains also follow accepted Internet standards that will help prevent trademark problems in the naming scheme.
- ❑ Most organizations break their domains into logical subdomains that correlate with the way their organization is structured.

Determining RDNs

Relative Distinguished Names (RDNs) are the parts that comprise the DN of an attribute. In general, when we talk about an RDN, we usually mean the left most part of a DN. The rest of the DN would be any of the other attributes that make up the DN. It's hard to say exactly what those would be, since there are no set rules on how to build a DN.

In the original X.500 specification, the common name (cn) attribute was the unique RDN. Of course, this strategy presented many of problems, because at the very least this would have required long DNs, and even then it might not prevent two different John Smiths sharing the same DN!

Again, we look to the existing Internet infrastructure in place to help us out. What we need is for our left-most part of the RDN to be something that is unique to the organization, which with the remainder of the RDN will make the DN unique within the LDAP namespace (or at least with a high degree of probability). Hopefully the system should already be in place to get this information, to reduce the load of creating infrastructure from scratch.

It is a widely accepted belief now that an RDN should not only be comprised of information that is already available, but that there should be something that makes the RDN unique to the user.

You are free to choose any system, but here are some possible solutions:

- ❑ Universally Unique Identifier (UUID)
- ❑ Personal security number
- ❑ User ID
- ❑ E-mail address

Universally Unique Identifier (UUID):

The **Universally Unique Identifier** (**UUID**), also known as the **Globally Unique Identifier** (**GUID**), is a system that was devised by the Network Computing System and later by the Open Software Foundation's Distributed Computing Environment (DEC). A UUID is a 128 byte number that uses an IEEE802 number block, usually available from a network card on a computer, plus part of the system time to derive a unique number. The human readable form of this number is converted into a hexidecimal digit, where the groupings are broken up by a dash (-). An example UUID is: f81d4fae-7dec-11d0-a765-00a0c91e6bf6. It is guaranteed to be unique until the about the year 5000. (Perhaps we should label this the "Year 5000 Problem".)

This system probably would not be useful for person entries (because the value would not generally be associated with the user except in this system), but would probably work when you are trying to designate a DN for a computer, printer or even a distributed computer program.

Example: dn: uuid=f81d4fae-7dec-11d0-a765-00a0c91e6bf6,dc=airius,dc=com

Personal Security Number

Most organizations assign an identification number to their members. They might even use a driver's license or Social Security Number. While this number is important for organizations to use as a unique ID in data processing, you may either want to hide it from anonymous acccess or you may be required to hide it for reasons of privacy or security. If the number must be hidden from anonymous access, it cannot be used in the distinguished name, because all of the parts of a DN will be visible in an anonymous search. If personal security is not an issue, this number would be a good candidate for inclusion in the DN:

Example: `dn: employeenumber=12301231,dc=airius,dc=com`

User ID

There isn't an organization thinking about using LDAP that doesn't already have user IDs assigned to its employees. The nice thing about user IDs is that they will be unique in any given system, but if you are trying to bridge two systems together, there is a likelihood that there will be name collisions. This is particularly true if the user IDs are based upon the name of the user. If you have a small organization or you are not bridging systems together, using user IDs is probably the safest bet.

Example: `dn: uid=scarter,dc=airius,dc=com`

Email address

The final solution is the one recommended in RFC 2377. This solution would use a user's Internet email address for user entries and the common name (cn) attribute for non-person entries. Internet email addresses (e.g. `mark@mjwilcox.com`) must be unique for the entire organization (actually for the world!) and the process for creating these addresses is an established practice. If when you create a new entry and the user doesn't already have an Internet email address, you can make one up. This address doesn't have to a valid one, just one that is unique. When looking for the user's email address, you should still look it up in the mail attribute. The email address doesn't even have to match up with the domain of the rest of the tree. For non-person entries (e.g. computers, rooms, etc) you can use the common name attribute, because there is little likelihood of a collision and the common name will likely be familiar for the users of the system.

Examples: `dn:uid=scarter@airius.com,dc=airius,dc=com`
          `dn:cn=Production Control Printer 1,dc=airius,dc=com`

Tree Branching

Organizations generally fall into a hierarchy, and this is generally the way organizational data is presented. This is why we use trees to describe LDAP data. Of course, how you break it down is up to you. The smart money is to allow for it to break down into both a logical pattern and another pattern that is optimized for lookup. Breaks in the tree (or branches if you prefer) occur with certain attributes in the DN. These include country, location, state, organization, organizational unit and domain component.

LDAP does not force you to make a shallow or a deep tree. You can decide how you want to branch it, for example, you can break by:

- ❑ Department
- ❑ Sub-net
- ❑ Function

Break by Department (organizationalUnit)

If you use this type of division, it will make more sense to your users, but it can result in a very long DN if you have many departments and sub-departments. This is also not recommended, because of the number of times an organization reorganizes.

```
Examples:    dn: uid=scarter,ou=Engineering,dc=airius,dc=com
             dn: uid=scarter,ou=Heating,ou=Environmental,ou=Engineering,
                 dc=airius,dc=com
```

Break by Sub-Net

This will follow your traditional network pattern but it might not make sense to your non-technical users, and also could result in a very long and complex DN.

```
Examples:    dn: uid=scarter,dc=airius,dc=com
             dn: uid=scarter,dc=heat,dc=env,dc=eng,dc=airius,dc=com
```

Break by Function (e.g. person, group)

Using this method, we are essentially grouping by an entry's function. For example, Sam Jones is a person, so he fills the function of 'People'. The printer in the administrative assistant's office fills the function of 'Printers'. When building the DN, include the function of the entry using the organizational unit attribute (ou). Now, you can include more than one ou value in the entry itself (and in the DN, but that's not recommended), so that besides saying Sam Jones is a 'People' entry, we could also say he works in accounting. By doing this, we make DNs more manageable, but we can also make searching faster, because we can have the server add an index for the ou attribute.

```
Examples:    dn: uid=scarter,ou=People,dc=airius,dc=com
             dn: cn=Printer 101,ou=Printers,dc=airius,dc=com
```

The diagram below shows the relationship between entries in a system where we use the Functional model. Here we see two entries – jsmith and scarter. Both are grouped together, because they fill the role of people in the organization, but they also have other functions such as accounting and sales, which are also part of their entries:

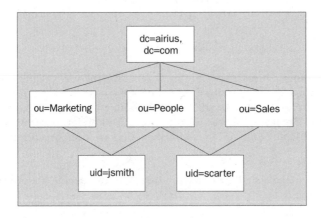

Adding your own Attributes/Objects

As you start to develop your own LDAP database, you will of course discover that the existing attributes and object classes don't meet all of your needs. You will need to add your own. Just like with any other type of database, modifying the schema is not something to be taken lightly, but if you must do it, modify the schema up front if possible. This will minimize the likelihood of modifying it later. If you need modifications, try to use auxiliary classes that you can add to particular entries without having to rewrite all of your entries which will be a very painful operation. (Auxiliary classes are classes that allow for extra attributes, without actually extending an already existing object class in an entry.)

Implementing an Upload Mechanism

So far, we have discussed how you might design your data and how to set up a basic LDAP server. Now let's look at the various means of uploading your data. If you are using a LDAP server that just provides a LDAP front-end to an existing directory service like NDS or NIS, you should be able to do business as usual. However, if you are going to use just straight LDAP, you have some decisions to make.

First, you need to determine how you will get your data. If you are lucky, you will already have a central data store you can draw from, and you will only have to concern yourself about a single LDAP server (for example, Netscape Directory Server or Microsoft Exchange), which makes synchronization less of a problem. However, you will probably have to draw your information from a variety of places and then feed that data into the LDAP server. It will also be likely that you will have to synchronize some of the data in the LDAP server with a non-LDAP system like a database. You want to keep the minimum data in this latter system, because it could bring you problems.

When developing your process, it is probably a good idea to set up a central RDBMS first, if you don't already have an existing data source. This system doesn't have to be elaborate – Microsoft Access with its simple visual Query Builder will work until your system outgrows it. The reason why using an RDBMS is helpful is because it makes a good 'clearing house' to put data into, in particular during the early stages of development. By developing relationships between data, you can start to see how your DIT should be designed, instead of trying to build it from scratch.

Synchronizing the LDAP database with other databases can be accomplished through various means. There is not a standard replication mechanism for LDAP, so each LDAP vendor has its own. Generally, these processes work fine for systems that are built by the same vendor. For different LDAP vendors, you must export the LDAP data to LDIF and then import into the other database (though there is an IETF committee working on standardized LDAP replication). To get LDAP data into an RDBMS, you will need to query an LDAP server and then convert the data returned into a different format, such as a comma-delimited text file. When synchronizing, you will need to determine which system is the master and stick to it.

It might be useful to look at some diagrams that illustrate these various relationships. The first diagram shows a system where the organization has decided to let public clients query LDAP, but does not allow any updates between LDAP and the client. Instead, the existing databases and directories (such as Sun's NIS or Novell's NDS) will export their data for import into the LDAP server via middleware applications which convert the different formats into LDAP data.

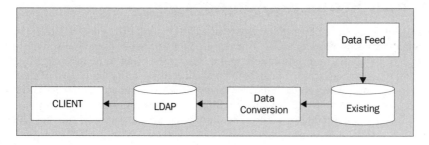

The following diagram shows a system similar to the one described above, except that the public client can do updates via LDAP and these updates will be processed back into the existing databases and directories:

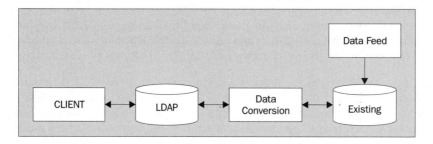

In the chapters that follow, where the various LDAP client APIs are discussed, we will cover how to use standard API functionality to add or modify entries and to synchronize systems.

Advanced Issues

There are other issues that you must decide during your implementation. These include what type of access you wish to allow for your LDAP data. LDAP access control is achieved by using ACLs. (Security will be covered in more detail in Chapter 12.)

Here are two example ACLs from the Netscape Directory Server sample LDIF file:

```
aci: (target ="ldap:///ou=People, o=airius.com")(targetattr =
      "userpassword || telephonenumber || facsimiletelephonenumber")(version 3.0;
    acl "Allow self entry modification";allow (write)(userdn = "ldap:///self");)

aci: (target ="ldap:///ou=People, o=airius.com")(targetattr !="cn || sn || uid")
                        (targetfilter ="(ou=Accounting)")(version 3.0;acl
              "Accounting Managers Group Permissions";allow (write)(groupdn =
                  "ldap:///cn=Accounting Managers,ou =groups,o=airius.com");)
```

The attribute starts with `aci:` and it has a `target` in the form of an LDAP URL (discussed in Chapter 6). The acronym `aci` stands for Access Control Instruction. The `targetattr` attribute defines which other attributes this particular ACL is protecting. It then has a comment, followed by the actions allowed and which bound entries are allowed to perform the action.

The first example ACL says that only entries that have `ou=People, o=airius.com` in their DN can have their password, telephone number or fax number changed by the user that matches that entry. For example, this means that Sam Carter can modify his own entry but not any other entry. The second says that users who are members of the group "Accounting Managers" can change any attribute, except `cn`, `sn` or `uid` of any entry that has contains an `ou` attribute of `Accounting`.

Each LDAP server has a slightly different ACL syntax, so check your server documentation before writing them out.

There are other security concerns to consider also – user authentication and encryption. Many LDAP v3 servers, including Sun's Directory Services LDAP server and Netscape's Directory Server, support the use of X.509 public-key based digital certificates. These certificates are issued by a trusted third party that verifies that someone is who they say they are, in a manner similar to a driver's license or a signature on a physical document. X.509 certificates are believed to be more secure than standard user IDs and passwords, because they are harder to imitate or steal. Unfortunately they are not foolproof and the infrastructure to manage them is not really in place yet to handle them effectively. (Having said that, I expect a surge in building this infrastructure as electronic commerce grows and organizations begin new projects after they fix their Year 2000 problems.)

Most Internet traffic occurs over public networks in clear text. This is what has made the Internet such an effective medium and has led to its growth and stability. However, it does leave your data vulnerable because anybody can read it (called 'snooping') and do what they please. So LDAP v3 supports **Secure Socket Layer (SSL)** and the **Simple Authentication and Security Layer (SASL)** to secure network traffic. SSL is a protocol that was developed by Netscape, but has become an official Internet standard and renamed Transport Layer Security (TLS). It uses X.509 digital certificates to set up the encrypted layer. This certificate not only encrypts all of the traffic between the client and server, but it also verifies to the client that the server is who it says it is. You can use different certificates for signing of documents and encryption. This is very important for improving the level of trust on the Internet. SASL is an Internet standard that allows plugging in any number of different services that both the client and server can speak, such as KRAM-MD5 and Kerberos.

The KRAM-MD5 makes a MD5 hash of a user's ID and password and then sends the ID and the constructed hash to server. The server then compares the hash from the client to the hash contained in the user's entry. This way you do not send a plain text password over the wire. The Kerberos system encrypts all of the data using a form of digital certificates. When a computer first connects to the network, it authenticates against a central Kerberos certificate server. If the Kerberos server authenticates the client computer, it issues a 'ticket' denoting that client computer is allowed on the network. This 'ticket' is used to authenticate the client against any Kerberos compliant server (which could be a mail server, LDAP server or a Windows 2000 server). The 'ticket' is used like a X.509 certificate to encrypt traffic between a client and host system. You should use one of these services (SSL/TSL or SASL) to protect your data 'over the wire'.

Summary

This chapter has covered a lot of ground, which forms the backdrop to subsequent chapters where we shall develop some real example code. Here is a summary of what we covered:

❑ Using LDIF to exchange data between LDAP accessible address books
❑ How to read LDIF
❑ Strategies for building your own LDAP server

Over the next few chapters, we are going to explore how to interact with LDAP services with our own applications. We will also discuss how to use existing LDAP clients to interact with LDAP services.

6

Programming with Netscape's C LDAP SDK

In this chapter we will be looking at how to develop LDAP applications using Netscape's C SDK. Along the way, we'll explore:

- ❑ Synchronous versus asynchronous operations
- ❑ Searching an LDAP server
- ❑ Using filter files
- ❑ Adding and deleting LDAP entries
- ❑ Modifying LDAP entries
- ❑ LDAP Authentication

We won't spend much time in this chapter concentrating on the details of the C API. This is because it has already been covered in excellent detail in the very first LDAP book, *LDAP: Programming Directory-Enabled Applications with Lightweight Directory Access Protocol* by Howes and Smith, published by MacMillan. Instead I will present a brief overview of the API, so we can spend more time discussing the Perl and Java SDKs, which have not been covered before.

> *Note that the examples in this chapter require the installation of the sample data, airius.ldif, that comes with the Netscape Directory Server (see Chapters 4 and 5). The examples also assume that you are using the default LDAP port 389.*

The Netscape C LDAP SDK

The Netscape C LDAP API is derived from the original University of Michigan API, which has become the reference API for LDAP. Netscape's C SDK has been rewritten for speed and bug fixes and includes a number of examples and documentation as well as the API libraries.

The University of Michigan API corresponds to version 2 of the LDAP protocol, and is defined in RFC 1823. Version 3.0 of Netscape's SDK corresponds to version 3 of the LDAP protocol, and is defined in `draft-ietf-ldapext-ldap-c-api-01.txt`: *"The C LDAP Application Program Interface".*

You can download the C LDAP SDK from one of two sources: the Netscape Directory Central site that is part of their DevEdge site at `http://developer.netscape.com/directory/`, or the Mozilla OpenSource Project site at `http://www.mozilla.org/directory/`.

The SDK contains examples, documentation, header files and pre-compiled libraries. The header file we will be using in this chapter is `ldap.h`, though there is also a second file `ldap_ssl.h` which we will come across in Chapter 12 when discussing the Secure Socket Layer and LDAP. The compiled library is called `nsldapss132v30`, and has `.dll` extension the Windows environment and a `.so` extension when used on Unix/Linux systems.

It was in May 1998 that the source code was released for the C SDK at `http://www.mozilla.org` as part of Netscape's Mozilla OpenSource project, which has also opened the source code for the Netscape Navigator Web browser. In August of the same year, Netscape opened the source to the Java LDAP SDK and also released PerLDAP, a Perl LDAP SDK. Opening the source code is as important for SDKs as it is for Web servers or operating systems, because SDKs, as their name suggests, are the basic toolkits from which developers build applications. They provide reliable code which the programmers can use to expose bugs in their own applications. SDK's also give developers the ability to optimize their distributions by removing parts they don't need.

There is not yet a standardized C++ library or wrapper to the C SDK at the time of writing. This is because most of the C SDK development has drawn from the Unix/Linux community where C++ is not used that much. Another reason why it's written in C instead of C++ is that the ANSI standard for C++ wasn't ratified until 1998, making it hard to develop an API that could reasonably be expected to compile on a wide range of compilers. Finally, most authentication systems that would be expected to add LDAP support were originally written in C.

A Brief Look at the LDAP C API

The most common operation to be performed by any applications will be to search an LDAP server. Any advanced LDAP applications use the search functions as a core function. The LDAP API has no concept of browsing or querying the properties of a single object, even these simple operations are both carried out by searching.

Essentially, all search functions take the following parameters:

- ❑   An LDAP connection handle
- ❑   The base to start the search from
- ❑   The scope of the search
- ❑   A search filter

Regardless of the type of search you are performing, you will get back one of the following types of results:

❑ One or more LDAP entries represented by an `LDAPMessage` structure.

❑ One or more LDAP search references, also represented by an `LDAPMessage` structure. These references are values that point to where the information you are looking for can be found. This type of information is called an **LDAP referral**.

❑ An error response, also represented by an `LDAPMessage` structure.

The LDAPMessage Structure

An `LDAPMessage` is a flexible data structure that shows the results of an LDAP operation: a set of LDAP search results, an LDAP entry or a referral. While this data type is declared in the `ldap.h` header file, it is not defined.

The actual structure of the `LDAPMessage` is dependent upon the functions called by the client application.

LDAPMessage Functions

These are the functions that build `LDAPMessage` structures:

ldap_search_ext_s() and ldap_search_ext()

The `ldap_search_ext_s()` and `ldap_search_ext()` functions are the API calls that perform a search against an LDAP server. One of these functions must be called first before any of the other `LDAPMessage` functions.

ldap_first_entry() and ldap_next_entry()

The `ldap_first_entry()` and `ldap_next_entry()` functions are the API calls that return a pointer to an `LDAPMessage` structure that represents an entry in the LDAP server. The difference between these functions is that you must call `ldap_first_entry()` first. You use these functions together so that you can go through an entire set of search results. To actually get attributes and values of a particular entry, you must call either the `ldap_get_dn()`, `ldap_first_attribute()` or `ldap_next_attribute()` functions. We will cover these functions in detail when we get to the section on searching the LDAP server.

ldap_first_reference() and ldap_next_reference()

The `ldap_first_reference()` and `ldap_next_reference()` functions are the API calls that return a pointer to an `LDAPMessage` structure that defines a search referral. A search referral is a LDAP message that says "The entry you are looking for is not contained in this LDAP server, but it might be found at this other LDAP server." We'll cover referrals in more detail in Chapter 12.

ldap_msgfree()

The `ldap_msgfree()` is the function that frees the memory that is currently being used by an `LDAPMessage` structure. This function should be called when you finished dealing with an `LDAPMessage` structure.

Determining LDAP Scope

When you perform a search, you must specify the base of the tree you want to start at, as well as the scope of the search. The scope defines exactly how much of the tree you want to search. There are three levels of scope, which are shown in the table overleaf:

Scope	Description
LDAP_SCOPE_SUBTREE	Starts at the base entry and searches everything below it including the base entry
LDAP_SCOPE_ONELEVEL	Only searches entries directly below the base entry
LDAP_SCOPE_BASE	Searches just the base entry.

The diagrams below illustrate the three possible scopes you can use for your search. The area of the directory trees enclosed in a box indicates where the search takes place. In the first case, everything below and including the search base is included:

LDAP_SCOPE_SUBTREE

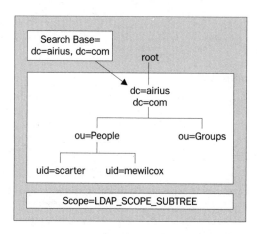

Here, only the level directly below the search base is searched:

LDAP_SCOPE_ONELEVEL

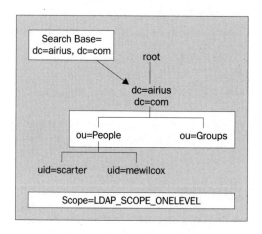

Here, only the base is searched. This is useful if you want to just get the attributes/values of just one entry.

LDAP_SCOPE_BASE

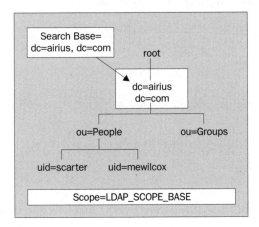

Initial LDAP Operations

Before you can perform any LDAP operation there are some basic housekeeping chores you must perform:

- ❑ The initializing of an LDAP connection
- ❑ Opening the connection

These operations are fairly straightforward.

Initialize an LDAP Handle (Connecting/Disconnecting)

You must first initialize an `LDAP` structure variable (also known as an LDAP handle) with the `ldap_init()` function call. This will return an `LDAP` data structure, which you then use when you need to perform any LDAP operation, including binding and searching.

```
#include <stdio.h>

#include "ldap.h" //the LDAP header file

...

LDAP *ld;

...

ld = ldap_init("localhost",389);
```

The `ldap_init()` function takes a hostname and a port number as its only parameters. The `LDAP` data structure maintains a record of the connection, the hostname, port and the last LDAP error code.

It will not be uncommon for your organization to have more than one LDAP server running for the purposes of either redundancy or speed optimization. The `ldap_init()` function allows you to pass more than one hostname in the function call. In this case, each hostname should be separated by a space. If an LDAP server does not use the default port (389, or 636 for SSL), then you specify the port in the *hostname:port* syntax. This is illustrated in the code extract below:

```
#include <ldap.h>
...
LDAP *ld;
...
int rc;

if ((ld = ldap_init("ldap.airius.com ldap2.airius.com:9389 ldap3.airius.com",
    389)) ==NULL)
{
   rc = ldap_get_lderrno(ld,NULL,NULL);
   fprintf(stderr,"ldap_init %s\n\n",ldap_err2string(rc));
   return (rc);
}
```

The `ldap_init()` function will attempt to connect to the first host and if that fails then it will attempt to connect to the next on the list. This makes it easy to build high availability clients if you have multiple LDAP servers. If you don't want to type 389 over and over again you can use the static `LDAP_PORT` variable that is defined in the `ldap.h` file.

When you are finished with your LDAP application you should disconnect from the server and free up the memory used in the `LDAP` data structure. To do this, you must use the `ldap_unbind()` or `ldap_unbind_s()` functions.

The `unbind()` functions take care of disconnecting and freeing any resources used by the `LDAP` data structure (specified by the `ld` variable below):

```
#include <ldap.h>

LDAP *ld;
int rc;
...

/* Now unbind,disconnect and free any resources */
if ( ldap_unbind( ld ) != LDAP_SUCCESS )
{
   rc = ldap_get_lderrno(ld,NULL,NULL);
   fprintf(stderr,"ldap_unbind %s\n\n",ldap_err2string(rc));
   return (rc);
}
```

Synchronous versus Asynchronous Operation

Before we discuss binding to a server, we should explain that the LDAP C SDK supports two basic types of operations – **synchronous** and **asynchronous**. You may have already heard of these terms in the context of "threaded" (asynchronous) and "non-threaded" (synchronous) operations. What we describe here is something similar. If you run an LDAP operation in a *synchronous* way, your application blocks until the operation is completed, which means that if you perform a search, you cannot do anything else until the search returns. On the other hand, in an asynchronous operation, your application can continue to do other things while the LDAP operation is being processed.

A synchronous operation can be viewed like this:

```
1. Connect to the LDAP server
2. Search the LDAP server
3. When the search returns call a function that does something not related to LDAP
4. Disconnect from the LDAP server
```

Here is a scheme that demonstrates an asynchronous operation:

```
1. Connect to the LDAP server.
2. Search the LDAP server
3. Is the search finished? If so go to step 6
4. While the LDAP server is searching, you can call a function that does something
   not related to LDAP
5. Goto step 3
6. Disconnect from the LDAP server
```

When looking at code, you can easily tell the difference between a synchronous and an asynchronous function – the *synchronous* function name will end with _s.

Synchronous operations are how we traditionally run our programs – we perform one activity, and only proceed to the next one, once the first is completed. This is fine, if the tasks are carried out quickly and efficiently. However, for slow applications, synchronous operation is not so good – your machine may be tied up in a long and complex search leaving you unable to do anything else at all. However, as we have just said, asynchronous operations allow us to perform more than one task at a time. You would normally want to do this when using a network – where operations can take a long time (e.g. the network might be busy, or the remote machine slow). In an asynchronous operation, you might set an LDAP search running, freeing your computer is to perform other tasks (e.g. query a database). It doesn't matter all that much how long the LDAP operation takes – you won't be sitting there waiting for it to return!

In this chapter, we will be using both of these types of operations in the coded examples.

Binding to the LDAP server

Access in LDAP is controlled by how the client application is bound to the LDAP server. The only bind method specified by the LDAP RFCs allows for simple authentication in which a user passes his or her distinguished name and password. The Netscape LDAP SDKs also support the use of SSL Personal Certificates and SASL. If any SASL provider supports encrypted authentication (such as Kerberos) with the server, then you can use that. See Chapter 12 for more information.

Unless otherwise specified, all the examples in this chapter will use simple authentication, because that is the most common. When you deploy a 'real' application, make sure that you understand the risks involved with any authentication system. LDAP also supports the ability to bind anonymously. To bind anonymously means that the connection is not associated with any particular entry in the system, the DN and password are set to NULL. Generally, the anonymously bound connection has very limited rights.

To get a better idea of how a bound LDAP connection can provide different results, let's take a look at the results from two searches that I carried out.

The first search, shows the results we get if we search an LDAPv3 server and get its configuration entry (dn: cn=config), but do not bind as a particular entry (an anonymous operation).

```
dn: cn=SNMP,cn=config
objectclass: top
objectclass: nsSNMP
cn: SNMP
nssnmpenabled: on
nssnmporganization:
nssnmplocation:
nssnmpcontact:
nssnmpdescription:
nssnmpmasterhost:
nssnmpmasterport:
```

Now let's see what happens if we authenticate to the server as the Directory Manager:

```
dn: cn=7-bit check,cn=plugins,cn=config
objectclass: top
objectclass: nsslapdPlugin
objectclass: extensibleObject
cn: 7-bit check
nsslapd-pluginpath: d:/netscape/ds4/lib/uid-plugin.dll
nsslapd-plugininitfunc: NS7bitAttr_Init
nsslapd-plugintype: preoperation
nsslapd-pluginid: NS7bitAttr
nsslapd-pluginversion: 4.0
nsslapd-pluginvendor: Netscape Communications
nsslapd-plugindescription: Enforce  7-bit clean attribute values
nsslapd-pluginenabled: on
nsslapd-backend: cn=ldbm
nsslapd-pluginarg0: uid
nsslapd-pluginarg1: mail
nsslapd-pluginarg2: userpassword
nsslapd-pluginarg3: ,
nsslapd-pluginarg4: o=airius.com

dn: cn=Binary Syntax,cn=plugins,cn=config
objectclass: top
objectclass: nsslapdPlugin
objectclass: extensibleObject
...
```

The results continue on for a couple of screens, but you get the idea.

The bind operations can be either synchronous or asynchronous. Remember the difference is that with synchronous operations, your program cannot do anything else until the operation is finished, while with asynchronous operations, your program can do other things while it waits for the operation to finish.

Synchronous Bind

The synchronous bind method is `ldap_simple_bind_s()`. (Recall that all synchronous functions have a `_s` suffix.) This function requires an LDAP structure handle, plus a user DN and password. If you wish to perform an anonymous bind, then you would just pass NULL as the values for the DN and password. We'll see how this works shortly. The LDAP data structure must never be NULL, otherwise your bind operation will fail. The bind function returns an integer representing an error code. Note that the error codes are defined by static global variables in `ldap.h`, so they are fairly easy to manage.

```
/*sync_bind.c
Exercise 6.1 - synchronous bind

usage: synch_bind
*/

#include <stdio.h>
#include <stdlib.h>
#include <string.h>
#include <time.h>

/* standard C ldap library */
#include "ldap.h"

#define MY_PROG "synch_bind"

#define MY_HOST      "localhost"
#define MY_PORT      389
#define MY_DN        "uid=scarter,ou=People,o=airius.com"
#define MY_PWD       "sprain"

void doWork();

main( int argc, char **argv )
{
    LDAP           *ld;
    int            rc,parse_rc = 0;

    printf("Testing %s \n",MY_PROG);

    /* First setup a LDAP connection */
    if ( (ld = ldap_init( MY_HOST, MY_PORT )) == NULL )
    {
        perror( "ldap_init" );
    }

    printf("connected to LDAP host %s on port %d\n",MY_HOST,MY_PORT);

    rc = ldap_simple_bind_s(ld,MY_DN,MY_PWD);
    doWork();

    if (rc != LDAP_SUCCESS )
    {
        fprintf( stderr, "LDAP Error: %s\n", ldap_err2string(rc));
    }
    else
    {
        printf("Bind successful!\n");
    }

    ldap_unbind(ld);
}

void doWork(void)
{
    printf("We're doing some Work\n");
}
```

All the doWork() function does here is print a short message. Of course, if the LDAP connection is slow, then the execution of this method would be stalled until the LDAP operation had been completed.

You should see the following output if you successfully bound to the LDAP server:

```
Testing sync_bind
connected to LDAP host localhost on port 389
We're doing some Work
Bind successful!
```

If you fail to bind to the server you should see something like this:

```
Testing synch_bind
connected to LDAP host localhost on port 389
LDAP Error: Invalid credentials
```

In order to perform an anonymous bind, we simply set the DN and the password to NULL for the call to ldap_simple_bind_s():

```
#define MY_HOST        "localhost"
#define MY_PORT        389
#define MY_DN   NULL
#define MY_PWD  NULL
```

The output from this example is exactly the same as that shown above.

What's Going On?

Before proceeding, let's take a brief look at what is happening in this example.

The first part of the code that we are interested in for LDAP is the following lines:

```
/* First set up an LDAP connection */
if ( (ld = ldap_init( MY_HOST, MY_PORT )) == NULL )
{
   perror( "ldap_init" );
}
```

In this step we initialize a connection to the LDAP server. It is always a synchronous function – there is no asynchronous option. The function requires a string that contains the value of an IP address or an FQDN that points to a host running the LDAP server. The second parameter is an integer value that is the port we are trying to connect on, normally 389. If the function succeeds it returns a pointer to an LDAP data structure, which is used internally by the API to represent an LDAP connection. If it fails (e.g. the function returns NULL), then we call the perror() function which will print out an error message.

The next part we are interested in is this section:

```
rc = ldap_simple_bind_s(ld,MY_DN,MY_PWD);

if (rc != LDAP_SUCCESS )
{
```

```
        fprintf( stderr, "LDAP Error: %s\n", ldap_err2string(rc));
}
else
{
    printf("Bind successful!\n");
}
```

The function `ldap_simple_bind_s()` binds (associates) the current LDAP connection to a particular entry in the LDAP server using the "Simple Authentication" method. The function requires the LDAP handle, the DN and password as parameters. The function will return an integer that will correlate to a particular LDAP result code. These LDAP result codes have constants defined for them so that they are easier to remember. It's easier to remember `INVALID_CREDENTIALS` than to remember the corresponding LDAP error code, 49.

If the result code which we have represented with the variable `rc` doesn't equal the `LDAP_SUCCESS` constant, that is LDAP result code 0, then we print out an error message and exit. The LDAP API function `ldap_err2string()` takes a LDAP result code and returns a string containing a more meaningful message. If the binding operation is successful then we are told so.

The final function we want to look at is this:

```
ldap_unbind(ld);
```

This function disconnects the application from the server. It takes an LDAP structure that is returned from the `ldap_init()` function that represents an LDAP connection and closes the connection down as we have said.

Asynchronous Bind

In network applications it is often useful, or even necessary, to be able to perform other operations while your network code runs. This is particularly true if your program is a GUI, like a Windows based application. This is because users often become nervous if they don't know whether or not the application is working. There can be no visual feedback during the whole time the network operation takes. In many circumstances, the whole application may appear to freeze. In a bind operation, you may wish to prepare for further operations on the assumption that the bind will be successful. This could involve things like making database connections, opening files or other time consuming tasks that can be taken care while the bind is occurring. You might also want to let GUI messages be processed while waiting for the operation to finish, so the application can update its screen appearance if necessary.

This bind operation is similar to the synchronous operations, except that you must make a call to `ldap_result()` every so often to check on the operation. You should also specify a time-out so that the operation aborts if inactive over a specified time-span. Note also that here we are using `ldap_simple_bind()` rather than `ldap_simple_bind_s()`.

Shown below is an example of an asynchronous user bind:

```
/*async_bind.c
Example 6.2 - asynchronous bind

usage: asynch_bind
*/
```

```
#include <stdio.h>
#include <stdlib.h>
#include <string.h>
#include <time.h>

/* standard C ldap library */
#include "ldap.h"

#define MY_PROG "asynch_bind"

#define MY_HOST        "localhost"
#define MY_PORT        389
#define MY_DN "uid=scarter,ou=People,o=airius.com"
#define MY_PWD "sprain"

void doWork();

main( int argc, char **argv )
{
    LDAP            *ld; /* LDAP connection structure */
    LDAPMessage     *result; /* structure that represents LDAP Messages */
    int             msg_id =0; /* use to keep track of LDAP operation */
    int             rc = 0; /* LDAP result code */
    int             finished = 0; /*Check if finished or not */
    struct timeval zerotime; /* time value used by asynchronous operations */

    /* Specify a timeout value */
    zerotime.tv_sec = zerotime.tv_usec = 0L;

    printf("Testing %s \n",MY_PROG);

    /* First setup a LDAP connection */
    if ( (ld = ldap_init( MY_HOST, MY_PORT )) == NULL )
    {
        perror( "ldap_init" );
    }

    printf("connected to LDAP host %s on port %d\n",MY_HOST,MY_PORT);

    msg_id = ldap_simple_bind(ld,MY_DN,MY_PWD);

    rc =0;
    while (finished == 0)
    {
        /* Do some other work here */
        doWork();

        rc = ldap_result( ld, msg_id, LDAP_MSG_ONE, &zerotime, &result );

        if( rc == -1)
        {
            finished =1;
            rc = ldap_get_lderrno( ld, NULL, NULL );
            fprintf( stderr, "ldap_result: %s\n", ldap_err2string( rc ) );

        }

        if(rc >=0)
        {
            finished = 1;
```

```
            if (ldap_result2error( result ) != LDAP_SUCCESS )
            {
                fprintf(stderr,"ldap_simple_bind: %s\n",ldap_err2string(rc));
            }
            else
            {
                printf ("Bind successful.\n");
            }
        }
    } /* end while*/

    ldap_unbind( ld );
}

void doWork(void)
{
    printf("We're doing some Work\n");
}
```

You should see output similar to this:

```
Testing asynch_bind
connected to LDAP host localhost on port 389
We're doing some Work
Bind successful!
```

Again, we can easily change the code to do an anonymous asynchronous bind, by simply setting the DN and the password to NULL:

```
#define MY_HOST        "localhost"
#define MY_PORT        389
#define MY_DN NULL
#define MY_PWD NULL
```

How Does This Code Work?

Well I had originally intended to show you that asynchronous LDAP operations allow you to do other tasks while the LDAP is working. But a combination of fast PCs and the performance enhancements in Netscape Directory Server 4, well it's too darn quick!. The operation always completed in a single cycle. For now, just take my word that asynchronous does allow you to do two things at once. The doWork() function was being executed at the same time as the LDAP binding operation.

From the above simple examples, you may well have started to think that asynchronous operations require more code than synchronous operations, and you would be correct. To get the flexibility of asynchronous operations requires a great deal of more work on your part.

Most of this code we have seen in the synchronous example. Let's take a look at the bits which are different. First we added the following section of code:

```
struct timeval zerotime;

/* Specify a timeout value */
zerotime.tv_sec = zerotime.tv_usec = 0L;
```

The `timeval` data type is a structure that represents time in a format that the LDAP SDK can understand (a `Long` integer). This structure is used to specify a timeout value for an asynchronous operation. Because we have set it to zero in this example, this tells the LDAP SDK that there is not a time limit for any of the asynchronous operations.

Our next operation is this line:

```
msg_id = ldap_simple_bind(ld, MY_DN, MY_PWD);
```

This bind function is very similar to the synchronous version. It takes a reference to LDAP connection `ld`, two strings, the DN and the password. The difference is that the function returns an integer that represents a reference to this LDAP operation. The LDAP SDK uses this ID to keep track of this particular LDAP operation. You can call several asynchronous operations at once and keep track of their progress through the use of the message IDs.

The next step we enter a `while` loop that continues until we set the `finished` variable to a non-zero value.

We can determine the status of the operation with this function:

```
rc = ldap_result( ld, msg_id, LDAP_MSG_ONE, &zerotime, &result );
```

This function requires a reference to an LDAP connection structure, the message ID of the particular operation we are interested in, a pointer to a structure representing a time out value, and a pointer to an `LDAPMessage` structure that contains the actual results of an operation (for example in a search, it would contain the results of that search).

The function returns an LDAP result code. While the operation is running it will be `NULL`. If a catastrophic error occurs (e.g. something the LDAP SDK is not expecting such as running out of memory on your machine), it will return −1. Otherwise it will return an LDAP result code that ranges from 0 to 97, all but zero being errors.

A Final Note About Authentication

If you specify a `NULL` as the password in a bind (either synchronous or asynchronous) then an anonymous bind will occur, an action specified in the LDAP RFCs. If you wish for a `NULL` password field not to bind, you must take care of this before making the bind in your application.

Searching an LDAP Server

The most common operation you are likely to perform on an LDAP server is searching. As we saw in an earlier chapter, searching is accomplished by specifying a search base, a scope and a filter. These are the essential parameters when searching. You also have the option to specify some extra options – e.g. you can specify the attributes you want back from the server. If you don't specify the attributes to return, the LDAP server returns all of the attributes your connection has permission to read. You can also set a search timeout and the maximum number of entries to return.

Introduction to filters

Filters take the form *attribute=value*, which can be enclosed in () if you prefer. Filters also accept Boolean expressions, wildcards (*), and equality tests (>=,<=,=,~=,=*). When you build filters, you can combine them together to make rather complex requests. For more information about filters, look up RFC 2254.

Simple Filters

Some examples of simple filters are shown in the table below:

Task	Filter
Search for an entry with a common name of Sam Carter	(cn=Sam Carter)
Search for all entries with a common name attribute ending in Carter	(cn=*Carter)
Search for all entries with Carter somewhere in their common name	(cn=*Carter*)
Search for entries that have surnames that are greater than or equal to Carter. This will return all the "Carters" as well as "Cartera", "Carterb" and so on through the alphabet	(sn>=Carter)
Search for entries that have surnames that are less than or equal to Carter, that is "Carter", "Carteq" and so on to the beginning of the alphabet	(sn<=Carter)
Search for entries that have surnames that are 'like' Carter. This would give you entries such as "Carver" and "Crater"!	(sn~=Carter)

Note that the operators less than (<) and greater than (>) are NOT defined.

Searches are either case-sensitive or case-insensitive depending upon the attribute. Some attributes (such as cn, sn) are *case insensitive*, so sn=Carter, sn=CARter and sn=carter would give the same results. Other attributes (such as labeledUri which contains a URL to a web site) are case sensitive. If you are not sure if the attribute is case-sensitive or not, you can check the server's schema.

Boolean Filters

Boolean (AND,OR,NOT) are represented as:

- ❑ & – AND
- ❑ | – OR
- ❑ ! – NOT

The AND and OR affect each set of parentheses () in the search filter, whereas the NOT only affects the first set of parentheses.

> Note that the Boolean filters &, | and ! come *before* the search filters to be operated on rather than between them. Also they can be applied to an unlimited number of search filters simultaneously, not just two.

Some examples of more complex filters, combined with logical operators, are shown in the table below:

Task	Filter
Search for entries with a user ID of `scarter` *and* including the object class `inetOrgPerson`	`(&(uid=scarter)(objectclass=inetOrgPerson))`
Search for all entries that have organizational units of Accounting *or* Engineering	`(|(ou=Accounting)(ou=Engineering))`
Search for all entries except those with a user ID of `scarter`	`(!(uid=scarter))`
Search for all entries that have surnames of Smith or Johnson and have an organizational unit of Accounting	`(&((|(sn=Smith)(sn=Johnson))(ou=Accounting))`

Synchronous Search

Let's first look at an example of a synchronous search, using the filter `(sn=carter)`:

```c
/*synch_search.c
Example 6.3 - synchronous searching

usage: synch_search
*/

#include <stdio.h>
#include <stdlib.h>
#include <string.h>
#include <time.h>

/* standard C ldap library */
#include "ldap.h"

#define MY_PROG "synch_search"

#define MY_HOST        "localhost"
#define MY_PORT        389
#define MY_SEARCHBASE  "o=airius.com"
#define SCOPE          LDAP_SCOPE_SUBTREE
#define FILTER         "(sn=Carter)"

void doWork();         // This function would be stalled while the LDAP operation
                       // takes place.
```

```
int test_work;

main( int argc, char **argv )
{
    LDAP            *ld;
    LDAPMessage     *result,*e;
    BerElement      *ber;
    char            *attribute;
    char            **vals;
    int             i,rc,parse_rc = 0;

    char *attribs[3];

    attribs[0]="cn";
    attribs[1]="mail";
    attribs[2]=NULL;

    printf("Testing %s \n",MY_PROG);

    /* First setup a LDAP connection */
    if ( (ld = ldap_init( MY_HOST, MY_PORT )) == NULL )
    {
       perror( "ldap_init" );
       exit(1);
    }

    printf("connected to LDAP host %s on port %d\n",MY_HOST,MY_PORT);

    /* This will use the options we have set above */
    rc = ldap_search_ext_s( ld, MY_SEARCHBASE, SCOPE, FILTER, attribs,0,NULL,NULL,
                                       LDAP_NO_LIMIT,0,&result);

    if ( rc != LDAP_SUCCESS )
    {
       fprintf( stderr, "ldap_search_ext: %s\n", ldap_err2string( rc ) );
       ldap_unbind( ld );
       exit(1);
    }

    doWork();

    printf("Total results are: %d\n",ldap_count_entries( ld, result));

    for (e = ldap_first_entry(ld, result); e != NULL; e = ldap_next_entry(ld,e))
    {
       printf("DN: %s\n",ldap_get_dn( ld, e ));

       /* Now print out the attributes and values of the search */
       for (attribute = ldap_first_attribute(ld, e, &ber);
            attribute != NULL; attribute = ldap_next_attribute(ld,e,ber))
       {
          if ((vals = ldap_get_values(ld, e, attribute)) != NULL )
          {
             for (i = 0;vals[i] != NULL;i++)
             {
                printf("\t%s: %s\n",attribute,vals[i]);
             }
             /*free memory that was used to store the values of the attribute */
             ldap_value_free(vals);
          }
```

```
            /* free memory used to store the attribute */
            ldap_memfree(attribute);
        }

        /* free memory used to store the value structure of the attribute */
        if ( ber != NULL )
        {
            ber_free( ber, 0 );
        }

        printf("\n");
    }

    if (rc != LDAP_SUCCESS )
    {
        fprintf( stderr, "LDAP Error: %s\n", ldap_err2string(rc));
    }

    ldap_msgfree( result );
    printf ("Search success!\n");
    printf("test_work is %d\n",test_work);
}

void doWork(void)
{
    test_work++;
}
```

The output from this function is shown below:

```
F:\ldap book\chapter 6\code\main>synch_search
Testing synch_search
connected to LDAP host localhost on port 389
Total results are: 4
DN: uid=scarter, ou=People, o=airius.com
        cn: Sam Carter
        mail: scarter@mail.airius.com

DN: uid=scarte2, ou=People, o=airius.com
        cn: Stephen Carter
        mail: scarte2@mail.airius.com

DN: uid=kcarter, ou=People, o=airius.com
        cn: Karen Carter
        mail: kcarter@mail.airius.com

DN: uid=mcarter, ou=People, o=airius.com
        cn: Mike Carter
        mail: mcarter@mail.airius.com

Search success!
test_work is 1

F:\ldap book\chapter 6\code\main>
```

What's Going On?

The set of code we want to look at is a variable declaration:

```
char *attribs[3];

    attribs[0]="cn";
    attribs[1]="mail";
    attribs[2]=NULL;
```

In the LDAP C SDK you can specify which attributes you want to have returned back from a search. Of course the attributes will only be returned if the entry that successfully match a search has these attributes and your client has sufficient access privileges. The list of attributes has to be an array terminated by a NULL attribute.

The next set of code we haven't seen before is as follows:

```
/* This will use the options we have set above */
    rc = ldap_search_ext_s( ld, MY_SEARCHBASE, SCOPE, FILTER, attribs,0,NULL,NULL,
                                            LDAP_NO_LIMIT,0,&result);
```

The function above is how we perform a synchronous search. The function takes

- ❏ A reference to an LDAP connection structure
- ❏ A string that represents the base entry we wish to start our search from
- ❏ An integer that represents the scope of the search
- ❏ A string that represents the search filter

These parameters are what I consider the *essential parameters* – any search must have non-NULL values for these fields The parameters after the search filter, starting with attribs affect the outcome of the search. These are the "extras". You can search the LDAP server without them (as we will find in Chapter 8, when we discuss the LDAP Java SDK). These parameters are:

- ❏ The array of attributes to get back from the search. If you wanted all of the attributes you would put a NULL here, if you don't want any attributes returned, you would pass the defined constant LDAP_NO_ATTRS.
- ❏ An integer (either 0 or 1) that specifies if you want to return the attribute names with the values or not – a value of 1 means that you DON'T want the attribute names returned back.
- ❏ A reference to any server controls (or extended server operations) we wish to ask to for. We'll cover server controls in Chapter 12.
- ❏ A reference to any client controls we wish to invoke
- ❏ A timeval structure that sets the time-out limit. We saw this type of structure in our asynchronous bind example. When set to LDAP_NO_LIMIT, there is no time-out.
- ❏ An integer that specifies how many entries we wish to be returned, a 0 means to return as many entries as the server will allow.
- ❏ A pointer to a LDAPMessage structure that will be set to the actual search results.

The search function will return an LDAP result code.

After you have called the search function and the operation was successful you must then get the results back. You do this with the ldap_first_entry() and ldap_next_entry() functions as we see in our next section.

```
    for (e = ldap_first_entry(ld, result); e != NULL; e = ldap_next_entry(ld,e))
```

The first function you must call is ldap_first_entry() which takes a reference to the LDAP connection and a reference to an LDAPMessage structure that represents the results of an LDAP search. It will return a chain of LDAPMessage structures that represent LDAP entries. The ldap_next_entry() also takes an LDAP connection handle and a pointer to a LDAPMessage structure that represents a series of LDAP entries.

The next step is to get the values of the attributes of the entry. The dn attribute is accessed differently from the rest of the attributes. To get the DN of an entry you use the `ldap_get_dn()` function which takes a reference to an LDAP connection and an `LDAPMessage` representing one LDAP entry. The `LDAPMessage` structure itself contains the entry data plus a pointer to the next entry or NULL if it is the last entry in the chain. This function will return a string. An example use of this function is in this line of code from our example:

```
printf("DN: %s\n",ldap_get_dn( ld, e ));
```

To get the individual attributes you must use the `ldap_first_attribute()` and `ldap_next_attribute()` functions. They work as a pair similar to the `ldap_first_entry()` and `ldap_next_entry()` functions. The `ldap_first_attribute()` function takes a reference to an LDAP connection, a reference to an LDAP entry and a pointer to a `BerElement` data structure. This data structure is used internally to define the values of the attribute according to the **Basic Encoding Rules** (BER), which are rules that have been defined through various Internet drafts for transmitting binary data over the Internet. The `BerElement` structure will be set to an array of attributes, the function `ldap_next_attribute()` retrieves the rest of these attributes, one at a time. Its parameters are the same, except that it expects a reference to a `BerElement` structure and not a pointer. Both of the `*attribute()` functions return a `LDAPMessage` structure representing an LDAP attribute. I told you that `LDAPMessage` structure was flexible!

Here is the code that retrieves the attributes of an entry:

```
/* Now print out the attributes and values of the search */
for (attribute = ldap_first_attribute(ld, e, &ber);
    attribute != NULL; attribute = ldap_next_attribute(ld,e,ber))
```

And here is the code to get the string values of a particular attribute:

```
if ((vals = ldap_get_values(ld, e, attribute)) != NULL )
{
   for (i = 0;vals[i] != NULL;i++)
   {
      printf("\t%s: %s\n",attribute,vals[i]);
   }
```

The `ldap_get_values()` function takes a reference to an LDAP connection, a reference to an LDAP entry and a reference to an LDAP attribute. The function returns a NULL terminated array of strings.

The above code assumes that the results of the search are printable text strings. If, however, the attribute's data is expected to be binary (such as a `jpegphoto`), you can get the values using the following syntax:

```
if( (list_of_photos = ldap_get_values_len( ld, e, "jpegphoto" ) ) != NULL )
```

The `ldap_get_values_len()` function takes a reference to an LDAP connection, a reference to an LDAP entry and the name of the target attribute you want, in this case `jpegphoto`.

It returns a NULL terminated array of `berval` data structures which have the form of:

```
struct berval {
    unsigned long bv_len; /* size of the stored values */
    char bv_val;          /* the actual data */
};
```

This structure contains the actual binary data of the attribute.

When you are finished, make sure you clean up after yourself (and release the resources used by the system to operate on your binary data, by calling the `ldap_value_free_len()` function.

Asynchronous Search

Searching is one area where you may well have a good reason to perform operations asynchronously, for example maximizing the speed of the search. It is not uncommon for users to have CPUs that run as high as 400 MHz (maybe even higher by the time you read this!) yet they still have to contend with networks that can take a long time to perform. The slowness of networks has nothing to do with the usage of CPU time – it is because network latency can be considerable. Asynchronous searches allow us to perform operations and deliver results back to users while the search is still being performed, enabling to user to work on the results he has, rather than waiting for all of them to download.

Like asynchronous binding, you perform the search and then periodically check to see how the operation is performing. You can get search results one at a time, all at the same time or get all received at the time the check was made. The `ldap_msgtype()` can be used to determine exactly what type of results you have received. Normally, you will perform operations as you receive results, either individually or in a batch.

```
/*async_search.c
Exercise 6.4 - asynchronous searching

usage: async_search
*/

#include <stdio.h>
#include <stdlib.h>
#include <string.h>
#include <time.h>

/* standard C ldap library */
#include "ldap.h"

#define MY_PROG "asynch_search"

#define MY_HOST        "localhost"
#define MY_PORT        389
#define MY_SEARCHBASE  "o=airius.com"
#define SCOPE          LDAP_SCOPE_SUBTREE
#define FILTER         "(sn=Carter)"

void doWork();

int test_work;

main( int argc, char **argv )
{
```

```
LDAP            *ld;
LDAPMessage     *result,*e;
BerElement      *ber;
char            *attribute;
char            **vals;
int             i,rc,parse_rc = 0;
int             msg_id = 0;
int             finished = 0;
int             total = -1;
char            *attribs[3];
struct timeval  zerotime;

/*Specify An Unlimited Search Time */
zerotime.tv_sec = zerotime.tv_usec = 0L;

attribs[0]="cn";
attribs[1]="mail";
attribs[2]=NULL;

printf("Testing %s \n",MY_PROG);

/* First setup a LDAP connection */
if ( (ld = ldap_init( MY_HOST, MY_PORT )) == NULL )
{
   perror( "ldap_init" );
   exit(1);
}

printf("connected to LDAP host %s on port %d\n",MY_HOST,MY_PORT);

/* This will use the options we have set above */
rc = ldap_search_ext(ld,MY_SEARCHBASE, SCOPE, FILTER, attribs, 0, NULL, NULL,
                                       NULL, LDAP_NO_LIMIT, &msg_id );

if ( rc != LDAP_SUCCESS )
{
   fprintf( stderr, "ldap_search_ext: %s\n", ldap_err2string( rc ) );
   ldap_unbind( ld );
   exit(1);
}

while ( finished == 0 )
{
   doWork();

   rc = ldap_result( ld, msg_id, LDAP_MSG_ONE, &zerotime, &result );

   if (rc == -1)
   {
      finished = 1;
      rc = ldap_get_lderrno( ld, NULL, NULL );
      fprintf( stderr, "ldap_result: %s\n", ldap_err2string( rc ) );
      ldap_unbind( ld );
      exit(1);
   }

   if (rc > 0)
   {
      total++;
```

```
            for (e = ldap_first_entry(ld, result);
                        e != NULL; e = ldap_next_entry(ld,e))
        {
            printf("DN: %s\n",ldap_get_dn( ld, e ));

            /* Now print out the attributes and values of the search */
            for (attribute = ldap_first_attribute(ld, e, &ber);
                    attribute != NULL; attribute = ldap_next_attribute(ld,e,ber))
            {
                if ((vals = ldap_get_values(ld, e, attribute)) != NULL )
                {
                    for (i = 0;vals[i] != NULL;i++)
                    {
                        printf("\t%s: %s\n",attribute,vals[i]);
                    }
                    ldap_value_free(vals);
                }
                ldap_memfree(attribute);
            }

            if ( ber != NULL )
            {
                ber_free( ber, 0 );
                ldap_msgfree(result);
            }
            printf("\n");
        }
    }

    /* Get final results */
    if (rc == LDAP_RES_SEARCH_RESULT)
    {
        finished = 1;
        parse_rc = ldap_parse_result( ld, result, &rc,NULL,NULL, NULL,NULL, 1 );
        if ( parse_rc != LDAP_SUCCESS )
        {
            fprintf(stderr, "ldap_parse_result: %s\n", ldap_err2string(parse_rc));
            ldap_unbind(ld);
            exit(1);
        }
        if ( rc != LDAP_SUCCESS )
        {
            fprintf(stderr, "ldap_search_ext: %s\n",ldap_err2string(rc));
            ldap_unbind(ld);
            exit(1);
        }
    }
}
    printf ("Search success!\n");
    printf ("Total entries found are: %d\n",total);
    ldap_unbind(ld);
    printf("test_work is %d\n",test_work);
}

void doWork(void)
{
    test_work++;
}
```

The output from this example is shown in the screenshot below:

```
F:\ldap book\chapter 6\code\main>asynch_search.exe
Testing asynch_search
connected to LDAP host localhost on port 389
DN: uid=scarter, ou=People, o=airius.com
        cn: Sam Carter
        mail: scarter@mail.airius.com

DN: uid=scarte2, ou=People, o=airius.com
        cn: Stephen Carter
        mail: scarte2@mail.airius.com

DN: uid=kcarter, ou=People, o=airius.com
        cn: Karen Carter
        mail: kcarter@mail.airius.com

DN: uid=mcarter, ou=People, o=airius.com
        cn: Mike Carter
        mail: mcarter@mail.airius.com

Search success!
Total entries found are: 4
test_work is 4374

F:\ldap book\chapter 6\code\main>_
```

Note that this is different from the last screen output – the value for `test_work`, here is 4374 – it was 1 before.

How Does This Code Work?

The asynchronous search works exactly like the synchronous search except that call to perform the actual search is a bit different – we are using `ldap_search_ext()`. Here is that code:

```
rc = ldap_search_ext(ld, MY_SEARCHBASE, SCOPE, FILTER, attribs, 0, NULL, NULL,
                                        NULL, LDAP_NO_LIMIT, &msg_id );
```

The main difference is that there is now a new extra parameter `&msg_id` which is a pointer to an integer that represents the message identifier for this operation to the SDK. We check to see if the operation is finished in the same manner as we did as the asynchronous bind, by making a call to `ldap_result()`. If there is any non-`NULL` value then we start processing the results. The search results are processed in the exact same fashion as a synchronous search. Note that asynchronous action is being demonstrated in that while the search is taking place, `doWork()` is incrementing `test_work` for each run of the `while` loop – over 4300 cycles!

Sorting

The results of a search should come back to you sorted by DN. However, you may wish to retrieve them sorted in a different manner, for example a list of names sorted by last name, or a set of data sorted by the last time a printer was used. In LDAP you can sort by a single attribute or by multiple attributes. If a particular attribute has multiple values, you can even sort the values of those attributes.

To sort by a single value you use the function `ldap_sort_entries()`. An example call to this function would look like this:

```
rc = ldap_sort_entries(ld, &result,sortby,strcmp);
```

This function starts with the usual parameters, the LDAP connection handle and an LDAP search results reference. The next attribute is a string that is set to the attribute you wish to sort by. The last parameter is a reference to a callback function. This last function will be used to determine the sort order. In the example above, which is the call we make in our next example, the standard string function `strcmp()` is used to sort our entries in ascending order. You call this function after you have your search results.

Let's look again at the synchronous search example, but this time we'll add the `roomNumber` to the attribute list, and sort the results by this new attribute. Note we are returning to synchronous searches:

```
/*sync_search_sort.c
Example 6.5 - synchronous searching with sort

usage: sync_search_sort
*/

...

main( int argc, char **argv )
{
    LDAP             *ld;
    LDAPMessage      *result,*e;
    BerElement       *ber;
    char             *attribute;
    char             **vals;
    char             *sortby = "roomNumber"; /* attribute to sort by */
    int              i,rc,parse_rc = 0;
    int              msg_id = 0;

    char *attribs[4];

    attribs[0]="cn";
    attribs[1]="mail";
    attribs[2]="roomNumber";
    attribs[3]=NULL;

    printf("Testing %s \n",MY_PROG);

/* First setup a LDAP connection */
    if ( (ld = ldap_init( MY_HOST, MY_PORT )) == NULL )
    {
        perror( "ldap_init" );
        exit(1);
    }

...

    /*strcmp is a standard string compare function that we are using as a
      callback function here */

    rc = ldap_sort_entries(ld, &result,sortby,strcmp);
    if ( rc != LDAP_SUCCESS )
    {
        fprintf( stderr, "ldap_search_ext: %s\n", ldap_err2string( rc ) );
        ldap_unbind( ld );
        exit(1);
    }
```

```
printf("Total results are: %d\n",ldap_count_entries( ld, result));

...
```

This code is almost identical to Example 6.3, except for the code outlined above in gray: a new character string `sortby`, the `attribs` array with four elements instead of three – to accommodate the extra attribute, and the `ldap_sort_entries()` function we have already described. The output for a simple sort should look like this:

```
Connected to LDAP host localhost on port 389
Total results are: 4
DN: uid=scarte2, ou=People, o=airius.com
        cn: Stephen Carter
        mail: scarte2@airius.com
        roomNumber: 2013

DN: uid=kcarter, ou=People, o=airius.com
        cn: Karen Carter
        mail: kcarter@airius.com
        roomNumber: 2320

DN: uid=mcarter, ou=People, o=airius.com
        cn: Mike Carter
        mail: mcarter@airius.com
        roomNumber: 3819

DN: uid=scarter, ou=People, o=airius.com
        cn: Sam Carter
        mail: scarter@airius.com
        roomNumber: 4612

Search Success!
```

Sort with Multiple Attributes

The next example shows you how to sort with multiple attributes. We do this with the `ldap_multisort_entries()` function. This function takes the same parameters as the `ldap_sort_entries()` function, except that you now pass a NULL terminated array of strings that lists the attributes you wish to sort on instead of a single attribute.

```
/*sync_search_sort_multi.c
Example 6.6 - synchronous searching sorting on multiple attributes

usage: sync_search_sort_multi
*/

#include <stdio.h>
#include <stdlib.h>
#include <string.h>
#include <time.h>

/* standard C ldap library */
#include "ldap.h"

...
```

```
char            *attribute;
char            **vals;
char            *sortby[3]; /* attribute to sort by */
int             i,rc,parse_rc = 0;
int             msg_id = 0;

char *attribs[4];

attribs[0]="cn";
attribs[1]="ou";
attribs[2]="telephoneNumber";
attribs[3]=NULL;

sortby[0] = "ou";
sortby[1] = "telephoneNumber";
sortby[2] = NULL;
```

. . .

```
/*strcmp is a standard string compare function that we are using as a
  callback function here */
rc =  ldap_multisort_entries(ld,&result,sortby, strcmp);
```

. . .

Once again, the only modifications you need to make are shown in gray. Note the array of sortby elements. Note also we are sorting first by organizational unit and then by telephone number. Running this code will produce output like this:

```
Connected to LDAP host localhost on port 389
Total results are: 4
DN: uid=mcarter, ou=People, o=airius.com
        cn: Mike Carter
        ou: Accounting
        ou: People
        telephoneNumber: +1 408 555 1846

DN: uid=scarter, ou=People, o=airius.com
        cn: Sam Carter
        ou: Accounting
        ou: People
        telephoneNumber: +1 408 555 4798

        telephoneNumber: +1 940 555 1234

DN: uid=kcarter, ou=People, o=airius.com
        cn: Karen Carter
        ou: Human Resources
        ou: People
        telephoneNumber: + 408 555 4675

DN: uid=scarte2, ou=People, o=airius.com
        cn: Stephen Carter
        ou: Product Development
        ou: People
        telephoneNumber: +1 408 555 6022


Search Success!
```

Sort an Attribute by Values

Not only can you sort the entries returned from a search, you can sort the values of a particular attribute or attributes of an entry. You do this with the `ldap_sort_values()` function like so:

```
rc = ldap_sort_values(ld, vals, strcmp);
        if (rc != LDAP_SUCCESS )
        {
            fprintf( stderr, "LDAP Error: %s\n", ldap_err2string(rc));
        }
```

This function takes a connection to the LDAP server, an array of attribute values, which are returned from the `ldap_get_values()` function, and a callback function, just as we used in the previous sort functions.

```
/*sync_search_sort_value.c
Exercise 6.7 - sorting by attribute value

usage: sync_search_sort_value
*/

#include <stdio.h>
#include <stdlib.h>
#include <string.h>
#include <time.h>

/* standard C ldap library */
#include "ldap.h"

...

    attribs[0]="cn";
    attribs[1]="mail";
    attribs[2]="objectclass";
    attribs[3]=NULL;

...

    // Remove the ldap_sort_entries() method and the if block that follows it

    printf("Total results are: %d\n",ldap_count_entries( ld, result));

    for (e = ldap_first_entry(ld, result); e != NULL; e = ldap_next_entry(ld,e))
    {
        printf("DN: %s\n",ldap_get_dn( ld, e ));
        /* Now print out the attributes and values of the search */
        for (attribute = ldap_first_attribute(ld, e, &ber);
            attribute != NULL; attribute = ldap_next_attribute(ld,e,ber))
        {
            if ((vals = ldap_get_values(ld, e, attribute)) != NULL )
            {
                rc = ldap_sort_values(ld, vals, strcmp);
                if (rc != LDAP_SUCCESS )
                {
                    fprintf( stderr, "LDAP Error: %s\n", ldap_err2string(rc));
                }
                for (i = 0;vals[i] != NULL;i++)
                {
                    printf("\t%s: %s\n",attribute,vals[i]);
                    ...
```

The main differences between this code and that of the previous example is that the
`ldap_sort_entries()` function has been removed, the `ldap_sort_values()` function is
inserted at the above place and the `attribs[2]` element has been set to `objectclass`. The output
below shows a list of the object classes for each of the selected entries:

```
DN: uid=scarter, ou=People, o=airius.com
        cn: Sam Carter
        mail: scarter@airius.com
        objectclass: person
        objectclass: inetOrgPerson
        objectclass: organizationalPerson
        objectclass: top

DN: uid=kcarter, ou=People, o=airius.com
        cn: Karen Carter
        mail: kcarter@airius.com
        objectclass: top
        objectclass: organizationalPerson
        objectclass: person
        objectclass: inetOrgPerson

DN: uid=mcarter, ou=People, o=airius.com
        cn: Mike Carter
        mail: mcarter@airius.com
        objectclass: person
        objectclass: top
        objectclass: inetOrgPerson
        objectclass: organizationalPerson

Search Success !
```

Working with Search Filter Files

When you are building applications, you cannot always rely on the fact that the end user will
understand LDAP syntax. Indeed, you may decide to provide your users with a neutral language
interface, where they can enter some words and then have you search the LDAP server.

The Netscape SDKs support the concept of filter configurations. These configurations are normally
stored in a text file and they provide a way to describe how you would like certain patterns searched.
For example, you might assume that a search text containing @ means that the user is looking for an
e-mail address. Then you can build the search filter as such.

Shown below is an example of a search filter file.

```
#search.conf
#Example Search filter
#This example is taken from Netscape's docs.

"people"

  "^[0-9][0-9-]*$"   " "   "(telephoneNumber=*%v))"   "phone number ends with"
```

"@"	" "	"(mail=%v)"	"e-mail address is"
		"(mail=%v*)"	"e-mail address starts with"

The lines starting with a # are comments. This example only has one group of filters, but is possible to make more complex search filter files by adding several filter groups. Each group is specified with a **tag**, which is on a line by itself and is in quotes. In the above example, the tag is "people". You should give the tag a descriptive name so that you can reference it programmatically.

The filter starts with a regular expression, for example "^[0-9][0-9-]*$", that defines the text to look for in the search. What this regular expression says that if the text starts with a number, followed by one or more numbers or dashes (-), but no other text, then it is a successful match. The next field is the delimiter (a space in this case), followed by the search filter that will be used – "(telephoneNumber=*%v))". This is followed by an optional description of the filter – "phone number ends with". The %v is the special variable that is replaced with the text, which is followed by the description of the particular filter.

> *If you are an old Perl or Unix hacker you probably have some experience with regular expressions. If you are new to regular expressions you should probably consult http://www.perl.com or do a Web search on regular expressions.*

To use the filter configuration files, you must first create a search configuration file that contains one or more filter groups, like in the example above. The file is a plain text file. In your application you must first open the file with the ldap_init_getfilter() function. This function takes a string that is the name of a LDAP filter configuration file. It returns a pointer to a LDAPFiltDesc structure that represents the data in the filter configuration file.

An example call to ldap_init_getfilter() would look like this:

```
if ( ( ldfp = ldap_init_getfilter( FILTER ) ) == NULL )
{
    perror( "Cannot open filter configuration file" );
    exit(1);
}
```

After you open the filter file, you can step through each filter with the ldap_getfirstfilter() and ldap_getnextfilter() functions. The ldap_getfirstfilter() function requires a reference to the filter configuration file's data, a string representing the name of the group you wish to use and a search string. The ldap_getnextfilter() function only requires the pointer to the filter configuration file. Both of these functions return a LDAPFiltInfo structure that looks like this:

```
typedef struct ldap_filt_info {
    char *lfi_filter;
    char *lfi_desc;
    int lfi_scope;
    int lfi_isexact;
    struct ldap_filt_info *lfi_next;
} LDAPFiltInfo;
```

Here is an example of how to step through a filter configuration file to retrieve all of the matching search filters:

```
for ( ldfi = ldap_getfirstfilter( ldfp, "people", buf );
          ldfi != NULL; ldfi = ldap_getnextfilter( ldfp ) )
```

Here is an example that uses the `LDAPFiltInfo` structure (named `ldfi`) to perform the search:

```
rc = ldap_search_ext_s( ld,MY_SEARCHBASE,ldfi->lfi_scope,ldfi->lfi_filter,
attribs,

0,NULL,NULL,LDAP_NO_LIMIT,0,&result);
```

Below is our search example again, this time modified to use the `search.conf` filter file:

```
/*sync_search_filter.c
Example 6.8 - using search filter files

usage: sync_search_filter
*/


...

#define MY_HOST          "localhost"
#define MY_PORT          389
#define MY_SEARCHBASE    "o=airius.com"
#define SCOPE            LDAP_SCOPE_SUBTREE
#define FILTER           "search.conf"    /* name of the file with the
                                             configuration information */

main( int argc, char **argv )
{
    LDAP            *ld;
    LDAPMessage     *result,*e;
    BerElement      *ber;
    char            *attribute;
    char            **vals;
    int             i,rc,parse_rc = 0;

    LDAPFiltDesc *ldfp; // pointer to the LDAP filter configuration file
    LDAPFiltInfo *ldfi; // data structure that contains the values of a LDAP Filter
    char buf[ 80 ] = "jc*@airius.com"; /* contains the search criteria */
    char *attribs[4];

    attribs[0]="cn";
    attribs[1]="mail";
    attribs[2]="ou";
    attribs[3]=NULL;

    printf("Testing %s \n",MY_PROG);

    /* First setup a LDAP connection */
    if ( (ld = ldap_init( MY_HOST, MY_PORT )) == NULL )
    {
        perror( "ldap_init" );
        exit(1);
    }

    printf("connected to LDAP host %s on port %d\n",MY_HOST,MY_PORT);
```

```
if ( ( ldfp = ldap_init_getfilter( FILTER ) ) == NULL )
{
    perror( "Cannot open filter configuration file" );
    exit(1);
}

for ( ldfi = ldap_getfirstfilter( ldfp, "people", buf );
        ldfi != NULL; ldfi = ldap_getnextfilter( ldfp ) )
{
    /* Use the selected filter to search the directory. */
    printf("filter is %s\n",ldfi->lfi_filter);
    rc = ldap_search_ext_s( ld,MY_SEARCHBASE,ldfi->lfi_scope,ldfi->lfi_filter,

attribs,0,NULL,NULL,LDAP_NO_LIMIT,0,&result);

    if ( rc != LDAP_SUCCESS )
    {
        fprintf( stderr, "ldap_search_ext: %s\n", ldap_err2string( rc ) );
        ldap_unbind( ld );
        exit(1);
    }

...

} // end for
ldap_msgfree( result );
printf ("Search success!\n");
}
```

There are quite a few more changes to the search file, as shown above. Note that we have changed the value of the `attribs[2]` element to "ou". Note also that we have specified the string "jc*@airius.com" as the search term, a convenient way of finding all Airius employees with the initials "JC". Part of the output will look something like this:

```
filter is (mail=jc*@airius.com*)
Total results are: 3
DN: uid=jcampaig, ou=People, o=airius.com
        cn: Jody Campaigne
        mail: jcampaig@airius.com
        ou: Product Development
        ou: People

DN: uid= jcampai2, ou=People, o=airius.com
        cn: Jeffrey Campaigne
        mail: jcampai2@airius.com
        ou: Human Resources
        ou: People

DN: uid=jcruse, ou=People, o=airius.com
        cn: Jim Cruse
        mail: jcruse@airius.com
        ou: Payroll
        ou: People
```

You also have the options to add prefixes and suffixes to your searches, built using search configuration files. One reason why you might want to add a prefix is so that you can specify an AND, OR or NOT to your searches. For example the prefix (&(ou=People) would limit output to just the People organizational unit. A reason why you would then would need a suffix is to make sure your parenthesis match up, so a suffix is often a closing parenthesis. This gives you the ability to build complex searches while still maintaining the simplicity of search configuration files. In this example we will refine the above filtered search to pick out the employee from the Payroll organizational unit:

```
/*sync search filter presuf.c
Example 6.9 - using prefixes and suffixes in your search

usage: sync search filter presuf
*/

...

#define PREFIX "(&(ou=payroll)"          //begin all search filters with this
#define SUFFIX ")"                        //end all search filters with this

...

    ldap_setfilteraffixes( ldfp, PREFIX, SUFFIX );

    for ( ldfi = ldap_getfirstfilter( ldfp, "people", buf );
            ldfi != NULL; ldfi = ldap_getnextfilter( ldfp ) )
    {
            /* Use the selected filter to search the directory. */
        printf("filter is %s\n",ldfi->lfi_filter);
...
```

The only difference between the previous search configuration file example and the one we looked at just now, is that we #define the prefix and suffix and then call the ldap_setfilteraffixes() function with these string constants as parameters. This function also takes a reference to the filter file, a string that is the search prefix and a string that is the search suffix. An example call to this function would look like this:

```
ldap_setfilteraffixes( ldfp, PREFIX, SUFFIX );
```

In our second example, we kept the same search text (jc*@airius.com) but this time we added a prefix of (&(ou=payroll and a suffix of ")". This says that the only successful matches will be those with an e-mail address starting with "jc" and ending with "@airius.com", and an ou attribute of "Payroll".

The output for this code should look something like this:

```
Testing synch_search
connected to LDAP host localhost on port 389
filter is (&(ou=payroll)(mail=jc*@airius.com))
Total results are: 1
DN: uid=jcruse, ou=People, o=airius.com
        cn: Jim Cruse
        mail: jcruse @airius.com
        ou: Payroll
        ou: People
```

```
filter is (&(ou=payroll)(mail=jc*@airius.com*))
Total results are: 1
DN: uid=jcruse, ou=People, o=airius.com
        cn: Jim Cruse
        mail: jcruse @airius.com
        ou: Payroll
        ou: People

Search Success !
```

Working with LDAP URLs

Within the past few years, a new vernacular has entered our everyday language – the language of the Internet. Many of us cannot go for one day without telling someone to go to `http://www.somewhere.com`. The LDAP committee of IETF realized the importance of URLs and devised an URL standard for LDAP. The reason why LDAP URLs are important is because of the importance of web browsers in our computing lives. Every major Internet protocol (e.g. http, mail, news, gopher, ftp, etc.) can be represented with a URL. To make LDAP as accessible as possible, it was necessary to come up with a way to represent LDAP operations via URLs, as specified in RFC 2255.

Here is an example LDAP URL:

```
ldap://localhost/o=Airius.com?cn,mail,telephoneNumber?sub?(sn=Carter)
```

Let's break this up into its component parts and see what each bit means:

- ❑ `ldap://` – the protocol. (For LDAP over SSL, use `ldaps://` instead.)
- ❑ `localhost` – the hostname, which can be a named host, an IP address etc.
- ❑ `o=Airius.com` – the search base.
- ❑ `cn,mail,telephoneNumber` – the list of attributes we wish to have returned.
- ❑ `sub` – search scope, which in this case corresponds to `LDAP_SCOPE_SUBTREE`,
- ❑ `(sn=Carter)` – the search filter
- ❑ `?` – delimit the sections of a LDAP URL.

From Netscape Communicator 4.5 or Microsoft IE 4, you can enter an LDAP URL into the browser and it will perform a search.

Here is an example screenshot of IE4 using the LDAP URL example from above:

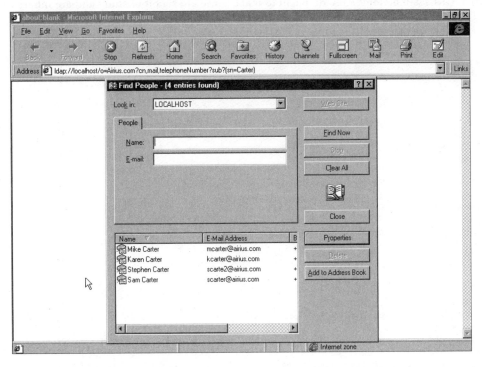

And here are the results in Netscape 4:

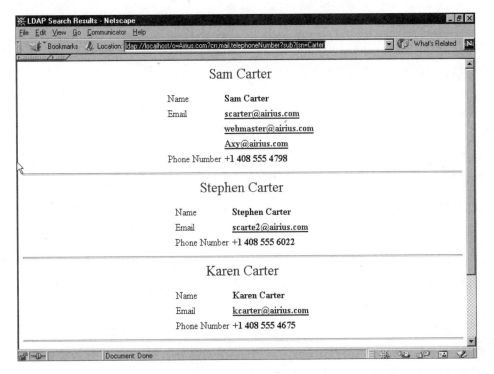

While LDAP URLs can be long, they do begin to make sense after a bit of study and are inherently more intelligible than your standard WWW CGI URL. Let's take one final look at the search example, and how we can modify it to use LDAP URLs:

```
/*sync_search_ldap.c
Example 6.10 - using LDAP URLs

usage: sync_search_ldap
*/

#include <stdio.h>
#include <stdlib.h>
#include <string.h>
#include <time.h>

/* standard C ldap library */
#include "ldap.h"

#define MY_PROG "sync_search_ldap"

#define MY_HOST         "localhost"
#define MY_PORT         389
main( int argc, char **argv )
{
    LDAP             *ld;
    LDAPMessage      *result,*e;
    BerElement       *ber;
    char             *attribute;
    char             **vals;
    int              i,rc,parse_rc = 0;
    int              msg_id = 0;
    char *url =
            "ldap://localhost/o=Airius.com?cn,mail,telephoneNumber?sub?(sn=Carter)";

    printf("Testing %s \n",MY_PROG);

    /* First setup a LDAP connection */
    if ( (ld = ldap_init( MY_HOST, MY_PORT )) == NULL )
    {
        perror( "ldap_init" );
        exit(1);
    }

    printf("connected to LDAP host %s on port %d\n",MY_HOST,MY_PORT);

    rc = ldap_url_search_s( ld, url, 0, &result);

    if ( rc != LDAP_SUCCESS )
    {
        fprintf( stderr, "ldap_search_ext: %s\n", ldap_err2string( rc ) );
        ldap_unbind( ld );
        exit(1);
    }

    printf("Total results are: %d\n",ldap_count_entries( ld, result));
...
```

The only difference between this search example and our previous is examples is this particular function call:

```
rc = ldap_url_search_s( ld, url, 0, &result);
```

The `ldap_url_search_s()` function is how you search an LDAP server using LDAP URLs. It takes an LDAP connection handle, a string representing the LDAP URL, an integer that represents whether to return attribute names or not (a zero means return attribute names) and a pointer to an `LDAPMessage` structure that will contain the results of the search. We can leave out the parameters for scope, search base, attributes to return and the filter because all of those items are contained in the LDAP URL.

Entry Modifications

While searching an LDAP directory is undoubtedly the most common task the average user will perform, there are going to be times when you will need to modify the entries in your database. This section will show you how to add an entry programmatically, modify those entries and then delete an entry. Even if you have access to an LDAP management interface such as the Netscape Console, you will still need to be able to modify the LDAP server from different clients for a variety of reasons. One reason is that your LDAP directory server may not be the authoritative reference for your organization – a person's true status in the organization will most likely be maintained elsewhere such as human resources. As data in that system changes (e.g. people are hired, people leave, people get married and change names, people change jobs in the organization, etc.), then you would need to take those changes from the human resources, and other authoritative data sources, and then apply them to your LDAP server. Thus you will need to be able to easily modify an LDAP database, add new entries and delete old ones.

Note that only synchronous examples are provided here.

Adding Entries

In previous chapters, we have seen how to go about entering data with the use of LDIF files. In this code example, we learn how to enter data from a program.

When you create an entry, you must bind as a user with the rights to complete the transaction. Normally there will be a set of LDAP server Directory Administrators who have these rights. You must make sure that the entry you are adding meets all of the schema criteria – that is to say it has non-zero values for the required attributes for its object class, otherwise the server is likely going to reject the operation. For more information on this see Appendix D.

Shown below is a short coded example demonstrating the process of adding a new entry:

```
/*add.c
Example 6.11 - synchronous adding

usage: add
*/

#include <stdio.h>
#include <stdlib.h>
#include <string.h>
#include <time.h>

/* standard C ldap library */
#include "ldap.h"
```

```
#define MY_PROG "add"

#define MY_HOST          "localhost"
#define MY_PORT          389
#define MY_DN            "uid=kvaughan,ou=People,o=airius.com"
#define MY_PWD           "bribery"

#define NEW_DN "uid=wilcox,ou=People,o=Airius.com"

main (int argc, char **argv )
{
   LDAP            *ld;
   LDAPMod         *mods[8];
   LDAPMod attribute1, attribute2, attribute3, attribute4,
           attribute5, attribute6, attribute7;
   char    *sn_values[] = { "Wilcox", NULL };
   char    *objectClass_values[] = { "top", "person", "organizationalPerson",
                             "inetOrgPerson", NULL };
   char    *cn_values[] = { "Mark Wilcox", NULL};
   char    *gn_values[] = { "Mark",NULL};
   char    *mail_values[] = {"wilcox@airius.com",NULL};
   char    *uid_values[] = {"wilcox",NULL};
   char    *ou_values[] = {"People","Human Resources",NULL};
   int     rc,parse_rc = 0;

   /* First setup a LDAP connection */
   if ( (ld = ldap_init( MY_HOST, MY_PORT )) == NULL )
   {
      perror( "ldap_init" );
      exit(1);
   }
   printf("connected to LDAP host %s on port %d\n",MY_HOST,MY_PORT);

   /* must bind to do any write operations */
   rc = ldap_simple_bind_s(ld,MY_DN,MY_PWD);
   if (rc != LDAP_SUCCESS )
   {
      fprintf( stderr, "LDAP Error: %s\n", ldap_err2string(rc));
      exit(1);
   }

   /* create the entry */

   attribute1.mod_op = LDAP_MOD_ADD;
   attribute1.mod_type = "sn";
   attribute1.mod_values = sn_values;

   attribute2.mod_op = LDAP_MOD_ADD;
   attribute2.mod_type = "objectclass";
   attribute2.mod_values = objectClass_values;

   attribute3.mod_op = LDAP_MOD_ADD;
   attribute3.mod_type = "cn";
   attribute3.mod_values = cn_values;

   attribute4.mod_op = LDAP_MOD_ADD;
   attribute4.mod_type = "givenname";
   attribute4.mod_values = gn_values;
```

```
    attribute5.mod_op = LDAP_MOD_ADD;
    attribute5.mod_type = "mail";
    attribute5.mod_values = mail_values;

    attribute6.mod_op = LDAP_MOD_ADD;
    attribute6.mod_type= "uid";
    attribute6.mod_values = uid_values;

    attribute7.mod_op = LDAP_MOD_ADD;
    attribute7.mod_type = "ou";
    attribute7.mod_values = ou_values;

    mods[0] = &attribute1;
    mods[1] = &attribute2;
    mods[2] = &attribute3;
    mods[3] = &attribute4;
    mods[4] = &attribute5;
    mods[5] = &attribute6;
    mods[6] = &attribute7;
    mods[7] = NULL;

    rc = ldap_add_ext_s( ld, NEW_DN, mods, NULL, NULL );

    if ( rc != LDAP_SUCCESS )
    {
        fprintf( stderr, "ldap_search_ext_s: %s\n", ldap_err2string( rc ) );
        ldap_unbind( ld );
        exit(1);
    }

    printf ("Operation success!\n");
}
```

What's Going On?

Most of the work in adding a new entry is actually building the entry itself externally. This means setting the distinguished name, adding all of the attributes and their values, etc. To actually add the entry is just a single function call, that of `ldap_add_ext_s()`. This function takes an LDAP connection handle, the DN, an array of `LDAPMod` structures representing the attributes of the entry, an optional array of server controls and an array of client controls – also optional. We'll talk about controls later in this chapter. The function returns an LDAP result code:

```
rc = ldap_add_ext_s( ld, NEW_DN, mods, NULL, NULL );
```

Attributes are represented with the `LDAPMod` data structure which looks like this:

```
typedef struct ldapmod {
    int mod_op;
    char *mod_type;
    union {
        char **modv_strvals;
        struct berval **modv_bvals;
    } mod_vals;

#define mod_values mod_vals.modv_strvals
#define mod_bvalues mod_vals.modv_bvals
} LDAPMod;
```

When using a `LDAPMod` structure, you define the `mod_op` variable, which uses an integer to tell the server what to do with this attribute (e.g. add, replace or delete entry). The `mod_type` variable is a string that contains the attribute's name. Finally the `mod_vals` variable accepts an array of strings or binary data depending upon the type of attribute, e.g. the attribute `sn` uses strings whereas the `jpegphoto` attribute uses binary data.

Here is some example code that builds a single attribute, `sn`. Note that `mod_op` only has the value `LDAP_MOD_ADD`:

```
attribute1.mod_op = LDAP_MOD_ADD;
attribute1.mod_type = "sn";
attribute1.mod_values = sn_values;
```

Run this code and an entry with the user ID of `wilcox` will have been added to the database. You can verify that this has happened by opening Directory Server and looking up the new entry under `People`.

Modifying an Entry

As well as adding data, it's likely that you'll need to change data from time to time, because users need to change their passwords, move to different offices, people get married and so on. The access control lists for the LDAP server will determine exactly which attributes/values can be modified by each user, hence the set of attributes that can be modified by the application will be determined by how that application is bound.

```
/*mod.c
Example 6.12 - synchronous modifications

usage: mod
*/

...

#define MY_PROG "mod"

#define MY_HOST        "localhost"
#define MY_PORT        389
#define MY_SEARCHBASE  "o=airius.com"
#define SCOPE          LDAP_SCOPE_SUBTREE
#define MY_DN          "uid=kvaughan,ou=People,o=airius.com"
#define MY_PWD         "bribery"
#define DN "uid=wilcox,ou=People,o=airius.com"

main (int argc, char **argv )
{
    LDAP        *ld;
    LDAPMod     *mods[3];
    LDAPMod     attribute1,attribute2;
    char        *mail_values[] = {"wilcox@mail.airius.com",NULL};
    char        *telephone_values[] = {"+1 940 555-1234",NULL};
    int         rc,parse_rc = 0;

    printf("Testing %s \n",MY_PROG);
    /* First setup a LDAP connection */
    if ( (ld = ldap_init( MY_HOST, MY_PORT )) == NULL )
    {
```

```
        perror( "ldap_init" );
        exit(1);
    }
    printf("connected to LDAP host %s on port %d\n",MY_HOST,MY_PORT);

    /* must bind to do any write operations */
    rc = ldap_simple_bind_s(ld,MY_DN,MY_PWD);
    if (rc != LDAP_SUCCESS )
    {
        fprintf( stderr, "LDAP Error: %s\n", ldap_err2string(rc));
        exit(1);
    }

    printf("bound to server\n");

    attribute1.mod_op = LDAP_MOD_REPLACE;
    attribute1.mod_type = "mail";
    attribute1.mod_values = mail_values;

    attribute2.mod_op = LDAP_MOD_REPLACE;
    attribute2.mod_type = "telephonenumber";
    attribute2.mod_values = telephone_values;

    mods[0] = &attribute1;
    mods[1] = &attribute2;
    mods[2] = NULL;

    /* perform modification */

    rc = ldap_modify_ext_s( ld, DN, mods, NULL, NULL );
    ldap_mods_free(mods,1);

    if ( rc != LDAP_SUCCESS )
    {
        fprintf( stderr, "ldap_search_ext: %s\n", ldap_err2string( rc ) );
        ldap_unbind( ld );
        exit(1);
    }

    printf ("Operation success!\n");
}
```

What's Going On?

Modification is similar to adding an entry. It uses the function `ldap_modify_ext_s()`, which takes the exact same parameters as the `ldap_add_ext_s()` function and returns a LDAP result code.

The difference is that your attributes may now contain different `mod_op` values. Besides the value of `LDAP_MOD_ADD`, which means to add a new entry, they may also contain the defined constant `LDAP_MOD_REPLACE`, which replaces the values of an existing attribute. If the attribute doesn't exist when the replace operation is called, it is added first, then the new values are given to that attribute. Alternatively, the value of `mod_op` can be `LDAP_MOD_DELETE`, which deletes all of the values of the attribute. Here is the first modification, that of the e-mail address:

```
attribute1.mod_op = LDAP_MOD_REPLACE;
attribute1.mod_type = "mail";
attribute1.mod_values = mail_values;
```

A word of caution about the LDAP_MOD_REPLACE option and multi-valued attributes; if you need to replace a single value of a multi-value attribute or add a new value to it, you must include all of the existing values you want to keep. Otherwise, when you do a replace with your single value, that single value will overwrite all of the existing values. For example say you have an entry which as the values of Mark Wilcox and Mark Edward Wilcox for the cn attribute. You decide you want to add the value Mark E. Wilcox to the attribute. For this operation to operate as you would expect, you must pass to the server an array that contains Mark Wilcox, Mark Edward Wilcox and Mark E. Wilcox.

Deleting an Entry

Eventually you will need to delete entries from your LDAP server. This might be because an employee leaves, or a printer is removed from service, etc. Just like adding or modifying an entry, a deletion can only be performed if you bind as a user with enough rights. In our example below user kvaughan is one of the Database Administrators, the only group who has rights to delete an entry. In general, deletions can only be performed by special accounts to prevent mistakes from occurring.

```
/*del.c
Example 6.13 - synchronous deletions

usage: del
*/

#include <stdio.h>
#include <stdlib.h>
#include <string.h>
#include <time.h>

/* standard C ldap library */
#include "ldap.h"

#define MY_PROG "del"

#define MY_HOST        "localhost"
#define MY_PORT        389
#define MY_SEARCHBASE  "o=airius.com"
#define SCOPE          LDAP_SCOPE_SUBTREE
#define MY_DN          "uid=kvaughan,ou=People,o=airius.com"
#define MY_PWD         "bribery"

#define DN "uid=wilcox,ou=People,o=airius.com"

main (int argc, char **argv )
{
    LDAP         *ld;
    int          rc,parse_rc = 0;

    printf("Testing %s \n",MY_PROG);
    /* First setup a LDAP connection */
    if ( (ld = ldap_init( MY_HOST, MY_PORT )) == NULL )
    {
        perror( "ldap_init" );
        exit(1);
    }
    printf("connected to LDAP host %s on port %d\n",MY_HOST,MY_PORT);

    /* must bind to do any write operations */
```

```
rc = ldap_simple_bind_s(ld,MY_DN,MY_PWD);
if (rc != LDAP_SUCCESS )
{
    fprintf( stderr, "LDAP Error: %s\n", ldap_err2string(rc));
    exit(1);
}

printf("bound to server\n");

/* perform deletion */
rc = ldap_delete_ext_s( ld, DN,NULL, NULL );

if ( rc != LDAP_SUCCESS )
{
    fprintf( stderr, "ldap_search_ext: %s\n", ldap_err2string( rc ) );
    ldap_unbind( ld );
    exit(1);
}

printf ("Operation success!\n");
}
```

What's Going On?

To delete an entry is very simple. You call the function `ldap_delete_ext_s()`, passing it a LDAP connection, a string representing the DN of the entry you wish to remove, plus the optional server and client controls. Once again it returns with an LDAP result code. Here is an example of a call to this function:

```
rc = ldap_delete_ext_s( ld, DN, NULL, NULL );
```

Working with Advanced Controls and Extended Operations

In LDAP version 3, the server developer has the ability to provide extra functionality called extended operations, an example of which would be to have the server sort the entries before returning them to the client. An LDAP client can determine what extended operations are available through the use of server controls.

LDAP clients can also posses some extended operations of its own such as a client side cache. More is said on this topic in chapter 12. However, one control I will present to you here is a user authentication routine.

A Working Authentication Routine

One rationale for implementing LDAP in your organization is to simplify user authentication. Most of your existing authentication systems are most likely either written in C or can make calls to an external C API either through a DLL on Windows or through Shared Objects on Unix. Thus understanding how to implement LDAP authentication in an application with the C SDK is very important.

The example in this section is taken from an article I wrote for Netscape ViewSource at (http://developer.netscape.com/viewsource/wilcox_ldap2.html).

The example shown below shows how easy it is to provide authentication in your applications with LDAP. It simply accepts a user ID and a password from the command line and checks that these pass:

```c
/*authenticate.c
Example 6.14 - authentication

usage: authenticate uid password
*/

#include <stdio.h>
#include <stdlib.h>
#include <string.h>
#include <time.h>

/* standard C ldap library */
#include "ldap.h"

#define MY_HOST          "localhost"
#define MY_PORT          389
#define MY_SEARCHBASE    "o=airius.com"

int authenticate();

int main( int argc, char **argv )
{
    /* for this test we will "set" the uid and passwords here
       had this been a real program, you would get them externally
       from a prompt
    */

    const char *uid = argv[1];
    const char *passwd = argv[2];
    char uid_filter[100]="uid=";
    int results = 1;

    if (argc < 3)
    {
        printf("usage: authenticate uid password\n");
        exit(1);
    }

    printf("Testing Authentication\n");

    // Need to build the search filter
    strcat(uid_filter,uid);

    printf("search filter is %s\n",uid_filter);

    results = authenticate(uid_filter,passwd);

    if (results == 0)
    {
        printf("you authenticated!\n");
    }
    else
    {
        printf("userid %s failed!\n",uid);
    }
}
```

```
int authenticate(char *uid filter,char *passwd)
{
    LDAP            *ld;
    LDAPMessage     *result, *e;
    char            *dn;
    int             value= 1;
    const char      *MY FILTER = uid filter;

    /* First setup a LDAP connection */
    if ( (ld = ldap init( MY HOST, MY PORT )) == NULL )
    {
        perror( "ldap_init" );
        return( 1 );
    }
    printf("connected to LDAP host %s on port %d\n",MY HOST,MY PORT);

    /* In LDAP v2 We must always authenticate as someone to do an operation.
       Here we authenticate as anonymous In LDAP v3 which Directory 3 & 4 support,
       you don't have to bind first, but it's good form.
    */
    if ( ldap_simple_bind_s( ld, NULL, NULL ) != LDAP_SUCCESS )
    {
        /*Special error method for LDAP */
        ldap perror( ld, "ldap_simple_bind_s" );
        return( 1 );
    }

    /* A bind in LDAP is accomplished by passing a Distinguished Name (DN) and
    the password. Of course people can't be expected to remember their DN. So
    instead we ask for the user ID (uid) and then search for the first entry
    that matches that user ID
    */

    if ( ldap search s( ld, MY SEARCHBASE, LDAP SCOPE SUBTREE,
        MY_FILTER, NULL, 0, &result ) != LDAP_SUCCESS )
    {
        ldap perror( ld, "ldap search s" );
        return( 1 );
    }

    /* Either LDAP Connection handle is bad or there are more than one user
      entry that matches the results
    */
    if (ldap_count_entries(ld,result)== -1)
    {
        ldap perror(ld,"ldap count entries");
        return(1);
    }
    if (e = ldap first entry(ld, result))
    {
        if ( (dn = ldap_get_dn( ld, e )) != NULL )
        {
            printf( "dn: %s\n", dn );

            /* if dn or password is empty but not null we need to throw it out
               here otherwise someone will successfully authenticate anonymously
            */
            if(strlen(dn) == 0) || (strlen(passwd) == 0))
            {
                printf("dn or password are empty.\n");
```

```
            return(1);
        }

        /* To test for authentication in LDAP, we do a bind. If it fails,
           the server will throw an error
        */
        if ( ldap simple bind s( ld, dn,passwd) != LDAP SUCCESS )
        {
            /*Special error method for LDAP */
            ldap perror( ld, "failed to authenticate" );
            return( 1 );
        }

        value = 0;
        /*call this to free memory */
        ldap memfree( dn );
    }
}

ldap_msgfree( result );
ldap_unbind( ld );
return( value);
}
```

What's Going On?

Doing authentication with LDAP is a bit different than with your traditional systems. For example in Unix we pass a user ID and password to a routine that returns true or false if the user ID and password match inside the password file. In LDAP, the equivalent call is to bind to the server. However, when we bind to the server in LDAP, it requires an entry's *distinguished name* as well as password. By now you know what a DN is and you will probably realize that no user could ever be expected to remember his or her full DN.

So when we write authentication routines that use LDAP, we still stick with tradition and ask for a user ID and password. Then we search the server for an entry that matches a particular ID. If we find a match, we then grab that entry's DN. Next we make a call to the ldap_simple_bind_s() function and check the LDAP result code that function returns to us. If it is success, we can assume the user ID/password match and that the user will be authenticated.

There is, however, one final catch! LDAP assumes an empty (but not NULL) password to mean you wish to bind to the server anonymously which in turn will result in a LDAP return code of "success", which of course it isn't. To prevent this you must check to make sure that you fail the authentication attempt before binding to the LDAP server.

I did that in this example like this:

```
/* if dn or password is empty but not null we need to throw it out
   here otherwise someone will successfully authenticate anonymously */
if ((dn == "") || (passwd == ""))
{
    printf("dn or password are empty.\n");
    return(1);
}
```

Summary

In this chapter, we have seen the basics of using the Netscape LDAP C API. In particular, we have focused on binding, searching, sorting entries, as well as manipulating the LDAP database by adding, deleting and modifying an entry.

LDAP client programming is where you will likely spend most of your time with LDAP development. While languages like Perl and Java seem to be making C programming appear like a dinosaur language, this is not the case. There are many more applications being developed in C than in Java. This is not to knock Java (as Java is the likely next major non-Windows programming language), but just a simple fact.

Also given that more and more operating systems makers are announcing native support for LDAP in their products, C LDAP client programming will grow in importance, because most systems programming is done in C.

Programming with the PerLDAP SDK

In this chapter, we will be exploring how to program LDAP clients with Perl. The Perl programming language has been a long time favorite for Unix system administrators, but has really come into prominence as the preferred language for developing Common Gateway Interface (CGI) applications for the web. Perl runs on just about every known operating system including all versions of Unix, Windows and Macintosh. For more information on the Perl language itself, you should check out the resources at the Perl homepage: `http://www.perl.com`.

There are some things to note about the PerLDAP SDK. The library requires that the Netscape C SDK be installed on your system. Since the C SDK is now an open source project, this shouldn't be a problem. At the time I'm writing this, the entire object-oriented wrappers around the C SDK were not entirely in place, so some functionality appears to be missing, but it's actually there – it's just not that pretty.

In particular, we will focus on:

❑ Connecting and binding to the LDAP server
❑ Searching an LDAP server
❑ LDAP URLs
❑ An LDAP WWW gateway

As in the previous chapter, the code examples presented here are based on the assumption that you have the sample data from `airius.ldif` *installed, with* `o=airius.com` *as your root, and that you are using the default port, 389. You will need to edit the code samples if this is not the case.*

First a Word From Our Sponsor

No this isn't a commercial, I just thought it would be a cute title for this section. I assume that if you are reading this chapter, you've at least heard of Perl, and probably have done at least a little bit of Perl programming. If not, I am assuming that you at least understand the basic tenets of programming and the concepts of object-oriented (OO) programming.

Perl is a bit different than your traditional computer language. The differences are largely derived from the fact that Perl was created by a linguist and not a computer scientist, and that it was designed to be an improvement upon the available tools that existed at the time for the lazy system administrator. (Laziness is what makes a good system administrator, after all why would we automate things if we weren't lazy?)

Again, if you are not familiar with Perl, I recommend you get a book on it, and there are many good ones out there, or you could grab an issue of the Perl Journal. At least scan through the www.perl.com web site.

The real issues I want to discuss are the concept of Perl modules and Perl's interface with C.

Perl Modules

Perl modules provide two services to the Perl programmer:

❑ They allow us to manage large development projects, in particular those that use code others have written, without having to worry about variable and function name collisions

❑ They allow for abstraction of applications – for example, we can call a method `printPage()` that sends text to a printer without caring exactly how `printPage()` actually gets the job done

Modules are to Perl what classes are to C++ and Java. In Perl, classes and modules are one and the same. Perl modules provide for object-oriented behavior in Perl if you want to use it, although you can also use modules like standard programming APIs and stick to just a procedural style without any object-oriented mechanisms. However, at the moment, Perl doesn't support traditional object-oriented mechanisms like private functions or variables within the language, like Java and C++ do.

In summary, the PerLDAP SDK is a Perl module, which is a collection of Perl code packaged in a way to make it easier to program with.

The way most of us see it, Perl has the following main strengths:

1. It is easy to use, in particular when compared to shell programming, where you need to connect together a series of command line utilities (something that is common in Unix but not so common in Windows)

2. Its text processing powers are second to no other language

3. It can easily interface with C (and vice versa), which makes it easy to improve the efficiency of Perl programs and to program in C when the need arises

The PerLDAP and C SDKs

The last point above is exactly what the PerLDAP SDK does. It is a Perl wrapper around the Netscape C SDK, which provides a fully functional interface to LDAP with the built in effectiveness of the C SDK. Most of the time you will use the OO interface to the SDK, but if you need to get access to the actual C SDK, you can. Indeed, you might want to, if you need to access a feature not yet implemented in PerLDAP, such as asynchronous functions. I'm often fond of saying that Perl makes C programming bearable. Or to quote another Perl saying, 'Perl keeps the easy things easy and the hard things possible.'

If you need to gain access to functions not specified in the OO interface, you should read the earlier chapter on the Netscape C SDK, as I will only discuss the Perl OO interface in this chapter.

Installing PerLDAP

You can get PerLDAP SDK from:

- ❑   `http://developer.netscape.com/directory/`
- ❑   `http://www.mozilla.org/directory`
- ❑   The Comprehensive Perl Archive Network (CPAN) at `http://www.perl.com/CPAN/`

At the time of writing, the Perl for Windows is available in two versions. One was built from the Perl source by Gurusamy Sarathy and the other was from a company called ActiveState. The ActiveState port doesn't always allow you to use all of the available modules for Perl, in particular those modules that required binding to a C library. ActiveState and the core Perl team are working on bringing both versions into a single standard, which should have been Perl 5.005. Unfortunately I couldn't get the PerLDAP to work with Perl 5.005 on Windows, so for the examples in this chapter, I used the 'pure' Windows Perl from Gurusamy Sarathy. To be honest the Perl team is working hard at getting full support on the ActiveState version, so by the time you read this, there should be only one version of Perl for Windows.

Summarized below are the steps you need to follow to get PerLDAP working on Windows NT (Windows NT 4 Workstation with Service Pack 3):

1.   Download Gurusamy Sarathy's Perl at:
     `ftp://ftp.cs.colorado.edu/pub/perl/CPAN/ports/win32/Standard/x86/perl 5.00402-bindist04-bc.zip`

2.   Install Perl following the instructions contained in the distribution

3.   Install the Netscape Directory SDK for C if you haven't already. Make sure that you put the file `nsldapssl32v30.dll` in the system32 directory of your Windows NT system directory (`WinNT`). If you wan to set this up for Windows 95, you put it the DLL in the system directory of your Windows directory.

4.   Get the PerLDAP distribution from `http://developer.netscape.com/directory/` (or any of the suggestions listed above) and unzip it.

5. Install the PerLDAP by typing `perl install-bin` at the command prompt inside the unzipped directory.

6. You can test to see if you have everything is working by using one of the example scripts that ships with PerLDAP. The easiest example to use without any prior knowledge is the `qsearch.pl` script which works almost exactly as the `ldapsearch` command line tool.

Here's an example of how to run it:

```
E:\perldap\examples>perl qsearch.pl -h localhost -p 389 -b "o=airius.com"
sn=Carter
```

7. If you still have trouble, try reading the PerLDAP FAQ at `http://www.mozilla.org/directory/` or asking at the PerLDAP newsgroup, which is available at the same URL.

PerLDAP Module Reference

PerLDAP is actually made up of several different modules, but you normally only interact with a single module, `Mozilla::LDAP::Conn`. This means that this is a module called `Conn` which has two parent classes (or modules, they mean the same thing in Perl), called `LDAP` and `Mozilla`.

Why is the first parent class called `Mozilla`? The reason is that `Mozilla` was the nickname of the original Netscape browser. (In fact, Netscape still refers to itself as `Mozilla` when communicating to the web server.) When Netscape opened the source to its browser, they named it the *Mozilla Project*. And PerLDAP was the first original product to come out of the opening of the Directory SDK sources, so that's why it's parent class is `Mozilla`.

Here are the four classes/modules for PerLDAP and an explaination of what each one does:

❑ `Mozilla::LDAP::Conn` – we use this class for most of our interaction with the server, including binding, searching and modifying

❑ `Mozilla::LDAP::Entry` – we use this class when dealing with individual LDAP entries and there are methods for getting/setting attributes, printing out the values as LDIF, etc

❑ `Mozilla::LDAP::API` – this class contains the wrappers around all of the functions in the C SDK and is used internally by PerLDAP

❑ `Mozilla::LDAP::Utils` – this class where routines that are useful to PerLDAP but don't really belong anywhere else get placed, such as the `ldapArgs()` function for processing command line arguments for LDAP routines

❑ `Mozilla::LDAP::LDIF` – this class comprises routines designed to make it easier to work with LDIF files

Connecting and Binding to the LDAP Server

The first thing you must do before you can access an LDAP server is to make a connection to it. As with many Perl functions, there is more than one way to do it. The right way is the one that works for your application.

To set up a new connection and a Perl object to perform operations against an LDAP server, you must create a reference to a `Mozilla::LDAP::Conn` object. When you create this object, you can specify the hostname of the LDAP server, the port, a distinguished name and password to bind as. You also have the option of using X.509 certificates for authentication if your server supports such an operation.

The parameters can either be specified one at time or by passing the options using a **hash**. We'll be looking at examples of both of these methods in just a moment. For Perl rulebook lawyers, a hash is actually an associative array, but most people call them *hashes* or *hash tables*. An associative array is like a traditional array, except that the key can be anything (such as a string), as opposed to just being an integer. The hash can be created by hand or by using the `Mozilla::LDAP::Utils::ldapArgs()` method, which constructs the hash by using command line arguments.

Note that you can trap the inability to establish a connection with the standard Perl syntax, `||` `die("...")`.

The code extract below shows how you can establish an LDAP connection object with scalar (singular) values:

```perl
#!/usr/local/bin/perl
#Import the most common PerLDAP modules
use Mozilla::LDAP::Conn;
use Mozilla::LDAP::Utils;
...

#This is an example of anonymous bind
#create connection
my $ldap = new Mozilla::LDAP::Conn("localhost",389,NULL,NULL) ;

#This is an example of authenticated bind
my $ldap = new
   Mozilla::LDAP::Conn("localhost",389,"uid=scarter,ou=People,o=airius.com",
                            "sprain") || die("Failed to establish an LDAP
connection.\n");
...
```

Here, we establish the connection and bind to the server by passing all of the necessary arguments to the `Mozilla::LDAP::Conn` constructor. These parameters are:

- ❑ The name of the server — `"localhost"`
- ❑ The port number — `389`
- ❑ The DN of the entry we wish to bind as — `"uid=scarter,ou=People,o=airius.com"`
- ❑ The entry's password — `"sprain"`

In the following extract, we are going to do the same thing, but instead of passing the parameters we will build a hash table first, where the keys are the names of the parameters the constructor is expecting. We then pass this hash table to the constructor, rather than the individual parameters, as we did above. For example, here is how we build the hash table:

```
my %ld = ();

#populate the hash
$ld->{"host"} = "localhost";
$ld->{"port"} = 389;
$ld->{"root"} = "o=airius.com";

#could bind as a user like this:
$ld->{"bind"} = "uid=scarter,ou=People,o=airius.com"
$ld->{"pswd"}= "sprain";

#this would bind anonymous
#$ld->{"bind"} = NULL;
#$ld->{"pswd"}= NULL;

#if you can use X.509 certificates, this is where you would put the BASE-64
encoded #string
$ld->{"cert"} = NULL;
```

After we have built the hash table, we can then pass it to the `Mozilla::LDAP::Conn` constructor like this:

```
my $ldap = new Mozilla::LDAP::Conn(\%ld) ||
                          die("Failed to establish an LDAP connection.\n");
```

The next example illustrates how you can establish an LDAP connection object with a hash table variable using the `ldapArgs()` utility method:

```
#!/usr/local/bin/perl
#Import the most common PerLDAP modules
use Mozilla::LDAP::Conn;
use Mozilla::LDAP::Utils;

#create hash
my %ld = ();

#populate hash
%ld = Mozilla::LDAP::Utils::ldapArgs()
|| die("Failed to establish an LDAP connection. \n");

#must pass hashes by reference
#create the connection object
my $ldap = new Mozilla::LDAP::Conn(\%ld);
...
```

The above extract uses the `ldapArgs()` method of the `Mozilla::LDAP::Utils` class. This method (a method in Perl can also be called a subroutine, use which ever term you feel most comfortable with) builds a hash table that you can pass to the `Conn` constructor. It builds this hash table using command line switches, the same command line switches you use when interacting with the standard LDAP command line tools (e.g. `ldapsearch` and `ldapmodify`) that go back to the original University of Michigan LDAP release. These switches are: `-b` *base* `-h` *host* `-D` *bind* `-w` *pswd* `-P` *cert filter*. So, if you are running a program, `sample.pl`, which uses this method to connect to LDAP, then you would need to call it like this:

```
perl sample.pl -b o=airius.com -h MyServer -p 389 -D
uid=scarter,ou=People,o=airius.com -w sprain
```

After you have established a connection object, you are ready to perform operations against the LDAP server.

Searching an LDAP Server

The most common operation to be performed by any application you will develop will be to search an LDAP server. Almost all advanced LDAP applications use the search functions as a core function. Essentially, all search functions take an LDAP connection handle, the base to start the search from, the scope of the search and a search filter. For more information on searching and determining the LDAP scope for searching, you should refer back to Chapter 6.

If the search is successful, it will return a `Mozilla::LDAP::Entry` object. You can then step through the search results using the `nextEntry()` method of this `Mozilla::LDAP::Entry` object.

Later in this section, we'll look at the various ways you can manipulate the values of this object to get back the attributes and values of each returned entry.

The Search Operation

In the majority of existing LDAP SDKs, the actual binding of the connection – the first step you must perform before doing any operation – is separate from the initial connection. In PerLDAP, however, this is not the case. The bind is made at the initial start of the connection, in the `new()` method call. This really doesn't pose any problems for us (or at least I haven't encountered any in my development so far), but it is different from, say, connecting with Directory SDK for Java. So, after you have created an LDAP object, you are connected to the LDAP server.

The way we actually perform the search is with the search method of the `Mozilla::LDAP::Conn` object. We must give it the search base, the scope and of course the filter to search.

After performing the search, we check to see if it actually returned any results with the `if (!$entry)` statement. If there are any returned, we then step through each result until there are no more. For each result, we print out the entire record with the `$entry->printLDIF()` statement. The `printLDIF()` function is a method of the `Mozilla::LDAP::Entry` object.

To demonstrate the difference between searching while using an anonymous bind and a search that has its connection with a bind to a particular entry, we will retrieve the LDAP server's configuration entry (`dn: cn=config`). First, let's see what happens when we perform an anonymous bind:

```perl
#!/usr/local/bin/perl
#search.pl
use strict;
use Mozilla::LDAP::Conn;

my $host = "localhost";
my $port = 389;
my $dn = "";
my $passwd = "";

#get the configuration schema for the server
my $base = "cn=config";

my $filter= "objectclass=*";
my $scope = "subtree";

#get LDAP connection
my $ldap = new Mozilla::LDAP::Conn($host,$port,$dn,$passwd)
                                        || die("Failed to open LDAP
connection.\n");

#this returns a Mozilla::LDAP::Entry object
my $entry = $ldap->search($base, $scope, $filter);

if (! $entry)
{
    print "Search failed. Try again\n";
}
else
{
    while ($entry)
    {
        #print out Entry
        $entry->printLDIF();
        $entry = $ldap->nextEntry();
    }
}
```

Running this code will produce the following output:

```
dn: cn=SNMP,cn=config
objectclass: top
objectclass: nsSNMP
cn: SNMP
nssnmpenabled: on
nssnmporganization:
nssnmplocation:
nssnmpcontact:
nssnmpdescription:
nssnmpmasterhost:
nssnmpmasterport:
```

In order to try out this example as an authenticated user, you only need to change two lines, to supply a DN and a password, for example:

```perl
my $dn = "cn=Directory Manager";
my $passwd = "password";
```

Clearly, you'll need to edit the script to use your own Directory Manager's password. Shown below is some example output from this second script – it's not all included, as there's so much or it, as you will see if you try out the example yourself.

```
dn: cn=7-bit check,cn=plugins,cn=config
objectclass: top
objectclass: nsslapdPlugin
objectclass: extensibleObject
cn: 7-bit check
nsslapd-pluginpath: d:/netscape/ds4/lib/uid-plugin.dll
nsslapd-plugininitfunc: NS7bitAttr_Init
nsslapd-plugintype: preoperation
nsslapd-pluginid: NS7bitAttr
nsslapd-pluginversion: 4.0
nsslapd-pluginvendor: Netscape Communications
nsslapd-plugindescription: Enforce  7-bit clean attribute values
nsslapd-pluginenabled: on
nsslapd-backend: cn=ldbm
nsslapd-pluginarg0: uid
nsslapd-pluginarg1: mail
nsslapd-pluginarg2: userpassword
nsslapd-pluginarg3: ,
nsslapd-pluginarg4: o=airius.com

dn: cn=Binary Syntax,cn=plugins,cn=config
objectclass: top
objectclass: nsslapdPlugin
objectclass: extensibleObject
```

When you perform a search on the LDAP server, it will return all of the attributes available to you for an entry by default. You can (and indeed should) save on bandwidth and client side resources by restricting the number of attributes you have returned to your client. You can do so like this:

```
my $entry = $ldap->search($base, $scope, $filter, 0, @attribs);
```

We now have two new parameters in the search() call: 0 and @attribs. The fourth parameter of the search() method specifies whether you want to return both values and attribute names or just the attribute names (the default is 0 and means that you want to return both). The @attribs argument is an array of attribute names representing the attributes you want to have returned by the search. The next example shows this in full detail:

```perl
#!/usr/local/bin/perl
#search.pl
use strict;
use Mozilla::LDAP::Conn;
use Mozilla::LDAP::Utils;
use Mozilla::LDAP::Entry;

my $host = "localhost";
my $port = 389;
my $dn = "";
my $passwd = "";
my $base = "o=airius.com";

my $filter =  "(sn=Carter)";
my $scope = "subtree";
```

```
my @attribs;
push(@attribs,"cn");
push(@attribs,"mail");
push(@attribs,"telephonenumber");

#get LDAP connection
my $ldap = new Mozilla::LDAP::Conn($host,$port,$dn,$passwd) || die("Failed to open
LDAP connection.\n");

#this returns a Mozilla::LDAP::Entry object
my $entry = $ldap->search($base, "subtree", "(sn=Carter)",0,@attribs);

if (! $entry)
{
    print "Search failed. Try again\n";
}
else
{
    while ($entry)
    {
        #print out Entry
        $entry->printLDIF();
        $entry = $ldap->nextEntry();
    }
}
```

This code will produce the following output:

As you can see, only the attributes that were specified in the @attribs array have been returned, that is, cn, mail and telephonenumber.

Modifying the LDAP Database

In this section, we are going to learn how to add new entries, modify existing entries and finally how to remove entries.

Add a New Entry

Remember that when we add a new entry, it must have all of the attributes required by the entry's object class and the optional attributes must be allowed by the entry's object class. This includes specifying all of the object classes, and the minimum of the required attributes for the object classes. If you do not follow these rules, the server should throw an error. I say *should* because the LDAP RFCs specify this behavior, but many LDAP servers (including Netscape's Directory Server) allow you to turn schema checking off. If you do this, you run a rather high risk of losing data integrity.

First, you create an entry with the `Mozilla::LDAP::Entry` object and set the distinguished name of that entry with the `setDN()` method on the entry object.

There are 2 ways of assigning attribute values:

❑ Set the attribute as a hash table, with the name of the attribute as the key – for example, `$entry->{'objectclass'} = ['top'];`.
❑ You can use the `addValue()` method, for example `$entry->addValue("sn","Wilcox");`.

Note that if you are setting an object class attribute that extends an existing object class, you must list all of the parent object class values. For example:

```
$entry->{'objectclass'} =
['top','person','organizationalPerson','inetOrgPerson'];.
```

Finally, you must bind as a user and the user must have proper rights to add a new entry. This whole process is illustrated in the code example below:

```perl
#!/usr/local/bin/perl
use strict;
use Mozilla::LDAP::Conn;
use Mozilla::LDAP::Utils;
use Mozilla::LDAP::Entry;

my $host = "localhost";
my $port = 389;

#a directory administrator
my $dn = "uid=kvaughan, ou=People, o=airius.com";
my $passwd = "bribery";
my $base = "o=airius.com";

#build the entry
my $entry = new Mozilla::LDAP::Entry();
$entry->setDN("uid=mwilcox,ou=People,o=airius.com");
$entry->{objectclass}= ["top","person","organizationalPerson","inetOrgPerson"];
$entry->addValue("cn","Mark Wilcox");
$entry->addValue("sn","Wilcox");
$entry->addValue("givenname","Mark");
```

```
$entry->addValue("mail","mwilcox\@airius.com");
$entry->addValue("ou","People");
$entry->addValue("ou","Accounting");
$entry->addValue("uid","mwilcox");

#get LDAP connection
my $ldap = new Mozilla::LDAP::Conn($host,$port,$dn,$passwd) || die("Failed to open
connect.\n");

$entry->printLDIF();
$ldap->add($entry);

#This will only be set if an error occurred
if ($ldap->getErrorCode())
{
    print $ldap->printError();
}
```

When run, this code will give the following output:

```
dn: uid=mwilcox,ou=People,o=airius.com
cn: Mark Wilcox
sn: Wilcox
givenname: Mark
mail: mwilcox@airius.com
ou: People
ou: Accounting
uid: mwilcox
```

You can confirm that the entry has been added by browsing the Directory Server.

Modify an Entry

You can also modify just particular attributes of an entry. When you do this, you have the option of adding new attributes, replacing the values of an existing attribute or deleting an attribute. Replacing a non-existent attribute is treated as the equivalent as adding a new one. Also, if there are multiple values for a particular entry, for example, someone has more than one common name, and you perform a replace with only a single value, all of the existing values will be removed.

You can get the current values of an entry in similar manner to the way you add values. Also, you can modify an entry using the same methods as you would when creating an entry from scratch. These would be by using methods like getDN(), getValue() or by hash.

As with an add operation, you must have the appropriate access rights to modify entries. It's also useful to know that in most LDAP servers, modification rights vary between entries. For example, in most systems, users can change their password, but not their name or user ID, whereas managers can change their names, contact information and so on. On the other hand, it usually takes a database administrator to perform operations like changing a user ID or distinguished name.

The code example below demonstrates how you could modify the entry we have just added for Mark Wilcox, to add an extra common name and to change the e-mail address:

```perl
#!/usr/local/bin/perl
use strict;
use Mozilla::LDAP::Conn;
use Mozilla::LDAP::Utils;
use Mozilla::LDAP::Entry;

my $host = "localhost";
my $port = 389;
my $dn = "uid=kvaughan, ou=Pesople, o=airius.com";
my $passwd = "bribery";
my $base = "o=airius.com";

#my @attribs;
push(@attribs,"cn");
push(@attribs,"mail");
push(@attribs,"telephonenumber");

#get LDAP connection
my $ldap = new Mozilla::LDAP::Conn($host,$port,$dn,$passwd) || die("Failed to open
connect.\n");

#this returns a Mozilla::LDAP::Entry object
my $entry = $ldap->search($base, "subtree", "(uid=mwilcox)",0,@attribs);

if (! $entry)
{
    print "Search failed. Try again\n";
}
else
{
    #print out Entry
    print "Old LDIF:\n";
    $entry->printLDIF();

    #now modify attribute
    $entry->{mail}=["bigboss\@airius.com"];
    $entry->{cn}=["Mark Wilcox","Mark E. Wilcox"];
    print"\nNew LDIF:\n";
    $entry->printLDIF();
    print "\nCN count:\n";

    #count number of Common Names
    print $entry->size("cn"),"\n";
    $ldap->update($entry);

    if ($ldap->getErrorCode())
    {
        print $ldap->printError();
    }
}
```

Running this code and you get the following output:

```
Old LDIF:
dn: uid=mwilcox,ou=People,o=airius.com
cn: Mark Wilcox
mail: mwilcox@airius.com
```

```
New LDIF:
dn: uid=mwilcox,ou=People,o=airius.com
cn: Mark Wilcox
cn: Mark E. Wilcox
mail: bigboss@airius.com

CN count:
2
```

You can verify the change in Directory Server:

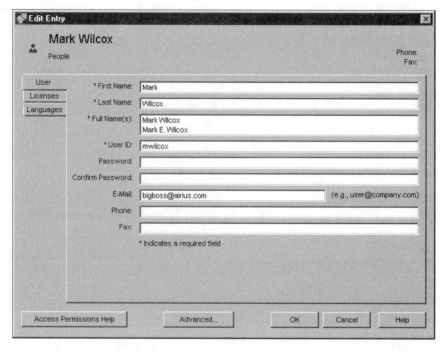

Remember how we have talked about the problems with replacing multi-valued attributes? (For example, if you replace a multiple-valued attribute with a single-valued one, it replaces all of the existing values) Let's look at an example of how to deal with that.

Say we have an entry for Sam Carter who has two values for his cn attribute, Sam Carter and Samuel Eugene Carter. Sam decides he would like to replace the "Eugene" with simply the initial "E.". To make this happen, our application must retrieve his entry from the server and make a copy of his current cn attribute. Then we must remove the offending value Samuel Eugene Carter from the value array and replace it with correct value Samuel E. Carter.

Here is the example program that does just that:

```
#!/usr/local/bin/perl
#multivaluemod.pl
use strict;
use Mozilla::LDAP::Conn;
```

```perl
my $host = "localhost";
my $port = 389;
my $dn = "cn=Directory Manager";
my $passwd = "jessica98";


#set the base to Sam Carter's entry for quick lookup
my $base = "uid=scarter,ou=People,o=airius.com";

#must have filter
my $filter = "uid=scarter";

#will only retrieve Sam's entry
my $scope = "base";

my @attribs;

$attribs[0] = "cn"; #we only want this attribute

my $bad_value = "Samuel Eugene Carter"; #value we want to replace
my $good_value = "Samuel E. Carter";   #our new value

#get LDAP connection
my $ldap = new Mozilla::LDAP::Conn($host,$port,$dn,$passwd) || die("Failed to open
connect\n");

#this returns a Mozilla::LDAP::Entry object
my $entry = $ldap->search($base, $scope, $filter,0,@attribs);

if (! $entry)
{
   die("Search failed.\n");
}
else
{
   #should only have 1 entry

   #get the current values of the CN
   my @cn = @{$entry->{'cn'}};

   #remove old value
   #replace "bad" value with "good" value
   $entry->removeValue("cn",$bad_value);
   $entry->addValue("cn",$good_value);

   # now add the modifications
   $ldap->update($entry);

   if ($ldap->getErrorCode())
   {
      print $ldap->printError();
   }


   #and print the new results
   my $new_entry = $ldap->search($base, $scope, $filter,0,@attribs);

   if (! $new_entry)
   {
      die("Search failed.\n");
   }
   else
```

```
        {
            $new_entry->printLDIF();
        }

    }
```

Delete an Entry

The procedure for deleting entries is quite straightforward. It removes an entry from the LDAP server's database. All you have to do is specify the distinguished name of the entry to be removed. The rights to do this are usually reserved to just a few people like the LDAP server administrators.

```perl
#!/usr/local/bin/perl
#delete.pl
use strict;
use Mozilla::LDAP::Conn;
use Mozilla::LDAP::Utils;
use Mozilla::LDAP::Entry;

my $host = "localhost";
my $port = 389;
my $dn = "uid=kvaughan, ou=People, o=airius.com";
my $passwd = "bribery";
my $base = "o=airius.com";
my $del_dn = "uid=mwilcox,ou=People,o=airius.com";

#get LDAP connection
my $ldap = new Mozilla::LDAP::Conn($host,$port,$dn,$passwd) || die("Failed to open
connect.\n");

$ldap->delete($del_dn);

if ($ldap->getErrorCode())
{
    print $ldap->printError();
}
else
{
    print "User deleted\n";
}
```

The following output confirms that the entry has been deleted:

```
User deleted
```

Once again you can verify this by browsing through the entries in the Directory Server:

LDAP URLs

As we discussed in the last chapter, the LDAP v3 committee designed the LDAP URL format so that you can specify all of an LDAP operation in a single string that can be used inside a web browser. This includes specifying the hostname, port, search base, scope, attributes to return, search filter and even binding.

Here is an example LDAP URL:

```
ldap://ldap.airius.com:389/o=airius.com?ou,cn,mail?sub?(sn=Carter)
```

Currently only the Netscape and Internet Explorer browsers versions 4 and above supports LDAP URLs directly. Most of the common LDAP SDKs support LDAP URLs, which enables you to use the simplicity of the URL format in any number of different LDAP client environments.

The following code example illustrates the usage of LDAP URLs from within a Perl program:

```perl
#!/usr/local/bin/perl
#url.pl
use strict;
use Mozilla::LDAP::Conn;
use Mozilla::LDAP::Utils;
use Mozilla::LDAP::Entry;

my $host = "localhost";
my $port = 389;
my $dn = "uid=kvaughn,ou=People,o=airius.com";
my $passwd = "bribery";
my $base = "o=airius.com";
my $filter ="(uid=scarter)";
my $scope = "sub";

my @attribs;
push(@attribs,"cn");
push(@attribs,"mail");
push(@attribs,"telephone");

#get LDAP connection
my $ldap = new Mozilla::LDAP::Conn($host,$port,"","")|| die("Failed to open LDAP
connection.\n");

#this returns a Mozilla::LDAP::Entry object
my $url = "ldap://$host:$port/$base?";
my $attribute;
foreach $attribute(@attribs)
{
    $url .=$attribute.",";
}

$url =~ s/,$//;
$url .= "?".$scope;
$url .= "?".$filter;
print "url: $url\n";
my $entry = new Mozilla::LDAP::Entry();
if ($ldap->isURL($url))
{
    $entry = $ldap->searchURL($url);
}
else
{
    die("$url is not a valid LDAP URL\n");
}

if (! $entry)
{
```

```
        print "Search failed. Try again\n";
   }
   else
   {
      while ($entry)
      {
          #print out Entry
          $entry->printLDIF();
          $entry = $ldap->nextEntry();
      }
   }
}
```

The output from this program looks like this:

```
url: ldap://localhost:389/o=airius.com?cn,mail,telephone?sub?(uid=scarter)
dn: uid=scarter, ou=People, o=airius.com
cn: Sam Carter
mail: scarter@airius.com
```

A WWW LDAP Gateway in Perl

The Perl programming language is being used in all sorts of pursuits. However, it will probably forever be linked with writing CGI programs for the World Wide Web. Because of this, our 'real world' example will be a very simple Perl/CGI WWW LDAP gateway.

The example is made up of two Perl scripts: `search.pl`, which performs the searching and `mod.pl`, which handles the modifications of entries.

To install this gateway you will need a Web server that lets you run CGI programs. As far as I know all major Web servers do let you do this pretty easy including Apache, Netscape Enterprise Server and Microsoft IIS.

> *You might be able to get this to run with the Microsoft Personal Web server, but from what I've read, that particular web server doesn't run Perl based CGI very well. Note that in order to run Perl scripts on IIS, you need to configure your properties so that* `.pl` *files are handled by* `perl.exe`. *You can do this by going to the Management Console and opening the* **Properties** *dialog for your web site. Go to the* **Home Directory** *tab and select* **Configure**. *On the* **App Mappings** *tab, enter the path for your executable, for example, C:\perl\bin\perl.exe %s %s. NB. The two* %s*'s are important and your scripts won't work without them. For more information on working with Perl5 and IIS4, check out the FAQ at* `http://www.whitecrow.demon.co.uk/steve/iis4.html`.

You'll need to add the `search.pl` and `mod.pl` to a CGI directory on your web server. Consult your server documentation on how to set this up if you don't know how. You start the application by browsing to `http://MyServer/mycgi-bin-dir/search.pl/`.

How Is This Going to Work?

Both of these examples use the `CGI.pm` module for handling the details of dealing with CGI from Perl. This module has been a standard part of Perl since version 5.004, but if you don't already have it you can get it from `http://www.perl.com/CPAN/`.

Search.pl

The first example program is called `search.pl`. Here is the full listing:

```perl
#!/usr/local/bin/perl
#search.pl
#search LDAP server
use CGI;     # CGI library
use CGI::Carp qw(fatalsToBrowser); #Echo error messages to browser and server log
use URI::URL;
use Mozilla::LDAP::Conn;  #LDAP module
use Mozilla::LDAP::Utils; #LDAP module

my $query = new CGI;

my $www_host = "localhost"; #hostname for your webserver
my $www_port = 80; #port number for your webserver

#parameters for the search - modify as appropriate
my $ldap_host = "localhost";
my $ldap_port = 389;
my $ldap_base = "o=airius.com";
my $dn = "";
my $pwd = "";

if ($query->request_method() eq "GET")
{
    #Build the search form
    print $query->header;
    print $query->start_html(-title=>'Search Form');
    print $query->h1("PerLDAP Search Gateway");

    my $action = $query->url;
    print $query->startform(-method=>'POST',
                            -action=>$action,
                           );
    print "<TABLE border=0>\n";
    print "<TR><TD>Enter LDAP Search Filter</TD><TD>";
    print $query->textfield('filter',"",50),"</TD></TR></TABLE>";
    print $query->br();
    print $query->submit();
    print $query->endform();
    print $query->end_html();
}
else
{
    print $query->header;
    print $query->start_html(-title=>'Search Results');
    my $filter = $query->param('filter');


    my $ldap = new Mozilla::LDAP::Conn($ldap_host,$ldap_port,$dn,$pwd) ||
                                die("Failed to open LDAP conenction.\n");

    my $entry = $ldap->search($ldap_base, "subtree",$filter);
    print $query->h1("LDAP Search Results");
    if (! $entry)
    {
        print "$filter did not return any results";
    }
    else
    {
```

```
          # I hacked this routine from the printLDIF routine
      while ($entry)
      {
          print "<TABLE border=3>";
          my $dn = $entry->getDN();
          my $uid = $entry->{uid}[0];

          #now hack dn so we can send it without losing dn
          my $test = "http://your_own_url_here/mod.pl?entry=$uid";
          my $url = new URI::URL($test);
          my $url_encode = $url->equery();
          print "<TR><TD>DN:</TD><TD> $dn </TD>";

          #only modify person entries
          if ($entry->hasValue("objectclass", "person", 1)){
              print "<TD><a href=\"$test\">Modify Entry</a></TR>";
          }
          else {
              print "</TR>";
          }

          print $query->br();
          my $attr;
          my @vals;
          #hacked this from PerLDAP internals
          foreach $attr (keys(%{$entry}))
          {
              @vals ="";
              next if ($attr =~ /^_.+_$/);
              next if $entry->{"_${attr}_deleted_"};
              grep((push(@vals,$_)), @{$entry->{$attr}});
              my $value;
              foreach $value(@vals)
              {
                  print "<TR><TD>$attr</TD><TD>$value</TD></TR>" unless \\
                  $value=~/^$/;
              }
          }
          print "</TABLE>";
          $entry = $ldap->nextEntry();
      }
      print $query->end_html();
  }
}
```

The first few lines of this example simply import all of the modules we need and declare all of the necessary variables to start the work. The first line that's interesting is this:

```
if ($query->request_method() eq "GET")
```

This tells us that if the method the browser used to call this script was with a "GET" as opposed to a "POST" (which is how we send form data to and from a web server), then we should print out our standard search form. This consists of a text box for the user to enter their search filter, and a button to submit the request.

Now, if the browser request is not a `"GET"`, then we assume it's sending a search request back to us. The search filter will be contained inside a form variable called `'filter'`. We can get the contents of that variable with this line of code:

```
my $filter = $query->param('filter');
```

After we have this data, we then perform a search the LDAP server in the traditional manner.

The difference comes in our output of the data. To make for a better looking web page, the code uses hidden tables for display. Unfortunately, the `printLDIF()` function doesn't give you a lot of flexibility in its output, so I peeked inside the code and (with some help from Leif Hedstrom, who wrote PerLDAP) I embedded the actual `printLDIF()` code inside the script, so that the necessary HTML table tags could be appended to get the desired output.

Here is that routine:

```
foreach $attr (keys(%{$entry}))
{
@vals ="";
next if ($attr =~ /^_.+_$/);
next if $entry->{"_${attr}_deleted_"};
grep((push(@vals,$_)), @{$entry->{$attr}});
my $value;
foreach $value(@vals)
{
print "<TR><TD>$attr</TD><TD>$value</TD></TR>" unless \\
$value=~/^$/;
}
}
```

To make it easier to quickly retrieve an entry from the server so that it can be modified, a link is included on the search results screen to allow the user to obtain the entry from the LDAP server for modification. We use the distinguished name to obtain the entry for modification as this gives the fastest possible lookup. Unfortunately, a DN can't be passed easily to a script because it contains characters (e.g. =) that mean something else in a CGI context, so it needs to be URL encoded, where special characters and spaces are translated to values that can be sent across to the web server. This value is then appended to the URL for the modification script. The code that does this is:

```
#now hack dn so we can send it without losing dn
my $test = "http://your_own_url_here/mod.pl?entry=$uid";
my $url = new URI::URL($test);
my $url_encode = $url->equery();
print "<TR><TD>DN:</TD><TD> $dn </TD>";

#only modify person entries
if ($entry->hasValue("objectclass", "person", 1)){
print "<TD><a href=\"$test\">Modify Entry</a></TR>";
}
```

This screen is the initial search screen:

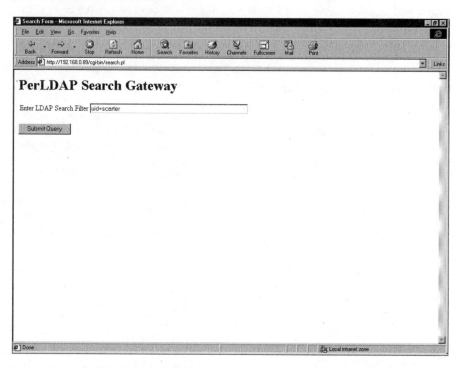

When you enter a search filer and press Submit Query, you should see this results screen:

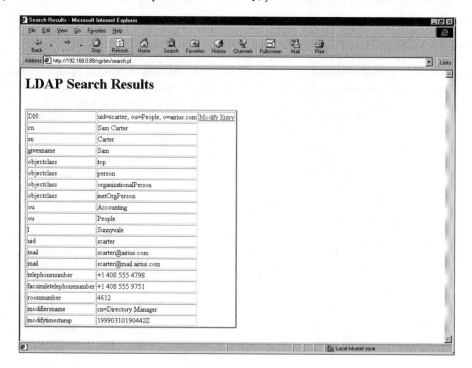

Mod.pl

This code may look complicated, but it is actually pretty simple. The full listing for `mod.pl` is shown here:

```perl
#!/usr/local/bin/perl
#mod.pl
#modify LDAP entry
use strict; # 'encourage' good programming
use CGI;      # CGI library
use CGI::Carp qw(fatalsToBrowser); #Echo error messages to browser and server log
use Mozilla::LDAP::Conn;  #LDAP module
use Mozilla::LDAP::Utils; #LDAP module

my $query = new CGI;

# Modify these for your own settings as appropriate
my $ldap_host = "localhost";
my $ldap_port = 389;
my $dn = "";
my $pwd = "";
my $ldap_base = "o=Airius.com";

if ($query->request_method() eq "GET")
{
    my $query_entry = $query->param("entry");

    #can modify if it is a not person entry
    my $filter = "(&(uid=$query_entry)(objectclass=*person))";

    print $query->header;
    print $query->start_html(-title=>'Modify Form');
    print $query->h1("PerLDAP Modify Gateway");
    my $action = $query->url;
    print $query->startform(-method=>'POST',action=>$action,);
    my $ldap = new Mozilla::LDAP::Conn($ldap_host,$ldap_port,$dn,$pwd) ||
                                   die("Failed to open a LDAP connection.");

    my $entry = $ldap->search($ldap_base,"subtree",$filter);

    if (! $entry)
    {
        die("Oops. You didn't enter a valid person filter.");
    }
    else {
        print "<TABLE border=0>\n";
        my $attr;
        my @vals;
        #hacked this from PerLDAP internals
        print "<TR><TD>dn</TD><TD>",$query->textfield("dn",
                                    $entry->getDN(),50),"</TD></TR>";
        foreach $attr (@{$entry->{"_oc_order_"}})
        {
            @vals ="";
            next if ($attr =~ /^_.+_$/);
            next if $entry->{"_${attr}_deleted_"};
            grep((push(@vals,$_)), @{$entry->{$attr}});
            my $value;
            my $out_string;
            foreach $value(@vals)
            {
```

```
                    #include separator for multi-values;
              $out_string = $value."I".$out_string unless $value=~ /^$/;
        }
     print "<TR><TD>$attr</TD><TD>",
                    $query->textfield($attr,$out_string,50),"</TD></TR>";
     }
   print "<TR><TD>DN</TD><TD>",
                         $query->textfield('mgr_dn',"",50),"</TD></TR>";
   print "<TR><TD>PASSWORD</TD><TD>",
               $query->password_field('mgr_password',"",50),"</TD></TR>";
   print "</TABLE>";
   print $query->submit();
   print $query->endform();
   print $query->end_html();
   }
}
else
{
   my $ldap = new Mozilla::LDAP::Conn($ldap_host,$ldap_port,$dn,$pwd) ||
               die("Failed to open a LDAP connection for modification.");
   my $entry = new Mozilla::LDAP::Entry();
   print $query->header;
   print $query->start_html(-title=>"LDAP Modify Results");
   my @attrs = $query->param;
   my $mgr_dn;
   my $mgr_password;
   foreach my $value (@attrs){
   if ($value eq "mgr_dn")
   {
      $mgr_dn = $query->param($value);
      next;
   }
   if ($value eq "mgr_password")
   {
      $mgr_password= $query->param($value);
      next;
   }
   if ($value eq "dn")
   {
      #print "USER DN:";
      #print $query->param($value),"<BR>";
      print $query->h1("Attempting to modify:");
      $entry = $ldap->search($query->param($value),"base",
                                          "(objectclass=*person)");
```

```
            if (! $entry)
            {
                die("Entered bad entry");
            }
            next;
        }
        else {
            my @vals = split(/\|/,$query->param($value));
            foreach my $val (@vals)
            {
                $entry->addValue($value,$val);
            }
        }
    }
}
#don't allow empty strings
if (($mgr_dn =~ /^$/) || ($mgr_password =~ /^$/))
{
    die("Failed to enter manager dn or password");
}

$ldap = new Mozilla::LDAP::Conn($ldap_host,$ldap_port,$mgr_dn,$mgr_password)
                || die("Failed to open a LDAP connection for modification.");
$ldap->update($entry);

if ($ldap->getErrorCode())
{
    print $query->h1($ldap->printError());
}
else
{
    print $query->h1($entry->getDN());
    print $query->h1("Entry updated");
}
}
```

If the request method is a "GET" (the user clicked on the link we built in our search results), then we send them back a standard HTML form where the attribute names are the labels, and the current attribute values are the form values. The user can then modify any of the values they wish, but these changes will only take affect if the user can bind to the server as an entry with the necessary rights. To allow them to bind to the server, we have two fields at the bottom of the form that allows them to enter a DN and password.

After the form is sent back to the server, we gather all of the form data and build a set of LDAP modifications, using code very similar to the examples covered earlier. Notice that on the LDAP modification, the attribute values are separated with a |. We bind to the server using the DN and password passed to us via the form and attempt an update of the entry. If the update succeeds, we tell the user so, otherwise we tell them that it did not and why. This example is a very basic gateway, but hopefully it provides enough useful code to get you started.

The modification data entry form looks like this:

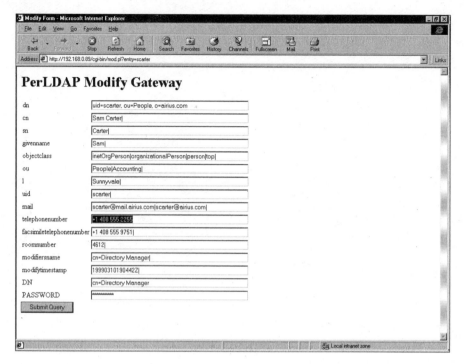

Summary

This chapter has introduced the Netscape PerLDAP SDK and looked at some of the advantages that Perl offers us. As with the last chapter, we have seen how to use the SDK to write some LDAP clients, implementing the basic functionality that we need. Finally, we saw how to use Perl to write an LDAP gateway for the web, allowing the user to search an LDAP server and modify the resulting entries.

The PerLDAP SDK is a very good start for a wrapper around the Netscape C LDAP SDK. By the time you are reading this, it should have already been improved and updated with more functionality. (At the time of writing, version 1.2 has just been released, though there aren't many new functions added but some bugs have been fixed.) PerLDAP version 2.0, which should be out around September 1999, is going to have new features, such as LDAP schema management and the ability to access Netscape Directory Server 4 configuration information. Netscape has already released some extra scripts written with the PerLDAP SDK, including the PerLDAP for Peoplesoft SDK, which is a set of tools written in Perl to make it easier to synchronize a Peoplesoft database with an LDAP database.

Peoplesoft is a set of software that is designed to make it easier to manage human resources information and is used by many organizations. Even if you don't use Peoplesoft, the PerLDAP for Peoplesoft SDK is useful to look at because it gives you a glimpse into one method of migrating information from legacy systems to an LDAP based system.

By providing an official LDAP module for Perl, Netscape has given LDAP developers a valuable 'duct tape' language to help build custom LDAP tools that we need to build and maintain our directory services.

Programming with the Netscape Directory SDK for Java

In this chapter, we will explore how to add LDAP capabilities to your Java applications. We will cover a variety of topics such as:

- Connecting and binding to an LDAP server
- Searching an LDAP server
- Sorting LDAP results
- Adding Entries
- Modifying Entries
- Deleting Entries
- LDAP URLs

Because there are many difficult bridges to cross when writing LDAP enabled Java applets (including browser security restrictions, differences in Java support between browsers and so on), we will only cover Java applications in this chapter. We will touch upon using LDAP from Java servlets in Chapter 13.

I'm assuming that you know the basics about Java (e.g. what packages and classes are, how to compile, etc.). If you need to read more about Java or take a refresher course, there are plenty of books on the subject out there, or you can visit the Java tutorial at `http://java.sun.com/`.

The Netscape Directory SDK for Java can be obtained from either `http://developer.netscape.com/directory/` or `http://www.mozilla.org/directory/`. This SDK has also been released as an open source project, so you have full access to the underlying source code (well all except for some utility libraries that are not essential to the SDK and were not released because they were purchased from the now defunct ORO Inc).

After unzipping the SDK distribution you will need to make sure that the following JAR files are in your CLASSPATH: ldapjdk.jar and ldapfilt.jar. Check with the documentation that comes with the Java Development Kit for your particular operating system to determine how to set your CLASSPATH. The Directory SDK for Java will work against any JDK 1.1 or later.

Most of my examples in this chapter are non-GUI based to keep the non-LDAP code to a minimum. There is nothing, however, to prevent them from being included in a GUI. Note that, as before, these examples use the sample data that comes with Netscape Directory Server.

Directory SDK for Java Packages and Classes

Before we dive into talking about the inner workings of the Directory SDK for Java, we should take a look at the relationship between the packages and classes that make up this SDK.

There are five main packages in the Netscape LDAP SDK for Java. They are:

- ❑ netscape.ldap – this package contains the essential classes that deal with 'core LDAP' including connecting, authentication, searching and modifying the LDAP data
- ❑ netscape.ldap.beans – this package contains classes that have been built as Javabeans, which are the component model of Java (similar to ActiveX)
- ❑ netscape.ldap.controls – this package contains classes that allow your applications to use server-side and client-side controls, which extend the functionality of standard LDAP operations
- ❑ netscape.ldap.util – this package contains classes that provide extra functionality that doesn't really fit in any other package, such as reading/writing LDIF files and Base64 encoding/decoding
- ❑ com.netscape.sasl – this package contains classes that allow your applications to use the Simple Authentication and Security Layer (SASL) protocol, which provides for more secure authentication mechanisms (we'll cover SASL in more detail in Chapter 12)

netscape.ldap Classes

Because we will spend so much of our time in the netscape.ldap package, it is useful to see a list of the classes therein and what they do. The information is summarized in the following tables.

Interfaces

Interface	Description
LDAPEntryComparator	Used to sort the results of a search.
LDAPRebind	Provides the implementation to authenticate to referred LDAP servers during a search referral.
LDAPSocketFactory	Provides different mechanisms for building a socket (e.g. network communication) that can talk LDAP. You would use this interface to add SSL support to your application.

Interface	Description
LDAPv2	Provides the basic functions that are listed in the LDAPv2 draft (RFC 1777).
LDAPv3	Extends the LDAPv2 interface and provides the basic functions that the LDAPv3 draft (RFC 2251) added to LDAPv2.

Classes

Class	Description
LDAPAttribute	Provides objects that represent individual attributes and their values.
LDAPAttributeSchema	Provides objects that represent the schema entry for a particular attribute.
LDAPAttributeSet	A collection class that allows you to get/set the attributes of a particular entry.
LDAPCache	Used to manage a client-side cache to improve search performance.
LDAPCompareAttrNames	Used to compare entries by the values of one or more attributes when sorting search results.
LDAPConnection	At the heart of the netscape.ldap package, this class is used to perform all of our LDAP operations (e.g. connecting, binding, searching and modifying).
LDAPControl	Provides access to an LDAP control, which we can use to access extra functions on the LDAP server.
LDAPDN	Allows us to manipulate distinguished names and relative distinguished names (such as getting the individual parts of a DN and RDN).
LDAPEntry	Allows us to interact with individual LDAP entries, including getting/setting attributes.
LDAPExtendedOperation	Allows us to use an LDAPv3 extended operation such as a persistent search.
LDAPMatchingRuleSchema	Allows us to interact with the schema entries that define how the server should match attributes (e.g. case sensitive, as a DN, etc).
LDAPModification	Allows us to define how an LDAP modification should be performed (which attributes should be replaced, deleted etc.)
LDAPModificationSet	Allows us to deal with a complete set of modifications to be made to an entry.

Table Continued on Following Page

Class	Description
LDAPObjectClassSchema	Represents a schema definition of a particular object class in the LDAP server.
LDAPRebindAuth	Defines how we can automatically re-authenticate ourselves to different LDAP servers during a search referral.
LDAPSSLSocketFactory	Returns an LDAP socket capable of operating over an SSL connection.
LDAPSSLSocketWrap Factory	Also returns an LDAP socket capable of operating over an SSL connection, but with a higher level of abstraction to the programmer.
LDAPSchema	Represents the LDAP server's schema and is how we modify or retrieve information about the schema.
LDAPSchemaElement	Represents a single element in the LDAP server's schema.
LDAPSearchConstraints	Represents 'constraints' you can place on a search (timeout setting, maximum number of results to return, etc).
LDAPSearchResults	Provides methods that allow us to do operate on the results of a LDAP search (getting individual entries, searching referrals, finding the number of entries returned, etc.)
LDAPSortKey	Provides information to the server for doing a server-side sort (which attributes to use for the sort, etc).
LDAPUrl	Handles LDAP URLs, discussed later in this chapter.

Exceptions

Exception	Description
LDAPException	General purpose exception class that is thrown when any LDAP operation that is performed is not successful (e.g. has an LDAP result code that is less than or greater than 0).
LDAPReferralException	Thrown when dealing when a search result. Returns an LDAP referral (discussed in Chapter 12).

Connecting and Binding to an LDAP Server

Most of the LDAP operations you will perform revolve around one particular class in the Java LDAP SDK, the LDAPConnection class. Objects of this class store the connection to the LDAP server and handle the authentication, as well as any operations like searching, modification and deletion. Most of the other classes in the SDK are accessory or utility classes for the LDAPConnection class. The only exceptions are the classes that deal with LDAPEntry objects.

The Connection

Before you can do any LDAP operations against an LDAP server, you must first create a reference to an `LDAPConnection` object like this:

```
LDAPConnection ldap = new LDAPConnection();
```

Then you can connect using the `connect()` method, passing the hostname and port like this:

```
ldap.connect("ldap.somewhere.com",389);
```

Binding (Authentication)

Anonymous Binding

After you connect, you should specify what type of user you are binding as. Some operations may be performed anonymously – and this is the default for the Directory SDK. Servers that only support LDAP v2 (such as Netscape Directory server 1.0 and early versions of OpenLDAP) require that you authenticate yourself, even if you are authenticating anonymously. You use the `authenticate()` method (of the LDAPConnection class) to bind to the server.

For an anonymous bind, the code would be:

```
ldap.authenticate("","");
```

Non-Anonymous Binding

You may wish to bind as a particular user, which is a requirement for any operation that will modify the server. You must bind with the DN of an entry and a password:

```
ldap.authenticate("uid=scarter,ou=People,o=airius.com","sprain");
```

If the authentication fails, an `LDAPException` will be thrown. Like all other exceptions in Java you must either catch the exception or rethrow it so that a superclass or method can deal with it.

LDAP v2 vs LDAP v3

By default, the Directory SDK for Java connects as an LDAPv2 client, so that it can interact with a wide variety of LDAP servers. If you know that your server supports LDAPv3, such as Netscape Directory Server 3 or 4, and in particular if you want to take advantage of server controls, then you need to specify that you are connecting as an LDAPv3 client.

You do this like so:

```
/* Specify the protocol version as our first parameter to let the server know we
are capable of doing LDAPv3. This will fail if the server cannot support LDAPv3 */
ldap.authenticate(3,"uid=scarter,ou=People,o=airius.com","sprain");
```

Connect and Bind in One Step

You can also be a bit lazy (in terms of less lines to type in your program) by connecting and binding in a single step by passing the DN and password in the `connect()` method, like this:

```
ldap.connect("localhost",389,"uid=scarter,ou=People,o=airius.com","sprain");
ldap.connect(3,"localhost",389,"uid=scarter,ou=People,o=airius.com","sprain");
```

Use a Clone and Save Some Bandwidth

The `LDAPConnection` class allows you to make a clone of itself. The clone object will share a single LDAP network connection (including the hostname, port and authentication information), but each operation will be considered separate. Any searches or modifications will happen independently of each other (no matter how many clones you have).

You should not make a clone until after you have connected your original `LDAPConnection` to the server, otherwise clones will not share the same network connection.

If you disconnect a clone, it appears as if the connection has closed to the clone, but the original LDAP connection is left unaffected. The only change occurs if you decide to rebind to the LDAP server. If you rebind inside a clone, it will create an entirely new and separate connection to the server.

This cloning capability allows you to conserve on network resources and object overhead, which can improve your application performance. Clone operations (and the entire Directory SDK) are thread safe. Here is an example of making a clone:

```
/*Call after ldap.connect() */
/* Dolly is the name of the first cloned sheep */
LDAPConnection dolly =  ldap.clone();
```

Further Operations

After you have bound and authenticated you are free to perform any of the various LDAP operations which we will be spending the rest of this chapter discussing.

Disconnect

After you are finished, you should disconnect from the server to free any resources on the server that might have been reserved for this connection. You disconnect like this:

```
ldap.disconnect();
```

Searching an LDAP Server

As we have seen in earlier chapters, searching is the key functionality of any LDAP application, and all search functions take an LDAP connection handle, the base to start the search from, the scope of the search and a search filter. See Chapter 6 for more details.

If the search is successful it will return an LDAPSearchResults object. You can then step through the search results using the next() method of this object. LDAPSearchResults implements the Enumeration interface.

Later in this section, we will show you the various ways you can manipulate the values of this object to access the attributes and values of each returned entry.

The Search Operation

We perform a search using the search() method of the LDAPConnection object, which returns a LDAPSearchResults object. There are four versions of the search method – or to be more exact two search methods and two that use LDAP URLs. There are also five additional read-only methods, which are really just base-level searches. The minimum required parameters are the search base, the scope and a filter, but there are also other parameters we can use to help manage the results.

Here is an example of a LDAP search:

```
LDAPSearchResults res = ld.search(base,scope,filter,null,false);
```

This method takes the following parameters:

❑   base – A string that represents the search base
❑   scope – An integer that represents the scope
❑   filter – A string that is the search filter.

The last two parameters deal with attributes. The spot that contains null takes a String array, which lists the name of the attributes you want to have returned from a search (null means to return all available attributes). The last parameter takes a boolean that specifies whether you want attributes and their values returned, or just the attribute names (false means to have both attributes and their values returned).

The LDAPSearchResults class is an extension of the standard Java Enumeration collection class, where each element it contains is an LDAPEntry object. To step through a set of search results you use some code like this:

```
/* Get the individiual results */
while (res.hasMoreElements())
{
LDAPEntry findEntry = null;
findEntry = (LDAPEntry) res.next();
```

To retrieve the DN of an entry you use the LDAPEntry class's getDN() method, like this:

```
findEntry.getDN();
```

In order for us to retrieve or display the attributes and values of a particular entry, we must get an LDAPAttributeSet from an LDAPEntry object:

```
LDAPAttributeSet attributeSet = findEntry.getAttributeSet();
```

An `LDAPAttributeSet` is a Java `Vector` collection that contains `LDAPAttribute` objects, which represent individual LDAP attributes. To step through the `LDAPAttributeSet`, you can use code that looks like this:

```
for (int i=0;i<attributeSet.size();i++)
{
LDAPAttribute attribute = (LDAPAttribute)attributeSet.elementAt(i);
```

You can also retrieve an individual attribute by name with the `getAttribute()` method of the `LDAPAttribute` class. The `getAttribute()` method takes a parameter that is a `String` variable set to the name of the attribute.

To get the attribute name you use the `getName()` method of the `LDAPAttribute` class:

```
attribute.getName();
```

An attribute can contain text or binary values. The `getStringValues()` and `getByteValues()` methods of the `LDAPAttribute` class will return a standard Java `Enumeration` object to you. If you use the `getStringValues()` method, each `Enumeration` element will contain a `String`, and if you use `getByteValues()`, each `Enumeration` element will contain an array of `byte` values.

Here is an example of getting the `String` values from an attribute:

```
Enumeration enumVals = attribute.getStringValues();
```

To show the difference the way the connection is bound can make on an operation, we are going to perform a search that will retrieve the configuration entry (`cn=config`) in the LDAP server, just as we have in the past two chapters. Our first example will be an anonymous search.

Anonymous Search

Shown below is the complete code listing for an anonymous search on an LDAP server using Netscape's Java SDK:

```
import netscape.ldap.*;
import java.io.*;
import java.util.*;

public class search_anon {

    public static void main(String args[])
    {
        /*define variables for the server and searching */
        String host = "localhost";
        int port = 389;
        String base = "cn=config";
        int scope = LDAPConnection.SCOPE_SUB;
        String dn = "";      //You can also use NULL here
        String pwd = "";     // You can also use NULL here
        String filter = "(objectclass=*)";

        LDAPConnection ld = null;
```

```
    try
    {
        ld = new LDAPConnection();

        /* connect to the server */
        ld.connect(host,port,null,null);

        /* Perform the search */
        LDAPSearchResults res = ld.search(base,scope,filter,null,false);

        /* Get the individiual results */
        while (res.hasMoreElements())
        {
            LDAPEntry findEntry = null;
            findEntry = (LDAPEntry) res.next();
            System.out.println("DN: "+findEntry.getDN());
            LDAPAttributeSet attributeSet = findEntry.getAttributeSet();

            for (int i=0;i<attributeSet.size();i++)
            {
                LDAPAttribute attribute =
                            (LDAPAttribute)attributeSet.elementAt(i);
                String attrName = attribute.getName();
                System.out.println( attrName + ":" );
                Enumeration enumVals = attribute.getStringValues();

                if (enumVals != null) {
                    while ( enumVals.hasMoreElements() ) {
                        String nextValue = ( String )enumVals.nextElement();
                        System.out.println( nextValue );
                    }
                }
            }
        }

        if (ld != null)
        {
            ld.disconnect();
        }
    }
    catch(LDAPException e)
    {
        e.printStackTrace();
    }
  }
}
```

The output of this program will look something like this:

```
DN: cn=SNMP,cn=config
objectclass:
top
nsSNMP
cn:
SNMP
nssnmpenabled:
on
```

```
nssnmporganization:
nssnmplocation:
nssnmpcontact:
nssnmpdescription:
nssnmpmasterhost:
nssnmpmasterport:
```

Authenticated Search

Our next example is the same search, but this time we will authenticate ourselves. The code is exactly the same, except for two minor changes. First, we need to specify a DN and a password in our variable declaration:

```
String dn = "cn=Directory Manager";
String pwd = "password";
```

And secondly, we need to call the `authenticate()` method of the `LDAPConnection` object before we perform the search:

```
    ...
        ld = new LDAPConnection();

        /* connect to the server */
        ld.connect(host,port,null,null);

        /* authenticate */
        ld.authenticate(dn,pwd);

        /* Perform the search */
        LDAPSearchResults res = ld.search(base,scope,filter,null,false);
    ...
```

By default, the search will return all of the attributes that can be retrieved according to the LDAP servers ACLs and what user the connection is bound as. In these first two examples, we are retrieving the `cn=config` entry from the LDAP server, but this time you have authenticated as a non-anonymous user (specifically the Directory Manager). The output should look something like this:

```
DN: cn=7-bit check,cn=plugins,cn=config
objectclass:
top
nsslapdPlugin
extensibleObject
cn:
7-bit check
nsslapd-pluginpath:
d:/netscape/ds4/lib/uid-plugin.dll
nsslapd-plugininitfunc:
NS7bitAttr_Init
nsslapd-plugintype:
preoperation
nsslapd-pluginid:
NS7bitAttr
nsslapd-pluginversion:
4.0
```

```
nsslapd-pluginvendor:
Netscape Communications
nsslapd-plugindescription:
Enforce  7-bit clean attribute values
nsslapd-pluginenabled:
on
nsslapd-backend:
...
```

Selecting Attributes

You can limit the attributes returned by passing an array of names of the attributes you wish to get back like we do here in our third example. Requesting only the attributes you need will speed up the search and reduce the memory requirements on your server and your client.

We are going to perform a more general search in this example, setting the search base to the o=airius.com, which is the root of the directory tree included in the sample Netscape database. We'll also use a search filter of sn=Carter.

We'll have to create an array (called attrs) to contain the list of attribute names we wish to retrieve. Later, when we make the call to the search() method we pass the attrs array with it as the fourth argument:

```
...
    String host = "localhost";
    int port = 389;
    String base = "o=airius.com";
    int scope = LDAPConnection.SCOPE_SUB;
    String dn = "";
    String pwd = "";
    String filter = "(sn=Carter)";

    LDAPConnection ld = null;

    try
    {
        ld = new LDAPConnection();
        ld.connect(host,port,dn,pwd);
        String attrs [] = {"cn","uid","mail"};

        LDAPSearchResults res = ld.search(base,scope,filter,attrs,false );

        while (res.hasMoreElements())
        {
...
```

When the above code is run, you will get output like this:

```
E:\WINNT\System32\cmd.exe                                    _ □ X

E:\Program Files\Netscape\ldapjava\packages>java search
DN: uid=scarter, ou=People, o=airius.com
cn:
Sam Carter
uid:
scarter
mail:
wilcox@mail.airius.com

E:\Program Files\Netscape\ldapjava\packages>
```

As you can see, the attributes returned here are the ones specified in the `attrs` array, that is, `sn`, `uid` and `mail`.

Search Constraints

Not only can you restrict what attributes you can get back, but you can also specify other factors on the search, such as the total number of results that are returned, how long the search can take and so on. This is through the use of the `LDAPSearchConstraints` class.

`LDAPSearchContraints` are unique for any given search, including searches performed over a cloned connection.

The next example is adapted from the previous one, but this time restricted it so that the search only returns three entries:

```
try
{
    ld = new LDAPConnection();
    ld.connect(host,port,dn,pwd);
    String attrs [ ] = {"cn","uid","mail"};
    int maxResults = 3;
    /*Get the existing Constraints for the current connection */
    LDAPSearchConstraints cons = ld.getSearchConstraints();
    cons.setMaxResults(maxResults);

    LDAPSearchResults res = ld.search( base, scope,
    filter, attrs, false,cons);

    System.out.println("Count is "+res.getCount());
    int x = 0;
    while ((res.hasMoreElements()) && (x < maxResults))
    {
      ...
```

This code produces the following output:

```
E:\WINNT\System32\cmd.exe                                          _ □ ×
E:\Program Files\Netscape\ldapjava\packages>java search
Count is 1
DN: uid=scarter, ou=People, o=airius.com
cn:
Sam Carter
uid:
scarter
mail:
wilcox@mail.airius.com
DN: uid=scarte2, ou=People, o=airius.com
cn:
Stephen Carter
uid:
scarte2
mail:
scarte2@airius.com
DN: uid=kcarter, ou=People, o=airius.com
cn:
Karen Carter
uid:
kcarter
mail:
kcarter@airius.com

E:\Program Files\Netscape\ldapjava\packages>
```

LDAP Database Modifications

In this section, we'll be looking at how to modify the data in your LDAP server using Netscape's Java LDAP SDK, including adding and deleting entries, as well as modifying existing ones.

Add an LDAP Entry

To add an entry is pretty simple. First, however, you must build the entry to be added. To do this, we use the following classes:

- ❑ LDAPEntry
- ❑ LDAPAttribute
- ❑ LDAPAttributeSet

The LDAPEntry contains all of the attributes and values for the entry. You build individual attributes with the LDAPAttribute class and then add each attribute you build to an object that is of the class LDAPAttributeSet. Finally, you add the LDAPAttributeSet to the LDAPEntry object.

For addition of an entry to succeed, the new entry must conform to the server's schema (unless the server administrator has schema checking turned off, which is a very bad idea). The connection must also be bound as the user who can add a new entry to the server.

```
import netscape.ldap.*;
import java.io.*;
import java.util.*;

public class add {

    public static void main(String args[])
    {
        String host = "localhost";
        int port = 389;
        String dn = "uid=kvaughan, ou=People, o=airius.com";
        String pwd = "bribery";
        String new_dn = "uid=mwilcox,ou=People,o=airius.com";
        String objectclass_values [] =
                    {"top","person","organizationalperson","inetorgperson"};
        String cn_values [] = {"Mark Wilcox"};
        String sn_values [] = {"Wilcox"};
        String givenname_values [] = {"Mark"};
        String ou_values [] = {"People","Accounting"};
        String uid_values [] = {"mwilcox"};
        String mail_values[] = {"wilcox@mail.airius.com"};
        LDAPAttributeSet attrib_set = null;
        LDAPAttribute attribute = null;
        LDAPEntry entry = null;

        LDAPConnection ld = null;

        try
        {
            ld = new LDAPConnection();

            /* must bind as a user with rights to write to the server */
            ld.connect(host,port,dn,pwd);
            attrib_set = new LDAPAttributeSet();
```

```
            attribute = new LDAPAttribute("objectclass",objectclass_values);
            attrib_set.add(attribute);

            attribute = new LDAPAttribute("cn", cn_values);
            attrib_set.add(attribute);

            attribute = new LDAPAttribute("sn", sn_values);
            attrib_set.add(attribute);

            attribute = new LDAPAttribute("givenname",givenname_values);
            attrib_set.add(attribute);

            attribute = new LDAPAttribute("mail", mail_values);
            attrib_set.add(attribute);

            attribute = new LDAPAttribute("ou",ou_values);
            attrib_set.add(attribute);

            attribute = new LDAPAttribute("uid",uid_values);
            attrib_set.add(attribute);

            /* create the entry object */
            entry = new LDAPEntry(new_dn,attrib_set);

            /* add the object */
            ld.add(entry);

            if (ld != null)
            {
                ld.disconnect();
            }
        }
        catch(LDAPException e)
        {
            e.printStackTrace();
        }
    }
}
```

Run this code and an entry for Mark Wilcox is added to the directory. This is confirmed by browsing through the Directory Server:

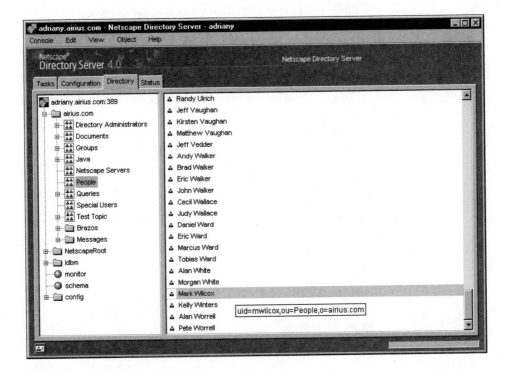

LDAP Entry Modifications

At some point, you are sure to need to make modifications to an LDAP entry. To do this, you use the `LDAPModificationSet` and the `LDAPAttribute` classes. You perform a modification in a similar fashion to creating a new LDAP entry from scratch. The biggest difference is that you must specify what type of modification this will be: either *add*, *replace* or *delete*.

Add is for when you need to add an attribute that doesn't yet exist in the entry. Replace is for changing the value or values of an existing attribute. If the attribute does not exist, replace behaves as add.

> *You should also be aware that if you perform a replace on an attribute that has multiple values, if you don't send the extra values along with your replacement value, they will all be removed. In the last chapter, we saw how this could be done with the PerLDAP SDK, but the same algorithm can be used in both Java and C.*

Finally, if you perform a delete, the attribute and all of its values will be removed.

As with the simple process of adding an entry, described earlier, you must be bound as a user with enough rights to perform these operations. Many administrators configure their databases with ACLs, so that all users can perform some modifications to their own entries, such as changing passwords. Then there are usually sub-administrators, who can add new entries and do things like change telephone numbers or addresses. Above these users are the database administrators themselves, who have full access to the system. Remember that all modifications must also conform with the server schema.

In this example, we are going to replace the existing `mail` attribute values and add a `telephonenumber` attribute to the Mark Wilcox entry. Here's the full listing for the modification example:

```java
import netscape.ldap.*;
import java.io.*;
import java.util.*;

public class mod {
    public static void main(String args[])
    {
        String host = "localhost";
        int port = 389;
        String dn = "uid=kvaughan, ou=People, o=airius.com";
        String pwd = "bribery";
        String entry_dn = "uid=mwilcox,ou=People,o=airius.com";
        String mail_values[] = {"wilcox@airius.com"};
        String telephone_values[] = {"940-555-2235"};
        LDAPAttribute attribute = null;
        LDAPModificationSet mods = null;

        LDAPConnection ld = null;

        try
        {
            ld = new LDAPConnection();

            /* must bind as a user with rights to write to the server */
            ld.connect(host,port,dn,pwd);

            mods = new LDAPModificationSet();
            attribute = new LDAPAttribute("mail",mail_values);
            mods.add(LDAPModification.REPLACE,attribute);

            attribute = new LDAPAttribute("telephonenumber",telephone_values);
            mods.add(LDAPModification.ADD,attribute);

            /* modify the object */
            ld.modify(entry_dn,mods);

            if (ld != null)
            {
                ld.disconnect();
            }
        }
        catch(LDAPException e)
        {
            e.printStackTrace();
        }
    }
}
```

The outcome of this transaction can be seen in Directory Server:

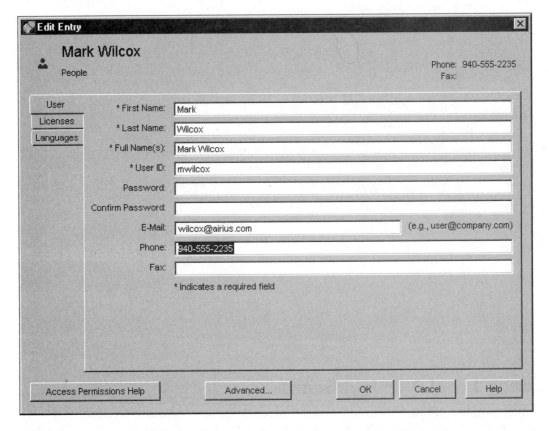

Delete an LDAP Entry

Deleting an entry is the simplest of the modifications you can do on an LDAP database. But of course, it is also a very powerful operation – so for safety reasons, deletions are usually reserved only for the database administrators.

All you must do is pass the distinguished name to the `LDAPConnection.delete()` method.

Shown below is a complete code example for deleting the very same entry that we created earlier for Mark Wilcox:

```
import netscape.ldap.*;
import java.io.*;
import java.util.*;

public class del {

    public static void main(String args[])
    {
```

```
                String host = "localhost";
                int port = 389;
                String dn = "uid=kvaughan, ou=People, o=airius.com";
                String pwd = "bribery";
                String entry_dn = "uid=mwilcox,ou=People,o=airius.com";

                LDAPConnection ld = null;

                try
                {
                   ld = new LDAPConnection();

                   /* must bind as a user with rights to write to the server */
                   ld.connect(host,port,dn,pwd);

                   /* delete the object */
                   ld.delete(entry_dn);

                   if (ld != null)
                   {
                      ld.disconnect();
                   }
                }
                catch(LDAPException e)
                {
                   e.printStackTrace();
                }
             }
       }
```

Netscape Java LDAP JavaBeans

Starting in version 1.1 of the Java programming language from Sun, the idea of JavaBeans was created. Beans are the component model for Java and are also designed to be used within a RAD (Rapid Application Development) GUI programming tool like Sun Workshop or Symantec Cafe. RAD development environments have a look and feel similar to the Microsoft Visual Basic environment.

Because we're concentrating on LDAP here, this example doesn't give a real flavor of JavaBeans programming, because JavaBeans are designed to be used in a visual editor. In a design tool that supports JavaBeans, you can configure the bean by assigning values to its properties and connecting the bean to other components through events and/or method invocations. The JavaBean specification defines interfaces which allow the design tool to discover all the properties, methods, and events which are available in the bean. So, although this example won't introduce all the aspects of programming with beans, you should at least be able to get an idea of how simple the default Netscape Java LDAP SDK beans are to use.

The example here uses the `LDAPIsMember` bean, which checks to see if a given user DN is a member of a given group (specified by its DN).

We are checking the following group:

```
cn=Accounting Managers,ou=groups,o=airius.com
```

We'll see if either "uid=scarter,ou=People,o=airius.com" or
"uid=mwilcox,ou=People,o=airius.com" are members of this group. Note that the bean
encapsulates the creation of an LDAPConnection, connecting to the server, authenticating,
searching, and evaluating the results. As a consequence, it is very easy to connect to other Java
components, applets or applications that do not know anything at all about LDAP.

In our JavaBeans example here, we are going to be demonstrating the use of the LDAPIsMember
bean, which ships with the Directory SDK for Java. This bean will tell you whether or not a DN is a
member of a given group.

Here is the full listing of the JavaBeans example:

```
import netscape.ldap.*;
import netscape.ldap.beans.*;

public class beanTest {

    public static void main(String args[])
    {
        String host = "localhost";
        int port = 389;
        String base = "o=airius.com";
        int scope = LDAPConnection.SCOPE_SUB;
        String group_dn ="cn=Accounting Managers,ou=groups,o=airius.com";
        String entry1 = "uid=scarter,ou=People,o=airius.com";
        String entry2 = "uid=mwilcox,ou=People,o=airius.com";

        LDAPIsMember bean1 = null;
        LDAPConnection ld = null;

        try
        {
            bean1 = new LDAPIsMember();
            bean1.setHost(host);
            bean1.setPort(port);
            bean1.setBase(base);
            bean1.setScope(scope);
            bean1.setGroup(group_dn); //specify which group to check

            bean1.setMember(entry1); //specify a user to check for membership

            if (bean1.isMember()) {
                System.out.println(entry1+" is a member");
            }
            else { System.out.println(entry1+" is not a member");}
                bean1.setMember(entry2);

            if (bean1.isMember()){
                System.out.println(entry2+" is a member");
            }
            else { System.out.println(entry2+" is not a member");}
        }
        catch(Exception e)
        {
            e.printStackTrace();
        }
    }
}
```

So what's going on here? Well, after we declare all the variables, there is the setup of the bean:

```
bean1 = new LDAPIsMember();
bean1.setHost(host);
bean1.setPort(port);
bean1.setBase(base);
bean1.setScope(scope);
bean1.setGroup("cn=Group1,ou=Groups,o=airius.com"); //specify which group to check
```

Next we specify the particular entry to check for membership:

```
String entry1 = "uid=scarter,ou=People,o=airius.com";
bean1.setMember(entry1);
```

Finally we perform the check to see if the member DN is actually a member of the group:

```
if (bean1.isMember()) {
System.out.println(entry1+" is a member");
}
else { System.out.println(entry1+" is not a member");}
```

The output from this code should look like the following screenshot:

LDAP Browser Example

In this penultimate example, we'll see a possible real world application that uses LDAP. It's an LDAP browser that uses the **JFC** (or **Java Foundation Classes**), which are now a standard part of Java, to provide a GUI search interface for an LDAP server.

It is made up of three primary classes and several smaller ones:

- ❏ LDAPBrowser – This is the primary class with the main() method. It sets up the GUI and handles the interaction with the user.
- ❏ LDAPHolder – This is an intermediary class that acts as a mediator between the LDAPBrowser and the LDAPFunctions class
- ❏ LDAPFunctions – This class contains all of the LDAP functions. While we could call all of the LDAP SDK functions directly, this class just makes the results easier to deal with.

Here is what main `LDAPBrowser` GUI should look like:

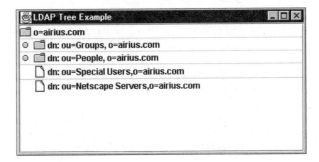

As you can see, it simply displays the `o=airius.com` root with all the organizational units under it in a 'tree' structure. If you double-click on **People**, for example, we can expand the tree and the screen should display all the people entries under the organizational unit, `ou=People`, like this:

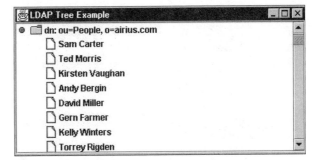

Double-clicking on an entry for one person then displays the information about that person:

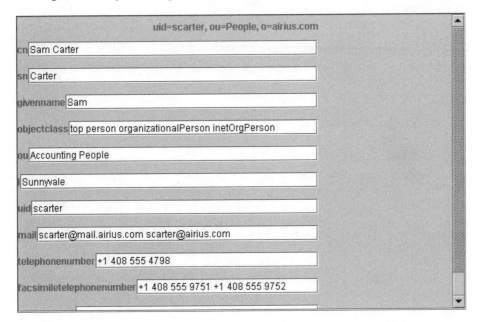

This screen displays all the attributes of the entry for Sam Carter.

Now let's take a look at the code that lies behind this browser application. This may seem a bit daunting, but the code is long for two reasons, one is because GUI programming takes up a lot of lines of space and second, because I've wrapped up a number of existing LDAP methods to make them easier to use in the browser classes.

Just take a drink of water, remember to breathe calmly and also remember that you don't have understand all of this in one sitting.

The first class we'll look at is the main one for the application – `LDAPBrowser`. Let's step through this code and see what each part does. The first thing we will do is import all of the packages and classes we need to compile and run our program:

```
import LDAPFunctions;
import LDAPHolder;
import java.util.Vector;
import java.util.*;
import netscape.ldap.*;

import javax.swing.*;
import javax.swing.tree.*;
import javax.swing.text.*;
import java.awt.event.*;
import java.awt.*;
import java.io.*;
```

Next we start with the actual class declaration for the primary class, `LDAPBrowser`:

```
public class LDAPBrowser extends JPanel
{
    private static String version = ".21";
```

The primary constructor for `LDAPBrowser` takes a hostname, a port number and a search base. This will then create a `JTree`, which is a JFC class that represents a visual tree structure (like Windows Explorer). The `JTree` will be placed inside a `JPanel`, because `LDAPBrowser` extends `JPanel`.

```
public LDAPBrowser(String host,int port,String base)
{
    JTree tree = new JTree();
    DefaultMutableTreeNode rootNode;
    DefaultMutableTreeNode parentNode;
    DefaultMutableTreeNode node;
    Font f;

    f = new Font("SanSerif",Font.PLAIN,24);
    setFont(f);
    setLayout(new BorderLayout());
```

Now we have the basic setup of our `JTree`, so we get some data for it. The root of the visual tree will be the search base, `o=airius.com`. Each branch will be the DN of every entry that has an `objectclass=organizationalUnit`. To determine this, we perform a standard LDAP search – except that the search is going through our `LDAPFunctions` class, which has functions built in to make it easier to deal with the results inside a GUI. We'll take a look at the code for `LDAPFunctions` shortly.

```
try {
    Vector results = null;
    LDAPFunctions lf = new LDAPFunctions(host,port,base);
    LDAPEntry entry = null;
    LDAPEntry personEntry =null;
    lf.connect();
    String personFilter;
    String ouFilter = "(objectclass=organizationalunit)";
    int size = 0;
    System.out.println("connected. Doing search.");
    results =
         lf.search(base,LDAPConnection.SCOPE_SUB,ouFilter,null,false);
    rootNode = new DefaultMutableTreeNode(base);
    System.out.println("past search");

    //replace this with warning dialog
    if (results == null){System.out.println("null returned.");
        System.exit(0);
    }
```

We have now got some search results, If not, we assume an error has occurred and exit the browser. We loop through our search results using the `LDAPHolder` class to store the results of the search. Just as `LDAPFunctions` was built to custom handle LDAP functions in this browser, `LDAPHolder` was specifically built to handle LDAP entry data for a `JTree`. We'll also be looking at the code for this class shortly.

The only real difference between displaying the results here and our earlier search examples is that now the data is being displayed inside a GUI instead of on the command line.

```
// we know first search will be "ou" or branches
for(int i=0;i<results.size();i++)
{
    System.out.println("inside for loop");
    entry = (LDAPEntry) results.elementAt(i);
    LDAPHolder lh = new LDAPHolder (entry);
    parentNode = new DefaultMutableTreeNode(lh,true);
    Vector ouVector = lh.getAttributeValues("ou");
    personFilter = new String("(&(objectclass=*)(ou="
                        +ouVector.elementAt(0)
                        +")(!(objectclass=organizationalunit)))");

    //now do a search for entries part of this ou
    Vector ouResults = lf.search(base,LDAPConnection.SCOPE_SUB,
                        personFilter,null,false);

    for (int z=0;z<ouResults.size();z++)
    {
        personEntry = (LDAPEntry) ouResults.elementAt(z);
        LDAPHolder plh = new LDAPHolder(personEntry);
        node = new DefaultMutableTreeNode(plh,false);
        parentNode.add(node);
    }
    rootNode.add(parentNode);
}
```

```
            System.out.println("past for loop");
            lf.disconnect();
            System.out.println("past disconnect");
            System.out.println("rootNode is "+rootNode.toString());
            tree = new JTree(rootNode);
            System.out.println("past jtree");
            tree.setFont(f);
```

This next line tells the Java Virtual Machine how to process double clicks on an item in the `JTree`:

```
            tree.addMouseListener(new DoubleClicker(this));
            add(new JScrollPane(tree),"Center");
        }
        catch(Exception e)
        {
          System.out.println(e.toString());
          System.exit(1);
        }
    }
```

The rest of this code is stuff used by JFC to build the GUI, such as setting the initial size of the `JPanel` that contains the `JTree`.

```
    public Dimension getPreferredSize()
    {
        return new Dimension(200,120);
    }
```

The main method sets up the `JFrame` (e.g. main windows) that will store all of the components:

```
    public static void main (String args[])
    {
        try {
            JFrame frame = new JFrame("LDAPBrowser Example version: "+version);
            LDAPBrowser panel = new LDAPBrowser("localhost",389,"o=airius.com");
            frame.setDefaultCloseOperation(JFrame.DO_NOTHING_ON_CLOSE);
            frame.setForeground(Color.black);
            frame.setBackground(Color.lightGray);
            frame.getContentPane().add(panel,"Center");
            frame.setSize(panel.getPreferredSize());
            frame.setVisible(true);
            frame.addWindowListener(new WindowCloser());
        }
        catch(Exception e){
            System.out.println(e.toString());
            e.printStackTrace();
            System.exit(1);
        }
    }
}
```

This class provides us with a window that displays the attributes and values of a particular entry in our tree. It determines which item was double clicked, and retrieves the data contained inside of that tree element (which is actually held by an `LDAPHolder` object). The panel that displays the data is called `LDAPPanel`.

```
class DoubleClicker extends MouseAdapter
{
    protected JPanel myPanel;
    DoubleClicker(){this.super();}
    DoubleClicker(JPanel panel){this.super();myPanel = panel;}
    public void mouseClicked (MouseEvent e)
    {
        try{
            JTree tree;
            Object item;
            TreePath path;
            tree = (JTree) e.getSource();
            path = tree.getPathForLocation(e.getX(),e.getY());
            item = path.getLastPathComponent();

            /*path object is just an Object
            convert to DefaultMutableTreeNode, then to LDAPHolder*/

            LDAPHolder lh =
                    (LDAPHolder)((DefaultMutableTreeNode)item).getUserObject();
            System.out.println("past lh");
            LDAPPanel entryPanel = new LDAPPanel(lh.getEntry());
            JFrame testFrame = new JFrame("LDAP Frame");
            JPanel displayPanel = new JPanel();
            JScrollPane jsp = new JScrollPane(entryPanel);
            testFrame.setForeground(Color.black);
            testFrame.setBackground(Color.lightGray);
            testFrame.addWindowListener(new LDAPWindowCloser());
            testFrame.getContentPane().add(jsp,"Center");
            testFrame.setSize(entryPanel.getPreferredSize());
            testFrame.setVisible(true);
            System.out.println("Double clicked on "+ item.toString());

            tree.scrollPathToVisible(path);
        }
        catch(NullPointerException npe) {
        }
    }
}

class WindowCloser extends WindowAdapter
{
    public void windowClosing(WindowEvent e)
    {
        Window win = e.getWindow();
        win.setVisible(false);
        win.dispose();
        System.exit(0);
    }
}

/*This class closes the LDAPPanel window */
class LDAPWindowCloser extends WindowAdapter
{
    public void windowClosing(WindowEvent e)
    {
        Window win = e.getWindow();
        win.setVisible(false);
        win.dispose();
    }
}
```

Next up is the class that handles the display of data held by a `LDAPHolder` object, `LDAPPanel`. It is called by `DoubleClicker`. Note that there's nothing new LDAP-wise in this section.

```java
//output entry data to screen
class LDAPPanel extends JPanel
{
    public LDAPPanel(String msg)
    {
        JLabel label;
        Font font;
        font = new Font("Serif",Font.PLAIN,8);
        setFont(font);
        setDoubleBuffered(true);

        label = new JLabel(msg);
        label.setFont(font);
        add(label);
    }

    public LDAPPanel(LDAPEntry entry)
    {
        JLabel label;
        JLabel blank = new JLabel();
        Font font;
        String msg;
        Box vBox;
        Box hBox;
        Component vGlue,vStrut,hGlue,hStrut;
        setDoubleBuffered(true);
        label = new JLabel(entry.getDN());

        vBox = Box.createVerticalBox();

        setLayout(new BorderLayout());
        add(vBox,"West");
        blank = new JLabel("     ");
        add(blank,"Center");

        vGlue = Box.createVerticalGlue();
        vBox.add(vGlue);
        vBox.add(label);
        vStrut = Box.createVerticalStrut(2);
        vBox.add(vStrut);

        LDAPAttributeSet entryAttrs = entry.getAttributeSet();
        Enumeration enumAttrs = entryAttrs.getAttributes();

        /* Loop on attributes */
        while ( enumAttrs.hasMoreElements() ) {
            LDAPAttribute anAttr = (LDAPAttribute)enumAttrs.nextElement();
            String attrName = anAttr.getName();
            label = new JLabel(attrName);

            hBox = Box.createHorizontalBox();
            vGlue = Box.createVerticalGlue();
            vBox.add(vGlue);
            vBox.add(hBox);
            vStrut = Box.createVerticalStrut(2);
            vBox.add(vStrut);
```

```
            hGlue = Box.createHorizontalGlue();
            hBox.add(hGlue);
            hBox.add(label);
            hStrut = Box.createHorizontalStrut(2);

            Enumeration enumVals = anAttr.getStringValues();
            StringBuffer dataBuffer = new StringBuffer();
            JTextField data_display;
            if (enumVals != null) {
                while ( enumVals.hasMoreElements() ) {
                    dataBuffer.append(( String )enumVals.nextElement()+" ");
                }
                data_display = new JTextField(dataBuffer.toString());
                hGlue = Box.createHorizontalGlue();
                hBox.add(hGlue);
                hBox.add(data_display);
                hStrut = Box.createHorizontalStrut(2);
                hBox.add(hStrut);
            }
        }
    }

    public Dimension getPreferredSize()
    {
        return new Dimension(300,400);
    }
}
```

The next class we're going to look at, LDAPFunctions, is a wrapper around the
netscape.ldap.* functions. In this class there are some additional get/set methods for host, port
and searchbase. Also, all of the search functions return a Vector instead of an Enumeration. (I
find dealing with Vectors easier than Enumeration objects. For example, you can get the size of a
Vector, but you can't with an Enumeration.)

There isn't anything new about LDAP programming in this class, but you might find it useful as a
'refresher' class as you skim through it – you should get another dose of how the classes and methods
work inside the Directory SDK for Java.

```
import netscape.ldap.*;
import java.util.*;
import java.util.Vector;

/* This class is some standard LDAP functions to make it easier to write LDAP
applications */
public class LDAPFunctions {
    private String ldapServer;
    private int ldapPort;
    private String bindDN;
    private String bindPassword;
    private String ldapOrgBase;
    private String ldapSearchBase;
    private LDAPConnection ld;

    public void connect() throws LDAPException {
        ld = null;
        ld = new LDAPConnection ();
        ld.connect(ldapServer,ldapPort);
    }
```

```java
    public void disconnect() throws LDAPException {
        if (ld != null) {
            ld.disconnect();
        }
    }

    public void authenticate() throws LDAPException {
        ld.authenticate(bindDN,bindPassword);
    }

    public void authenticate(String bindDN, String bindPassword) throws
                                                            LDAPException
    {
        ld.authenticate(bindDN,bindPassword);
    }

    public Vector search(String base,int scope,String filter,String attrs[],
                                    boolean attrsOnly) throws LDAPException
    {
        System.out.println("I'm in search 1 ");
        Vector v = new Vector();
        LDAPSearchResults results =
                                ld.search(base,scope,filter,attrs,attrsOnly);
        while (results.hasMoreElements()){
            System.out.println("results next element");
            v.addElement((LDAPEntry) results.next());
            System.out.println("past addElement()");
        }
        return v;
    }

    public Vector search(String base, int scope, String filter,
            String attrs[], boolean attrsOnly, LDAPSearchConstraints cons)
                                                        throws LDAPException
    {
        try{
            System.out.println("I'm in search 2");
            LDAPSearchResults results = null;
            Vector v = new Vector() ;
            results = ld.search(base,scope,filter,attrs,attrsOnly,cons);
            while (results.hasMoreElements()){
                v.addElement(results.next());
            }
        return v;
        }
        catch(NullPointerException ne){
            return null;
        }
    }

    public Vector lfsearch(LDAPUrl url) throws LDAPException {
        LDAPSearchResults results = null;
        Vector v = new Vector();
        results = ld.search(url);
        while (results.hasMoreElements()){
            v.addElement(results.next());
        }
    return v;
    }
```

```java
public Vector search(LDAPUrl url, LDAPSearchConstraints cons) throws
                                                      LDAPException
{
    LDAPSearchResults results = null;
    Vector v = new Vector();
    results = ld.search(url,cons);
    while (results.hasMoreElements()){
        v.addElement(results.next());
    }
    return v;
}

public void addEntry(LDAPEntry entry) throws LDAPException {
    ld.add(entry);
}

public void removeEntry(String dn) throws LDAPException {
    ld.delete(dn);
}

public void setLdapServer(String ldapServer){
    this.ldapServer = ldapServer;
}

public String getLdapSearchBase(){
    return ldapSearchBase;
}

public void setBindDN(String bindDN){
    this.bindDN = bindDN;
}

public String getBindPassword(){
    return bindPassword;
}

public void setBindPassword(String bindPassword){
    this.bindPassword = bindPassword;
}

public String getBindDN(){
    return bindDN;
}

public void setLdapSearchBase(String ldapSearchBase){
    this.ldapSearchBase = ldapSearchBase;
}

public String getLdapOrgBase(){
    return ldapOrgBase;
}

public void setLdapPort(int ldapPort){
    this.ldapPort = ldapPort;
}

public int getLdapPort(){
    return ldapPort;
}
```

```
public void setLdapOrgBase(String ldapOrgBase){
    this.ldapOrgBase = ldapOrgBase;
}

public String getLdapServer(){
    return ldapServer;
}

public LDAPFunctions(){
}

public LDAPFunctions(String ldapServer, int ldapPort, String ldapOrgBase)
{
    this.ldapServer = ldapServer;
    this.ldapPort = ldapPort;
    this.ldapOrgBase = ldapOrgBase;
}

public LDAPFunctions(String ldapServer, int ldapPort,String ldapOrgBase,
                                    String bindDN,String bindPassword)
{
    this.ldapServer = ldapServer;
    this.ldapPort = ldapPort;
    this.ldapOrgBase = ldapOrgBase;
    this.bindDN = bindDN;
    this.bindPassword = bindPassword;
}

/*This method is to test this class */
public static void main(String args[])
{
    LDAPFunctions lf = new LDAPFunctions("localhost",389,"o=airius.com");
    Vector results = null;
    LDAPEntry entry;
    try
    {
        lf.connect();
        String filter = "cn=Sam Carter";
        String attrs[] = new String[3];
        int size = 0;
        LDAPUrl url = new LDAPUrl("ldap://airwolf/uid=bjensen," +
                        "ou=People,o=Airius.com?cn,mail,telephoneNumber");
        attrs[0] = "cn";
        attrs[1] ="mail";
        attrs[2] = "telephonenumber";
        System.out.println("connected. Doing search.");
        results =
            lf.search("o=airius.com",LDAPConnection.SCOPE_SUB,filter,null,false);
        System.out.println("done search.");
        //      results = lf.lfsearch(url);
        if (results.size() > 0) {size = results.size();}
        for (int i=0;i<size;i++)
        {
            entry = (LDAPEntry)results.elementAt(i);
            if(entry != null){ System.out.println(entry.toString());}
        }
        lf.disconnect();
        System.exit(0);
    }
```

```
        catch(Exception e)
        {
            e.printStackTrace();
            System.exit(1);
        }
    }
}
```

The `LDAPHolder` class is designed to hold the data for an LDAP entry inside a `JTree`. When the entry is listed as an entry on the tree, only it's DN or Common Name is shown (depending whether or not it's an `organizationalUnit`). When a user double-clicks on a tree element, its full entry is displayed, and the entry is stored inside this class. Again nothing new with LDAP is shown in this class, it's just a plain storage class.

> *If I was going to put this into production, I don't think I would hold all of the data inside this class. Instead I would hold just the DN and Common Name here. When a request came in to display the full entry, I would then grab the entry from the server, using the DN of the entry as my search base.*

```
import java.util.Vector;
import java.util.Hashtable;
import java.util.Enumeration;
import netscape.ldap.*;

/*Some functions to make it easier to deal with LDAP data for my LDAPBrowser
application*/
public class LDAPHolder {

    private Hashtable attribHash ;
    private netscape.ldap.LDAPEntry entry;
    private boolean isBranch; // define if branch entry or not

    public LDAPHolder() {}

    public LDAPHolder(LDAPEntry entry) throws LDAPException
    {
        attribHash = new Hashtable();
        this.setEntry(entry);
    }

    public netscape.ldap.LDAPEntry getEntry(){
        return entry;
    }

    public String toString(){
        Vector v = (Vector)attribHash.get("cn");
        if (v == null) {String s = "dn: "+this.getDN();return s;}
        else{
            return (String) v.elementAt(0);
        }
    }

    /** This gets the entry and sets the attribHash table up. */
    public synchronized void setEntry(netscape.ldap.LDAPEntry entry) throws
                                                     LDAPException
    {
```

```
        System.out.println("inside setEntry");
        this.entry = entry;
        Vector v = null;
        System.out.println("past entry, past null");
        attribHash.put("dn",entry.getDN());
        System.out.println("dn is "+entry.getDN());

        LDAPAttributeSet entryAttrs = entry.getAttributeSet();
        Enumeration enumAttrs = entryAttrs.getAttributes();

        /* Loop on attributes */
        while ( enumAttrs.hasMoreElements() ) {
            v = new Vector();
            LDAPAttribute anAttr = (LDAPAttribute)enumAttrs.nextElement();
            String attrName = anAttr.getName();
            Enumeration enumVals = anAttr.getStringValues();
            if (enumVals != null) {
                while ( enumVals.hasMoreElements() ) {
                    String aVal = ( String )enumVals.nextElement();
                    v.addElement(aVal);
                }
            }
            attribHash.put(attrName,v);
        }
    }

    public String getDN()
    {
        return (String) attribHash.get("dn");
    }

    public Vector getAttributeValues (String attribute)
    {
        try
        {
            return (Vector) attribHash.get(attribute);
        }
        catch (NullPointerException npe)
        {
            return null;
        }
    }
}
```

If you try compiling and running this code (available from the Wrox Press web site), you should be
able to see something like the example GUI shown at the beginning of this section, that allows you to
browse through that data in the `airius.com` directory.

Authenticating Through LDAP

If you want to use an LDAP server as an authentication database for your Java applications, you can.
This final example application is one that I wrote for a column in *Netscape ViewSource*
(`http://developer.netscape.com/viewsource`).

On the command-line to the application, you pass a user ID (username, typically) and a password. The application searches as anonymous for an entry with a matching uid attribute under o=airius.com. If more than one match is found, then authentication is considered to fail. If there is exactly one match, then authentication needs to succeed with both the DN of that entry and the password provided on the command line. Note that for this to work, access permissions in the database must be set up to allow anonymous searches under o=airius.com, which is the case with for the sample airius.ldif database provided with Netscape Directory Server 3.x and 4.x.

Here is the code:

```
import netscape.ldap.*;

/*
    ldapAuth.java
    usage: ldapAuth uid password
*/

public class ldapAuth {

    public static boolean authenticate(String uid,String pwd)
    {
        boolean status = false;
        LDAPConnection ld = new LDAPConnection();
        LDAPEntry findEntry = null;
        String dn = null;
        String MY_HOST = "localhost";
        int MY_PORT = 389;
        String MY_SEARCHBASE = "o=airius.com";
        String MY_FILTER = "uid=" + uid;

        try {
            ld.connect( MY_HOST, MY_PORT );
            LDAPSearchResults res = ld.search(
                MY_SEARCHBASE,LDAPConnection.SCOPE_SUB,MY_FILTER,null,false);

            System.out.println("getCount is "+res.getCount());
            // more than 1 user matching filter, fail.
            if (res.getCount() != 1) { return false;}

            if (res.hasMoreElements()) {
                findEntry = res.next();
                dn = findEntry.getDN();

                System.out.println("dn is "+dn);
                //prevent anonymous connections
                if ((dn == "") || (pwd == "")) { return false;}
                //now attempt to bind to server
                ld.authenticate(dn,pwd);

                //if ld.authenticate doesn't throw an exception we passed
                status = true;
            }
        }
        catch(LDAPException e) {
            System.out.println(e.toString());
        }
        catch(Exception x) {
            x.printStackTrace();
```

```
        }
        return status;
    }

    public static void main (String args[]) {
        if (args.length <2) {
            System.out.println("usage ldapAuth userid password");
            System.exit(1);
        }

        String uid = args[0];
        String passwd = args[1];
        boolean status = authenticate(uid,passwd);
        if (status) {
            System.out.println(uid+" authenticated!");
        }
        else {
            System.out.println(uid+" failed!");
        }
        System.exit(0);
    }
}
```

If you type the following command:

```
java ldapAuth kvaughan bribery
```

Then this is the output you would get:

Summary

We have looked at various aspects of using the Netscape Directory Java SDK in this chapter, examining the usual functionality you would want from a directory application, including searching for and modifying entries. Toward the end of the chapter, we saw an example of a more 'real life' browser application, created using the JFC.

The Java programming language is a very popular language for doing development on the Internet. And LDAP appears to be well on the way to becoming *the* directory service protocol for the Internet. The Netscape Java LDAP SDK is a very well built and powerful toolbox to use for building LDAP aware Java applications.

Bear in mind that we have hardly scratched the surface of what's possible with this LDAP SDK. In future chapters, we will come back to using Java to demonstrate more advanced topics like client caching and extended server operations.

Programming with the LDAP Provider in the Sun JNDI

In this chapter, we're going to learn how to build LDAP clients using the Sun **Java Naming and Directory Interfaces** (**JNDI**). If you are, or have been, doing any work with the Enterprise JavaBeans or Java Messaging SDKs you will need to become familiar with JNDI because these SDKs require it. JNDI is also interesting because it provides for a standard mechanism for storing persistent Java objects on the network. It also allows you to work with other network services besides LDAP, including Sun's NIS and Novell's NetWare Directory Service (NDS).

In this chapter, we will focus on how to use JNDI to access LDAP data. We will learn how to:

- ❑ Search an LDAP server
- ❑ Add and delete LDAP entries
- ❑ Modify existing entries
- ❑ Use a different LDAP service provider
- ❑ Store and retrieve Java objects in an LDAP server

What is JNDI?

The JNDI SDK is conceptually different from, say, the Netscape Directory SDK for Java. The latter is designed to provide low-level access to the LDAP protocol. It forces the server to speak LDAP, which means that the server developer has to worry about how to translate from a different protocol (for example Lotus Notes) to a standard one. On the other hand, JNDI is designed to make the application developer responsible for the protocol used to communicate between the client application and the server. It does try to make things easy by creating a specific set of methods that your application can use, regardless of the underlying protocol used. The way all this is accomplished is through the use of **service providers**.

Our first diagram shows the relationship between an application, JNDI, JNDI providers and directory servers. Note how JNDI separates the user from having to directly access the servers.

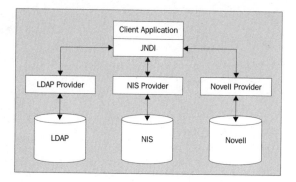

In our next diagram we see the relationship between a client application and the Netscape LDAP SDK for Java. Here, the client has to manipulate the LDAP server using the SDK. There is no intervening layer to do the hard work for it.

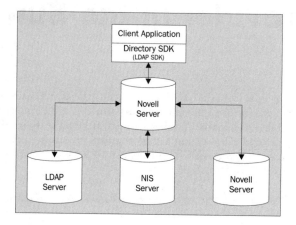

There is a broad similarity between the way JNDI providers interact with applications and the way database drivers relate to clients using Java Database Connectivity (JDBC). They are special middle-tier software applications that shield the user from having to communicate directly with underlying system APIs. At the time of writing, JNDI has providers for:

❑ LDAP
❑ The local file system (regardless if whether it is Unix or Windows NT)
❑ Novell's NDS
❑ Sun's NIS/NIS+

The list of providers is growing fast.

The use of a JNDI provider to communicate with the underlying LDAP server means that when you test out your LDAP client application on a local desktop, you do not even need an LDAP server. You could, for example, use the File System provider, and then scale your application up to a full LDAP server when you are ready for production by simply switching JNDI providers.

Just as you can change underlying protocols by changing providers, you can also choose service providers from different vendors that supply the same service. As we'll see later on in the chapter, both Sun and IBM supply a JNDI provider for LDAP.

Where JNDI really shines is the ability to maintain **object persistence** on the network. This is the ability to store the exact state of a Java object somewhere on the network and then restore that object at a later date with its state intact, even from a different machine. By **exact state**, we mean that the object's methods and the values of all its variables are preserved intact from the moment of storage until retrieval. Java has supported object persistence since JDK version 1.1, but it wasn't until JNDI that we could take advantage of object persistence on the network.

> *If you are developing standard directory service applications in Java, for example, storing white pages information, I urge you to give JNDI, Netscape's Java LDAP SDK and Microsoft's Java ADSI a look.*

You can get the JNDI SDK from Sun Microsystems at `http://java.sun.com/products/`. Follow the instructions supplied to show you to how to install JNDI and to set your environment up to run it. JNDI only works with JDK 1.1 and higher.

Naming Service versus Directory Service

Before we proceed, we should describe the difference between a naming service and a directory service. A naming service simply provides a mechanism for providing a unique name to a similar set of entries. For example the Internet domain name system is a naming service. Through the use of Fully Qualified Domain Names (FQDN) such `www.unt.edu`, it is highly unlikely that two separate organizations will own the same name. When we add a new domain to the Internet, agencies such as the InterNIC ensure that the domain name does not match any other. Inside each network, the network administrators ensure that as each new host is brought on to the Internet, each machine has its own unique name as well.

While each host on the Internet has its own unique name, this name is useless unless it can be resolved into an IP address. The DNS system, that is the system that resolves domain names into IP addresses, is a type of a directory service. As we have said before, a directory is optimized for very fast lookup. One way to achieve this is to make sure that each entry in the directory has a unique name, which is provided via a naming service.

In summary, you can have a naming service without a directory service, but you can't have a directory service without a naming service.

JNDI Class Structure

Just as we did with the Directory SDK for Java, we will take a brief look at the packages and classes that make up the JNDI SDK.

- ❑ `javax.naming` – this package that allows applications to interact with naming services.
- ❑ `javax.naming.directory` – this allows applications to interact with both directory and naming services. It is derived from the `javax.naming` package.

❑ `javax.naming.spi` – this is the package JNDI service providers use to interact with `javax.naming.*` packages. It enables different providers to be plugged in with an overlying JNDI API.

We will be using the `javax.naming` and `javax.naming.directory` packages, so it would be useful to have a quick reference to the interfaces and classes that these packages contain.

javax.naming

Interfaces

❑ `Context` – defines the methods needed to access and modify the JNDI environment a particular application might be in (e.g. items such as hostname, port, user ID, etc)

❑ `Name` – defines methods for providing for a standard name for an object

❑ `NameParser` – defines methods that can break a hierarchical name (such as an LDAP entry's DN) into it constituent parts

❑ `NamingEnumeration` – defines methods that are used to provide a back list of objects by the classes in the `java.naming.*` packages

❑ `Referenceable` – only implemented by classes that can provide references back to themselves (that is they can provide an address to a storage location that is not bound to the directory server)

Classes

❑ `BinaryRefAddr` – provides a binary data type that represents the location of an object such as the BER encoded LDAP location of an object or a handle to a serialized Java object.

❑ `Binding` – allows the association of a name, such as `cn=MyJavaObject,ou=Java,o=airius.com`, to a specific object

❑ `CompositeName` – enables the creation of an object name from multiple namespaces (e.g. attributes of an object might be stored in LDAP and on a file system)

❑ `CompoundName` – supplies a hierarchical namespace such as that of LDAP

❑ `InitialContext` – represents the initial environment (e.g. LDAP, NIS, file system, etc.) that the application will be accessing

❑ `LinkRef` – represents a `Reference` object which has a value that is a name, called the link name, that is bound to a single name inside a context (in the case of LDAP, the value of a link name would be an entry's DN)

❑ `NameClassPair` – represents a name which is associated with a fully qualified package name of an object, e.g. `cn=String->java.lang.String`

❑ `RefAddr` – represents a `Reference` object that contains a name and address of an object that represents communications protocol such as "NT Printing Services"

❑ `Reference` – an object that is stored OUTSIDE the naming and directory services

❑ `StringRefAddr` – denotes the string form of an address necessary for a communications system, such as a hostname or a URL

Exceptions

❑ AuthenticationException – is called when we fail to authenticate to a naming or directory service

❑ AuthenticationNotSupportedException – is thrown when we attempt to call an unsupported authentication mechanism (e.g. we try to use SSL when the LDAP server only supports simple authentication)

❑ CannotProceedException – is thrown when the operation has reached a point where it cannot proceed any further (e.g. it received a search referral to a different LDAP server)

❑ CommunicationException – occurs when we lose connectivity to the server

❑ ConfigurationException – occurs when there is something wrong with the configuration of the service provider

❑ ContextNotEmptyException – is thrown when you try to delete a Context object which is not empty (e.g. you try to remove an organizationalUnit attribute and there are still entries present containing that attribute)

❑ InsufficientResourcesException – is thrown when resources are not available for the server or the client to process the request (e.g. you could have exceeded an administrative quota, be out of memory, etc)

❑ InterruptedNamingException – is thrown when an error occurs while a naming operation is being invoked

❑ InvalidNameException – occurs when the name of an object is not allowed by the underlying naming service (if you are using LDAP, this would be thrown if you specify an invalid DN)

❑ LimitExceededException – is thrown whenever a user or server limit is reached, a connection timeout for instance

❑ LinkException – is thrown whenever there is a problem with a link

❑ LinkLoopException – is thrown whenever a link to a reference is also a link back to the original caller

❑ MalformedLinkException – occurs whenever an invalid link name is provided for an operation

❑ NameAlreadyBoundException – is thrown whenever an attempt is made to bind an object to a name that is already in use

❑ NameNotFoundException – is thrown whenever an object cannot be found because the name of the object doesn't exist or cannot be found given the current context

❑ NamingException – is the superclass of all exceptions thrown by the Context and DirContext interfaces

❑ NamingSecurityException – is the superclass of all security related exceptions thrown by the Context and DirContext interfaces

❑ NoInitialContextException – is thrown when an initial context cannot be located

❑ NoPermissionException – occurs when the application attempts to perform an operation that it doesn't have the necessary rights for

❑ NotContextException – is thrown when the application attempts to operate on an object who's bound name is either in the wrong context, or doesn't have a context, and a context is required to complete the operation

❑ OperationNotSupportedException – is thrown when the application attempts to perform an operation which the underlying naming or directory service doesn't provide.

❑ `PartialResultException` – occurs when the operation was unable to return the complete results, but instead gave a partial answer (for example the application could not find `uid=scarter,ou=People,o=airius.com`, but could find `ou=People,o=airius.com`, which would be the partial result of the search)

❑ `ReferralException` – is thrown when an LDAP referral is returned in an operation

❑ `ServiceUnavailableException` – is thrown when the particular naming or directory service is not available (e.g. you can connect to the host, but there is not a service running on the connected port)

❑ `SizeLimitExceededException` – occurs when a result is too large for the given size limit

❑ `TimeLimitExceededException` – is thrown when the operation failed to finish before a given time limit

javax.naming.directory

Interfaces

❑ `Attribute` – defines a single attribute of an object

❑ `Attributes` – defines a collection of `Attribute` objects

❑ `DirContext` – an interface to a directory service

Classes

❑ `BasicAttribute` – represents a simple implementation of the `Attribute` interface

❑ `BasicAttributes` – stores a collection of `BasicAttribute` objects

❑ `InitialDirContext` – represents the initial context for directory server operations

❑ `ModificationItem` – represents an object for use in a directory service modification operations

❑ `SearchControls` – represents controls we can present to the server to extend the standard directory service functions, such as sorting the search results

❑ `SearchResult` – represents the results of a directory service search operation

Exceptions

❑ `AttributeInUseException` – occurs when an attempt is made to add an attribute to an entry when one of the same name already exists

❑ `AttributeModificationException` – is thrown when an attempt is made to make a modification that violates the directory service schema

❑ `InvalidAttributeIdentifierException` – is thrown when an incorrect attribute name is supplied

❑ `InvalidAttributesException` – is called when trying to add an attribute that violates the directory service schema

❑ `InvalidAttributeValueException` – occurs when trying to add a value to an attribute that violates the directory service schema

❑ `InvalidSearchControlsException` – is thrown when an incorrect search control is passed to the directory service

- ❏ `InvalidSearchFilterException` – is thrown when an incorrect search filter is passed to the directory service
- ❏ `NoSuchAttributeException` – occurs when you attempt to get or set the value of an attribute that doesn't exist
- ❏ `SchemaViolationException` – is thrown when you attempt any other operation that violates the directory service schema

Connecting to an LDAP Server

As we have discovered in previous chapters, before you can perform any type of operation on an LDAP sever, you must first obtain a reference and a network connection to the LDAP server, and you must also specify how you wish to be bound to the server – either anonymously or as an authenticated user.

Connecting

In JNDI, you must first obtain a reference to an object that implements the `DirContext` interface. In most applications we will use an `InitialDirContext` object which takes a hash table as a parameter. The hash table, which is a type of data structure where environment variables are set programmatically, can itself contain a number of different references. It should have, at the very least, a reference to a field with the key `Context.INITIAL_CONTEXT_FACTORY` containing a value of the fully qualified class name of the service provider. It should also contain the hostname and the port number to the LDAP server. You supply the latter information using the `Context.PROVIDER_URL` key, containing the protocol, hostname and port number in this form: `ldap://localhost:389`.

This is best illustrated using an example.

```
Hashtable env = new Hashtable();

//Specify which class to use for our JNDI provider
env.put(Context.INITIAL_CONTEXT_FACTORY, " com.sun.jndi.ldap.LdapCtxFactory");

//Specify host name and port number
env.put(Context.PROVIDER_URL, "ldap://localhost:389");

//Get a reference to a directory context
DirContext ctx = new InitialDirContext(env);
```

We first create a `Hashtable` object to store our environmental variables for our directory service:

```
Hashtable env = new Hashtable();
```

Next we specify the fully qualified package name of our JNDI provider:

```
env.put(Context.INITIAL_CONTEXT_FACTORY, "com.sun.jndi.ldap.LdapCtxFactory");
```

Then we must specify the hostname and port number to our LDAP server:

```
env.put(Context.PROVIDER_URL, "ldap://localhost:389");
```

Finally we get a reference to our initial directory context with a call to the `InitialDirContext` constructor, giving it our `Hashtable` as its only parameter.

```
DirContext ctx = new InitialDirContext(env);
```

Binding

If you use the default values, the connection will be bound as anonymous. For some operations, however, you will need to be bound as a particular user. Recall that access rights to the directory tree are controlled by how you are bound.

You can specify authentication by including the `Context.SECURITY_AUTHENTICATION`, `Context.SECURITY_PRINCIPAL`, and `Context.SECURITY_CREDENTIALS` keys in the hash table passed to the `InitialDirContext` object.

Here is some example syntax, illustrating a non-anonymous bind:

```
Hashtable env = new Hashtable();

//Specify which class to use for our JNDI provider
env.put(Context.INITIAL_CONTEXT_FACTORY, "com.sun.jndi.ldap.LdapCtxFactory");

//This sends the id and password as plain text over the wire
env.put(Context.SECURITY_AUTHENTICATION,"simple");
env.put(Context.SECURITY_PRINCIPAL,MGR_DN);
env.put(Context.SECURITY_CREDENTIALS,MGR_PW);

//Get a reference to a directory context
DirContext ctx = new InitialDirContext(env);
```

Once again we create a `Hashtable` object and specify which JNDI provider we will be using. To specifically bind to the server we must provide the environment with the method for our authentication (e.g. "simple", SSL , or SASL). Then we must specify the DN and the password of the entry we wish to bind as:

```
env.put(Context.SECURITY_AUTHENTICATION,"simple");
env.put(Context.SECURITY_PRINCIPAL,MGR_DN);
env.put(Context.SECURITY_CREDENTIALS,MGR_PW);
```

Finally we create the `DirContext` object as before.

Searching an LDAP Server

As we have seen in the previous three chapters, the most common operation to be performed by any application is searching an LDAP server – JNDI offers yet another different way of achieving this. In JNDI, we use the `search()` method of the `DirContext` interface, which returns a `NamingEnumeration` object, if the search is successful.

Later in this section we will show you the various ways you can manipulate the values of this object to get back attributes and values of each returned entry.

The Search Operation

We perform a search using the `search()` method of an object that implements the `DirContext` interface, such as the `InitialDirContext` class. The minimum number of parameters which must be supplied are the search base and a search filter – much the same as the previous SDKs we have covered. There are other parameters we can use to help us manage the results.

You should note that in the other LDAP APIs, you must specify the scope as a parameter in the search methods. In JNDI, however, the scope is set in the `SearchControls` object, which is an optional third parameter of the `search()` method. By default it is set to `subtree`. For more information on search scope, I refer you to the fuller discussion in Chapter 6.

Our first example will show a very simple search example, where the search filter is `sn=Carter`. This will return all entries that have a surname, that is the attribute specified by `sn`, of Carter. This first example is an anonymous search.

Most of the examples here are non-GUI based. However, there is nothing to prevent them from being included in a GUI. The final example in this chapter will show how to store GUI components in an LDAP server.

```
// Example 9.1
// Standard anonymous search

import java.util.Hashtable;
import java.util.Enumeration;

import javax.naming.*;
import javax.naming.directory.*;

public class JNDISearch
{
    // initial context implementation
    public static String INITCTX = "com.sun.jndi.ldap.LdapCtxFactory";
    public static String MY_HOST = "ldap://localhost:389";
    public static String MY_SEARCHBASE = "o=Airius.com";
    public static String MY_FILTER = "(sn=Carter)";

    public static void main(String args[])
    {
        try
        {
            //Hashtable for environmental information
            Hashtable env = new Hashtable();

            //Specify which class to use for our JNDI provider
            env.put(Context.INITIAL_CONTEXT_FACTORY, INITCTX);
            // Specify host and port to use for directory service
            env.put(Context.PROVIDER_URL, MY_HOST);

            //Get a reference to a directory context
            DirContext ctx = new InitialDirContext(env);
```

```
        //specify the scope of the search
        SearchControls constraints = new SearchControls();
        constraints.setSearchScope(SearchControls.SUBTREE_SCOPE);

        //perform the actual search
        //we give it a searchbase, a filter and a the constraints
        //containing the scope of the search
        NamingEnumeration results =
                              ctx.search(MY_SEARCHBASE,MY_FILTER,constraints);

        //now step through the search results
        while (results != null && results.hasMore())
        while (results != null && results.hasMore())
        {
            SearchResult sr = (SearchResult) results.next();
            String dn = sr.getName();
            System.out.println("Distinguished Name is "+dn);

            Attributes attrs = sr.getAttributes();

            for (NamingEnumeration ne = attrs.getAll();ne.hasMoreElements();)
            {
                Attribute attr = (Attribute)ne.next();
                String attrID = attr.getID();

                System.out.println(attrID+":");
                for (Enumeration vals = attr.getAll();vals.hasMoreElements();)
                {
                    System.out.println("\t"+vals.nextElement());
                }
            }
            System.out.println("\n");
        }
    }
    catch(Exception e)
    {
        e.printStackTrace();
        System.exit(1);
    }
    }
  }
}
```

The output from this code example is shown in the screenshot:

```
Distinguished Name is uid=scarter, ou=People
facsimiletelephonenumber:
        +1 408 555 9751
        +1 408 555 9752
telephonenumber:
        +1 408 555 4798
givenname:
        Sam
sn:
        Carter
l:
        Sunnyvale
roomnumber:
        4612
ou:
        Accounting
        People
mail:
        scarter@mail.airius.com
        scarter@airius.com
uid:
        scarter
cn:
        Sam Carter
-- More --
```

How a JNDI Search is Performed

After we get initial context, set by the variable `ctx`, we next specify the scope of our search. If we don't specify a scope, JNDI will assume a scope of `subtree`, so these next two lines are actually redundant but is useful to show you how to specify the scope:

```
SearchControls constraints = new SearchControls();
constraints.setSearchScope(SearchControls.SUBTREE_SCOPE);
```

After we specify the scope we can perform the actual search like this:

```
NamingEnumeration results = ctx.search(MY_SEARCHBASE,MY_FILTER,constraints);
```

The `NamingEnumeration` class is equivalent to the `SearchResults` class in the Netscape Directory SDK for Java.

Each element in a `NamingEnumeration` object will contain a `SearchResult` object which we can retrieve like this:

```
SearchResult sr = (SearchResult)results.next();
```

The `SearchResult` is equivalent to an `LDAPEntry` object in the Netscape Directory SDK for Java. We can get the DN of an entry like this:

```
String dn = sr.getName();
```

To get the attributes of an entry you use the `getAttributes()` method of the `SearchResult` class like this:

```
Attributes attrs = sr.getAttributes();
```

This will return an object that implements the `Attributes` interface. (The `InitialDirContext` class returns a `BasicAttributes` object.)

After we create an `Attributes` object, which, as you may recall, is a collection class, we can then step through the elements using a `NamingEnumeration` object like this:

```
for (NamingEnumeration ne = attrs.getAll();ne.hasMoreElements();)
{
  Attribute attr = (Attribute)ne.next();
  String attrID = attr.getID();
  System.out.println(attrID+":");
  for (Enumeration vals = attr.getAll();vals.hasMoreElements();)
  {
     System.out.println("\t"+vals.nextElement());
  }
  ...
```

Each element in the `Attributes` object is an object that has implemented the `Attribute` interface. (The `InitialDirContext` class uses `BasicAttribute` objects.) The `getID()` method of the `Attribute` interface returns the name of the attribute. The `getAll()` method, also of the `Attribute` interface, returns a standard Java `Enumeration` object, which we can then access to get the values of the individual attribute.

In every LDAP server, there are certain attributes that are not going to be available to anonymous users because of the access controls on the server. There are also certain attributes that may only be available to certain privileged users – pay scale, for example, may only be visible to human resources.

The next example shows how we can do an authenticated search:

```
// Example 9.2
// Standard authenticated search

...

    public static String MY_HOST = "ldap://localhost:389";
    public static String MGR_DN = "uid=kvaughan, ou=People, o=airius.com";
    public static String MGR_PW = "bribery";
    public static String MY_SEARCHBASE = "o=Airius.com";
    public static String MY_FILTER = "(sn=Carter)";

    public static void main(String args[])
    {
        try
        {
            //Hashtable for environmental information
            Hashtable env = new Hashtable();

            //Specify which class to use for our JNDI provider
            env.put(Context.INITIAL_CONTEXT_FACTORY, INITCTX);
            env.put(Context.PROVIDER_URL, MY_HOST);

            //Security Information
            //authenticates us to the server
            env.put(Context.SECURITY_AUTHENTICATION,"simple");
            env.put(Context.SECURITY_PRINCIPAL,MGR_DN);
            env.put(Context.SECURITY_CREDENTIALS,MGR_PW);

            //Get a reference to a directory context
            DirContext ctx = new InitialDirContext(env);

            SearchControls constraints = new SearchControls();
            constraints.setSearchScope(SearchControls.SUBTREE_SCOPE);
    ...
```

This second search example is exactly the same as the first one, except that we have authenticated ourselves to the server, using the user ID kvaughan.

If you try compiling and running this example, you'll see that it produces the same output as before. Note that by default the LDAP server returns all of the attributes for a search. There may, however, be occasions when we don't want this, because we are only concerned with particular attributes.

In our third example, we ask to only be shown the common name (cn) and e-mail address (mail) attributes:

```
// Example 6.3
// Search return with specified results

...
```

```java
public class JNDISearch
{
    // initial context implementation
    public static String INITCTX = "com.sun.jndi.ldap.LdapCtxFactory";
    public static String MY_HOST = "ldap://localhost:389";
    public static String MY_SEARCHBASE = "o=Airius.com";
    public static String MY_FILTER = "(sn=Carter)";

    //specify which attributes we are looking for
    public static String MY_ATTRS[] = {"cn","mail"};

    public static void main(String args[])
    {
        try
        {
            //Hashtable for environmental information
            Hashtable env = new Hashtable();

            //Specify which class to use for our JNDI provider
            env.put(Context.INITIAL_CONTEXT_FACTORY, INITCTX);
            env.put(Context.PROVIDER_URL, MY_HOST);

            //Get a reference to a directory context
            DirContext ctx = new InitialDirContext(env);

            SearchControls constraints = new SearchControls();
            constraints.setSearchScope(SearchControls.SUBTREE_SCOPE);

            NamingEnumeration results =
                            ctx.search(MY_SEARCHBASE,MY_FILTER,constraints);

            while (results != null && results.hasMore())
            {
                SearchResult sr = (SearchResult) results.next();
                String dn = sr.getName()+", "+MY_SEARCHBASE;

                System.out.println("Distinguished Name is "+dn);
                Attributes ar = ctx.getAttributes(dn,MY_ATTRS);

                if (ar == null)
                {
                    System.out.println("Entry "+dn+
                    " has none of the specified attributes\n");
                }
                else
                {
                    for (int i =0;i<MY_ATTRS.length;i++)
                    {
                        Attribute attr = ar.get(MY_ATTRS[i]);
                        if (attr != null)
                        {
                        System.out.println(MY_ATTRS[i]+":");
                        for (Enumeration vals = attr.getAll();vals.hasMoreElements();)
                            {
                                System.out.println("\t"+vals.nextElement());
                            }
                        }
                    System.out.println("\n");
                }
            ...
```

The difference between this code and our earlier example searches is that we now limit the number of attributes we want retrieved.

First we created a `String` array that listed the attributes we wanted like this:

```
public static String MY_ATTRS[] = {"cn","mail"};
```

To retrieve this set of attributes we use the `getAttributes()` method of the `DirContext` interface, providing the DN of a specific entry and the array of attributes like this:

```
Attributes ar = ctx.getAttributes(dn,MY_ATTRS);
```

We can retrieve a particular `Attribute` object from an `Attributes` object like this:

```
Attribute attr = ar.get("cn");
```

I want to point out that retrieving a specific set of attributes from an individual entry is very quick, but this is not very practical for general searching. In a general LDAP search, the end user is not going to know the existing distinguished names of the entries they are looking for. So we will have to search the LDAP server and retrieve a set of entries. In JNDI (as opposed to the Netscape Directory SDK for Java), this search will return all of the attributes associated with each individual entry. If we then make subsequent call to `getAttributes()`, this will require another call to the LDAP server to get back the set of attributes. This is inefficient because it requires us to user extra memory for all of the attributes and extra bandwidth for the extra communication.

This inefficiency arises from the fact that JNDI is designed to provide multi-protocol access to directory services and its primary goal is to facilitate storage of Java objects on the network. It is *not* a general purpose directory service API.

Because we have just specified the common name and mail attributes this time, the resulting output from the code should look like this:

LDAP Server Modifications

We can also use JNDI to add new entries to the server, delete entries as well as modify existing entries.

Adding Entries

Using JNDI to add entries to an LDAP server is in fact more difficult than it is with other LDAP SDKs. This is because JNDI's primary goal is to allow the storage and retrieval of Java objects over the network. A consequence of this is that a programmer must go through some extra hoops, such as creating a Java class for each type of entry you want to add to the LDAP server. This section is presented to contrast JNDI with the other SDKs that we have discussed. We will look at how to add and modify a simple entry in the LDAP server. Later in the chapter we'll learn how to use the LDAP server as an object store.

To store an entry in an LDAP server using JNDI, you must first bind an object to a DN. This means that each object (whether this a simple person entry or a serialized Java class) we store in the server must have a DN associated with it. This is not an entirely new concept to us because every entry in an LDAP server must have a DN.

To store even a simple entry in the LDAP server, we must create a class that implements the `DirContext` interface.

As with any other LDAP SDK the process of adding an entry can only be performed by an authenticated user, though when it comes to storing Java objects, these authentication rules can be a bit more flexible.

Our next code sample shows a very simple `Person` class that implements the `DirContext` interface. Most of the methods in the interface are not actually implemented because we don't need them for our very simple example here. I derived this class from the `Drink.java` example found in the JNDI tutorial at `http://java.sun.com/products/jndi/tutorial`.

> *New objects must also conform to the LDAP server's schema, or the entries will not be added.*

I think will be easier to explain how to add an entry with JNDI if I explain the code as we go along. The complete source code for this example can be found on the Wrox web site, in a file called `Person.java`.

```
// Example 9.4
// Person class
```

First is our `Person` class declaration; note that we state that we will implement the methods for the `DirContext` interface.

```
public class Person implements DirContext
{
    String type;
    Attributes myAttrs;
```

Next we have our constructor. Note that it takes several strings that we use to build a `inetOrgPerson` object class. If we were going to use this code in a production environment, I would instead require a DN and a `Hashtable` object containing attribute/value(s) pairs.

```
//Person("mewilcox","Mark","Wilcox","ou=Accounting","mewilcox@airius.com");
public Person(String uid,String givenname,String sn,String ou,String mail)
{
    type = uid;
```

We will use the `BasicAttributes` class to store our attributes and their values. The `BasicAttributes` class stores attributes using the `BasicAttribute` class. By specifying `true` in the `BasicAttributes` constructor we are telling it to ignore the case of attribute names when doing attribute name lookups.

```
myAttrs = new BasicAttributes(true);
```

To add a multi-valued attribute we need to create a new `BasicAttribute` object which requires the name of the attribute in its constructor. We then add the values of the attribute with the `add()` method.

```
Attribute oc = new BasicAttribute("objectclass");
oc.add("inetOrgPerson");
oc.add("organizationalPerson");
oc.add("person");
oc.add("top");

Attribute ouSet = new BasicAttribute("ou");
ouSet.add("People");
ouSet.add(ou);

String cn = givenname+" "+sn;
```

Finally we add all of our attributes to the `BasicAttributes` object.

```
myAttrs.put(oc);
myAttrs.put(ouSet);
myAttrs.put("uid",uid);
myAttrs.put("cn",cn);
myAttrs.put("sn",sn);
myAttrs.put("givenname",givenname);
myAttrs.put("mail",mail);
}
```

When the following method is called it will return our `BasicAttributes` object when requested by a name in the form of a `String`. It is designed to only return the attributes of a specific entry, but since this class will only hold one entry, it's not actually going to be called. The following variations of `getAttributes()` are included for illustrative purposes:

```
public Attributes getAttributes(String name) throws NamingException
{
    if (! name.equals(""))
    {
        throw new NameNotFoundException();
```

```
    }
      return myAttrs;
  }
```

This method does the same thing as above but is only called when the name is passed as a `Name` object.

```
public Attributes getAttributes(Name name) throws NamingException
{
    return getAttributes(name.toString());
}
```

This next version of `getAttributes()` returns only the attributes listed in the `String` array `ids`. The first parameter should be a DN:

```
public Attributes getAttributes(String name, String[] ids)
throws NamingException
{
    if (! name.equals(""))
    {
        throw new NameNotFoundException();
    }

    Attributes answer = new BasicAttributes(true);
    Attribute target;
    for (int i = 0; i < ids.length; i++)
    {
        target = myAttrs.get(ids[i]);
        if (target != null)
        {
            answer.put(target);
        }
    }
    return answer;
}
```

The next method does the same as the other `getAttributes()` methods except it takes a `Name` object as well as the array `ids`:

```
public Attributes getAttributes(Name name, String[] ids)
throws NamingException
{
    return getAttributes(name.toString(), ids);
}
```

This very simple function is used for serialization:

```
public String toString()
{
    return type;
}
```

The following lines illustrate a few of the methods that a JNDI service provider, such as the `InitialDirContext` class, would use to provide an application with services, such as reading entries from the directory or authenticating to the server. As they are not going to be used in this example, a full list is not given. However the complete list is included with the full source code at the Wrox web site.

```
public Object lookup(Name name) throws NamingException
{
    throw new OperationNotSupportedException();
}

public Object lookup(String name) throws NamingException
{
    throw new OperationNotSupportedException();
}

public void bind(Name name, Object obj) throws NamingException
{
    throw new OperationNotSupportedException();
}
...
```

And here is the program that uses the `Person` class to add an entry for Mark Wilcox to the LDAP server:

```
// Example 9.5
// Adding an object to an LDAP server

import java.util.Hashtable;
import java.util.Enumeration;

import javax.naming.*;
import javax.naming.directory.*;

public class JNDIAdd
{
    // initial context implementation
    public static String INITCTX = "com.sun.jndi.ldap.LdapCtxFactory";

    public static String MY_HOST = "ldap://localhost:389";
    public static String MGR_DN = "uid=kvaughan, ou=People, o=airius.com";
    public static String MGR_PW = "bribery";
    public static String MY_SEARCHBASE = "o=Airius.com";

    public static void main(String args[])
    {
        try
        {
            //Hashtable for environmental information
            Hashtable env = new Hashtable();

            //Specify which class to use for our JNDI provider
            env.put(Context.INITIAL_CONTEXT_FACTORY, INITCTX);

            env.put(Context.PROVIDER_URL,MY_HOST);
            env.put(Context.SECURITY_AUTHENTICATION,"simple");
            env.put(Context.SECURITY_PRINCIPAL,MGR_DN);
            env.put(Context.SECURITY_CREDENTIALS,MGR_PW);
```

```
        //Get a reference to a directory context
        DirContext ctx = new InitialDirContext(env);

        Person p = new Person("mewilcox", "Mark", "Wilcox", "ou=Accounting",
                                              "mewilcox@airius.com");

        ctx.bind("uid=mewilcox,ou=People,o=airius.com", p);
    }
    catch(Exception e)
    {
        e.printStackTrace();
        System.exit(1);
    }
  }
}
```

As you can see this method of adding an entry to the LDAP server is very different from the other LDAP SDKs we have used. One we have connected and bound and created a `DirContext` object, we must create a new Java object that implements the `DirContext` interface such as our `Person` class like this:

```
Person p = new Person("mewilcox", "Mark", "Wilcox", "ou=Accounting",
                                  "mewilcox@airius.com");
```

Then we associate a name, specifically the DN of the entry, with this object in our current context with the `bind()` method of the `DirContext` interface like this:

```
ctx.bind("uid=mewilcox,ou=People,o=airius.com", p);
```

The `InitialDirContext` class will then perform the LDAP addition operation. It will retrieve all of the attributes we have stored in our entry and add them to the server. Because we used the `BasicAttribute` class to build our attributes, they will be retrieved using the standard name/value pairs we have seen in every other LDAP SDK.

Modifying Entries

As we have seen in previous chapters, there comes a time when LDAP entries need to be updated, for example:

- ❑ A user needs to change his password
- ❑ Someone changes his or her name
- ❑ People switch jobs, and change offices

In JNDI, modifications to an entry are made with the `ModificationItem` and `BasicAttribute` classes. When you make a modification, it can be one of ADD, REPLACE or DELETE. A REPLACE will add an attribute if it doesn't exist.

You should also be aware that if you perform a replace on an attribute that has multiple values, if you don't send the extra values along with your replacement value, they will all be removed. In Chapter 7 we learned how to do this with the PerLDAP SDK, but the same algorithm can be used using C, Java and JNDI.

As we have said previously, modifications must be performed by an authenticated user and the range of modifications will be determined by the rights the bound entry has on a particular entry. For example, users can generally change their passwords but nothing else, while administrative assistants can change telephone numbers and mailing addresses. Finally, it takes a database administrator to do things like change a user ID.

The code shown below demonstrates how we can modify the attributes of the `Mark Wilcox` entry that we added in the previous example:

```
// Example 9.6
// Modifying an entry

import java.util.Hashtable;
import java.util.Enumeration;

import javax.naming.*;
import javax.naming.directory.*;

public class JNDIMod
{
    // initial context implementation
    public static String INITCTX = "com.sun.jndi.ldap.LdapCtxFactory";

    public static String MY_HOST = "ldap://localhost:389";
    public static String MGR_DN = "uid=kvaughan, ou=People, o=airius.com";
    public static String MGR_PW = "bribery";
    public static String MY_SEARCHBASE = "o=Airius.com";

    public static void main(String args[])
    {
        try
        {

            ...

            //Get a reference to a directory context
            DirContext ctx = new InitialDirContext(env);

            ModificationItem[] mods = new ModificationItem[2];

            Attribute mod0 = new BasicAttribute("telephonenumber","940-555-2555");
            Attribute mod1 = new BasicAttribute("l", "Waco");

            mods[0] = new ModificationItem(DirContext.REPLACE_ATTRIBUTE,mod0);
            mods[1] = new ModificationItem(DirContext.ADD_ATTRIBUTE,mod1);

            //DirContext.DELETE_ATTRIBUTE not shown here
            ctx.modifyAttributes("uid=mewilcox,ou=People,o=airius.com", mods);
        }
        ...
```

To modify an entry first create an array of two `ModificationItem` objects. The `ModificationItem` takes a modification type (add, replace or delete) and an `Attribute` object such as `BasicAttribute`. Here is a simple example that does two things. First it changes the telephone number, i.e. replaces an old value with a new one, as specified by the `DirContext.REPLACE_ATTRIBUTE` flag. Secondly, it adds a new attribute to the entry, a locality (the `l` attribute), with a value of "Waco". The `DirContext.ADD_ATTRIBUTE` flag allows this to take place:

```
Attribute mod0 = new BasicAttribute("telephonenumber","940-555-2555");
Attribute mod1 = new BasicAttribute("l", "Waco");

mods[0] = new ModificationItem(DirContext.REPLACE_ATTRIBUTE,mod0);
mods[1] = new ModificationItem(DirContext.ADD_ATTRIBUTE,mod1);
```

The actual modification is performed by the `DirContext` method, `modifyAttributes()`, as follows:

```
ctx.modifyAttributes("uid=mewilcox,ou=People,o=airius.com", mods);
```

Deleting Entries

Eventually, you will need to remove entries from you LDAP server. This is easily accomplished by calling the `destroySubContext()` method of the `DirContext` interface, with the distinguished name of the entry that needs to be removed. Normally, delete operations are restricted to the LDAP database administrators.

Here is an example of deleting an entry:

```
// Example 9.7
// Delete Entry

import java.util.Hashtable;
import java.util.Enumeration;

import javax.naming.*;
import javax.naming.directory.*;

public class JNDIDel
{
    // initial context implementation
    public static String INITCTX = "com.sun.jndi.ldap.LdapCtxFactory";

    public static String MY_HOST = "ldap://localhost:389";
    public static String MGR_DN = "cn=Directory Manager";
    public static String MGR_PW = "jessica98";
    public static String MY_SEARCHBASE = "o=Airius.com";

    public static String MY_ENTRY = "uid=mewilcox, ou=People, o=airius.com";

    public static void main(String args[])
    {
        try
        {
            ...

            //Get a reference to a directory context
            DirContext ctx = new InitialDirContext(env);

            ctx.destroySubcontext(MY_ENTRY);
        }
        catch(Exception e)
        {
```

```
            e.printStackTrace();
            System.exit(1);
        }
    }
}
```

The only real difference in the code in this example and the rest of our examples is this line:

```
ctx.destroySubcontext(MY_ENTRY);
```

This will remove the entry in the LDAP server, specified by the parameter MY_ENTRY.

Using a Different Provider

As we saw earlier in this chapter, JNDI allows us to change service providers easily without having to rewrite our entire application. In this section, you should see just how easy this is.

In our example here, we are going to use the **IBM JNDI Directory Service Provider**, which is a fully LDAP version 3 compliant provider. When JNDI was initially released, the Sun provider was only LDAPv2 compliant. In late 1998, Sun released a fully LDAPv3 compliant JNDI provider.

The IBM provider was developed as part of the IBM AlphaWorks project, which is a web site devoted to Research and Development for computing, primarily in Java (http://www.alphaworks.ibm.com). While the AlphaWorks name is designed to let users know that the products are not commercially supported, many of them, like this JNDI provider, work very well. Some of them have even started to appear in IBM's commercial products – for example, the High Performance Compiler and the XML parser. Perhaps this JNDI LDAP provider will be one of those by the time you read this.

This example is the same simple search example from earlier except that it uses the IBM LDAP JNDI provider. Once the IBM JNDI provider is installed, all you have to do is change one line from this:

```
static String INITCTX = "com.sun.jndi.LDAPCtxFactory";
```

to this:

```
static String INITCTX = "com.ibm.jndi.LDAPCtxFactory";
```

Everything else should work as expected. Well, let me say this with one caveat. If you are working in the US, everything else does work as expected. However, unbeknown to me, the IBM provider requires some Secure Socket Layer code which they can't ship to developers overseas because the US government considers the exporting of encryption code on the same level as exporting nuclear weapons. So if you are outside of the US, you will just have to read along. I don't make the rules, I just live by them. Just remember that not all providers will be created equal, so not all providers will have all of the same functions as the other. The only way that I know of determining the capabilities of providers is by reading their provided documentation.

So if you live in the States, try this example out. It is exactly the same as the search example 9.3, but with just one code change:

```
// Example 9.8
// Search using IBM's JNDI LDAP Provider

import java.util.Hashtable;
import java.util.Enumeration;

import javax.naming.*;
import javax.naming.directory.*;

public class JNDISearch
{
...
```

```
    //Use IBM's JNDI LDAP Package instead
    public static String INITCTX = "com.ibm.jndi.LDAPCtxFactory";
```

Using JNDI and LDAP to Store Java Objects

In the final part of this chapter, we'll see how easy it is to store and restore Java objects in an LDAP server using JNDI. This is important in enterprise distributed computing, because it means you can create a central repository for classes that perform certain tasks you need in your everyday business. The logic of the classes are called **business rules**, and the classes themselves are called **business objects**. In the past, we had to recreate these rules for each application. Now, with JNDI and the forthcoming Enterprise JavaBeans, we are able to create classes that implement these rules once, store them in an LDAP server and recreate them in our Java applications as we need them.

In order to store a Java object, an LDAP server must support the Java JNDI schema. This schema ships with the JNDI SDK and will likely appear by default in LDAP servers by the time you read this. Alternatively you can turn off the schema checking facility in Directory Server. Objects to be stored must support the Java Serialization interface called Serializable. This is simple to implement. All you have to do is say that your class implements the Serializable interface and that's it. For more information on this topic consult your favorite Java resource such the official Java site at http://java.sun.com/, or Ivor Horton's *Beginning Java 2* published by Wrox Press.

Storing and Restoring Methods

To store a Java object in LDAP, you just need to pass the following simple line of code:

```
    ctx.bind("cn=JSlider,ou=Java,o=airius.com",slider);
```

Here, ctx is a reference to a Java object that implements the DirContext interface. The first parameter in the bind() method is the distinguished name of the LDAP entry and the final parameter is the Java object to be stored, in this case, slider.

And that's it.

We covered adding an LDAP entry earlier in the chapter, but this is an "add" with a difference. The slider object is actually an instance of the JFC component JSlider. This piece of code takes the current state of the slider variable and serializes it to the LDAP server. It is stored as a JavaObject object class entry in the LDAP server.

To get a reference to that object from the server you do the following:

```
JSlider my_slider = (JSlider)ctx.lookup("cn=JSlider,ou=Java,o=airius.com");
```

This will return to you a fully working JSlider complete with the state of the JSlider (the position of the slider on the scale) when it was stored.

And to remove the object you just make a call like this:

```
ctx.unbind("cn=JSlider,ou=Java,o=airius.com");
```

Authentication Control

Because you are storing your objects in an LDAP server, you can take advantage of LDAP access controls to provide a fine grain of security to your Java objects. For example, you might just want specific users to be able to store the actual objects, application administrators perhaps, but allow anyone to get access to them. You definitely would want to restrict the ability to delete the objects, because a lot of work may have gone into the creation of the object in the first place and removing it would erase all of that work, not to mention how many applications the deletion might break.

Another popular reason to store your objects in LDAP is that you can use Secure Socket Layer (SSL) to transmit your objects. This protects them from being stolen 'over the wire' and because SSL includes verification of the parties, it can help prevent a 'man-in-the-middle' attack where someone might try to sneak in a malicious piece of code to crash your application, or steal data. Security and LDAP will be discussed in more detail in Chapter 12.

Not the Whole Story

In our example, we are storing the entire Java object in the LDAP server. This might not always be the best way to store Java objects – either to save disk space, network bandwidth or other reasons. JNDI also supports the concept of *References*.

Prepare Schema

The JNDI SDK ships with an LDAP schema that you can use so you can store Java objects in your LDAP server. You will need to see your LDAP server's instructions for manually adding schema updates, or look up Appendix D on schema modification, because I include an example application that modifies the schema using Java. You might also want to turn schema checking off, which is fine for testing, but it's not recommended for production use because your data could get corrupted.

You will also need to create a new organizational unit called ou=Java under the o=airius.com root. This would be a good chance for you try out your LDAP programming skills in adding a new entry to your LDAP server.

Example Application

The example application that is presented here is called TUG, which stands for *Totally Useless GUI*. It does nothing except show you how to store a Java object (in this case a JFC Slider) into a LDAP server and retrieve that object.

Here is a diagram that shows you the relationship of object serialization, LDAP and JNDI:

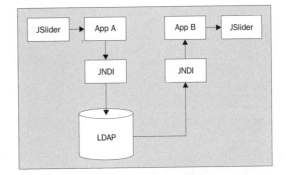

This example uses the Sun LDAP JNDI provider and the Java Foundation Classes, that is Swing. It draws a frame with a panel that contains a `JSlider` and two `JButtons`:

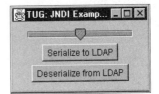

When you click on the Serialize to LDAP button this will set the slider to its 15 position and then stores it in the LDAP server:

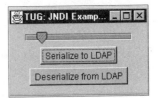

After you have serialized the slider, search your LDAP server for the entry `cn=JSlider,ou=Java,o=airius.com` and you will see it there. The junk that is displayed as the attribute values is the Base64 encoding of the Java object's serialized state.

When you click on the Deserialize from LDAP button, a new frame opens up. On this new frame, you'll see a non-modified `JSlider` and then see the deserialized `JSlider`, which should set itself to the same position as the original `JSlider`:

The screenshot on the right shows the deserialized slider object. The window shows the position of the slider when it was serialized, at position 15, as the bottom of the two sliders. The top one can be moved as before, though it doesn't actually do anything. I told you this GUI was useless and if you haven't tried out the code, you really won't get the full experience! However, when you do run it, you'll be amazed at how easy it is to store and retrieve Java objects using LDAP. At the click of the mouse, TUG is stored on the server, at the click of the mouse it is retrieved again.

Now let's take a look at the code to show how TUG works:

Again since the code is so long and most if it is devoted to building the GUI, I will highlight the JNDI sections.

```
// Example 9.9
// Storing Java objects to LDAP with JNDI

import com.sun.java.swing.*;
import com.sun.java.swing.tree.*;
import com.sun.java.swing.text.*;

import java.awt.event.*;
import java.awt.*;
import java.io.*;
import java.util.*;

import javax.naming.*;
import javax.naming.directory.*;

//Totally Useless GUI
//Demonstrates the use of Serializing objects in JNDI
public class TUG extends JPanel
{
```

Initialize our static JNDI variables.

```
    // initial context implementation
    public static String INITCTX = "com.sun.jndi.ldap.LdapCtxFactory";

    public static String MY_HOST = "ldap://localhost:389";
    public static String MGR_DN = "uid=kvaughan, ou=People, o=airius.com";
    public static String MGR_PW = "bribery";
    public static String MY_SEARCHBASE = "o=Airius.com";

    public JSlider slider = null;

    // TUG constructor, creates slider and two buttons and enables mouse
    public TUG ()
    {
        slider = new JSlider();

        Button b1 = new Button("Serialize to LDAP");
        Button b2 = new Button("Deserialize from LDAP");

        b1.addMouseListener(new serializeTUGClicker(this));
        b2.addMouseListener(new deserializeTUGClicker(this));
        add(slider);
        add(b1);
        add(b2);
    }

    // sets size of TUG GUI
    public Dimension getPreferredSize()
    {
        return new Dimension(200,120);
    }
```

This method serializes TUG to the LDAP server:

```
public void serializeTUG()
{
    try
    {
```

Here the JNDI environment is initialized:

```
        //Hashtable for environmental information
        Hashtable env = new Hashtable();

        //Specify which class to use for our JNDI provider
        env.put(Context.INITIAL_CONTEXT_FACTORY, INITCTX);

        env.put(Context.PROVIDER_URL,MY_HOST);
        env.put(Context.SECURITY_AUTHENTICATION,"simple");
        env.put(Context.SECURITY_PRINCIPAL,MGR_DN);
        env.put(Context.SECURITY_CREDENTIALS,MGR_PW);
```

Get our initial context.

```
        //Get a reference to a directory context
        DirContext ctx = new InitialDirContext(env);
```

Change our `JSlider` value.

```
        //do something to show we had a modified slider
        slider.setValue(15);
        updateUI();
```

Store our `JSlider` object in the LDAP server.

```
        //now bind our JSlider
        System.out.println("getValue is "+slider.getValue());
        ctx.bind("cn=JSlider,ou=Java,o=airius.com",slider);
    }
    catch(Exception e)
    {
        e.printStackTrace();
        System.exit(1);
    }
}
```

This method retrieves our serialized `JSlider` from the LDAP server.

```
public void deserializeTUG()
{
    try
    {
        //Hashtable for environmental information
        Hashtable env = new Hashtable();
```

```
              //Specify which class to use for our JNDI provider
              env.put(Context.INITIAL_CONTEXT_FACTORY, INITCTX);

              env.put(Context.PROVIDER_URL,MY_HOST);
              env.put(Context.SECURITY_AUTHENTICATION,"simple");
              env.put(Context.SECURITY_PRINCIPAL,MGR_DN);
              env.put(Context.SECURITY_CREDENTIALS,MGR_PW);

              //Get a reference to a directory context
              DirContext ctx = new InitialDirContext(env);
```

Here we retrieve our `JSlider` object with the `lookup()` method of the `DirContext` interface.

```
              //Now get our slider back from the LDAP server
              JSlider my_slider =
                          (JSlider)ctx.lookup("cn=JSlider,ou=Java,o=airius.com");
              System.out.println("getValue is "+slider.getValue());
```

And this is where we delete the `JSlider` entry. If you want to unload TUG but don't want to delete it from the server, you can comment out this line.

```
              ctx.unbind("cn=JSlider,ou=Java,o=airius.com");
```

Finally we display the retrieved `JSlider` object.

```
              //Now put it back on the screen
              my_slider.setValue(my_slider.getValue());

              System.out.println("getValue is "+slider.getValue());
              JFrame frame = new JFrame("TUG Deserialization Window");
              JPanel panel = new JPanel();
              //Another slider to demonstrate that we have a new one
              JSlider temp_slider = new JSlider();
              panel.add(temp_slider);
              panel.add(my_slider);
```

The rest of the code deals entirely with the GUI handling methods.

```
              frame.setDefaultCloseOperation(JFrame.DO_NOTHING_ON_CLOSE);
              frame.setForeground(Color.black);
              frame.setBackground(Color.lightGray);
              frame.getContentPane().add(panel,"Center");

              frame.setSize(new Dimension(200,100));
              frame.setVisible(true);
              frame.addWindowListener(new TUGWindowCloser());updateUI();
          }
      catch(Exception e)
      {
          e.printStackTrace();
          System.exit(1);
      }
  }
```

The `main()` function creates the TUG object and draws the GUI:

```java
    public static void main(String args[])
    {
        try
        {
            JFrame frame = new JFrame("TUG: JNDI Example Application");
            TUG panel = new TUG();

            frame.setDefaultCloseOperation(JFrame.DO_NOTHING_ON_CLOSE);
            frame.setForeground(Color.black);
            frame.setBackground(Color.lightGray);
            frame.getContentPane().add(panel, "Center");

            frame.setSize(panel.getPreferredSize());
            frame.setVisible(true);
            frame.addWindowListener(new WindowCloser());
        }
        catch(Exception e)
        {
            System.out.println(e.toString());
            e.printStackTrace();
            System.exit(1);
        }
    }
}

// close window and exit
class WindowCloser extends WindowAdapter
{
    public void windowClosing(WindowEvent e)
    {
        Window win = e.getWindow();
        win.setVisible(false);
        win.dispose();
        System.exit(0);
    }
}

// close the deserialized TUG window
class TUGWindowCloser extends WindowAdapter
{
    public void windowClosing(WindowEvent e)
    {
        Window win = e.getWindow();
        win.setVisible(false);
        win.dispose();
    }
}

// method that performs the serialization of TUG in response to the mouse click
class serializeTUGClicker extends MouseAdapter
{
    protected TUG myTUG;
    serializeTUGClicker(){this.super();}
    serializeTUGClicker(TUG aTUG){this.super();myTUG = aTUG;}

    public void mouseClicked (MouseEvent e)
    {
        try
        {
```

```
                myTUG.serializeTUG();
            }
            catch(NullPointerException npe) {}
        }
    }

    // method that performs the deserialization of TUG in response to the mouse click
    class deserializeTUGClicker extends MouseAdapter
    {
        protected TUG myTUG;
        deserializeTUGClicker(){this.super();}
        deserializeTUGClicker(TUG aTUG){this.super();myTUG = aTUG;}

        public void mouseClicked (MouseEvent e)
        {
            try
            {
                System.out.println("Mouse Clicked");
                myTUG.deserializeTUG();
            }
            catch(NullPointerException npe) {}
        }
    }
```

Summary

In this chapter we have explored how to search and manipulate an LDAP server using the Java Naming and Directory Interfaces (JNDI). We have seen that it operates in quite a different way to the other SDKs covered in this book, especially the Netscape LDAP Java SDK. We have used JNDI classes and interfaces to add, modify and delete a simple entry. We have also demonstrated the purpose for which JNDI was developed – to store Java objects on the server that can be loaded and unloaded from the client console. We showed this with a simple, but ultimately useless example, TUG. Finally JNDI providers for LDAP have been produced by Sun and also by IBM and we showed how simple it is to change from one provider to another.

Programming with the ADSI SDK

10

ADSI is Microsoft's **Active Directory Service Interfaces**. It is similar in concept to Sun's Java Naming and Directory Interface (JNDI) that we looked at in the last chapter. It is designed by Microsoft to provide a common API for programming to a variety of directory services, and at the present time is specific to Windows. The power of ADSI lies in the fact that it based on Microsoft's Component Object Model (COM).

> *If you haven't encountered COM before, then don't worry. I'm going to explain a bit about it in this chapter — enough for you to follow the examples presented here. If you want to find out more, there are many good books on the subject. You could also check out the introduction to COM that comprises chapters 1 and 2 from* Professional COM Applications with ATL, *available for download from the Wrox Press web site at* http://www.wrox.com.

The fact that ADSI is based on COM means that the ADSI SDK can be used very easily by any programming language that understands COM, and there are a lot of them. For example, you can use ADSI from C, C++, Visual Basic, Java, and scripting languages, such as VBScript. If that doesn't impress you, then just think that this also means you can even use ADSI to access an LDAP directory service from an Excel or Word macro!

This chapter will follow much the same format as previous chapters — we'll spend a bit of time looking at what ADSI is, then go through some practical examples showing how to do various operations on LDAP directories using ADSI, such as adding and modifying entries.

Because ADSI is based on COM, we need to learn a bit about COM before we can learn about ADSI. COM's a really deep subject — there have been whole books written about it — but here we'll just touch on the surface of it enough to know what's going on in ADSI.

Also, don't get confused between ADSI and Active Directory — they might have similar names, but they are different. Active Directory is the LDAP directory service that forms a core part of the new Windows 2000 operating system, whereas ADSI is a standard for accessing different directory services.

We'll be looking briefly at Active Directory at the end in this chapter.

About ADSI

We're going to start off by looking at what ADSI is before we go on to the background of how it works. Then we will move on to some examples of ADSI programming.

So, let's see what ADSI can do for us. The diagram below shows how ADSI fits in between your client and a directory service:

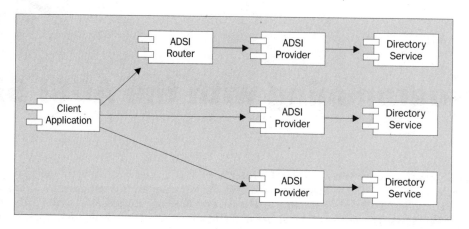

The client here is the same as throughout the rest of this book – it's the application you've written to access a directory service. First of all, the client will probably talk to something called the **ADSI router**. Remember that ADSI is a standard for getting to lots of different directory services. That means you could have several different directories on your computer, so when you attempt to bind to an object, the first thing ADSI has got to do is figure out which directory you want to access. The ADSI router is a bit of software (actually a DLL) which is able to browse through the ADSI providers on your system and tell you which ones are present. If you're not sure what ADSI provider you want, then you'll have to use the ADSI router. On the other hand, if you do know the name of the provider, you'll most likely by-pass the router altogether, and talk straight to the provider. This is why there is an extra link in the diagram that goes from the client straight to the providers.

An **ADSI provider** can be thought of as the ADSI wrapper around a directory service. It accepts requests from the client that are made using the various functions offered by ADSI, and converts the request into whatever communications mechanism that directory service understands. The provider can then talk to the directory service and pass the results back to the client. The result is that the client can really talk to any directory for which an ADSI provider exists, using exactly the same API calls. To some extent, this is very similar to what LDAP tries to do.

The differences between LDAP and ADSI are:

- ❑ ADSI actually defines the API calls as part of its standard. LDAP broadly defines the protocols by which the clients should talk to the directory services, but largely leaves the actual API up to the individual implementation.
- ❑ In terms of sophistication of language, ADSI is a high level standard. You can talk to ADSI from many languages, something that is not possible with the LDAP API.

This all sounds a bit theoretical, so in the next section, we'll look at some examples of ADSI providers, which should make it clearer how this all works in practice.

The ADSI Providers

ADSI providers can come in two flavors:

❑ Ones that Microsoft have written, which you'll usually get automatically when you install ADSI, although what you get will, to some extent, depend on how your system is set up.

❑ Third party providers, written by independent software vendors. There will probably be quite a few of these written over the next few years

One of the aims of ADSI is to unify directory access, so Microsoft are hoping that, whenever anyone writes a new directory service, they will also write an ADSI provider around it, so that client applications can use ADSI to talk to the directory. However, at the moment, ADSI is still new and so the only important ADSI providers are those Microsoft has written. These are sometimes known as the **system providers**, and they include:

❑ The LDAP provider
❑ The WinNT provider
❑ The NDS provider
❑ The IIS provider

So, let's have a look at these in a bit more detail.

The LDAP Provider

This is the one that we're really interested in, because it's the one we'll be using for the examples later on. You can think of this provider as being like a protocol converter – i.e. it converts LDAP to ADSI and vice versa. Using this provider, you should be able to talk to any LDAP directory using ADSI instead of an LDAP API. It does mean there's an extra layer between your client and the directory service, but Microsoft claim this layer is very thin and won't add significantly to your processing time. Whether this claim is true is more controversial – I've seen conflicting reports about this on the Internet. Directories that you'd typically access using the LDAP provider include Active Directory, the Exchange Server Directory, and Netscape Directory Server.

The WinNT Provider

This is an unusual one, in that it doesn't actually really have a directory service behind it. It gathers together information from the various computers on your local network, for example, user accounts, services, groups and so on, and combines this information so that it all *looks* like it's coming from a directory. The point is really that Active Directory will be a central directory of information on Windows 2000, but Windows NT 4.0 doesn't have such a directory. However, if you use the WinNT provider, you can program applications as if there really is a directory of all your resources, just like Active Directory. Cunning, huh? You can use the WinNT provider to do things like modify user accounts or monitor resources, such as printers on your network.

The NDS Provider

NDS is Novell's NetWare Directory Services, which we looked at in Chapter 1, and it comes as no surprise to know that this is the provider you would use to talk to NDS! If you have computers on your network running NDS, then you can use ADSI to communicate with NDS using this provider.

The IIS Provider

IIS is Microsoft's Internet Information Server. It's the software that processes all the requests from browsers if you have a web site hosted on your machine. Internally, IIS maintains a directory of virtual directories, security and configuration information for the IIS server. The IIS provider – yep, you got it – let's you access the IIS directory using ADSI.

You can probably see from this discussion that there are a lot of things that ADSI providers can do. Typically, they wrap around a directory service, but clearly, they don't have to. If required, you can write a provider that fakes a directory to make things easier for clients, just like the WinNT provider does. I wouldn't be surprised to find in the future that ISVs are producing directories intended for Windows, for which the directory service itself is an ADSI provider.

Active Directory Browser

The easiest way to see what directories look like using ADSI is to use one of the general-purpose ADSI browsers Microsoft has written. Of these, the most powerful one is an application that goes by the name `adsvw.exe`. It's also known as the Active Directory Browser (Microsoft trying to confuse us about the distinction between ADSI and Active Directory again!). This is actually part of the Windows 2000 beta, but you can run it on its own on Windows NT 4.0.

The ADSI Directory Structure

When you first start up the Active Directory Browser, you should see a dialog like this:

If you then select ObjectViewer, another dialog box appears asking you for the object at the root of the tree to be displayed:

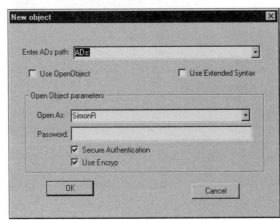

If you type in ADs: for the object, you can see all the ADSI providers installed on your machine. If you type in something more specific, you can limit the tree to any particular provider, or even to a sub-tree within that provider. Checking the box marked Use OpenObject indicates that you want to supply a username and password. This is what the resulting screen looks like on my machine:

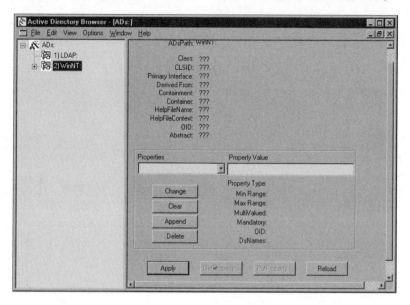

As you can see, it's a pretty standard Explorer style user interface, with the left hand pane showing the tree structure of a directory down to the selected object, and the right hand pane showing details of the object.

The main thing to notice about it is how all the different providers actually appear as children of a single object, ADs:, giving the appearance of one single huge directory that encompasses everything else. ADs: is the ADSI router. It's also known as the **namespaces object**, because it contains all the various ADSI namespaces. Confusingly, the objects immediately below it in the hierarchy are termed the **namespace objects**, reflecting that each of them heads one namespace. In the screenshot above, you can see that both LDAP and WinNT providers are installed.

> *Note that there is a third provider, Sample, which is a sample ADSI provider written by Microsoft to illustrate how to write an ADSI provider. It features a small registry-based directory of people.*

Note that the WinNT provider has a box next to its name indicating that there are further entries inside it, whereas the LDAP provider does not. Due to a restriction of LDAP, it is generally not possible to browse LDAP providers on a system. You have to know the name of the provider you are looking for and supply it explicitly. Because of this, the LDAP namespace object is unable to detect which objects are inside it, and so appears as empty.

However, if you do specify a pathname in the New object dialog box, you can still get to LDAP directories, for example, you can simple give the LDAP URL for the root directory on your LDAP server.

The following screenshot, from the Active Directory Browser, shows how you can use ADSI to look specifically at the LDAP directory `o=airius.com`:

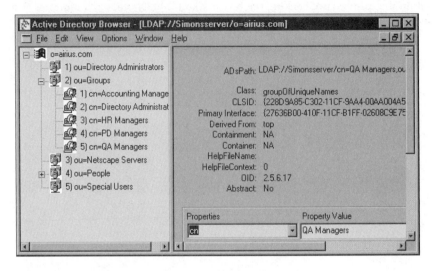

Querying a Directory

If instead of selecting ObjectViewer in the first dialog, you select Query, you can do a search of a directory. In this case, you should see a dialog box like this:

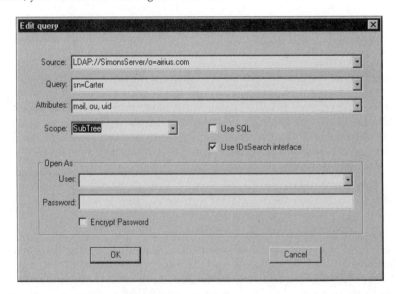

Here, the ADsPath is specified to the Directory Server called `o=airius.com` running on your local machine, that is `localhost`. If you're wondering, ADsPath is just what we call pathnames to ADSI objects that are in a format that ADSI providers can understand. The search finds everyone with a surname of `Carter`, and should return the e-mail, organizational unit and user ID attributes which are displayed. The scope is anywhere within the directory. Recall that the search scope is discussed in Chapter 6.

There a also a dialog box for preferences on various advanced options for the search, but it's usually OK to leave these blank, as I've done here:

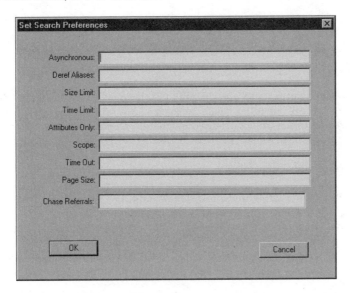

With this search specified, these are the results:

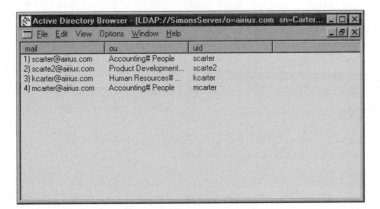

Installing Active Directory Browser

`adsvw.exe` comes automatically with Windows 2000 beta. It was not shipped with NT 4.0, but if you have a Windows 2000 beta CD, you can extract it on to your hard drive and run it as normal. Just run the command prompt, change directory to whichever directory you want `adsvw.exe` to reside in, and type in the command:

```
Extract PATHNAME/adsvw.ex_
```

PATHNAME is the path to the folder on the CD in which `adsvw.ex_` resides.

`adsvw.exe` should also be available with Windows 2000 when it's released, though Microsoft have indicated they intend to replace it with a Microsoft Management Console snap-in which will perform a similar function.

The ADSI Object Model

Now that we've seen what ADSI can do for you and how its directories are structured, it's time to move on to look at the theory behind how it works and how to write applications using it.

A Word About COM

COM is a standard for how applications and objects talk to each other. COM is all about objects, so if you've programmed in any object-oriented language, or even in Visual Basic, you'll have no trouble understanding this. In most traditional object-oriented languages, an object is simply something that has properties (data) and methods (functions). Properties are the things that define the state the object is in and methods are the things the object can do. As we have seen, this contrasts with the idea of an object in a directory, which has only properties.

In order to understand ADSI, we need to know a few things about COM. In this chapter, we'll be focussing on programming ADSI clients from Visual Basic and scripting languages, so this section will cover the ADSI object model from a Visual Basic programmer's perspective. If you already know any COM, you'll probably be surprised by some of the details that are left out. I won't say anything about reference counting or GUIDs, or any of the sorts of things that C++ programmers working with COM need to understand – precisely because you don't need those things in order to program with COM using Visual Basic.

Visual Basic and scripting languages to a large extent hide what's going on inside COM from the programmer. This means that if you're going to write COM clients (which is what your ADSI client applications are) in these languages, then you don't really need to know anything about how COM works. To understand how ADSI objects are designed, however, you need to know a bit about COM interfaces, which are discussed later on in this chapter. So, if you want to use ADSI from Visual Basic, this chapter will cover everything you need to know.

ADSI COM Objects

In this section, we're going to see how ADSI objects work with a couple of examples. Let's see how, in Visual Basic, you get an object in a directory using ADSI:

```
Dim objLDAP As Object
Set objLDAP = GetObject("LDAP://MyServer/o=airius.com")
```

If you're a Visual Basic programmer, the first thing that you'll notice is there's actually nothing new here! GetObject() is not a special ADSI function – it's a function that gets used all the time in Visual Basic to retrieve COM objects. You give it a name, and it finds the COM object which matches that name. The previous line, with the Dim statement, simply declares the variable. By declaring it as type Object, we're simply saying that it's a COM object of some description.

So, the only interesting bit in the above code extract is the pathname supplied to `GetObject()`. When the computer sees the pathname, it tries to figure out what it means. It does this by looking at the first component – in this case, `LDAP:`. It knows it's looking for some kind of COM object, so it looks round your system (i.e. the registry and a few other places) to see if it can create a COM object that answers to the name, LDAP. If you've got ADSI installed on your system, then it'll discover it can do this – so it goes ahead and creates an instance of this object. Now the object that answers to the name `LDAP:`, just happens to be – wait for it – ADSI's LDAP provider. More accurately, the LDAP provider itself isn't an ADSI object, it's a dynamic link library (DLL) that hosts a COM object known as the LDAP namespace object. And it's this object which gets instantiated.

> *If you've only programmed on Unix, you may not have heard of DLLs before. They are libraries that can be linked in at run time rather than link time, similar to* `.so` *files (Shared Libraries) on Unix*

So, we have the LDAP namespace object. What does the computer do then? It hands the entire remainder of the `ADsPath` over to that object. Basically it says, "This is as far as I can get. You figure out what the rest of this funny name means." The LDAP namespace object will look at the rest of the pathname, which says `MyServer/o=airius.com`. It knows from this that it's looking for an LDAP directory service running on a machine called `MyServer`. And because there's no port number specified, it knows to look on the default LDAP port, 389. Once it's got that directory service, it will internally use the LDAP API to locate the object with the distinguished name `o=airius.com` and bind to it.

Now, all that probably sounds very complicated, but the beauty of it is that that's all taken care of for you. All you have to do is supply the correct `ADsPath` to the standard Visual Basic call `GetObject()`, and you've got the object in the directory.

ADsPaths

The principle behind `ADsPaths` is fairly simple. They start with the name of the provider, and add `://`. Everything after that is determined by the provider – you have to look in the documentation for that particular provider to find out how the rest of the pathname works. However, most providers use a fairly intuitive format. Let's look at some examples to gain a better idea of how this works.

Firstly, if you don't know which provider to use, you can use the path `ADs:`, which will simply hook you up to the ADSI router.

For the WinNT provider, you can use paths such as `WinNT://MyDomain/MyComputer/Me`. This will get you to the local user account called `Me`, on the computer called `MyComputer`, which is a member of the domain `MyDomain`.

We have already seen one example of an `ADsPath` for the LDAP provider. Here's another one: `LDAP://SERVERNAME:444/uid=Mark,ou=people,o=airius.com`. The pathname has a more complex syntax because you need to specify the name of the server and the port number, and what follows is a typical LDAP path with comma separators. Only if you are looking for an LDAP server that runs on the default port of 389, do you simply supply the server name. Once you've got that far, the rest of the `ADsPath` is simply the distinguished name of the required object in the directory.

Here is another LDAP example: `LDAP://dc=MyDomain,dc=com`. Here, the server name has been omitted completely, so LDAP will look for the nearest installation of Active Directory. This will probably be the Active Directory that controls the domain of which your local computer is a member. Incidentally, this example illustrates one of the few special connections between ADSI and Active Directory. They are different (honest!) but it seems Microsoft can't resist anything that helps you to access their own LDAP directory! In this latter example, the `ADsPath` is the `ADsPath` of the domain object for the domain `MyDomain.com`.

Here is one final example: `GC://dc=MyDomain,dc=com`. `GC:` is a special prefix that indicates the **global catalogue**, which is a part of Active Directory. It contains some of the data in Active Directory, but with many of the attributes for each object omitted. This can speed up searching. If you use a pathname beginning with `GC:`, you will still hook up to Active Directory, you will still be using the LDAP provider, but the provider will know that you want to perform a fast search using only the global catalogue rather than the entire Active Directory database. This is an exception to the rule that you attach to a provider by specifying the name of the provider followed by a colon, and is accomplished by some clever registry entries.

Wrapping Directory Objects

We now know how to use VB to bind to an ADSI COM object. I just want to go over the significance of the object we've bound to a bit more carefully. Shown below is the same Visual Basic snippet we saw earlier, but this time adding an extra line that asks for the object's name:

```
Dim objLDAP As Object
Set objLDAP = GetObject("LDAP://MyServer/o=airius.com")
Debug.Print objLDAP.Name
```

Now just take a moment to compare this with the equivalent C code that uses the LDAP API:

```
LDAP            *ld;    // declare to an LDAP structure
int             rc;     // integer to store LDAP error codes

// connect to server. If it fails, print error message
if ( (ld = ldap_init( MyServer, 389 )) == NULL )
    {
        perror( "ldap_init" );
    }

rc = ldap_simple_bind_s(ld, MY_DN, MY_PWD);   //bind to the server
```

Do you notice something different about how the line that gets the object's RDN works, that is apart from the fact that they're in different languages? Well in the LDAP C example, we've only bound to the directory. We have to specify the name of the server in the `if` statement, and then specifically bind to it in a separate function call. In the Visual Basic ADSI example, the connection and bind are carried out in the same call after the `objLDAP` object has been created. The object does the job for us. We can then use the object as we so wish. Here we ask for its name, hence the syntax: `objLDAP.Name`.

That's partly what object-oriented programming is about: breaking the program into self-contained chunks – objects, which do the dirty work of processing API calls leaving the user free to do other things. If you look back over the last two chapters you'll see that both the Java and JNDI SDKs use the same principle.

There's one crucial point to understand here, which also applies to Java and JNDI, and that is the object you have – the entity called `objLDAP` in the above example – is not the object in the directory. It's a proxy object within your program that wraps the object in the LDAP directory. In the specific case of ADSI, it's actually a COM object that you're program talks to. The COM object understands how to access the object in the LDAP directory using the LDAP API, so that you don't have to worry about it.

Since what we've got is a COM object, we need to understand some of the special rules about how COM objects work.

Understanding COM Interfaces

As we've seen already, an 'object' in terms of the object-oriented programming model, is something that has methods and properties which can carry out a series of API calls without the user being aware. COM, however, introduces an extra layer of abstraction. Instead of the object itself exposing the properties and methods, the object has a number of **interfaces**, and it is the interfaces which expose the properties and methods. To some extent, you can regard an interface as just a way of grouping together properties and methods, though as we'll see later, it does have more significance than that.

To see how this works in practice, let's examine the most common interface used in ADSI, `IADs`. `IADs` defines the following properties:

Property	Description
Name	The name of the object. For LDAP, this is the object's relative distinguished name.
ADsPath	The object's `ADsPath`.
GUID	A GUID (otherwise known as a UUID) that uniquely identifies the object's class. Note that this *not* the same as the `objectGuid` attribute, which uniquely identifies the instance of the object.
Class	The class of the object. For LDAP, this is the same as the `objectclass` attribute.
Schema	This is the `ADsPath` of an object known as a class object, which contains the full definition of the class our object belongs to.
Parent	The `ADsPath` of the object in the directory that contains this object. This property allows you to easily navigate up the directory tree.

And the following methods:

Method	Description
Get()	Returns the value(s) of a named property.
Put()	Sets the value(s) of a named property.

Method	Description
GetEx()	Returns the value(s) of a named property. Similar to Get(), but returns the results in a slightly different format. GetEx() is useful if you don't know whether the property is single or multi-valued.
PutEx()	Sets the value(s) of a named property. Contains various options that are useful for multi-valued properties. For example, using PutEx(), you can replace all the values, remove a value from the list, add a new value or clear all the values.
SetInfo()	Updates the property cache.
GetInfo()	Retrieves the property cache.
GetInfoEx()	Selectively retrieves certain named properties from the property cache.

There are several new concepts here in these descriptions of what the methods do, but don't worry about them for the moment. Right now what interests us is that this is *the* definition of the interface, IADs. What this means is if you have any COM object which implements IADs, then you know automatically that you can call up any of these methods. You don't know for certain what will happen when you call them – that much is entirely up to the particular object concerned. For example, ADSI namespace objects and the ADSI router generally don't have a schema, and will often return an error if you attempt to access their Schema property. The point is, however, that if IADs is implemented, then these properties and methods are available.

Why am I making such a big issue of this? The reason is that this is defining principle of COM. Once an interface is defined, the set of properties and methods it exposes is set in stone. It must never, ever, be changed. A COM interface is often described as being a contract between the client and server for this reason. Even if you later on decide an interface isn't quite what you wanted, you can't change it because of the risk of breaking existing software using it. You just have to define a new interface instead. Which is why, for example, if you look up the ADSI documentation, you'll find an interface IPropertyValue, and another interface, IPropertyValue2.

The other point about COM and interfaces is that you *never* talk directly to an object. You always talk to it through one of its interfaces. Take a look at our Visual Basic snippet again:

```
Dim objLDAP As Object
Set objLDAP = GetObject("LDAP://MyServer/o=airius.com")
Debug.Print objLDAP.Name
```

The line that declares objLDAP as an Object is actually doing something more precise than that. It's declaring that objLDAP refers to a special interface called IDispatch. IDispatch is a general-purpose interface intended to allow Visual Basic and scripting clients to find out what other interfaces are actually supported and call up methods on them. In Visual Basic (but not VBScript) I could equally well have written the code like this:

```
Dim objLDAP As IADs
Set objLDAP = GetObject("LDAP://MyServer/o=airius.com")
Debug.Print objLDAP.Name
```

This will work the same, but will run a bit more efficiently, because I've effectively told the computer that IADs is the interface I will be using, which saves it a bit of work at run time in figuring out how to call the Name property.

For more information on how you can program COM using Visual Basic read VB COM: Visual Basic 6 Programmer's Introduction to COM *by Thomas Lewis, published by Wrox Press.*

Interface Inheritance

COM interfaces support inheritance. If interface A inherits from interface B, this means that A must implement all the properties and methods of B, as well as its own properties and methods. This isn't something that should bother us too much. I've mentioned it to simply stop any COM gurus shouting at me for misleading you. You see, I've actually missed out some of the properties and methods of IADs in my list above. I gave you all the IADs ones, but forgot to mention that IADs is derived from the standard COM interface, IDispatch. The fact that it derives from IDispatch means that scripting clients are able to use the IDispatch methods to indirectly call the IADs methods. So, we could also list the extra IDispatch methods along with the IADs ones, but they're not relevant to understanding how ADSI works. If you're really interested, you can look it up in any COM book.

Well that's the story for interfaces. Let's get back to the main meat of this chapter – ADSI.

The Property Cache

Some of the IADs methods mention something called the **property cache**. This is an attempt to cut down on the network traffic. An ADSI object exists in the same process as your client, so it's very efficient to carry out operations that effect only the client and the ADSI object. The overhead is not really any more significant than a normal function call within a program. On the other hand, the directory service will almost certainly exist in a separate process, in all probability on a separate machine. Heck, if you're using the Internet, it's not inconceivable that you could be sitting in California carrying out operations on a directory located in Australia. Communication between your ADSI COM object and the directory itself is therefore likely to be considerably slower, so we really need to try to cut down on the number of network calls that actually go over the wire.

The property cache is ADSI's attempt to get round this. Each ADSI object maintains its own local copy of some or all of the properties (that is attributes) that the corresponding directory object has – this is the property cache. When you read from or write to any of these attributes, using any of the ADSI object's properties or most of the ADSI object's methods, including Get(), Put(), GetEx() and PutEx(), you are actually only reading from or writing to the property cache. When you have finished your changes and want them written to the directory itself, you call IADs::SetInfo(), which writes whatever happens to be in the property cache to the actual directory. This is more efficient because everything gets written in one single network call. If you don't call SetInfo(), then your changes will never make it to the directory, and so will be lost as soon as your client exits.

Similarly, it's generally good practice to call GetInfo() when you first obtain your object. This copies the data from the directory into your property cache. It's not absolutely necessary to call GetInfo(), because most ADSI methods will detect any attempt to read from an uninitialized property cache and automatically call GetInfo() for you. GetInfoEx() is a way of being even more efficient – if you know in advance that you're only interested in certain properties, you can call GetInfoEx(), specifying exactly which ones you want, and only those properties will be copied into your property cache.

Programming with ADSI

We've now got to the point where we've covered enough theory of ADSI. It's time to get stuck into some practical examples of how to carry out common operations with ADSI. As with the previous chapters, these examples use the sample data that comes with Netscape Directory Server. The server is running on port 389 of the computer, `localhost`, which means that the `ADsPath` for the directory is `LDAP://localhost/o=airius.com`.

Running these examples requires an installation of ADSI 2.5, which you can download from the Microsoft web site, `http://www.microsoft.com`. When you install ADSI, you will automatically get the WinNT and LDAP providers. If your computer is running Windows 2000 (or a version of the beta) then you will have ADSI installed automatically. In your Visual Basic projects, you'll need to add the ADSI type library to the list of references, which can be done very easily by going to Tools | References and clicking on the Active DS Type Library check box. Note that this is not necessary if you are using VBScript.

The beauty of this is that once you've installed the directory server and ADSI, there's nothing more to be done. ADSI will be able to talk to the LDAP directory automatically. The only point you may have to watch is that if your computer is a domain controller running Windows 2000, then you might find that port 389 is already in use by Active Directory and you need to select another port for any other LDAP server. It's hard to be certain of this yet because (at the time of writing) Windows 2000 hasn't been released – so when you have it you should check the documentation for it.

Binding and Authenticating

We've already seen in Visual Basic how to do a simple bind to an object, using the `GetObject()` function. This function supplies default credentials to the directory service. What the term "default credentials" means depends on the particular ADSI provider. Often it will mean that the default user credentials of the account from which you are running the client are assumed. But for LDAP, it is simply the equivalent to performing an anonymous bind (i.e. supplying `NULL` credentials).

Unusually, supplying credentials is something that is harder to do in Visual Basic than in C++. There is no single function to do this. Instead, there is (wait for it) another interface, `IADsOpenDSObject`. `IADsOpenDSObject` has no properties and just one method, `OpenDSObject()`, which returns the object for which the `ADsPath` has been supplied, binding to it using the supplied credentials.

The `IADsOpenDSObject` interface is normally exposed by just one COM object in each directory, the namespace object. This means that to bind to an object as an authenticated user, you will first have to bind to the namespace object using default credentials, then use its `IADsOpenDSObject::OpenDSObject()` method to supply the actual credentials to the object you want. The `OpenDSObject()` method requires the `ADsPath` of the object, your username and password, and an integer which indicates roughly the level of encryption required. To keep things simple here, we'll keep that as zero:

```
Dim objNamespace As IADsOpenDSObject
Set objNamespace = GetObject("LDAP:")

Dim objLDAP As IADs
Set objLDAP = objLDAPns.OpenDSObject("LDAP://localhost/ou=people, o=airius.com",_
                              "cn=Directory Manager", "password", 0)
```

Now it's time to go onto some fully functional examples. The first few of these are Visual Basic projects, with a simple interface consisting of a form with a single list box that looks like this:

Retrieving Entries

IADs is the main ADSI interface and is very crucial for this reason: an ADSI object always implements IADs.

IADs gives you all the methods you need to retrieve any property for which you already know the name. If you don't know the name of the property you're looking for, or you just want to browse all the properties, then it's a bit more complicated. We'll treat these two cases separately.

Retrieving Known Attributes

If you do know the names of the properties, then it's easy. The standard six properties exposed by IADs (summarized in the section *Understanding COM Interfaces*) can simply be treated as variables. Any other properties can be obtained using Get() or GetEx() on specifying the name of the property.

I've added code to the Form_Load() function, called when the application starts up, which adds data from the LDAP server to the list box. This example prints out several properties.

You are reminded that this code is available for download from the Wrox web site.

```
' Example 10.1
' LookUpKnown.vbp

Private Sub Form_Load()

' bind to directory object ou=people, o=airius.com
Dim objLDAP As IADs
Set objLDAP = GetObject("LDAP://localhost/ou=people,o=airius.com")

' retrieve standard IADs properties
List1.AddItem "Name (RDN)of object is     " & objLDAP.Name
List1.AddItem "ADsPath of object is " & objLDAP.ADsPath

' retrieve a single valued property
List1.AddItem ""
List1.AddItem "Single-valued property:"
List1.AddItem "Value of ou is       " & objLDAP.Get("ou")
```

```
' retrieve a multi-valued property
List1.AddItem ""
List1.AddItem "Multi-valued property: objectClass: Values are"
Dim objClasses
objClasses = objLDAP.Get("objectClass")
For Each Value In objClasses
    List1.AddItem Value
Next

End Sub
```

This code starts by displaying the name and the ADsPath. These are standard properties that are defined as part of the IADs interface, so we can just treat them as variables. Then we move on to have a go at a single valued property defined in the schema, ou, using the Get() method on the IADs object. This returns the value of the property requested, ready to put in the list box.

Finally, we display a multi-valued property, in this case, the objectclass attribute. Because it's multi-valued, it will be returned as an array of values – which there's an extra variable defined, objClasses, to hold the array. We can use a For Each loop to iterate through the values.

Clear enough? Here are the results:

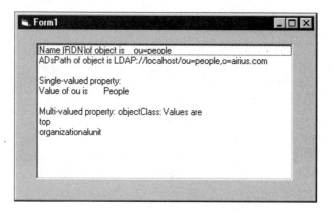

Retrieving All Attributes

If we don't know the names of the properties, then we've got more of a problem. One approach is to use the schema, which relies on us getting the ADsPath of the class object.

The class object implements another interface, IADsClass, which exposes a number of properties concerned with the schema. Two of these are called MandatoryProperties and OptionalProperties, which respectively return lists of the names of the required and optional properties objects of the class that we have. We can then pass these names as parameters to IADs::Get(). The code looks like this:

```
' Example 10.2
' LookUpUnknown.vbp

Private Sub Form_Load()

' bind to directory object ou=people, o=airius.com
Dim objLDAP As IADs
Set objLDAP = GetObject("LDAP://localhost/ou=people,o=airius.com")

' locate schema
Dim objSchemaADsPath
objSchemaADsPath = objLDAP.Schema
List1.AddItem "ADsPath of class object is " & objSchemaADsPath

'bind to schema object
Dim objSchema As IADsClass
Set objSchema = GetObject(objSchemaADsPath)

'list mandatory properties and values
List1.AddItem ""
List1.AddItem "MANDATORY PROPERTIES"
For Each property In objSchema.MandatoryProperties
    List1.AddItem property
    Dim AttrValues
    AttrValues = objLDAP.GetEx(property)
    For Each Value In AttrValues
        List1.AddItem "        " & Value
    Next
Next

End Sub
```

Here, we've bound to the object as normal, and then used the property `IADs::Schema` to get the `ADsPath` of the schema object, and bound to this object specifying the `IADsClass` interface. Armed with this information, we can step through the list, requesting each named property from our original object. Notice that `GetEx()` is used, which will always return an array of values, even for single valued properties. We need to do this because we don't immediately know which of the properties are single valued. The advantage of this is that we are always able to step through the array displaying the values, without having to test how many values there are first.

For simplicity, the above code example only displays the mandatory properties. In principle, the optional properties can be dealt with in exactly the same way, except you use the `OptionalProperties` property of the class schema object. However, there is an extra complication in this case, because some of the optional properties may not have any values set — that is, after all, the point of an optional property! If no value has been set, then the call to `GetEx()` will raise an error, which needs to be handled, complicating the code somewhat.

Here's the output from the above code:

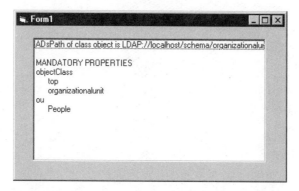

There is, incidentally, an alternative way of enumerating through all the properties. An ADSI object normally exposes another interface, `IADsPropertyList`, which has methods to enumerate all the properties. This approach is simpler, but produces slightly different results, in that it will only retrieve the properties that are actually in the property cache. This means, for example, that you won't get any data back concerning optional properties for which the object does not have a value. Depending on what you want to do with the data this could be an advantage or a disadvantage.

> *We're not going to cover using `IADPropertyList` here, because it involves learning another three interfaces (`IADsPropertyList`, `IADsPropertyEntry` and `IADsPropertyValue2`), and we only have one chapter on ADSI! But if you're interested, the information is in the MSDN.*

Modifying Entries

Modifying an entry in your LDAP server using ADSI is simply a case of using the `IADs::Put()` method for single valued properties, or `PutEx()` for multi-valued properties. The only significant point to remember is the to call `SetInfo()` to update the actual directory after you've changed the values in the cache. The following example demonstrates the modification of the description property for Sam Carter's entry.

Setting properties is something for which you generally need higher access rights than for looking up properties. So in this example we need to actually authenticate to the directory. In the code example below, the authentication is done as the directory manager – an easy choice because the directory manager has access to modify virtually anything in the Netscape sample database. Here the directory manager has a password of 'password', but obviously you'll need to adjust this for you own:

```
' Example 10.3
' ModifyEntries.vbp

Private Sub Form_Load()

' bind to directory object uid=scarter, ou=people, o=airius.com
' authenticating as the directory manager
Dim objLDAPns As IADsOpenDSObject
Set objLDAPns = GetObject("LDAP:")
```

```
Dim objLDAP As IADs
Set objLDAP = objLDAPns.OpenDSObject("LDAP://localhost/ou=people, o=airius.com",_
                          "cn=Directory Manager", "password", 0)

' retrieve standard IADs properties
List1.AddItem "Name (RDN)of object is    " & objLDAP.Name
List1.AddItem "ADsPath of object is " & objLDAP.ADsPath

'set a property
objLDAP.Put "description", "what a lovely object"
objLDAP.SetInfo
List1.AddItem "Description is now " & objLDAP.Get("description")

End Sub
```

And the results of this code are:

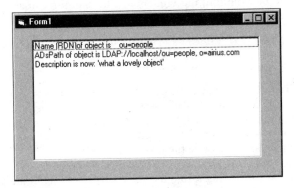

Browsing the Directory

LDAP itself doesn't really have any concept of browsing a directory. So if you want to implement this kind of functionality, you must do a search specifying a scope of one-level with a filter of (objectclass=*). Similarly, LDAP doesn't have any separate concept of retrieving the results from one specified object. If that's what you want to do, you actually do a search with a scope of base only.

ADSI differs in both of these respects. If you want to retrieve any property of a particular object, then you can use the IADs methods, and if you want to browse down the directory hierarchy, then you can use the IADsContainer interface. This is implemented by every ADSI object which can contain other objects. In other words, if the object in the directory is a container, then the corresponding ADSI object will implement both the IADs and IADsContainer interfaces.

IADsContainer exposes the following properties:

Property	Description
Count	Returns the number of objects that the container object holds
Filter	A filter that determines which class of child objects we are interested in

And the following methods:

Method	Description
GetObject()	Returns an ADSI COM object corresponding to the child of this container, which has the supplied RDN.
Create()	Creates a new COM object of the given name and class. This object will be written to the directory itself (in other words, a corresponding new object will be created in the directory) when SetInfo() is called on the new object.
Delete()	Deletes the named object, which must be a child of the container. This deletion happens in the directory immediately.
MoveHere()	Moves an object, which can be anywhere else within the same directory, to be a child of this container. This method can also be used to rename an object.
CopyHere()	Same as MoveHere(), except that it makes a copy of the object, leaving the original in place as well.

You can probably see from this list that IADsContainer is the interface to use for doing things like moving objects around your directory. It also has a GetObject() method that allows you to obtain a specific child object as long as you know the name of it. But from the list above, there doesn't seem to be anything that lets you get a list of all the child objects if you don't already know their names — which is what we need if we are to browse the directory.

In fact, ADSI objects support browsing through a standard COM technique known as **enumerators**. What this means is that if you're programming in Visual Basic or VBScript, you can use Visual Basic's For Each loop to list the contents of a container. The code for this browse example is shown below:

```
' Example 10.4
' Browse.vbp

Private Sub Form_Load()

' bind to object and list its children
Dim objContainer As IADsContainer
Set objContainer = GetObject("LDAP://localhost/ou=people,o=airius.com")

For Each person In objContainer
    List1.AddItem person.Name
    List1.AddItem person.Class
Next

End Sub
```

So, if you're using Visual Basic you don't actually need a separate COM method to do browsing at all. As you can see, implementing this kind of functionality is really very straightforward.

The results from this code look like this:

The code above will retrieve all objects no matter what class they are. If we only want to retrieve objects of a certain class, or classes, we can do this by setting the `Filter` property of the `IADsContainer` interface. So, for example, if we want to restrict our output to objects that are people, we must modify the above code to read:

```
' bind to object and list its children
Dim objContainer As IADsContainer
Set objContainer = GetObject("LDAP://localhost/ou=people,o=airius.com")

objContainer.Filter = Array("inetOrgPerson")
For Each person In objContainer
    List1.AddItem person.Name
    List1.AddItem person.Class
Next
```

Note that a filter here is simply a list of classes and it is *not* the same thing as an LDAP search filter. At the moment, we're talking about browsing, not searching. You should also note that an array is used here because the filter is a list of names – you might want to retrieve information about more than one class.

Unfortunately, there's no point giving a screenshot for the above code, because it's exactly the same as the previous screenshot. *All* entries in the container ou=people,o=airius.com have the object class inetOrgPerson – so you'll just have to believe that the filter really does work! A filter would be useful in cases were some entries within ou=people,o=airius.com belong to a particular object class and others don't.

Adding Entries

If you look back at the table summarizing the methods of the IADsContainer interface, you should be able to guess what the method we're going to need next is – IADsContainer::Create(). The main points to note with this method is that you call Create() on the container of the object you want to create, and that you must subsequently call SetInfo() on the COM object that you've just created to actually add the corresponding directory object. This gives you a chance to set the values of the appropriate properties, which you need to do to ensure that your new object does not break the schema rules of the directory – in which case the call to SetInfo() will fail. Recall that the directory service will refuse to create an object that doesn't satisfy the schema.

The next couple of examples are in VBA rather than Visual Basic. The code below is a little Excel macro that creates a new organizational unit, called Another OU in the Netscape sample directory.

> *If you haven't actually written Excel macros before, you need to go to the* Tools | Macros | Visual Basic Editor *to type it in.*

Here's the macro:

```
' AdsCreate.txt

Sub ADsCreate()
' creates an ADSI object

Dim objNamespace
Set objNamespace = GetObject("LDAP:")

Dim objContainer
Set objContainer = objNamespace.OpenDSObject("LDAP://localhost/o=airius.com",
"cn=Directory Manager", "password", 0)

Dim objOU
Set objOU = objContainer.Create("organizationalUnit", "Another OU")

objOU.Put "objectClass", Array("top", "organizationalUnit")
objOU.Put "ou", "thingies"

objOU.SetInfo

' now show some data for the new object
Range("A1").Select
ActiveCell.FormulaR1C1 = "Name"
Range("B1").Select
ActiveCell.FormulaR1C1 = objOU.Name

Range("A2").Select
ActiveCell.FormulaR1C1 = "ADsPath"
Range("B2").Select
ActiveCell.FormulaR1C1 = objOU.ADsPath

Range("A3").Select
ActiveCell.FormulaR1C1 = "ou"
Range("B3").Select
ActiveCell.FormulaR1C1 = objOU.ou

End Sub
```

Here are the results of this code:

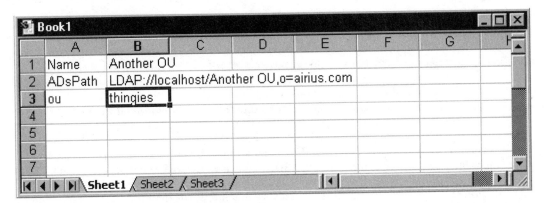

Neat, huh! I bet you didn't realize you could do this with Excel!

Deleting Entries

This is similar to adding entries, except that it's simpler – there are no properties to set (obviously!) and no need to call `SetInfo()` because the deletion is instantaneous. Here's the code to do it, again in Excel:

```
' AdsDelete.txt

Sub ADsDelete()
' deletes an ADSI object
Dim objNamespace
Set objNamespace = GetObject("LDAP:")

Dim objContainer
Set objContainer = objNamespace.OpenDSObject("LDAP://localhost/o=airius.com",_
             "cn=Directory Manager", "password", 0)

objContainer.Delete "organizationalUnit", "Another OU"

End Sub
```

Searching

We've left searching until last because of all the operations it's the most complex one to carry out in ADSI if you are using scripting clients.

ADSI defines an interface to carry out searching, `IDirectorySearch`, but it is not accessible to scripting clients. This is because – without going into too much detail – scripting languages use a slightly indirect method of calling COM methods, which uses the `IDispatch` interface. The upshot of this is that scripting clients can only call methods on interfaces that are derived from `IDispatch`. Most COM interfaces satisfy this requirement, but `IDirectorySearch` doesn't.

So, how can you carry out searching with ADSI? The answer is – if you're using Visual Basic or scripting languages – you don't. You use another SDK, known as **ActiveX Data Objects** (**ADO**). ADO is very similar in concept to ADSI. It is a set of COM objects and interfaces that allow you access to data. The difference is that whereas ADSI is geared very much towards directories, ADO is aimed more at conventional databases.

Whereas in ADSI you would connect to a particular provider, in ADO you connect to a data source – which for practical purposes is pretty much the same thing as far as the client is concerned. The actual data sources will be different, though. A common data source used with ADO is the SQL Server database. Another one is the ADSI ADO provider. This *isn't* an ADSI provider – it's an ADO data source, but it's a data source, which takes its data by hooking up to whatever ADSI provider you specify when you first connect to it. It's a somewhat indirect route – in the case of LDAP the process is as follows. Data gets passed from the LDAP directory to your client, first via the LDAP API, then the ADSI ADO provider, then through OLE DB (a lower level set of interfaces which ADO sits on top of), and finally through ADO. Complex but it works – and it does enable you to carry out searching!

Unfortunately, because this involves a fair bit more learning to get familiar with ADO, we don't have space here to go into full details of how to do this, but there is a good sample in the ADSI section of the Platform SDK documentation.

Remember, however, that this only applies to LDAP searches for which a complex search filter is required, or for which the scope is `subtree`. In order to carry out an LDAP search with a scope of `base` or `one-level`, and for which the filter is no more complex than specifying one or more object classes, you would use the `IADs` and `IADsContainer` methods to obtain the results more simply.

Introduction to Active Directory

Active Directory is the name Microsoft has given to its next generation directory services for Windows 2000. Active Directory really has a dual role. On the one hand, it is an LDAP directory, but at the same time it actually forms a replacement for Windows NT domains and is seen as a competitor to Novell's NDS.

Active Directory is intended as a directory of network resources. This means it will contain details of computers, printers, groups and user accounts. However, because it also contains data for all the security permissions, this means that it can actually be used as the directory on which the new Windows 2000 domains will be based.

It has really been introduced in response to a lot of criticism that the NT domain model previously used to control the sharing of resources across a network was inadequate for large enterprises, because of its lack of a central directory. As a result of this, Windows NT 4.0 has primarily been used on stand-alone workstations and in small networks. It's failed to make significant inroads into the market for very large enterprises, where Unix systems still dominate.

Since the new Windows 2000 operating system has yet to be released at the time of writing, it's hard to assess the actual performance of Active Directory. However, its features include the following:

- ❑ Replication
- ❑ Installation information
- ❑ Security ACLs
- ❑ Domain trees and forests
- ❑ Extensible schema

Replication

In order to improve performance, the directory may be replicated across multiple servers. The servers hosting the directory all have an equal status as domain controllers. There is no such thing as a primary domain controller, as there is with NT 4.0 domains, which hold ultimate authority.

Having multiple servers hosting the directory raises the usual problem of keeping all servers up to date. Active Directory uses a flexible model, in which it is OK for some copies of the directory to be out of synch for a short time. In other words, a modification made to the directory may take a while before it is propagated across all the servers. The copies of the directory are updated at frequent intervals, and a sophisticated algorithm is used to determine which of the copies of the directory is the most up to date. This is the one propagated to the other servers.

Installation Information

Active Directory will contain information about the software that is installed on the network. This information will be used in conjunction with a new application, the Windows Installer, to ease the process of installing software. One of the new features resulting from this is it will be possible to install components of an application on demand. This means that there will be no need to install all components when the software is first installed, but if an attempt is made to use a component that hasn't been installed, the Windows Installer will step in and automatically install it first.

Security ACLs

Information about security permissions will be maintained through Access Control Lists (ACLs) and Access Control Entries (ACEs). It will be possible to put separate access control lists around not just individual directory entries, but around individual attributes, so that users can be granted or denied access to individual attributes. This clearly gives a very fine granularity of authorization control.

Domain Trees and Forests

Active Directory supports the organization of NT domains into domain trees. A tree of domains allows sub-domains to be created for sections of an organization, with some security permissions being passed down the tree. This will make it easier for organizations to subdivide their networks. A forest is a set of domains that share schema and configuration information, but don't have a common parent domain.

Extensible Schema

The Active Directory schema can be freely modified or extended, so you can store your own classes of objects in it, if the standard Microsoft schema classes are not suitable for your purposes.

Summary

ADSI is a pretty deep subject, and the Component Object Model, on which it is based, is even deeper. We've done no more than scratch on the surface of it here. I hope it's enough to give you some idea of the potential power of ADSI, and how easy it can be to use ADSI to access LDAP directories, especially from Visual Basic and VBA and Excel. The fact that Microsoft have chosen ADSI as the recommended means of accessing Active Directory pretty much guarantees that ADSI will become a widely used means of accessing LDAP directories over the next couple of years.

Alternative LDAP SDKs and Tools

Over the last five chapters, we have discussed the primary APIs and SDKs that you can use to add LDAP functionality to your own applications. In this chapter, we will discover some different LDAP SDKs and various existing tools that you can use in your LDAP applications. Most of the subject matter in this chapter covers additional features of existing products, simple tools and demonstrations of language extensions. Some are fairly new technologies that you may not be familiar with.

The reason why I'm adding this chapter is that you might be using applications or programming in languages that we haven't covered yet, and you need to know that LDAP is available to you even if you cannot use, or do not want to use, one of the existing LDAP SDKs. For example you might be one of the hundreds of programmers out there, developing web applications using the PHP language. If you are worried that you may have to throw all that work out because you want to use LDAP, well don't be. PHP supports LDAP. Or you might be a Perl programmer who doesn't want to use the PerLDAP SDK because it requires the Netscape Directory SDK for C. You can still access LDAP from "pure" Perl, with Graham Barr's Net::LDAP module. There are also tools presented here that give you access to LDAP from ODBC and Server-Side JavaScript.

Here's what we'll cover in this chapter:

- ❑ Standard LDAP command line tools
- ❑ The Perl Net::LDAP API
- ❑ PHP web programming language
- ❑ PS Enlist (ODBC)
- ❑ SSJSLDAP SDK
- ❑ ColdFusion

LDAP Command Line Tools

The LDAP command line tools have been a part of standard LDAP packages ever since LDAP first appeared. Every LDAP server distribution that I know of comes with its own versions of the standard tools – the University of Michigan, for instance, OpenLDAP and Netscape etc., and they all operate in very much the same way. Learning how to use these tools is essential if you are going to be building clients for LDAP, or administrating an LDAP server. They have been thoroughly tested and debugged, and so they provide a useful, quick and easy way to test out LDAP search filters and modifications, without the need to develop software programs. The two utilities, that are fairly ubiquitous, are ldapsearch and ldapmodify.

ldapsearch

The ldapsearch command line tool was developed as an example client for the original LDAP API from the University of Michigan. A version of it is included with just about every type of LDAP development kit, for example you will find an ldapsearch executable in the Tools directory of the Netscape SDK for C. It is very simple to operate, indeed its simplicity is what makes it the best tool to build your LDAP queries when you are developing fuller LDAP clients.

The ldapsearch command is used like this:

```
ldapsearch -b "my_search_base" "(search filter)"
          [-h ldaphost -p ldapport
           -D "dn to bind as"
           -w "password"
           -s "list of attributes to return"]
```

A basic example would be:

```
ldapsearch -b "o=airius.com" "(sn=Carter)"
```

This would return all of the entries that have Carter as the value of their sn attribute.

By default, the ldapsearch tool will look for an LDAP server on the local machine (localhost), so you will usually need to specify the host, for example:

```
ldapsearch -h ldap.myhost.com -p 389 -b "o=airius.com" "(sn=Carter)"
```

Sometimes you will need to search as an authenticated user in order to see attributes that are not presented when you are bound as an anonymous user (such as the user password or perhaps salary).

```
ldapsearch -h ldap.myhost.com -p 389 -D "cn=Directory Manager" -w "mypassword" -b
"o=airius.com" "(sn=Carter)"
```

By default, the search results will return all of the attributes and values in the entry. To limit those results you can use the -s parameter. In the example below, we would return only the uid of each resulting entry:

```
ldapsearch -b "o=airius.com" "(sn=Carter)" -s uid
```

The output from such a search would look something like this:

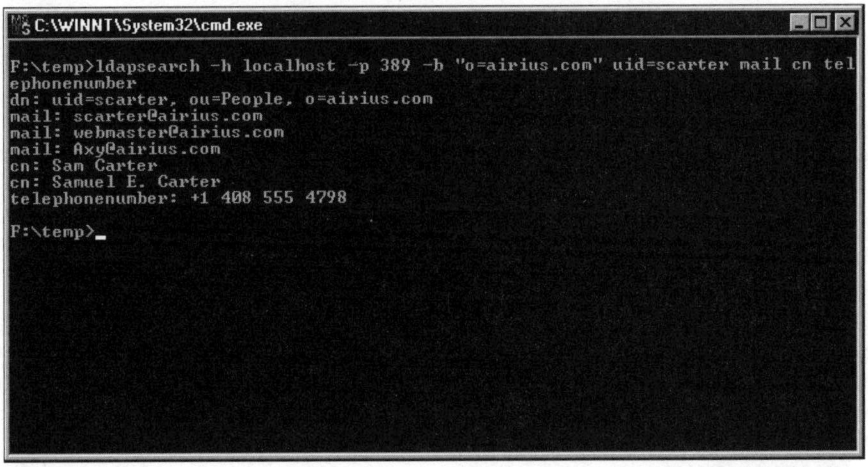

ldapmodify

The `ldapmodify` tool allows you to add new entries, as well as modifying existing ones. Suppose you want to add an new entry that is stored in LDIF format in a file called `add.ldif`. You could do this with the following line:

```
ldapmodify -h ldap.myhost.com -p 389 -D "uid=kvaughan, ou=People, o=airius.com" -w
"bribery" -a -f add.ldif
```

Two new switches can be seen here, `-a` which is the go-ahead signal to carry out the modification, and `-f` which tells the tool to add the new entry as the specified file. The file `add.ldif` that is being used in the above command is shown below. It is in the standard LDIF format that we have seen in earlier chapters:

```
dn: uid=mewilcox,ou=People,o=airius.com
cn: Mark Wilcox
sn: Wilcox
givenname: Mark
uid: mewilcox
mail: mewilcox@mail.airius.com
```

To change an attribute, you would use the following syntax:

```
ldapmodify -h ldap.myhost.com -p 389 -D "uid=mewilcox, ou=People, o=airius.com" -w
"bobby"
dn: uid=mewilcox, ou=People, o=airius.com
changetype: modify
replace: userpassword
userpassword: newpassword
\n\n
```

The syntax for a `ldapmodify` is as follows. First you must specify the DN of the entry you wish to change. Next you must tell it what type of modification you wish to make with the `changetype` parameter. The value for `changetype` is either `add`, `modify`, or `delete`. Next you indicate which attribute you are going to modify – in this case we are going to replace the `userpassword` attribute. On the following line the new password is entered. Finally you end the entry with two carriage returns, which is represented above as `\n\n` – this is required for `ldapmodify` to complete its operation.

Net::LDAP

The Net::LDAP module was developed by Graham Barr. The difference between Net::LDAP and PerLDAP is that Net::LDAP doesn't require you to have any C libraries installed on your system. All you need is a Perl interpreter, version 5.004 or later, for it to work. It should be noted that any version of Perl before 5.004 is considered a security risk, so you shouldn't be using it anyway. Since Perl is found on all flavors of Unix, on Windows and Macintosh systems, and even mainframes, this library has a wide variety of platforms it can run on. I've personally used both Net::LDAP and PerLDAP in production environments with great success, so you can choose the LDAP module for Perl that you feel most comfortable with. Choose Net::LDAP for its ease of portability, or PerLDAP when you want the extra speed a C based API gives you, because either one will serve you just fine.

Using Net::LDAP

You can get Net::LDAP from the Comprehensive Perl Archive Network (CPAN) at `http://www.perl.com/CPAN/`. Documentation for the SDK is contained in the modules that make up the SDK in a format called Plain Old Documentation (or POD) which is the standard way of providing documentation for Perl modules. Check with your Perl distribution to see how to translate POD into the format of your choice (which can range from plain text to HTML and postscript format). Graham also maintains a listserv for Net::LDAP users to subscribe to and send messages to. The address is `perl-ldap-request@mail.med.cornell.edu`.

The next example shows you the basics of programming with `Net::LDAP`.

```
#Exercise 11.1
#!/usr/local/bin/perl
#search.pl with Net::LDAP
use Net::LDAP;

$ldap = new Net::LDAP('localhost');

$ldap->bind ;      # an anonymous bind

$mesg = $ldap->search (
                  base   => "o=airius.com",
                  filter => "(sn=Carter)"
                ) or die ("Failed on search.$!");

foreach $entry ($mesg->all_entries) { $entry->dump; }

$ldap->unbind;     # end session
```

To create a new Net::LDAP object you use the standard new syntax and provide the constructor with a hostname, and optionally a port number, the default being 389. You can authenticate to the server anonymously with a call to the `bind` method. The `search` method in its most simple form (as shown above) takes a base and a filter, in a comma pair. The symbol `=>` is a fancy way of denoting a comma. Finally to disconnect from the server, you make a call to the `unbind` method which takes no parameters.

The `search()` method returns a `Net::LDAP::Message` object from which you can process LDAP result codes, referrals and entries. A call to the `Net::LDAP::Message` method, `all_entries` returns an array of `Net::LDAP::Entry` objects. To display their contents as LDIF you can use the `dump` method of the `Net::LDAP::Entry` object.

The next example shows a bound search:

```
#Exercise 11.2
#!/usr/local/bin/perl
#search.pl with Net::LDAP
use Net::LDAP;

$ldap = new Net::LDAP('localhost');

$ldap->bind (
            dn       => 'uid=kvaughan, ou=People, o=airius.com',
            password => 'bribery'
            ) || die $@;

$mesg = $ldap->search (
                    base   => "o=airius.com",
                    filter => "(sn=Carter)"
                    ) or die ("Failed on search.$!");

foreach $entry ($mesg->all_entries) { $entry->dump; }

$ldap->unbind;   # end session
```

The only difference between this example and the one above is the call to the `bind()` function:

```
$ldap->bind (
            dn       => 'uid=kvaughan, ou=People, o=airius.com',
            password => 'bribery'
            ) || die $@;
```

We simply give it an entry's DN and password, just as with any other LDAP SDK. For those unfamiliar with Perl, the $@ is not a typo – it displays the error message of the call fails.

Next we restrict the search, by adding limits.

```
#Example 11.3
#!/usr/local/bin/perl
#search.pl with Net::LDAP
use Net::LDAP;

$ldap = new Net::LDAP('localhost');
```

```
$ldap->bind (
                dn        => 'uid=kvaughan, ou=People, o=airius.com',
                password => 'bribery'
                ) || die $@;

@attrs = ['uid','mail'];
$mesg = $ldap->search (
                        base   => "o=airius.com",
                        filter => "(sn=Carter)",
                        attrs => @attrs
                        ) or die ("Failed on search.$!");

foreach $entry ($mesg->all_entries) { $entry->dump; }

$ldap->unbind;    # end session
```

To limit the attributes in a search you must build an anonymous array like this:

```
@attrs = ['uid','mail'];
```

And pass it to the search method like this:

```
$mesg = $ldap->search (
                        base   => "o=airius.com",
                        filter => "(sn=Carter)",
                        attrs => @attrs
                        ) or die ("Failed on search.$!");
```

The output for this example should look something like this:

```
-------------------------------------------------
dn: uid=scarter, ou=People, o=airius.com
uid: scarter
mail: scarter@airius.com
-------------------------------------------------
dn: uid=scarte2, ou=People, o=airius.com
uid: scarte2
mail: scarte2@airius.com
-------------------------------------------------
dn: uid=kcarter, ou=People, o=airius.com
uid: kcarter
mail: kcarter@airius.com
-------------------------------------------------
dn: uid=mcarter, ou=People, o=airius.com
uid: mcarter
mail: mcarter@airius.com
```

As with all the APIs discussed in this book we can add an entry:

```
#Exercise 11.4
#!/usr/local/bin/perl
#add.pl with Net::LDAP
use Net::LDAP;

$ldap = new Net::LDAP('localhost');
```

```
$ldap->bind (
                dn        => 'uid=kvaughan, ou=People, o=airius.com',
                password => 'bribery'
            ) || die $@;
```

```
my $dn = "uid=mewilcox,ou=People,o=airius.com";
my @objectclasses = ['top','person','organizationalperson','inetOrgperson'];
my @cn = ['Mark Wilcox'];
my @givenname = ['Mark'];
my @mail = ['mewilcox@airius.com'];
my @telephonenumber = ['+1 555 5555'];
my @ou = ['People','Accounting'];
my $sn = "Wilcox";
my $uid = "mewilcox";

$msg = $ldap->add ($dn,
            attr => [ 'uid' => $uid,
                      'sn' => $sn,
                      'objectclass' => @objectclasses,
                      'givenname' => @givenname,
                      'cn'   => @cn,
                      'mail' => @mail,
                      'telephonenumber' => @telephonenumber
                    ]
            ) || warn "failed to add entry. $!" ;

print "msg is $msg\n";

$ldap->unbind;
```

To add a new entry you must pass in the attributes to the `attr` parameter of the add() method which belongs to the Net::LDAP object. You can provide the attributes as either scalar values (those variables who's names start with a $ and can contain text or binary data) or anonymous arrays (which we talked about in our limiting attribute example). Here is an example of this:

```
my @ou = ['People','Accounting'];
my $sn = "Wilcox";
my $uid = "mewilcox";

$msg = $ldap->add ($dn,
            attr => [ 'uid' => $uid,
                      'sn' => $sn,
                      'objectclass' => @objectclasses,
                      'givenname' => @givenname,
                      'cn'   => @cn,
                      'mail' => @mail,
                      'telephonenumber' => @telephonenumber
                    ]);
```

Note that we build the entry and add it to the server in one step, as opposed to two separate steps in most of the other LDAP SDKs.

The only output is the following message:

```
msg is Net::LDAP::Add=Hash(0xa48704
```

Now we come to modify an entry:

```
#Example 11.5
#!/usr/local/bin/perl
#mod.pl with Net::LDAP
use Net::LDAP;

$ldap = new Net::LDAP('localhost');

$ldap->bind (
            dn        => 'uid=kvaughan, ou=People, o=airius.com',
            password => 'bribery'
            ) || die $@;
```

```
my $dn = "uid=mewilcox,ou=People,o=airius.com";

my @mail = ['mewilcox@mail.airius.com','mewilcox@airius.com'];

$ldap->modify ($dn,
            replace =>{ 'mail' =>@mail}
            ) || warn "failed to add entry. $!" ;
```

```
$ldap->unbind;
```

This is very straightforward. You use the modify() method of the Net::LDAP object to change the values of an attribute in a LDAP entry. You can specify a replace, add or delete.

Finally the delete operation is as follows:

```
#Exercise 11.6
#!/usr/local/bin/perl
#del.pl with Net::LDAP
use Net::LDAP;

$ldap = new Net::LDAP('localhost');

$ldap->bind (
            dn        => 'uid=kvaughan, ou=People, o=airius.com',
            password => 'bribery'
            ) || die $@;
```

```
my $dn = "uid=mewilcox,ou=People,o=airius.com";

$ldap->delete ($dn) || warn "failed to delete entry\n.";
```

```
$ldap->unbind;
```

To delete an entry, you simply pass a DN to the delete() method of the Net::LDAP object.

As you can see, Net::LDAP module is a is pretty easy to use and can do just about anything you need. It's still undergoing active development and likely will continue to be used even alongside PerLDAP, if for nothing else, because of its independence from the C SDK. This is because sometimes getting the C libraries and the Perl modules to communicate properly is not easy – especially if you use systems that have no existing binary of the C SDK.

PHP

PHP is a language that has grown from a simple duct tape of shell scripts, to a pretty well developed web application development language, comparable to ColdFusion, but without the visual development tools. You can't argue with its price (free) and it's open source, so it has gained a great deal of popularity. It's available on all flavors of Unix and Windows NT. It has the ability to connect to a variety of databases and uses a syntax that is a combination of Perl and shell scripting. PHP also allows you to link in C libraries which increase the range of applications that it can be used in, including LDAP support. For more information consult the PHP documentation at
`http://www.php.net/`.

One of the reasons why PHP has gained so much popularity, is that it is a very easy language to learn, looking similar to JavaScript and HTML. This can be very important to novice web developers who may have not had any formal training in traditional programming languages. More sophisticated developers like PHP because, for a simple language, it is very versatile – able to be used with ODBC and LDAP for example, yet is quick and efficient. It lacks the complexity that you get with traditional Perl, C or Java based CGI programming. PHP was built to do one task well – that is to develop web enabled applications without learning a full programming language.

Using PHP-LDAP

PHP is can be downloaded from `http://www.php.net/`. To use LDAP from PHP you will need to have installed the Netscape Directory SDK for C (which we talked about in Chapter 6). On Unix, you will have to download the source code and compile PHP from scratch and if you want to have LDAP support, you will need to compile PHP with this option set – see the documentation that comes with PHP for instructions on how to do this with your particular flavor of Unix. For Windows NT, you have to get the precompiled binary files which already include LDAP support.

There is excellent documentation downloadable from the PHP site and they maintain a listserv for PHP support and development.

If you have used the Directory SDK for C, you will find using LDAP in PHP very similar.

Here are some simple examples. First a search with an anonymous bind:

```
//Exercise 11.7

<?php
    // basic sequence with LDAP is connect, bind, search, interpret search
    // result, close connection

    echo "<h3>LDAP query test</h3>";
    echo "Connecting ...";
    $ds=ldap_connect("localhost");  // must be a valid LDAP server!
    echo "connect result is ".$ds."<p>";

    if ($ds)
    {
        echo "Binding ...";
        $r=ldap_bind($ds);      // this is an "anonymous" bind, so no DN is supplied
        echo "Bind result is ".$r."<p>";
```

```
      echo "Searching for (sn=Carter)";
      // Search surname entry
      $sr=ldap_search($ds,"o=airius.com","(sn=Carter)");
      echo "Search result is ".$sr."<p>";

      echo "Number of entries returned is ".ldap_count_entries($ds,$sr)."<p>";

      echo "Getting entries ...<p>";
      $info = ldap_get_entries($ds, $sr);
      echo "Data for ".$info["count"]." items returned:<p>";

      for ($i=0; $i<$info["count"]; $i++)
      {
          echo "dn is: ". $info[$i]["dn"] ."<br>";
          echo "first cn entry is: ". $info[$i]["cn"][0] ."<br>";
          echo "first email entry is: ". $info[$i]["mail"][0] ."<p>";
      }

      echo "Closing connection";
      ldap_close($ds);

   }
   else
   {
      echo "<h4>Unable to connect to LDAP server</h4>";
   }
?>
```

The syntax may look unfamiliar, but what the example is doing certainly is not. You connect to the LDAP server with the `ldap_connect()` function, which returns a handle to an LDAP connection. You then search with the `ldap_search()` function, which takes a reference to a LDAP connection, a search base, a filter, and other parameters, just like the examples with other LDAP SDKs. The `ldap_search()` function returns a handle to a `SearchResults` structure. We can get the individual results by calling `ldap_get_entries()`. This function takes a handle to an LDAP connection and the `SearchResults` structure and returns a multi-dimensional array. You can get access to individual attributes and their variables by using syntax like this: `$info[0]["cn"][0]` which will return the value of the `cn` attribute of the first entry in the search results. The output for this code is as follows:

```
LDAP query test

Connecting... connect result is 1

Binding... bind result is 1

Searching for (sn=Carter) search result is 2

Number of entries returned is 4

Getting entries...

Data for 4 items returned:

attribute is
first cn entry is: Sam Carter
first email entry is: scarter@airius.com
```

```
first cn entry is: Stephen Carter
first email entry is: scarte2@airius.com

first cn entry is: Karen Carter
first email entry is: kcarter@airius.com

first cn entry is: Mike Carter
first email entry is: mcarter@airius.com

Closing connection
```

Now a search where you specifically bind to the server using the `ldap_bind()` function:

```php
//Exercise 11.8

<?php
    // basic sequence with LDAP is connect, bind, search, interpret search
    // result, close connection

    echo "<h3>LDAP query test</h3>";
    echo "Connecting ...";
    $ds=ldap_connect("localhost");  // must be a valid LDAP server!
    echo "connect result is ".$ds."<p>";

    if ($ds) {
        echo "Binding ...";
        $r=ldap_bind($ds,"uid=kvaughan, ou=People, o=airius.com","bribery");
        echo "Bind result is ".$r."<p>";
```

You can bind to the server by passing a DN and a password to the `ldap_bind()` function like this:

```php
$r=ldap_bind($ds,"uid=kvaughan,ou=People,o=airius.com","bribery");
```

The rest of the code and the output is very much the same as in the previous example.

Now we add an entry.

```php
//Exercise 11.9

<?php
    $ds=ldap_connect("localhost");

    if ($ds)
    {
        $r=ldap_bind($ds,"uid=kvaughan, ou=People, o=airius.com", "bribery");

        // prepare data
        $info["cn"]="Mark Wilcox";
        $info["sn"]="Wilcox";
        $info["givenname"]="Mark";
        $info["ou"]="People";
        $info["ou"]="Accounting";
        $info["uid"]="mewilcox";
        $info["mail"]="mewilcox@mail.airius.com";
        $info["objectclass"][0]="top";
        $info["objectclass"][1]="person";
        $info["objectclass"][2]="organizationalPerson";
        $info["objectclass"][3]="inetOrgPerson";
```

```
        $dn = "uid=mewilcox,ou=People,o=airius.com";
        $r=ldap_add($ds, $dn, $info);

        echo $dn." user added";
        ldap_close($ds);
    }
    else
    {
        echo "Unable to connect to LDAP server";
    }
?>
```

To add an entry, you must be bound to the server as an entry with modification rights. You first build a multidimensional array that contains the attributes and values, then pass this array along with a reference to an LDAP connection and a DN of the new entry to the `ldap_add()` function. On completion of the addition, an LDAP result code $r is returned. The output is just one line:

```
uid=mewilcox,ou=People,o=airius.com user added.
```

You can verify that the entry has been added by looking in Directory Server or by doing a command line search with `ldapsearch`.

Now let's modify the entry we just added:

```
//Exercise 11.10

<?php
    $ds=ldap_connect("localhost");

    if ($ds)
    {
        $r=ldap_bind($ds,"uid=kvaughan, ou=People, o=airius.com", "bribery");

        // prepare data
        $dn = "uid=mewilcox,ou=People,o=airius.com";
        $info["mail"]="wilcox_the_greatest@airius.com";

        $r=ldap_modify($ds, $dn, $info);

        echo $dn." user modified";
        ldap_close($ds);
    }
    else
    {
        echo "Unable to connect to LDAP server";
    }
?>
```

You modify the entry using the same multidimensional array we used to add it, but this time we use the `ldap_modify()` function. Unlike other LDAP SDKs, which allow you to specify an add, replace or delete of an attribute, PHP only supports replace. Once again the output is one single line:

```
uid=mewilcox,ou=People,o=airius.com user modified.
```

You can verify that the entry has been added by looking in Directory Server or by running `ldapsearch`.

Finally we can delete the entry:

```php
//Exercise 11.11

<?php
    echo "<h3>LDAP query test</h3>";
    echo "Connecting ...";
    $ds=ldap_connect("localhost");  // must be a valid LDAP server!
    echo "connect result is ".$ds."<p>";

    if ($ds)
    {
        echo "Binding ...";
        $r=ldap_bind($ds,"uid=kvaughan, ou=People, o=airius.com","bribery");

        echo "Bind result is ".$r."<p>";
        $dn = "uid=mewilcox,ou=People,o=airius.com";
        ldap_delete($ds,$dn);
        echo "User deleted<br>";
        echo "Closing connection";
        ldap_close($ds);
    }
    else
    {
        echo "<h4>Unable to connect to LDAP server</h4>";
    }
?>
```

To delete an entry you pass a reference to an LDAP connection and a DN to the `ldap_delete()` function. You must, of course, bind as Directory Manager in order to carry out this transaction. The output is as follows:

```
LDAP query test

Connecting... connect result is 1

Binding... bind result is 1

User deleted

Closing Connection
```

PS Enlist (Accessing LDAP from ODBC)

PS Enlist is a unique LDAP client product made by Persistent Systems Private Limited who are based in Pune, India. Persistent Systems is primarily an international consulting company specializing in software development. Their URL is http://www.pspl.co.in/PSEnList. What makes PS Enlist so unique is that it allows you to search LDAP data using ODBC calls. ODBC (Open Database Connectivity) is a standard interface that has been promoted by Microsoft for accessing databases from a standard API. While ODBC has been ported to various Unix platforms it is much more common to find and use ODBC on the Windows platform.

The provision of an ODBC interface to LDAP makes it very easy to perform LDAP searches with any tool that can access ODBC, such as Visual Basic or Delphi. However, I think the biggest benefit you'll receive from a product like this is the ability to access LDAP data from Microsoft Office applications.

Why is this important? Because one of the most common uses for databases is in mundane tasks like storing addresses for use in mailing labels and form letters. This is one reason why databases proliferate within an office environment – people build their own databases in something like FoxPro or Access, usually with the same information as another department in the organization. Even if they don't, there are still problems in maintaining the systems, in particular as people leave the organization. One of the reasons you will want to create a LDAP database is to centralize the management of address book data. Often, the reason people don't want LDAP is because they can't access them via ODBC. Now with PS Enlist you can.

Using PS Enlist

The steps you follow to use PS Enlist are as follows:

1. Create an ODBC data source that maps to an LDAP server. PS Enlist comes with a handy tool that allows you to map LDAP attributes to ODBC data elements. You can even assign a primary key based on one of the attributes in your entry.

2. Connect to the ODBC source and act on it as if it were an ordinary database.

The following screenshots are just for illustration.

Shown below is where you select an LDAP enabled ODBC data source using PS Enlist:

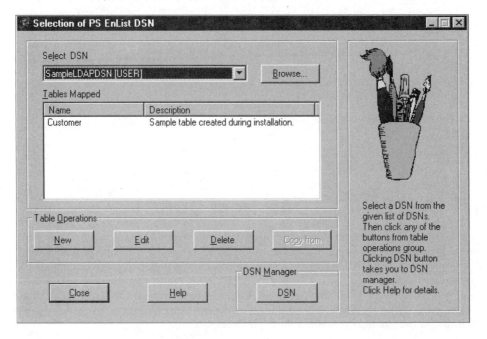

In the screenshot above we specify which ODBC data source we wish to link LDAP to. Then we create at least one new table in our database to hold the LDAP data. We can have several new tables, each of which provides a different view of the data in our LDAP server.

Here is where you specify essential LDAP information:

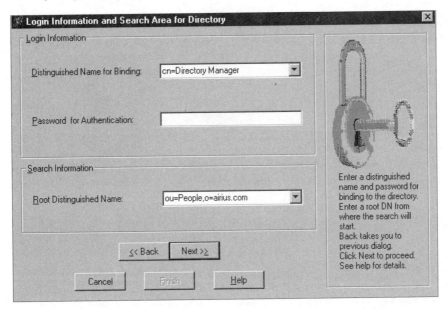

Using the screen above you specify how you wish to bind to the server and specify which part of the tree to draw your data from, that is the search base.

Then you select LDAP object classes for each of the tables in your database:

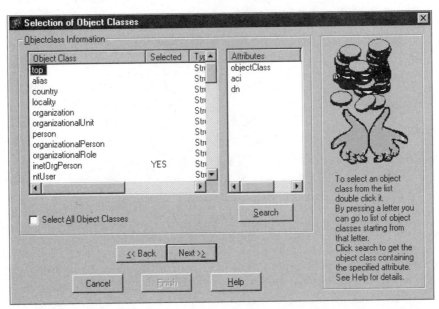

The screenshot above shows the screen that allows you to pick which particular type of entries you wish to retrieve from the LDAP server for a particular table in your data source. Currently you can only pick one type of object class per table.

Here, you can see how attributes for each object class can be mapped to individual fields in the table:

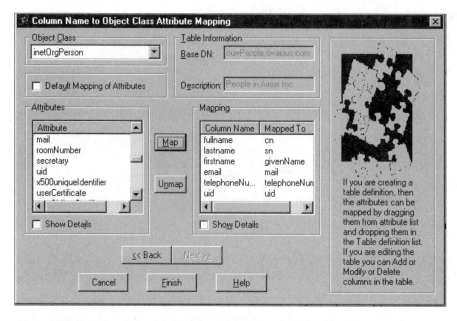

After you have chosen your object class, you can then map selected attributes to fields in your table. You can choose to keep the attribute names as field names or you can supply new names that mean more to the end user.

There is also search functionality provided:

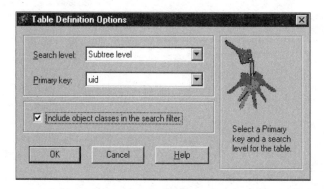

After you have selected your object class and mapped your entries, you must define which attribute is going to be your table's primary key. Then you can click OK and this will populate your table. When this process is complete, you can search the table just as you would a traditional ODBC data source, except that the data will actually be retrieved from a LDAP server. However, PS Enlist does not yet support the ability to support updates and modifications of LDAP data via ODBC.

Admittedly going between LDAP and ODBC can be a bit troublesome because the data models are different, but it probably will make LDAP more accessible while ODBC is still being used. Microsoft only support ODBC because so many clients currently use it, and for that reason the future of PS Enlist looks fairly secure in the short term. In the longer term, however, the newer technologies OLE DB and ADSI look set to render ODBC obsolete.

Server-Side JavaScript – LDAP SDK

SSJS is the server-side cousin to the JavaScript programming language that is very popular for developing interactive web pages inside web browsers. SSJS is found in the Netscape Enterprise and FastTrack web servers. It is designed to be a replacement for standard CGI programming and to make it easier to enable database access over the web. SSJS predates Microsoft's Active Server Pages (ASP) and Allaire's ColdFusion. However, it's not as popular as either of these products.

If you are not familiar with Server-Side JavaScript, then you will need to look up Netscape's online documentation at `http://developer.netscape.com/docs`.

SSJS, however, is used frequently by developers who use the Netscape SuiteSpot server line for their development purposes. In part this was because server-side Java in the form of Java servlets didn't really become popular until the Enterprise 3.5.1 release in mid-1998.

The SSJSLDAP SDK is how I originally got involved in LDAP programming and was the first step I took towards becoming an LDAP guru. I originally created it because I needed a way to search LDAP data over the web, and I couldn't get any of the Perl LDAP SDKs to work – this was over a year before PerLDAP's release. At that time, there wasn't a way to use the just-released Java Servlet API for the Solaris version of the Enterprise Server, but I knew about SSJS and that JavaScript had a mechanism to talk to Java (called LiveConnect), and so SSJSLDAP was born.

SSJSLDAP uses the Netscape Java LDAP SDK. It consists of a JavaScript source file (LDAP.js) and a single Java class, `SSJSLDAP.class`. The Java class is a simple wrapper class that is needed because JavaScript doesn't yet handle things like exceptions.

By the time you read this, SSJSLDAP should be on `http://www.mozilla.org`, but it will for sure be at my site, `http://www.mjwilcox.com`.

Using SSJSLDAP

In this section, we're going to look at some examples using the SSJSLDAP SDK – which is included with the source code examples that accompany this book, available from the Wrox Press web site.

You need to have a copy of Netscape Enterprise web server to use this library.

Summarized below are the steps you need to follow to get the SDK set up on your system and to try out the following examples:

1. Download the Netscape LDAP Java SDK and install it on your system (http://devedge.netscape.com/directory)

2. Go to the directory `<Enterprise server root>\plugins\java`.

3. Make a directory there called `local-classes`, if it doesn't already exist.

4. Copy the `ldapfilt.jar` and `ldapjdk.jar` files into the local-classes directory and then unzip them. This will create a `netscape` and a `com` directory. In a future version of the Enterprise Server, you won't have to unzip the jar files.

5. Create directory `<server root>\plugins\java\local-classes\org\mozilla\ssjs`

6. Place the `SSJSLDAP.class` file in this directory.

7. Restart the Enterprise Server.

8. When you compile your web file for your SSJS applications, just make sure that you include the `LDAP.js` file when you run the JavaScript Compiler.

The library contains working examples for searching and modifying the LDAP database. These are similar in nature to the full Netscape LDAP SDK for Java so I'm not going to go in much detail here.

To connect to the LDAP server you must create an initial reference to the LDAP object like this:

```
/* Grab an LDAP object */
var ldap = new
LDAP(project.host,parseInt(project.port),project.searchBase,parseInt(0),

project.mgr_dn,project.mgr_pw);
```

I'll just show some portions of code that demonstrate how these are done. First, here is the simple search:

```
var searchFilter = "cn=Sam Carter";
var attributeArray = new Array();
//make sure we start out with clean attributes.
ldap.connection.attributes = new java.util.Vector();
ldap.connection.attributes.addElement("cn");
ldap.connection.attributes.addElement("sn");
ldap.connection.attributes.addElement("givenname");
ldap.connection.attributes.addElement("mail");
ldap.connection.attributes.addElement("telephone");
var attributeArray = new Array();
attributeArray = ldap.doSearch(searchFilter,ldap.connection.attributes,1);
var LDAP_RESULTS = ldap.getLDAPErrorCode();
write("LDAP_RESULTS= "+LDAP_RESULTS+"<BR>");
write(ldap.getErrorMessage()+"<Br>");
if (LDAP_RESULTS == 52) {
write("error in connection");
write("trying to reconnect");
redirect('init.htm');
}
```

To search the LDAP server you use the `doSearch()` function. This takes a search filter, a Java `Vector` that lists the attributes you want returned, and an integer which gives you the total number of results returned. We must use a `Vector` instead of a JavaScript array because the latter are not true data types. JavaScript arrays are objects in JavaScript, and the LiveConnect mechanism cannot change a JavaScript array to a Java array. Also, you also cannot create true Java arrays from inside JavaScript. As a result of this, we create a Java `Vector`, which is similar to a JavaScript array, and pass that to my SSJSLDAP functions. Inside SSJSLDAP, a routine exists that translates a Java Vector into a Java array. What is returned is a standard JavaScript array.

And here is an example showing how you can add an entry:

```
var givenname = new Packages.java.lang.String(request.givenname);
var sn = new Packages.java.lang.String(request.sn);
var uid = new Packages.java.lang.String(request.uid);
var userpassword = new Packages.java.lang.String(request.userpassword);
var mail = new Packages.java.lang.String(request.mail);
var ou = new Packages.java.lang.String(request.ou);
var dn = "uid="+uid+",ou=People,o=Airius.com";
var temp_cn = givenname+" "+sn;
var cn = new Packages.java.lang.String(temp_cn);

var attrib_set = new Packages.netscape.ldap.LDAPAttributeSet();
var attribute = new Packages.netscape.ldap.LDAPAttribute("objectclass");
attribute.addValue("top");
attribute.addValue("person");
attribute.addValue("organizationalPerson");
attribute.addValue("inetOrgPerson");
attrib_set.add(attribute);

var attribute = new Packages.netscape.ldap.LDAPAttribute("givenname");
attribute.addValue(givenname);
attrib_set.add(attribute);

var attribute = new Packages.netscape.ldap.LDAPAttribute("sn");
attribute.addValue(sn);
attrib_set.add(attribute);

var attribute = new Packages.netscape.ldap.LDAPAttribute("cn");
attribute.addValue(cn);
attrib_set.add(attribute);

var attribute = new Packages.netscape.ldap.LDAPAttribute("uid");
attribute.addValue(uid);
attrib_set.add(attribute);

var attribute = new Packages.netscape.ldap.LDAPAttribute("ou");
attribute.addValue(ou);
attribute.addValue("People");
attrib_set.add(attribute);

var attribute = new Packages.netscape.ldap.LDAPAttribute("userpassword");
attribute.addValue(userpassword);
attrib_set.add(attribute);

var attribute = new Packages.netscape.ldap.LDAPAttribute("mail");
attribute.addValue(mail);
attrib_set.add(attribute);
```

```
ldap.connection.addEntry(dn,attrib_set)

var LDAP_RESULTS = ldap.getLDAPErrorCode();
write("LDAP_RESULTS= "+LDAP_RESULTS+"<BR>");
write(ldap.getErrorMessage()+"<Br>");

if (LDAP_RESULTS == 52) {
write("error in connection");
write("trying to reconnect");
redirect('init.htm');
}

//I have stumbled on a bug in the modify code.
//The LDAP server doesn't show an error, but the SDK is throwing one.
//So I'll wait for fix later
if ((LDAP_RESULTS != 0) && (LDAP_RESULTS != 20)){
write ("LDAP error code: "+ldap.getLDAPErrorCode());
write(ldap.getErrorMessage());
}
else{
write("Entry Added");
}
```

When we add a new entry, we create it using the same steps as we did in Chapter 8. The only difference is that we pass it to the `connection.addEntry()` function which handles any exceptions that might get thrown during the add since JavaScript cannot handle Java exceptions.

Modifying an entry is done like this:

```
//in "real life" get the dn from the user who has authenticated to the server
// e.g. request.remote_user
var entrydn = request.entrydn;
var attribute = request.attribute;
var value = request.value;
ldap.addAttribute(entrydn,attribute,value);
```

We modify by using the `addAttribute()` function of the SSJSLDAP object. It takes a DN, an attribute name and a value, which can be either a scalar JavaScript value or a Java `Vector`.

And this is how you go about deleting an entry:

```
var entrydn = request.entrydn;
ldap.deleteEntry(entrydn);
```

To delete an entry you simply specify a DN to the `deleteEntry()` function.

If you are using SSJS for your application development and you need LDAP support, then I suggest you check out this library. It's not perfect, but it should give you a sound basis for further development.

As for the future of the library, well, let's say it's murky. There future of SSJS is not clear at the time of writing, made even murkier now that Sun will be investing in the development of the servers, and I think the general SDKs (Java, C, PerLDAP) are more useful. Server-side Java and Perl are more portable and popular development languages, so that's where I would personally rather concentrate on development.

Allaire's ColdFusion

Allaire's ColdFusion web-database development language and development environment is the premiere web-database system in use today. It is extremely popular and uses an HTML-like syntax, which is fairly easy to pick up, although using it can result in some messy programming. When you see the syntax, you'll probably think that the system cannot be very powerful. Yet you will likely be amazed at everything ColdFusion supports and how easily it does it. ColdFusion runs on Windows NT and Solaris with a Linux version being developed.

You can find out more information about ColdFusion at http://www.allaire.com.

One of the things that ColdFusion supports is LDAP and in my day job we've used this support with great success. We originally used LDAP as a central database for user authentication for restricted web sites. When we needed to build web-database applications that needed authentication control, we decided to test out LDAP and ColdFusion. I can personally attest to the success of this endeavor. Now, instead of having to worry about setting up extra tables in our databases plus with a custom authentication program for each of our applications, we just take our LDAP templates and port them to our new application. This is not the prettiest code reuse method, but it does save an extra day or two of work. In addition, our users now don't have to keep up with an extra user ID. In fact, the success of this movement led to our implementation of a standard enterprise user ID.

We don't have space here to discuss how to build ColdFusion applications, but we'll just look at some basic code that allows us to search and modify an LDAP database.

Probably the best way to get started is to use the LDAP Wizard in ColdFusion Studio 4. A 30 day evaluation copy is available for download from http://www.allaire.com/products/. The wizard will generate three files, one for viewing, one for editing and one for action. The view page simply displays an entry. The edit page allows you to modify an entry and the action page contains the code that processes requests to step through the entries in a search or perform the modifications.

ColdFusion uses an HTML-like markup language called CFML (ColdFusion Markup Language) that enables you to develop ColdFusion applications using a language that you're probably familiar with. CFML may sound like a limitation, but it has turned into an incredibly powerful tool. I'm not a ColdFusion expert myself, but I have seen developers who work for me turn out ColdFusion applications that can generate GIF and JPEG images on the fly, FTP files to remote servers and send native SMTP mail. The only other language environment that carries out such a range of task with comparative ease is the Perl programming language.

Here is an example code snippet of accessing LDAP using ColdFusion.

```
<!--- retrieve DNs for all viewed records --->
   <CFLDAP NAME="GetDNs"
          SERVER="pollux.acs.unt.edu"
          PORT="389"
          USERNAME=""
          PASSWORD=""
          ACTION="query"
          START="ou=People,o=unt.edu"
          SCOPE="oneLevel"
          ATTRIBUTES="dn"
          TIMEOUT="20"
                  FILTER="sn=Wilcox"
   >
```

The `CFLDAP` tag is how you specify all of your LDAP operations. The parameters should, by now, be pretty self-explanatory. The `ACTION` parameter is what determines if the operation is a search (e.g. query) or a modification.

Conclusion

In this chapter, we have seen a whole host of miscellaneous tools and SDKs that you can use to create your LDAP clients.

- ❑ Command line tools – to search and modify LDAP servers without the need to create custom programs
- ❑ Net::LDAP – a portable Perl LDAP SDK that does not require C header files and binaries
- ❑ PHP – a new language for creating simple web applications
- ❑ PS Enlist – enables LDAP searches through ODBC
- ❑ SSJSLDAP SDK – another useful way of accessing LDAP, this time through Netscape Enterprise Server
- ❑ Allaire's ColdFusion – a web-database development environment that naturally supports LDAP

If there is one thing that should be obvious from this chapter (and the last 5 chapters) is that no matter your programming language, environment or operational requirements, there is an API, SDK or tool that will allow you to operate against a LDAP server. This should hopefully remove any remaining concerns about the availability of LDAP tools.

12

Referrals, Replication, Security and LDAP Controls

In this chapter, we are going to cover several topics that are going to be implemented by the more advanced user of LDAP. They are also topics that show you the true power of LDAP. By the end of this chapter, you should certainly see why LDAP is *the* directory service protocol for the Internet.

We will cover:

❑ **Referrals** – these give us the ability to have one search span multiple LDAP servers

❑ **Server Replication** – this gives us the ability to replicate portions of one LDAP server across other servers for improved performance and reliability

❑ **Access Control Lists** (ACLs) – these allows to control how people interact with our LDAP data

❑ **Secure Socket Layer Protocol** – this protocol encrypts our transactions over the network

❑ **Simple Authentication and Security Layer Protocol** – this protocol allows us to define authentication and encryption methods besides SSL

Referrals

Back in Chapter 1, we discussed how LDAP was derived from X.500 and that X.500 was primarily designed to be a global directory service. You might also remember that we talked about the Domain Naming Service and how it has become a global directory service. The reason why DNS has become a global directory service is not because each DNS server contains an entire set of hostnames and IP addresses, but because each DNS server has the ability to pass a single search request to another one that can answer the request. The requests are passed on until an answer is found. This is accomplished because each DNS server knows the location of at least one other DNS server, and DNS clients can pass this search to each successive DNS server. Well, referrals (sometimes called smart referrals in the literature) are the means by which we can accomplish this same feat in LDAP.

A **referral** is returned when an LDAP server doesn't contain the entry(s) that a client needs (either as a result of a search or of an attempted modification), but the server does know the location of another server that might be able to fulfill the request. Referrals appeared in the LDAP v3 specification, and although they sound complicated, they are relatively easy to implement.

The referral is built with the `referral` object class, which has only one required attribute, called `ref`, which is an LDAP URL pointing to the server that contains the real object. Each `referral` object's `ref` attribute can have several values that can represent several different servers. This is for reliability and performance reasons – for example, one server might be a shorter network 'hop' to your client than another.

Here is an example of a referral object in LDIF:

```
dn: ou=Mail,o=airius.com
objectclass: top
objectclass: organizationalUnit
objectclass: referral
ref: ldap://exchange.airius.com/o=exchange.airius.com
ou: Mail
```

This example says that for any LDAP query where `ou=Mail,o=airius.com` is involved, then the LDAP server should return this referral. The referral states that the real object lives at the LDAP URL, `ldap://exchange.airius.com/o=exchange.airius.com`.

One reason why we might want to set up a referral is if we have several LDAP servers on our network, but we want the end-user only to have to interact with a single entity. For example, suppose that we have two LDAP servers on our network. One is a Netscape Directory Server, which we use to store essential contact information and user authentication for our network. Our primary organizational e-mail server is a Microsoft Exchange Server, which has an LDAP interface. To keep all of our e-mail addresses easy to remember, we end all of them as `@airius.com`, but in reality they are stored in Exchange as `@exchange.airius.com` (for example, `scarter@airius.com` is expanded to `scarter@exchange.airius.com`).

Referrals and Clients

When an LDAP operation returns a referral, the client has the option to ignore the referral or follow it. When a client decides to follow a referral, it has the option to specify how many referrals it will follow. Suppose a referral on Server A points to a referral on Server B, which in turn points to a final entry on Server C. If a client follows the referral on Server A, then it can specify how long the referral operation will take and any special binding instructions (for example, bind as a particular user on Server A, but on any referrals only bind anonymously).

Here is a diagram that shows what a referral operation looks like:

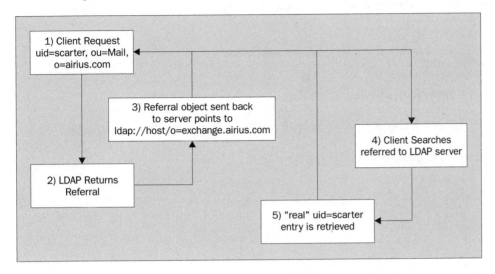

Now we'll look at an example using the Netscape LDAP Java SDK. In this example, our client will handle the referral on its own. Note that the Java SDK contains a special exception called `LDAPReferralException`, and when your client gets this exception, it can use the `getURLs()` method of the `LDAPReferralException` to get all of the referral URLs. Now, if you just follow the URL, this may be a successful operation. If you are performing a search, say for a user that is under `ou=Mail, o=airius.com`, then you will have to do a new search that uses the original filter and a base of the distinguished name of the referral URL. Then you can go on your merry way.

OK, the first part we have seen before. We just set up our variables and make a connection with the LDAP server:

```
import netscape.ldap.*;
import netscape.ldap.util.*;
import java.io.*;
import java.util.*;

public class search {

  public static void main(String args[])
  {
    String host = "localhost";
    int port = 389;
    String base = "o=airius.com";
    int scope = LDAPConnection.SCOPE_SUB;
    String dn = "";
    String pwd = "";
    String filter = "uid=scarter";

    LDAPConnection ld = null;
    LDAPSearchResults res = null;

    try
    {
      ld = new LDAPConnection();
      ld.connect(host,port,dn,pwd);
      String attrs [] = null;
```

First, we want to tell the SDK that we will not follow referrals automatically. Instead, we wish to handle referrals on our own (the SDK will now throw an `LDAPReferralException` for us to process):

```
LDAPSearchConstraints cons = ld.getSearchConstraints();
cons.setReferrals(false);
```

We now search just as we always have:

```
res = ld.search( base, scope, filter, attrs, false,cons);
```

Begin to process the results as you would any other search:

```
LDAPEntry findEntry = null;
while (res.hasMoreElements())
{
  findEntry = null;
  try
  {
    findEntry = (LDAPEntry)res.next();
    System.out.println("DN: "+findEntry.getDN());
    LDAPAttributeSet attributeSet = findEntry.getAttributeSet();

    for (int i=0;i<attributeSet.size();i++)
    {
      LDAPAttribute attribute =
                        (LDAPAttribute)attributeSet.elementAt(i);
      String attrName = attribute.getName();
      System.out.println( attrName + ":" );

      Enumeration enumVals = attribute.getStringValues();
      if (enumVals != null) {
        while ( enumVals.hasMoreElements() ) {
          String nextValue = (String)enumVals.nextElement();
          System.out.println( "\t" + nextValue );
        }
      }
    }
  }
}
```

Now the code really changes. If during the processing of search results, we encounter a `Referral` object, the SDK will throw an `LDAPReferralException` that we must handle:

```
catch (LDAPReferralException ref)
{
  System.out.println("inside referals");
```

The referrals will come in the form of LDAP URLs that point to the DN of the entry on the new server. This is probably not the entry we really want (that is, the entry on the server that the referral points to is just an `organizationalUnit` object, and the entry(s) we are interested in lie 'below' that object).

In our example here, we are assuming that the entry we get passed in a referral is the search base to look in the new server.

```
LDAPUrl url[] = ref.getURLs();
LDAPConnection temp = new LDAPConnection();
for (int i=0; i< url.length; i++)
  {
  try{
    System.out.println("url["+i+"] is "+url[i].getDN());
```

Make a new LDAP connection using the hostname and port from the referral:

```
temp.connect(url[i].getHost(),url[i].getPort());
System.out.println("connected");
```

Now we perform a new search, using the DN of the referral we have received as our search base. After we perform the search, we handle the results just as we would a non-referred search. Note that we have chosen not to handle a referral in our search that is based on the referral object. There is nothing to prevent the server from throwing us a new referral, but we have chosen not to accept any new referrals.

```
LDAPSearchResults temp_res =
        temp.search(url[i].getDN(),scope,filter,attrs,false);
System.out.println("performed search");
if (temp_res.hasMoreElements())
  {
    System.out.println("Found results");
    findEntry = (LDAPEntry) temp_res.next();
    LDAPAttributeSet attributeSet=findEntry.getAttributeSet();
    for (int x=0;x<attributeSet.size();x++)
      {
        LDAPAttribute attribute =
                        (LDAPAttribute)attributeSet.elementAt(x);
        String attrName = attribute.getName();
        System.out.println( attrName + ":" );

        Enumeration enumVals = attribute.getStringValues();

        if (enumVals != null) {
          while ( enumVals.hasMoreElements() ) {
            String nextValue = ( String )enumVals.nextElement();
            System.out.println( "\t" + nextValue );
          }
        }
      }
  }
catch(LDAPException x)
  {
    System.out.println("Problem in handling referal connection");
    System.out.println(x.toString());
    System.exit(1);
  }
    }
  }
}
```

```
            if (ld != null)
            {
              ld.disconnect();
            }
            System.out.println("finished!");
            System.exit(0);
        }
        catch(LDAPException e)
        {
            e.printStackTrace();
            System.exit(1);
        }
        catch (Exception e)
        {
            e.printStackTrace();
            System.exit(1);
        }
    }
}
```

Here is what the results would look like if you run the search referral example:

```
DN: uid=scarter, ou=People, o=airius.com
cn:
        Sam Carter
sn:
        Carter
givenname:
        Sam
objectclass:
        top
        person
        organizationalPerson
        inetOrgPerson
ou:
        Accounting
        People
l:
        Sunnyvale
uid:
        scarter
mail:
        scarter@airius.com
telephonenumber:
        +1 408 555 4798
facsimiletelephonenumber:
        +1 408 555 9751
roomnumber:
        4612
inside referals
url[0] is o=exchange.airius.com
connected
performed search
Found results
ou:
        Accounting
        People
mail:
```

```
            scarter@exchange.airius.com
    objectclass:
            top
            person
            organizationalPerson
            inetOrgPerson
    ...
```

Server Replication

The LDAP specification allows for a mechanism to be established to replicate data between LDAP servers. You may need to do this for:

- ❑ Better reliability
- ❑ Better performance
- ❑ More flexible security

Reliability

If you have your data stored on multiple servers and a hardware failure should occur, you can always switch clients to one of your backup machines

Performance

If your network is very busy or strung out over a wide area (at various parts of the country or even in different countries around the world), you may wish to place copies of the database closer to clients. Netscape does this for their e-mail servers. They store the actual mailbox location in LDAP, so that their employees can have 'business card' addresses (for example, `mewilcox@netscape.com`) instead of having to publish their 'real' address (for example, `mewilcox@box1.mcom.com`). To speed the LDAP lookup, they place a copy of their directory servers on each e-mail server box.

Security

The LDAP security model is flexible and secure, but you may wish to provide an extra layer of protection by allowing public access to a particular subset of your database. To prevent mishaps of ACLs or even a direct hack attempt on the machine, you may wish to only store the particular subset of the directory on a particular machine, perhaps even on the public side of a firewall.

Unfortunately, as yet, there is no true standard for LDAP replication (but the IETF directory group is working on it). As far as I know, all modern LDAP servers come with the ability to replicate in some form. In the University of Michigan and OpenLDAP servers, there is a separate server program called `slurpd` that is the replication server. The Netscape Directory Server has their replication services built into the server. If you are using a proprietary server product such as Novell Directory Services (which provides a LDAP interface), then you can use their existing tools to replicate their internal data.

Replication in Netscape Directory Server

In the Netscape Directory Server (version 4), you can use the Replication Agreements screen to configure your LDAP servers for replication. This includes the ability to set up a server as a supplier of information, a consumer of information or both. For example, you may have one LDAP server that is the master source for e-mail addresses and another server which is the master source for physical contact information (mailing addresses, telephone numbers and so on). You would like for both servers to have a copy of each other's information locally to improve lookup performance and to have a backup set of data in case one of the servers should fail. In this case, both servers would be consumers and suppliers (providers) of information. You can specify if you want to supply/consume an entire tree or part of a tree.

Here is a screenshot from Netscape Directory Server of the menu that sets up the basic consumer information:

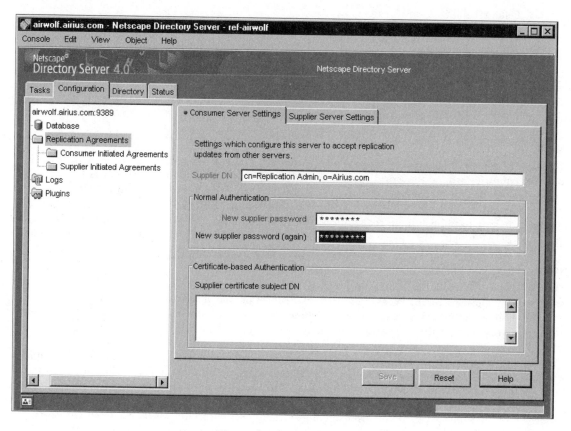

And here is the screenshot of the basic supplier information screen:

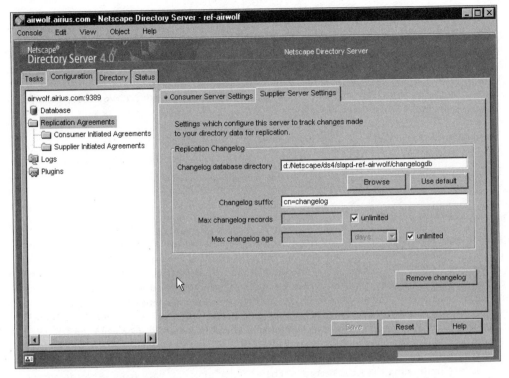

To configure the actual replication, you must set up either Consumer Initiated Agreements or Supplier Initiated Agreements. Information on how to set up these agreements is available from the online help.

Finally, when you are using server replication, you must decide how you will deal with the following situations:

❑ Updates – Can updates occur on any consumer server, or only on the master? If they can occur on the consumer servers, how will you update the master? What happens if two different independent consumer updates occur on the same entry?

❑ Master failure – What happens if the master server should go down? Does a consumer server become a master? Do you continue to process updates? If you process updates how do you update the master once it's back on-line?

Typically, most LDAP servers can handle some lag between updates and data discrepancies between supplier and consumer. That is, it's OK to have data discrepancies, as long as you know which server is the true 'master' of the data and that updates occur regularly to the client. In the end, it will likely depend not only on the particular LDAP server, but also on the particular application, as to how sensitive you, the LDAP administrator, will be to supplier/consumer updates.

Securing LDAP

In this section, we'll cover how to protect the individual entries in the LDAP server through the use of Access Control Lists, how to encrypt our data with the Secure Socket Layer protocol and provide for alternative authentication mechanisms with the Simple Authentication and Security Layer protocol.

When you are implementing LDAP (or any other network information resource) you must consider how you will protect your data in three key areas:

- ❑ The data inside the system (e.g. individual entries)
- ❑ The data transfer between client and host (e.g. communication over the network)
- ❑ Determining who a client is (e.g. client authentication)

Access Control Lists

With ACLs, you gain the power to give Joe the ability to see and modify all of an entry, and restrict Jill to just being able to read an entry, and you can limit the number of possible attributes of an entry an anonymous user can see. By default, all of the data in the tree is restricted so that the *only* user that can see, compare, read or modify it is the Directory Manager (that is the super-user account of the database). When you employ ACLs, you are in fact giving abilities to certain entries or group of entries. For example, you might specify that end-users can modify their passwords and telephone numbers, but only their area's database manager can add or remove an end-user from the LDAP server. You can also give rights to an entire group of users.

In LDAP, ACLs are built using the `aci` attribute. The actual syntax can vary from server to server. Because there is not a standard syntax for ACLs, this does pose some problems in exchanging data between LDAP servers. Every LDAP compliant server that I know about accepts LDIF files for data exchange, and because they can accept LDIF, this means that it is easy to share data between LDAP servers, regardless of the differences in implementation or a replication standard. However, there is not a standard for ACLs, so your restrictive permissions on one server might be ignored on another, which could lead to problems with data security and data access (the people who should have access to the data might not be able to get to it).

Here is an example that shows a Netscape ACL in LDIF:

```
aci: (target ="ldap:///ou=People, o=airius.com")(targetattr !="cn || sn || uid")
(targetfilter ="(ou=Accounting)")(version 3.0;acl "Accounting Managers
Group Permissions";allow (write)(groupdn = "ldap:///cn=Accounting Managers,
ou=groups,o=airius.com");)
```

The following table explains the parts of a Netscape ACL:

ACL Label	ACL Value
target	A DN in LDAP URL format (without the hostname)
targetattr	A search filter of attributes this ACL affects
targetfilter	This ACL only affects entries that match this filter

ACL Label	ACL Value
version	The version of the ACL (3.0 is for DS 3 & 4)
acl	A comment
allow	A list of modifications (e.g. write, read, search, compare, etc.)
bind DN	This ACL is only effective for bound entries that match this DN

If you want a more formal definition, Jeff Hodges of Stanford University has written a paper, *ABNF Definition of Netscape Directory Service ACI Attribute Value Syntax*, which you can find at `http://www.stanford.edu/group/networking/directory/doc/NS-DS-ACI-Syntax-ABNF.txt`. This paper is not a standard — it's just a guide that LDAP developers can reference when writing applications for the Netscape Directory Server.

Shown below are the ACLs (in LDIF) for the `o=airius.com` and `ou=People,o=airius.com` entries in the example `airius.ldif` file that comes with Netscape Directory Server 4. First, the `o=airius.com` entry:

```
dn: o=airius.com
objectclass: top
objectclass: organization
o: airius.com
```

The ACL shown below gives the anonymous user read-only access to every attribute under the `o=airius.com` base, except for `userPassword`, which an anonymous user can't see at all:

```
aci: (target ="ldap:///o=airius.com")(targetattr !="userPassword")
(version 3.0;acl "Anonymous read-search access";
allow (read, search, compare)(userdn = "ldap:///anyone");)
```

The next ACL allows members of the group `Directory Administrators` full access to every attribute and entry in the `o=airius.com` tree:

```
aci: (target="ldap:///o=airius.com") (targetattr = "*")
(version 3.0; acl "allow all Admin group"; allow(all) groupdn
          = "ldap:///cn=Directory Administrators, ou=Groups, o=airius.com";)
```

An now let's look at the `ou=People,o=airius.com` entry:

```
dn: ou=People,o=airius.com
objectclass: top
objectclass: organizationalunit
ou: People
```

This ACL says that each user can change their password, telephone number and fax number:

```
aci: (target ="ldap:///ou=People, o=airius.com")
(targetattr ="userpassword || telephonenumber || facsimiletelephonenumber")
(version 3.0;acl "Allow self entry modification";
allow (write)(userdn = "ldap:///self");)
```

The next is a bit more complicated, and allows managers of each department to modify entries that belong to that department. For example, the group `Accounting Managers` the ability to modify those entries with an `ou` value of `Accounting`, except for the attributes common name (cn), last name (sn) and user ID (uid):

```
aci: (target ="ldap:///ou=People, o=airius.com")(targetattr !="cn || sn || uid")
(targetfilter ="(ou=Accounting)")
(version 3.0;acl "Accounting Managers Group Permissions";
allow (write)(groupdn = "ldap:///cn=Accounting Managers,
ou=groups,o=airius.com");)

aci: (target ="ldap:///ou=People, o=airius.com")(targetattr !="cn || sn || uid")
(targetfilter ="(ou=Human Resources)")
(version 3.0;acl "HR Group Permissions";
allow (write)(groupdn = "ldap:///cn=HR Managers,ou=groups,o=airius.com");)

aci: (target ="ldap:///ou=People, o=airius.com")(targetattr !="cn ||sn || uid")(
targetfilter ="(ou=Product Testing)")
(version 3.0;acl "QA Group Permissions";
allow (write)(groupdn = "ldap:///cn=QA Managers,ou=groups,o=airius.com ");)

aci: (target ="ldap:///ou=People, o=airius.com")(targetattr !="cn || sn || uid")
(targetfilter ="(ou=Product Development)")
(version 3.0;acl "Engineering Group Permissions";
allow (write)(groupdn = "ldap:///cn=PD Managers,ou=groups ,o=airius.com");)
```

ACLs can seem a bit crazy to look at and luckily most commercial LDAP servers provide a friendlier interface. However, understanding ACLs is crucial for proper management of an LDAP server.

Protecting Data Over the Wire

The Internet was originally designed with the notion that the network itself was secure, because everyone using it knew everyone else. Nowadays, this way of thinking is seen to be very naïve, but you must understand that the Internet protocols were built with the idea in mind of just trying to get the thing to work, so security was not the top priority. The original developers knew one another, and they never really expected the work they did to become the worldwide phenomenon it has. When you live and work among your friends, you don't worry too much about locking your front door. Luckily, the TCP/IP protocols can carry about anything we need and it is very simple to encrypt our data over the wire.

While there are many encryption and security schemes out there, the LDAP specification allows for two:

- ❑ Secure Socket Layer (SSL)
- ❑ Simple Authentication and Security Layer (SASL)

Both of these are now Internet standards.

Introducing the Secure Socket Layer

The **Secure Socket Layer** (SSL) protocol was created by Netscape to secure traffic over the World Wide Web. SSL has become the *de facto* standard for encrypting all manners of Internet traffic. While it began life as a proprietary protocol, Netscape always intended to make it an open standard and that is what it has become. The new standard is called Transport Security Layer, though it is still popularly referred to as the Secure Socket Layer.

SSL connections allow for both **encryption** and **verification**. (Encryption simply means garbling the connection so that someone who 'sniffs' the traffic can't understand it.) The encryption uses something called public-key encryption. When you think of encryption, you probably think of James Bond movies and secret decoder rings. These types of encryption schemes rely on a single key to do all of the encryption and decryption. If this key is compromised, your entire encryption scheme is busted. The Allied powers in World War II scored some of their largest victories because they were able to break or capture the key. In public-key encryption, there are two keys – a private key and a public key. The private key is kept out of public circulation, while the public key is designed to be given out in the open.

Public Keys

Let's look at an example to try to clarify this. Suppose Bob has a private and public key, and he puts his public key out on his web site. Alice wants to send Bob a message and doesn't want anyone else to read it but Bob. So, she gets Bob's key from his Web site and then she uses it to encrypt her message. Next she sends Bob the message. Now, if Craig intercepts this message, he can't decode it even if he has a copy of Bob's public key, because only Bob's private key can decode the message.

There is one problem in the public key stage, however. How do you really know that it's Bob's key? Perhaps Craig hacked his way into Bob's site and put his own public key there. Now when Craig intercepts Alice's message, he can read it.

There are two ways to limit the likelihood of this type of attack. One is that public keys should have a short life span. That is, they should be considered invalid after a certain period of time (for example, 6 months). After this time, the expired public key should be considered untrustworthy. The second method is to have one or more digital signatures on a public key to vouch that it is genuine. For example, Bob and Alice know both know Mark. Mark visits Bob one night and Bob shows him his public key. Alice already has a copy of Mark's public key. So Mark digitally signs Bob's public key – he leaves a unique value that can only be generated by his public key. Now when Alice gets a copy of Bob's public key, she can see that is has also been signed by Mark, so she decides she can trust it.

If you are thinking, "Gee, this stuff is relying a whole bunch on trust and isn't that asking for a lot?", you must realize that most of our lives are based on implicit trust. We trust that when we fly on an airplane that the airplane crew are trained and know what they are doing. We trust that when we order a bouquet of flowers over the phone for our mothers on Mother's Day, that the person on the other end taking our credit card number, is indeed a florist. I'm sure you can think of plenty of other examples.

The 'digital signing' of a public-key by a third-party to vouch for its validity is not that much different than the Federal Aviation Administration giving a pilot a license to fly. We trust that the FAA knows what a person needs to know to fly an airplane full of people, so when the FAA issues a person a pilot's license, we then assume that person is OK to be our pilot.

Secret Keys

One other problem with using encryption with public-keys is that it can take an enormous amount of time to verify each message. That is why the SSL protocol uses both public-key and secret-key encryption. After the client and server have decided that they can talk to each other, they can then send each other the necessary information for generating **secret keys** (much like the decoder rings of old science fiction comic books), because secret-key encryption is much faster.

While you usually only think of server authentication when you think of SSL, it is also possible to use it for client authentication. In this section however, we'll focus on connecting to the server using SSL.

Laws on Encryption

Before we go much further, we need to talk a bit about encryption and the United States government. The US government views the exporting of encryption programs the same way it views exporting a weapon. Right or wrong, the US government believes that if encryption tools fell into the hands of 'the bad guys', then they might not be able to defeat them because 'the bad guys' could talk in complete secrecy. To ensure that the US government (primarily the National Security Agency) can always read encoded transmissions, it is against the law for a US based company to export a piece of software with greater than 40-bit encryption. 40-bit encryption means the size of the number that is used to generate the key. The bigger the bit number, the harder it is to break the encryption code. Currently it takes a network of 400 MHz Pentiums a few minutes to crack a 40-bit code. If you took the same algorithm, but used a 128-bit number instead, it would take the same network longer than the universe's known existence to break the code.

On a final note, if a programmer was to take the code they wrote for their encryption program and published it in a book, then that would be OK. Once it's published as a book, it then is protected by the US Constitution's first Bill of Rights – Freedom Of Speech. As the comedian Yackov Smirnov, once said "What a Country!"

I only mention this because I know many of you will probably be reading this outside of the United States and so many of these SSL examples may not work.

Command line Utilities

Certain versions of the standard command line utilities like those from Netscape (for U.S. users anyway), allow you to connect using SSL, provided you give them a path to a certificate database, like the one that ships with Netscape Communicator. (Both US and international versions of Communicator should have a certificate database, but your command line tools may not support SSL.)

Here is an SSL connection of the standard `ldapsearch` utility:

```
ldapsearch -Z -P /path/to/certdatabase -b "o=airius.com" "sn=Carter"
```

How SSL Works

SSL can be used to encrypt traffic over any open network. All SSL transactions occurs in 6 steps:

1. The client sends the server its SSL protocol version (e.g. SSLv2 or SSLv3), some random data, its maximum bit size (e.g. 40-bit or 128-bit) plus some other information needed for doing an SSL transaction.

2. The server sends back a similar set of data to the client, except that it also sends the client a copy of the server's certificate and its public key. The server's certificate contains information that 'vouches' for the server's identity.

3. The client decides whether or not the server can be trusted. (See the next section, *How a Client Determines A Server's Trustworthiness.*)

4. If the client doesn't trust the server, it disconnects from it. If, however, the client does trust the server, then it sends back an initial secret key that is signed with the server's public key.

5. The server decrypts the message and can also ask for client SSL authentication (this latter part is optional). The server then sends back some information that the client and server will use to encode their messages, including measures to reduce the likelihood of any data tampering in between the client and server.

6. The client and server carry on their normal transaction except that is now encrypted with SSL.

How a Client Determines A Server's Trustworthiness

As part of the negotiation process of setting up an SSL connection (a process called the 'SSL Handshake'), the server will send the client a **certificate**.

A certificate is record of some key information that the client can use to determine whether or not the server can be considered trustworthy. This record must meet four criteria to be considered 'OK':

7. The certificate's expiration date must be on or after today's date.

8. The Certificate Authority that issued the certificate must be trusted.

9. The public key of the Certificate Authority that issued the certificate must validate the digital signature of the Certificate Authority that is on the certificate.

10. The domain name that is listed in the certificate must match the server's domain name.

Here is an example of server certificate as presented in Netscape Communicator:

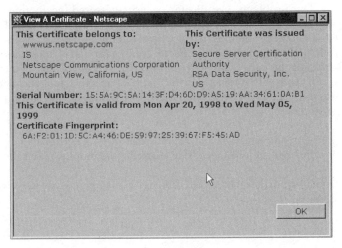

You can retrieve a server's certificate by clicking on the closed "lock" in the lower left hand corner of the Navigator browser window.

What is a Certificate Authority

A Certificate Authority is an organization or person who issues certificates. Several companies make commercial software for issuing and managing certificates. There are even some freeware certificate generation/management resources, such as the SSLeay project.

Generally, a Certificate Authority will be a third party that has done some checking to verify a site before issues a certificate. For example, Verisign, the leading server certificate supplier, will require proof of your company's incorporation, a letter from your CEO or designate on company letterhead and will contact your organization's human resources department to verify that your organization's Verisign contact person is actually employed by your organization. Only after all of these criteria are met (plus a payment) does Verisign issue the certificate. In fact, they are one of the few Certificate Authorities that all major SSL clients, such as Netscape and IE, already accept 'out of the box'. You can read more about Verisign at http://www.verisign.com.

If you don't want to spend the money and time to go through a company like Verisign, you can become your own Certificate Authority. What this means is that you can issue certificates internally for your own servers. Netscape, Microsoft and Verisign all make products that you can use to issue your own certificates. However, if you do this, your SSL clients (such as Netscape Communicator and Microsoft Internet Explorer) will not immediately recognize you as a Certificate Authority, so your users will have to recognize you as one. (Netscape and Internet Explorer both have mechanisms for adding new Certificate Authorities.)

A Certificate Authority doesn't just have to issue server certificates, they can also issue client certificates. Client certificates are considered a more secure form of authentication than standard user IDs and passwords, because they take one more possible human point of failure out of the picture. As we mentioned way back in Chapter 1, passwords are not a perfect authentication system because people pick ones that are easy to guess, they give them out to strangers, they write them down, and the password can be stolen while being transferred over the network. Certificates on the other hand, cannot be forgotten or easily faked. There is the possibility they could be stolen, but usually this means that the thief must have physical access to the machine.

However, certificates do have their problems. Certificates are usually stored locally on hard disks. A user might get a new computer, or their hard disk could crash, or they erase the file, and a new certificate must be generated. Another problem is that if a certificate is stored locally on the computer and the user leaves their machine unattended, then someone could gain illegal access to a machine by simply pressing a button that sends the certificate, no password guessing involved. You can store certificates on smart cards (ID badges with magnetic strips that contain the actual certificate), but then you would have to put smart card readers on everyone's machines, come up with software that can read the smart card data and so on.

The Certificate Authority can revoke both server and client certificates. A certificate might be revoked if it is stolen, lost or otherwise compromised (for example, the employee left the company).

The infrastructure of Certificate Authorities who must issue and managing certificates is called the Public Key Infrastructure (PKI).

Adding SSL Encryption to Your LDAP Server

Most commercial LDAP servers provide the ability to use SSL (OpenLDAP plans support for SSL in a future version).

Since we have used Netscape Directory Server as our reference LDAP server for this book, we might as well look at some screen shots demonstrating how to request an SSL server certificate. You will actually need to contact a company like Verisign or purchase your own certificate management software to get a server certificate.

> *Verisign (`http://www.verisign.com`) do allow you to get a test certificate for free, which you can use if you wish to try out for yourself the following code example using SSL. You can install the certificate using the wizard discussed in this section.*

You can use the Netscape Certificate Wizard to generate your request. I'm not going to show you the entire wizard, just some of the key steps. Here is where you start up the wizard:

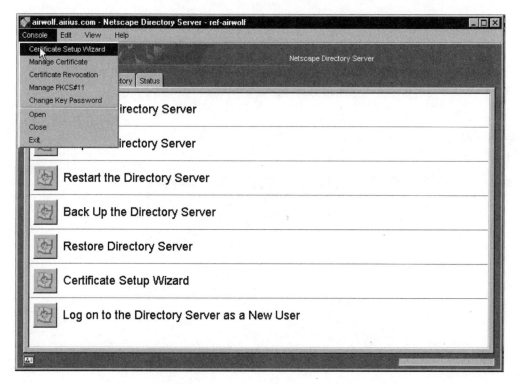

The next step is to choose how you will create your keys, either using a software method or a hardware method, such as a card that supports the US government FORTEZZA standard. If you already have a certificate, you can choose to install it here:

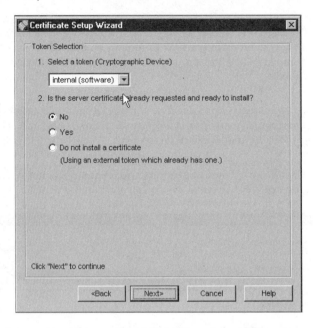

A couple of screens later we can set up a Trust Database where will store our private key and our certificate. This database should be considered as a private database as your user password file.

Near the end of the wizard, you will be asked who you want to use as your Certificate Authority:

Most Certificate Authorities allow you to send your certificate request by e-mail or by filling out a form on a web page. Before you can send the e-mail or fill in the certificate request form web page, you need to generate the actual request. This final screenshot shows the information you must provide before sending the request:

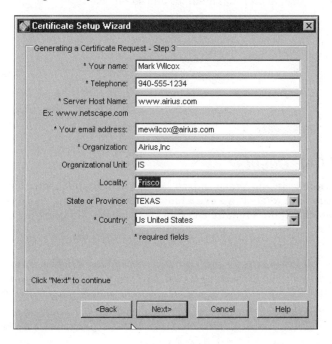

Note that if you have a server with an aliased name (for example, `www.airius.com` and `www1.airius.com`), you must get two separate certificates, because a server certificate is only good for one server hostname.

After you gone through the wizard, it will generate a message like this (this particular message is for an e-mail request, but the web form result would look similar).

```
Certificate request has been generated.

The mail that you should send is in the file d:\temp\mailtmp.367
It contains the To, Subject and Reply-To fields.  Please use your mailer to enter
the rest of the file as the body of the message. When the response arrives, you
can use the Install a Certificate form to put it in place.

To: www@unt.edu
Subject: Certificate request
Reply-To: mewilcox@airius.com

Webmaster: mewilcox@airius.com
Phone: 940-555-1234

Common-name: www.airius.com
Email: mewilcox@airius.com
Organization: Airius,Inc
Org-unit: IS
Locality: Frisco
State: TEXAS
Country: Us
```

The actual certificate request is a BASE-64 encoded string of the data above, plus some information that specifies the maximum key size, encryption methods and so on.

```
-----BEGIN NEW CERTIFICATE REQUEST-----
MIIBIzCBzgIBADBpMQswCQYDVQQGEwJVczEOMAwGA1UECBMFVEVYQVMxDzANBgNV
BAcTBkZyaXNjbzETMBEGA1UEChMKQWlyaXVzLEluYzELMAkGA1UECxMCSVMxFzAV
BgNVBAMTDnd3dy5haXJpdXMuY29tMFwwDQYJKoZIhvcNAQEBBQADSwAwSAJBAOdI
o9WUDo2GQKn9GJfy8d6e02wziogPJi0rofkYbgddndmgypFsZwjN9agNvu0x7Q2q
gqfuxsjGvUgWX8MMWJcCAwEAAaAAMA0GCSqGSIb3DQEBBAUAA0EAptPKuBkjrmbk
WES6qURm4X4dVTEqDCiwfc8F7vxI9P+K3qwnZn4sDUGz0AALExnfj0V+8+PYmMmX
a+3L2aX1gA==
-----END NEW CERTIFICATE REQUEST-----
```

Writing SSL Capable LDAP Clients

Our next example shows how to write our synchronized search client from Chapter 6 using an SSL connection. It really only requires a total of two extra function calls, `ldapssl_client_init()` and `ldapssl_init()`. Note that it does require a certificate database. I'm using the one that comes with Netscape Communicator.

If you are wondering why that I constantly use the Netscape Communicator database is because it's handy, common, free and makes management of the database pretty easy. This is important because for your clients to use SSL, the CA that signed the certificate must be recognized in the database. The easiest way to import a CA is by using Netscape Communicator.

This example is written in C because the Netscape C SDK comes with SSL support 'out of the box' from http://developer.netscape.com/directory. The Java version requires a third party SSL package, unless you wish to restrict your Java LDAP development to applets running in Netscape Communicator. This lack of support in the Java version is because of the way SSL must be handled in Java and the tight export restrictions on encryption technologies in the United States.

Most of this code we have seen before, it's our standard search code, but this time it will connect over SSL. The new bits of code have been highlighted (note that you need to #include the header, ldap_ssl.h):

```c
/*synch_search_ssl.c
usage: synch_search_ssl

synchronous searching
*/

#include <stdio.h>
#include <stdlib.h>
#include <string.h>
#include <time.h>

/* standard C ldap libary */
#include "ldap.h"
#include "ldap_ssl.h"

#define MY_PROG "synch_search_ssl"

#define MY_HOST        "localhost"
#define MY_PORT        389
#define MY_SEARCHBASE  "o=airius.com"
#define SCOPE LDAP_SCOPE_SUBTREE
#define FILTER         "sn=Vaugh*"

int main( int argc, char **argv )
{
    LDAP           *ld;
    LDAPMessage    *result,*e;
    BerElement     *ber;
    char           *attribute;
    char           **vals;
    int            i,rc,parse_rc = 0;
    int            msg_id = 0;
    char *attribs[4];

    attribs[0]="cn";
    attribs[1]="mail";
    attribs[2]="objectclass";
    attribs[3]=NULL;

    printf("Testing %s \n",MY_PROG);

    /* First set up an LDAP connection */
    if ( ldapssl_client_init( "/path to Communicator's/cert7.db", NULL ) < 0) {
        printf( "Failed to initialize SSL client...\n" );
        return(1);
    }
```

```
      /* get a handle to an LDAP connection */
      if ((ld = ldapssl_init( "localhost", LDAPS_PORT, 1 )) == NULL) {
         perror( "ldapssl_init" );
         return(1);
      }

   printf("Connected to LDAP host %s on port %d\n",MY_HOST,LDAPS_PORT);

   rc = ldap_search_ext_s(ld,MY_SEARCHBASE,SCOPE,FILTER,attribs,0,NULL,
                                    NULL,LDAP_NO_LIMIT,0,&result);

   if ( rc != LDAP_SUCCESS ) {
      fprintf( stderr, "ldap_search_ext: %s\n", ldap_err2string( rc ) );
      ldap_unbind( ld );
      exit(1);
   }


   printf("Total results are: %d\n",ldap_count_entries( ld, result));

   for (e = ldap_first_entry(ld, result); e != NULL; e =
                                        ldap_next_entry(ld,e))
   {
      printf("DN: %s\n",ldap_get_dn( ld, e ));

      /* Now print out the attributes and values of the search */
      for (attribute = ldap_first_attribute(ld, e, &ber); attribute != NULL;
                        attribute = ldap_next_attribute(ld,e,ber))
      {
         if ((vals = ldap_get_values(ld, e, attribute)) != NULL ) {
            if (rc != LDAP_SUCCESS ) {
               fprintf( stderr, "LDAP Error: %s\n", ldap_err2string(rc));
               exit(1);
            }

            for (i = 0;vals[i] != NULL;i++) {
               printf("\t%s: %s\n",attribute,vals[i]);
            }
            ldap_value_free(vals);
         }
         ldap_memfree(attribute);
      }

      if ( ber != NULL ) {
         ber_free( ber, 0 );
      }

      printf("\n");
   }

   if (rc != LDAP_SUCCESS ) {
      fprintf( stderr, "LDAP Error: %s\n", ldap_err2string(rc));
      exit(1);
   }

   ldap_msgfree( result );
   printf ("Search success!\n");
   return (1);
}
```

Let's spend a moment looking at exactly what the new code does. First we must set up the LDAP SDK to use SSL by providing the location of a certification database, here we are using the one that comes with Netscape Communicator:

```
/* First set up an LDAP connection */
if ( ldapssl_client_init( "/path to Communicator's/cert7.db", NULL ) < 0) {
printf( "Failed to initialize SSL client...\n" );
return(1);
}
```

Then, we connect just as we would with any other LDAP connection, except that we use the `ldapssl_init()` function and the port should be 636, which is the default LDAP SSL port:

```
/* get a handle to an LDAP connection */
if ((ld = ldapssl_init( "localhost", LDAPS_PORT, 1 )) == NULL) {
perror( "ldapssl_init" );
return(1);
}
```

Simple Authentication and Security Layer (SASL)

SSL is a great way to improve the security of your network if you are building from scratch. However, you might already have legacy systems that you want to use, or you may wish to implement a different system than SSL. The **Simple Authentication and Security Layer** (SASL) is a protocol designed to define a common way for authentication systems to communicate over a network.

To use SASL, you will most likely have to develop something custom for your server before you can even attempt to write a client. Check with your server's documentation to see if it supports SASL and what you have to do to enable it.

I only know for sure that Netscape supports SASL directly but it doesn't come with any SASL functions enabled, so instead you must write your own server plugins (applications that are written to extend the Directory server's basic functionality). The Netscape C and Java SDKs both support SASL authentication and the PerLDAP should support it in a future version. Because SASL is not widely implemented and each instance will be different, there won't be any examples presented here.

SASL was designed to support two important existing authentication mechanisms from the start:

- ❑ Kerberos
- ❑ MD-5

Kerberos is a system designed to provide encryption and secure login for a network. When a server wishes to use Kerberos, a certificate is granted to that server and an entry is made in the Kerberos database. When a user logs onto the network, he/she is authenticated by the Kerberos server (but is not authenticated by Kerberos, instead Kerberos uses another system for the actual authentication, which could still be LDAP). If the authentication succeeds, then a 'ticket' is stored by the user's client machine. As the user interacts with services on the network, this 'ticket' is passed to the Kerberos compliant server, which in turn looks up the ticket in the Kerberos database to determine whether or not this user is valid, and comes from the same machine that issued the ticket. If so, then the user is authenticated to the system. Kerberos is a popular system, but has not been widely implemented because it requires a lot of people and machine resources to manage. This might change after the release of Windows 2000, which will require Kerberos to run. If you want to find out more about the details of Kerberos, you should check out the paper on the subject at:
`http://nii.isi.edu/publications/kerberos-neuman-tso.html`

The second system SASL was designed to support was the MD-5 hashing algorithm. MD-5 is not a network encryption scheme, but instead is designed to make it harder for people to steal passwords. (A network encryption scheme attempts to make it harder for anyone to steal any piece of data.) The term *MD-5* means the algorithm that is used to make a hash of the user's password. Under this system, the user enters their user ID and password to the client. The client then makes an MD-5 hash of the password and passes the user ID and hashed password to the server. The server looks up the entry that matches the user ID and compares the entry's password hash to the hash that was passed to it. If they match, then the user is authenticated. The MD-5 algorithm is designed so that it is highly unlikely that two different strings will make the same hash, and so that the slightest change (just one character) results in a very different hash. MD-5 is a very popular algorithm for use in encryption schemes and verification of data. It is however finally showing some weakness (its hashes are not as unique as we once believed).

Alternatives such as using a double MD-5 hash and the SHA-1 (Secure Hash Algorithm) have been proposed, with SHA-1 the likely future replacement. (SHA-1 support is already available in most LDAP servers, including Netscape Directory Server and OpenLDAP.) Using MD-5 to hash the password before sending it to the server doesn't prevent a person from 'sniffing' the network and stealing it, because the data is still going across the network in plain text. If a password was stolen over the network, a person could still gain access by writing a client that sent the stolen hash to the server. It does however, prevent the possibility of taking that stolen 'password' and using it on systems that still use plain text passwords, because the odds of being killed by a rogue asteroid are better than guessing the string that made up the hash.

SASL Psuedo Code

Before we leave this section, let's take a quick look at the steps that take place during an SASL transaction:

1. The client contacts the server and says it's capable of doing a particular SASL mechanism.

2. The server sends information back to the client saying that it supports the particular SASL mechanism. Otherwise, the server says it doesn't support the particular SASL mechanism and the transaction ends.

3. The client sends information back to the server that performs the SASL mechanism (e.g. Kerberos ticket, MD-5 hash).

4. The server either authenticates the client or sends back a message stating that the authentication failed.

If you are looking for more information on this, SASL is defined in RFC 2222. Jeff Hodges maintains a digest of an SASL (specifically Kerberos, but in general about SASL) conversation on the Netscape Directory Developers newsgroup, which you can find at:
http://www.stanford.edu/group/networking/directory/doc/KerberosAnalysis.txt.

Working with LDAP Controls

The developers of the LDAP protocol had the foresight to realize that because of competition, LDAP server vendors and developers would want to add extra features to their servers. They also didn't want to come back to the committee table to come up with another version of the LDAP protocol, much like we have to for HTML. Instead, they came up with the concept of **extended operations** and **controls**.

Under HTML, if a browser vendor decided they wanted a new tag, they added it. There is not a mechanism to tell other browsers how to handle this tag. This meant that web developers were put into the bind of developing pages that might not display as well (if at all) on some browsers. In LDAP on the other hand, server developers are free to extend their server functionality (they might want to add full featured transaction control including rollbacks for their LDAP server, for example). LDAP clients that wish to take advantage of these features can send a message to the server asking to use this transaction operation when performing their updates. The server can respond back by either using the control, or telling the client that it doesn't support that particular control. There is even a mechanism for a client to query a server to determine what types of controls it supports.

In summary, an extended operation is a feature added to an LDAP server that goes beyond the standard functionality of LDAP. Your clients access these extended operations by using server controls.

You can query the server to determine what controls it supports. To do this, you must set the scope to `BASE`, the search base as blank (`" "`) and the filter as `"objectclass=*"`. The attribute you are looking for is `supportedControl`.

> *To develop your own operations you'll need to read your server's documentation.*

In this section, we'll see one of the more common operations – the server-sort control, using the Netscape Directory SDK for Java just for convenience. This control will sort the results on the server as opposed as sorting them on the client. By default, there is no sorting on the client or server, so you have to specify this yourself.

To do the sort you use the `LDAPSortKey` and `LDAPSortControl` objects of the Netscape LDAP Java SDK. The `LDAPSortControl` contains an array of the `LDAPSortKeys`. You pass the `LDAPSortControl` as part of the `LDAPSearchConstraints` object in the `search()` method of the `LDAPConnection` object.

When you build the `LDAPSortKey`, you just need to pass the attribute name you want. If you want to sort in ascending order, you just pass the name. If you want to go in descending order you must put `"-"` in front of the attribute name.

If you want to sort on more than one attribute, you must first build up a set of `LDAPSortKey` objects and then pass them to an array of `LDAPSortKeys`. Let's see how all this works in a coded example.

Since this another long example, I'll break the code up by presenting my comments along the way.

```
import netscape.ldap.*;
```

Note that we need to import the package that contains the classes that support using LDAP controls, `netscape.ldap.controls`:

```
import netscape.ldap.controls.*;

import netscape.ldap.util.*;
import java.io.*;
import java.util.*;

public class sort {

  public static void main(String args[])
  {
    String host = "localhost";
    int port = 389;
    String base = "o=airius.com";
    int scope = LDAPConnection.SCOPE_SUB;
    String dn = "";
    String pwd = "";
    //String filter = "cn=*C*";
    String filter = "sn=Carter";

    LDAPConnection ld = null;
    LDAPSearchResults res = null;

    try
    {
      ld = new LDAPConnection();
      ld.connect(host,port,dn,pwd);

      String attrs [] = {"cn","sn","givenname","uid"};
```

First, we need to create the keys we will use for sorting using the `LDAPSortKey` class, which takes an attribute name to sort by. In this case, we'll sort by `givenname`. By default, the sort is in ascending order, but you can put a minus sign (-) in front of the attribute name you wish to sort by, to reverse the sort order.

```
/* Create sort keys that specify the sort order. */
LDAPSortKey sortByFirstName = new LDAPSortKey("givenname");
LDAPSortKey sortByUID = new LDAPSortKey("-uid");
LDAPSortKey[] sortOrder = {sortByFirstName,sortByUID};
```

Next, we build our control. The SDK hides us from the fact that to enable the control, we must specify the control by its object identifier (OID), which we discussed in Chapter 3. The OID for the server sort control is `1.2.840.113556.1.4.473`. We must send this plus an array of the values that go with the control, in this case the list of attributes we wish to sort by:

```
/* Create a server control using that sort key. */
LDAPSortControl sortCtrl = new LDAPSortControl(sortOrder,true);
LDAPSearchConstraints cons = ld.getSearchConstraints();
```

The next line of code takes care of sending the control to the server, and then the rest of the code is similar to what we've seen already:

```
      cons.setServerControls(sortCtrl);

      res = ld.search( base, scope, filter, attrs, false,cons);

   LDAPEntry findEntry = null;
   while (res.hasMoreElements())
   {
      findEntry = (LDAPEntry)res.next();
      System.out.println("DN: "+findEntry.getDN());

      LDAPAttributeSet attributeSet = findEntry.getAttributeSet();

      for (int i=0;i<attributeSet.size();i++)
      {
         LDAPAttribute attribute=(LDAPAttribute)attributeSet.elementAt(i);
         String attrName = attribute.getName();
         System.out.println( attrName + ":" );

         Enumeration enumVals = attribute.getStringValues();
         if (enumVals != null) {
            while ( enumVals.hasMoreElements() ) {
               String nextValue = ( String )enumVals.nextElement();
               System.out.println( "\t" + nextValue );
            }
         }
      }
   }
}
//ignore referrals in this example
catch(LDAPReferralException x) {}
catch(LDAPException e)
{
   e.printStackTrace();
   System.exit(1);
}
catch (Exception e)
{
   e.printStackTrace();
   System.exit(1);
}

try{
   if (ld != null)
   {
      ld.disconnect();
   }
   System.out.println("finished!");
   System.exit(0);
}
catch (LDAPException e1)
{
   e1.printStackTrace();
   System.exit(1);
}
   }
}
```

#### Chapter 12

The results of this program should look something like this:

```
DN: uid=kcarter, ou=People, o=airius.com
cn:
        Karen Carter
sn:
        Carter
givenname:
        Karen
uid:
        kcarter
DN: uid=mcarter, ou=People, o=airius.com
cn:
        Mike Carter
sn:
        Carter
givenname:
        Mike
uid:
        mcarter
DN: uid=scarter, ou=People, o=airius.com
cn:
        Sam Carter
sn:
        Carter
...
```

Summary

Throughout this penultimate chapter, we have been looking at some of the more advanced features that you can take advantage of in your LDAP applications. In particular, we have seen:

- ❏ What referrals are and how they work
- ❏ When and why we would want to implement replication
- ❏ Using access control lists and how they can give granular control over who can access the data in an LDAP server and what level of access they have
- ❏ How to secure data 'over the wire', including the use of encryption using public and private keys
- ❏ How SSL works in practice with a coded example of searching an LDAP server over an SSL connection
- ❏ How you can extend the functionality of LDAP applications using LDAP controls

These are some of the more interesting and complex areas of LDAP programming/development, and should give you an idea of the power and the scope that LDAP offers.

13

LDAP Cookbook

Well we've definitely covered a lot of ground so far. While I've done my best to show you example applications where appropriate, this final chapter is basically a collection of practical LDAP examples demonstrating some of the various aspects of LDAP that have been covered throughout the book.

While these examples are written in Perl or Java, there's nothing that prevents them from being written in something else. For the most part, these are general examples that hopefully you'll find useful. I plan to start making a large 'cookbook' of examples as part of my on-going **Project PLUMS**. PLUMS stands for **Practical LDAP User Management System**. This pet project of mine is designed to collect together a number of free, open-source tools and algorithms that LDAP administrators/developers need to make LDAP fit into their organization. While LDAP does not have to be limited to user data, I think that LDAP's main purpose in most organizations is going to be to centralize the management of users. Thus I decided to call it a 'User Management System'.

LDAP programming generally is not hard, but why keep re-inventing the wheel?

Project PLUMS can be found on my web site at http://www.mjwilcox.com.

DumpTree

One of the most frequently asked questions on the LDAP newsgroups and list servers of which I am a member is how to display the members of certain 'branch', such as a department. This particular example is designed to show you one possible way of displaying this information.

The Perl script shown below takes an organizationalUnit and then dumps all of the members of that unit onto the screen. You could substitute the organizationalUnit attribute for any attribute you wish, such as location (l) or organization (o). As before, I'll step through this code, discussing the important bits as they appear.

```
#!/usr/local/bin/perl
# dumpTree.pl
# Given a ou, it will dump records to the screen
# usage dumpTree.pl "organizational unit"

use Mozilla::LDAP::Conn;
use Mozilla::LDAP::Utils;
```

Get the `organizationalUnit` from the command line.

```
my $term = shift;

my $host = "localhost";
my $port = 389;
my $dn = "";
my $passwd = "";
my $base = "o=airius.com";

my $filter = "(ou=$term)";
my $scope = "subtree";

my @attribs;
push(@attribs,"cn");
push(@attribs,"mail");
push(@attribs,"telephonenumber");

#get LDAP connection
my $ldap = new Mozilla::LDAP::Conn($host,$port,$dn,$passwd) || die("Failed to open
LDAP connection.\n");
```

Next, we perform the search:

```
#this returns a Mozilla::LDAP::Entry object
my $entry = $ldap->search($base, "subtree", $filter,0,@attribs);
```

Then do a very simple display:

```
if (! $entry)
{
   print "Search failed. Try again\n";
}
else
{
   while ($entry)
   {
      #print out Entry
      $entry->printLDIF();
      $entry = $ldap->nextEntry();
   }
}
```

So, if you type in the command line something like this:

```
c:\ perl dumpTree.pl Accounting |more:
```

Then you should get an output like this:

```
C:\WINNT\System32\cmd.exe                                    _ □ ×
dn: uid=scarter, ou=People, o=airius.com
cn: Sam Carter
mail: scarter@airius.com
telephonenumber: +1 408 555 4798

dn: uid=tmorris, ou=People, o=airius.com
cn: Ted Morris
mail: tmorris@airius.com
telephonenumber: +1 408 555 9187

dn: uid=dmiller, ou=People, o=airius.com
cn: David Miller
mail: dmiller@airius.com
telephonenumber: +1 408 555 9423

dn: uid=gfarmer, ou=People, o=airius.com
cn: Gern Farmer
mail: gfarmer@airius.com
telephonenumber: +1 408 555 6201

dn: uid=jwallace, ou=People, o=airius.com
cn: Judy Wallace
mail: jwallace@airius.com
telephonenumber: +1 408 555 0319
-- More  --
```

GetGroups

Another common question that I see is, "How do you print out the members of a group?" This script presented in this section is the answer to that question. You simply give the script a group name and it will print out all of the members. This includes all of the members of any groups that are members of the group. There is not a theoretical limit to this script, though I have only tried it to a depth of three levels.

Here is the code for `GetGroups.pl`:

```perl
#!/usr/local/bin/perl
# getGroups.pl
# Given a group name, it will print out all members, including
# members of groups that are members of the original group.
# Prints out the common name of the member instead of their dn
# to make it a bit more user friendly
# usage getGroups.pl "group name"
use Mozilla::LDAP::Conn;  #LDAP module
use Mozilla::LDAP::Utils; #LDAP module

#Some Variables to Set
my $term  = shift;
my $ldap_host = "localhost";
my $ldap_port = 389;
my $ldap_base = "o=airius.com";

#we're doing an anonymous search
my $dn = "";
my $pwd = "";
```

A group is only considered a group if it has an `objectclass` attribute value of `groupofuniquenames`.

```
my $filter = "(&(objectclass=groupofuniquenames)(cn=$term))";

#now do the first search
my $ldap = new Mozilla::LDAP::Conn($ldap_host,$ldap_port,$dn,$pwd)
                        || die("Failed to open LDAP conenction.\n");

my @attribs = ("objectclass","uniquemember","cn");
my $entry = $ldap->search($ldap_base, "subtree", $filter, 0, @attribs);

#print out results
if (! $entry)
{
    print "$filter did not return any results";
}
else
{
```

Pass each entry to a subroutine called `printMembers()` for display.

```
    while ($entry)
    {
        &printMembers($entry);
        $entry = $ldap->nextEntry();
    }
}

# printMembers
sub printMembers
{
    my $entry = shift; #this will be an LDAPEntry object
    print "\ndn: ",$entry->getDN(),"\n";
```

Members of the group are stored as the values of the `uniquemember` attribute. The value will be a DN of an entry in the LDAP server:

```
    my @members = @{$entry->{uniquemember}};
    #now get the entry from the server
    my $temp_ldap=new Mozilla::LDAP::Conn($ldap_host,$ldap_port,$dn,$pwd)
                            || die("Failed to open LDAP connection.\n");
    for $member (@members)
    {
```

By setting the search base to the DN of a `uniquemember` value and the scope to `"base"`, the filter is actually irrelevant (the server will ignore it). It will retrieve the entry that matches the DN very quickly.

```
    my $temp_entry = $temp_ldap->search($member,"base",
                    "objectclass=*",0,@attribs);
```

Here, we print out the common name of the member entry:

```
        print "member is ",@{$temp_entry->{cn}},"\n" unless ! @{$temp_entry->{cn}};
        if (! $temp_entry)
        {
            print "$member not a valid entry\n";
        }
        else
        {
```

Next, we need to check to see if the member entry is a group itself. We determine this by see whether it has a value of `groupofuniquenames` in its `objectclass` attribute. If so, then pass this DN to the `printMembers()` subroutine (in effect creating a recursive operation):

```
            #Check to see if uniquemember is a group or not
            #if so then print out the values
            if ($temp_entry->hasValue("objectclass", "groupofuniquenames",1))
            {
                print "\nSubgroup of: ",$entry->getDN(),"\n";
                &printMembers($temp_entry)
            }
        }
    }
}
```

Here is some example output from this script:

```
C:\WINNT\System32\cmd.exe

F:\cookbook>perl searchgroup.pl "accounting managers"
dn: cn=Accounting Managers,ou=groups,o=airius.com
member is Sam Carter
member is Ted Morris
member is HR Managers

Subgroup of: cn=Accounting Managers,ou=groups,o=airius.com

dn: cn=HR Managers,ou=groups,o=airius.com
member is Kirsten Vaughan
member is Chris Schmith
member is Directory Administrators

Subgroup of: cn=HR Managers,ou=groups,o=airius.com

dn: cn=Directory Administrators, ou=Groups, o=airius.com
member is Kirsten Vaughan
member is Robert Daugherty
member is Harry Miller

dn: cn=Accounting Managers,ou=groups,o=exchange.airius.com

F:\cookbook>
```

Dealing with Images

One of the most exciting aspects of LDAP is that it is able to store and retrieve binary data such as images. In this example, we will deal with images stored in the JPEG format.

Storing photographs is important in a large organizational setting where it is impossible to know who everyone is. While name-badges with photographs are popular, these can still be faked, but storing the image in LDAP allows your security personnel to retrieve that image using a standard LDAP client with the ability to display images, such as the client built into Netscape Communicator.

You may also wish to store photos for other purposes. LDAP might be an easy way to put photos in a web accessible database for an on-line real-estate sales site, for example, or for insurance purposes. Perhaps you run an on-line dating service and you would like to give your clients the ability to store their photos in the system. The possibilities are endless.

The program shown below, `loadJPEG`, is a command line program just to make it easier to show the actual loading of the image. Its companion class, `viewJPEG` is a Java Swing application that displays an image.

```
import netscape.ldap.*;
import java.io.*;
import java.util.*;

//load a JPEG photo file into LDAP as a modify
public class loadJPEG
{
    public static void main(String args[])
    {
        byte jpeg_data[] = null;
```

First, we must open the file containing our JPEG encoded photograph as a `RandomAccessFile` object, which is a standard Java object designed for fast operations over binary data. After have opened the file, we read the entire file into an array of `byte` objects:

```
        //first load the photo as read only
        try{
            RandomAccessFile raf = new RandomAccessFile("mark_wilcox.jpg","r");
            jpeg_data = new byte[(int)raf.length()];
            raf.readFully(jpeg_data);
            System.out.println("read jpeg_data");
        }
        catch(IOException ioe)
        {
            ioe.printStackTrace();
            System.exit(1);
        }
        //LDAP stuff below
        String host = "localhost";
        int port = 389;
        String base = "o=airius.com";
        int scope = LDAPv2.SCOPE_SUB;
        String dn = "uid=kvaughan, ou=People, o=airius.com";
        String pwd = "bribery";
        String entry_dn = "uid=scarter,ou=People,o=airius.com";

        LDAPAttribute attribute = null;
        LDAPModificationSet mods = null;
        LDAPConnection ld = null;
```

```
        try
        {
            ld = new LDAPConnection();

            // must bind as a user with rights to write to the server
            ld.connect(host,port,dn,pwd);
```

After we have the data loaded into our array, it's actually a simple step to insert the photo into our server. We simply create a new `LDAPModificationSet`, as well as a new `LDAPAttribute`, giving it the name of our attribute, `jpegPhoto`, and the array containing the data. Then we add the newly minted `LDAPAttribute` object to the `LDAPModificationSet` object (specifying a replace modification type here). Finally, we pass the `LDAPModificationSet` to the `LDAPConnection`'s `modify()` method, along with the DN of the entry to which we wish to add the photo:

```
            mods = new LDAPModificationSet();
            attribute = new LDAPAttribute("jpegPhoto",jpeg_data);
            mods.add(LDAPModification.REPLACE,attribute);

            // modify the object
            ld.modify(entry_dn,mods);
            if (ld != null)
            {
                ld.disconnect();
            }
        }
        catch(LDAPException e)
        {
            e.printStackTrace();
        }
    }
}
```

Our next class, `viewJPEG`, allows us to retrieve the entry and will display it in a simple GUI window:

```
import netscape.ldap.*;
import netscape.ldap.util.*;

import javax.swing.*;
import javax.swing.text.*;
import java.awt.event.*;
import java.awt.*;

import java.io.*;
import java.util.*;

//view JPEG photos
public class viewJPEG extends JPanel
{
    viewJPEG(String host,int port,String base,String uid)
    {
        super();
        int scope = LDAPConnection.SCOPE_SUB;
        String dn = "";
        String pwd = "";
        String filter = "uid="+uid;
```

```
LDAPConnection ld = null;

Font f;
f = new Font("SanSerif",Font.PLAIN,24);
.setFont(f);

// setLayout(new BorderLayout());
try
{
    ld = new LDAPConnection();
    ld.connect(host,port,dn,pwd);
```

We search as we would a normal entry:

```
String attrs [] = {"cn","jpegPhoto"};

LDAPSearchResults res = ld.search( base, scope, filter, attrs, false );

while ( (res.hasMoreElements())
{
    LDAPEntry findEntry = null;
    findEntry = (LDAPEntry)res.next();

    //get the CN attribute
    LDAPAttribute cn_attribute = findEntry.getAttribute("cn");
    //get the jpegPhoto attribute
    LDAPAttribute jpeg_attribute = findEntry.getAttribute("jpegPhoto");

    //print CN values
    Enumeration enumVals = cn_attribute.getStringValues();
    JLabel cn_label = new JLabel("Common Name:");
    add(cn_label);
    if (enumVals != null) {
        while ( enumVals.hasMoreElements() ) {
            String nextValue = ( String )enumVals.nextElement();
            JTextField data_display = new JTextField("cn: "+nextValue);
            add(data_display);
        }
    }
}
```

Here is the 'meat' of this program. In every other search example we have seen so far, we have only dealt with text values. To get the values of a binary attribute such as `jpegPhoto`, we must use the `getByteValues()` of the `LDAPAttribute` class. This will return an `Enumeration` object, where each entry in the enumeration is an array of `byte` objects:

```
//display jpeg photo
enumVals = jpeg_attribute.getByteValues();

if ( enumVals != null ) {
    while ( enumVals.hasMoreElements() ) {
        byte data[] = (byte []) enumVals.nextElement();
```

The next three lines create an image that can be displayed in a window with the data contained in the `jpegPhoto` attribute:

```
                    ImageIcon icon= new ImageIcon(data);

                    JLabel jpeg_label = new JLabel(icon);
                    add(jpeg_label);
                }
            }
        }

        if (ld != null)
        {
            ld.disconnect();
        }
    }
    catch(LDAPException e)
    {
        e.printStackTrace();
    }
    catch (Exception e)
    {
        e.printStackTrace();
        System.exit(1);
    }
}

public Dimension getPreferredSize()
{
    return new Dimension(400,400);
}

public static void main(String args[])
{
    if ( args.length < 1 )
    {
        System.out.println("usage viewJPEG uid");
        System.exit(0);
    }
    String uid = args[0];
    int version = 1;
    JFrame frame = new JFrame("viewJPEG "+version);
    viewJPEG panel = new viewJPEG("localhost",389,"o=airius.com",uid);
    frame.setDefaultCloseOperation(JFrame.DO_NOTHING_ON_CLOSE);
    frame.setForeground(Color.black);
    frame.setBackground(Color.lightGray);
    frame.getContentPane().add(panel,"Center");
    frame.setSize(panel.getPreferredSize());
    frame.setVisible(true);
    frame.addWindowListener(new WindowCloser());
    }
}

class WindowCloser extends WindowAdapter
{
    public void windowClosing(WindowEvent e)
    {
        Window win = e.getWindow();
        win.setVisible(false);
        win.dispose();
        System.exit(0);
    }
}
```

Here is an example screenshot of the `viewJPEG` program. It's an exciting photograph of your author, who's posing as his alter-ego, Sam Carter. All you have to do is supply the `scarter uid` as a command line argument:

Now that I have shown you a Java GUI, here is a screenshot taken using Netscape Communicator (only versions 4.5 or later actually shows an image). Hopefully, you are now seeing some of the potential for this ability. With an LDAP server and a client like Netscape Communicator, you could very quickly create a web based image 'database', without needing to interface with CGI, ASP or any other server side programming tool!

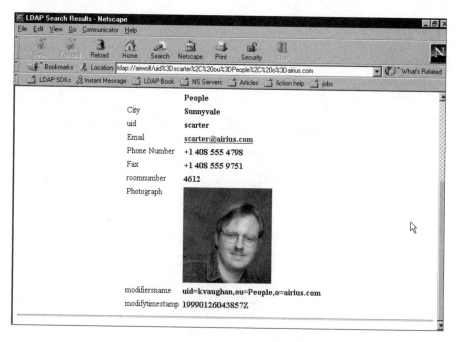

Document Management

LDAP doesn't necessarily just have to be used to store data about people. It can also be used to manage other resources. One possible application could be for document management. For the purposes of this discussion, a document is anything that has been created as a text document and is designed to be read. This reading could be stored on-line or in a hardcopy version stored somewhere (like in your organization's library).

This type of document management system is useful if you have a collection of documents that you wish to make available to an audience and you want to provide a standardized mechanism for searching the collection.

LDAP provides the ability to construct a standard set of records that can be searched via various LDAP clients. An interesting (and very advanced) project would be to develop a server plug-in that actually enables LDAP clients to search Z39.50 servers. Z39.50 is a standard for enabling the distributed searching of standard library card catalogs.

In this example, we will be using the `document` object class and a Java program called `docManager`. This program is fairly simple, with just enough functionality to demonstrate what we need for a basic document management system.

The first screen is blank and the user has the option to either complete the record and then add it, or to just enter a term or two to search the system.

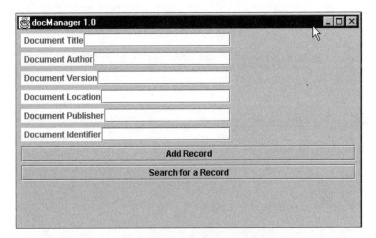

To add a record, the user fills in all of the fields and then clicks on the Add Record button:

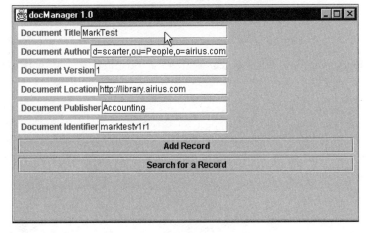

After you have added some entries, you'll probably want to be able to search. You can enter a term in one or more of the fields and `docManager` will search the LDAP database for documents that match those values. This is a very simplistic search and not a very good GUI for returning values. For a real program, you'd probably want a drop down menu of results or a table or something else.

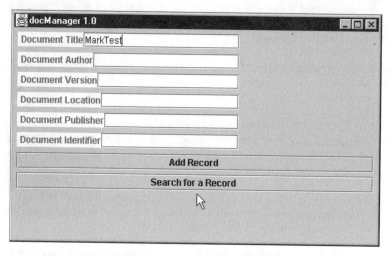

And here are the results:

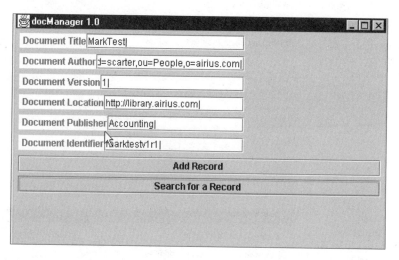

Because this is stored in LDAP, we can search the document records with a standard LDAP client, such as the `ldapsearch` command line utility.

Note the `pilotObject` is a non-standard `objectclass` attribute that is the parent of the `document` object class in the Netscape Directory Server. If you are using an LDAP server that doesn't have this object, you can always create your own document object class.

Shown below is some typical output from searching documents with `ldapsearch`:

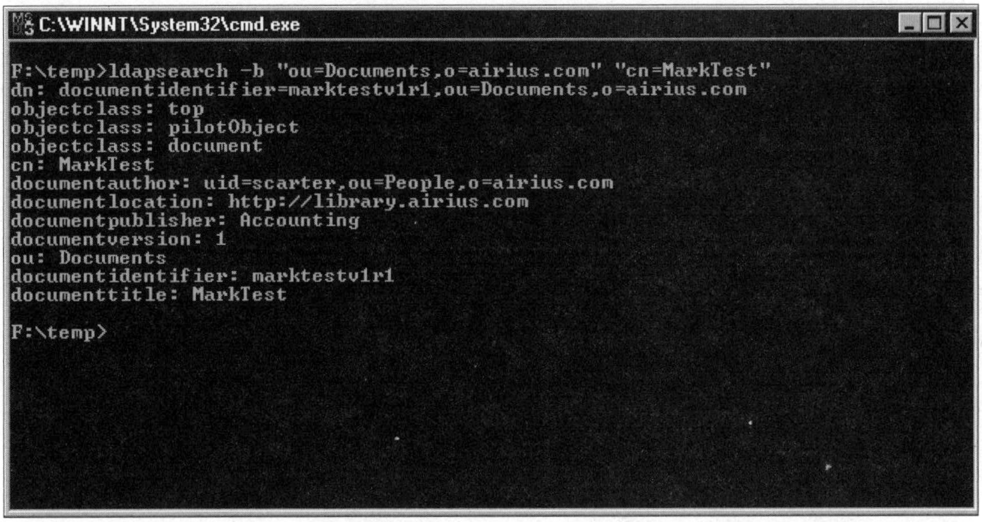

```
C:\WINNT\System32\cmd.exe                                      _ □ ×

F:\temp>ldapsearch -b "ou=Documents,o=airius.com" "cn=MarkTest"
dn: documentidentifier=marktestv1r1,ou=Documents,o=airius.com
objectclass: top
objectclass: pilotObject
objectclass: document
cn: MarkTest
documentauthor: uid=scarter,ou=People,o=airius.com
documentlocation: http://library.airius.com
documentpublisher: Accounting
documentversion: 1
ou: Documents
documentidentifier: marktestv1r1
documenttitle: MarkTest

F:\temp>
```

Because the document index is stored in LDAP, you can use LDAP's beneficial attributes of security, replication and its distributed nature to provide a very rich document warehouse.

These types of traditional database roles are ones I think LDAP will take on as it becomes a more popular technology, particularly when the application extends beyond the local network and onto an Extranet or the Internet. Let's now take a look at the code for `docManager`:

```java
//docManager
//document management system that uses LDAP
//as its database system

import java.util.Vector;
import java.util.*;
import netscape.ldap.*;

import com.sun.java.swing.*;
import com.sun.java.swing.tree.*;
import com.sun.java.swing.text.*;
import java.awt.event.*;
import java.awt.*;
import java.io.*;
```

Our first class, `docManager`, is the data entry and data viewing panel and is our primary class:

```java
public class docManager extends JPanel
  {
    displayPanel titlePanel;
    displayPanel authorPanel;
    displayPanel versionPanel;
    displayPanel locationPanel;
    displayPanel idPanel;
    displayPanel publisherPanel;
```

```
    public docManager()
    {
        setLayout(new GridLayout(10,1,5,5));
        setBorder(BorderFactory.createEmptyBorder(5,5,5,5));

        // setLayout(new BoxLayout(this,BoxLayout.Y_AXIS));
        setDoubleBuffered(true);

        titlePanel = new displayPanel("Document Title");
        authorPanel = new displayPanel("Document Author");
        versionPanel = new displayPanel("Document Version");
        locationPanel = new displayPanel("Document Location");
        publisherPanel = new displayPanel("Document Publisher");
        idPanel = new displayPanel ("Document Identifier");
        JButton addButton = new JButton("Add Record");
        addButton.addMouseListener(new addClicker(this));
        JButton searchButton = new JButton("Search for a Record");
        searchButton.addMouseListener(new searchClicker(this));

        add(titlePanel);
        add(authorPanel);
        add(versionPanel);
        add(locationPanel);
        add(publisherPanel);
        add(idPanel);
        add(addButton);
        add(searchButton);
    }

    public Dimension getPreferredSize()
    {
        return new Dimension(500,300);
    }

    public static void main(String args[])
    {
        double version = 1.0;
        JFrame frame = new JFrame("docManager "+version);
        docManager panel = new docManager();
        frame.setDefaultCloseOperation(JFrame.DO_NOTHING_ON_CLOSE);
        frame.setForeground(Color.black);
        frame.setBackground(Color.lightGray);
        frame.getContentPane().add(panel,"Center");
        frame.setSize(panel.getPreferredSize());
        frame.setVisible(true);
        frame.addWindowListener(new WindowCloser());
    }
}
```

The next class, addClicker, is called (unsurprisingly) when the user clicks on the Add a Record button:

```
class addClicker extends MouseAdapter
{
    protected docManager myPanel;
    addClicker(){this.super();}
    addClicker(docManager panel){this.super();myPanel = panel;}
```

```
    public void mouseClicked (MouseEvent e)
    {
      try{
          String host = "localhost";
          int port = 389;
          String base = "o=airius.com";
          int scope = LDAPConnection.SCOPE_SUB;
          String dn = "cn=Directory Manager";
          String pwd = "jessica98";
```

Here, we get the values of the text fields in the panel:

```
          String titleText = myPanel.titlePanel.data_display.getText();
          String authorText = myPanel.authorPanel.data_display.getText();
          String locationText = myPanel.locationPanel.data_display.getText();
          String publisherText = myPanel.publisherPanel.data_display.getText();
          String versionText = myPanel.versionPanel.data_display.getText();
          String idText = myPanel.idPanel.data_display.getText();
```

Then, we create a new DN for our entry:

```
          String new_dn = new String("documentidentifier="+idText+",
                                        ou=Documents,o=airius.com");

          String objectclass_values [] = {"top","pilotObject","document"};
          String cn_values [] = {titleText};
          String author_values [] = {authorText};
          String location_values [] = {locationText};
          String ou_values [] = {"Documents"};
          String version_values[] = {versionText};
          String publisher_values [] = {publisherText};
          String identifier_values[] = {idText};
          String title_values[] = {titleText};

          LDAPAttributeSet attrib_set = null;
          LDAPAttribute attribute = null;
          LDAPEntry entry = null;

          LDAPConnection ld = null;

          ld = new LDAPConnection();
```

The following line sets up the connection to the LDAP server:

```
          ld.connect(host,port,dn,pwd);
```

This bit of code is building the attributes for our entry:

```
          attrib_set = new LDAPAttributeSet();

          attribute = new LDAPAttribute("objectclass",objectclass_values);
          attrib_set.add(attribute);

          attribute = new LDAPAttribute("cn", cn_values);
          attrib_set.add(attribute);
```

```
            attribute = new LDAPAttribute("documentauthor", author_values);
            attrib_set.add(attribute);

            attribute = new LDAPAttribute("documentlocation",location_values);
            attrib_set.add(attribute);

            attribute = new LDAPAttribute("documentpublisher",publisher_values);
            attrib_set.add(attribute);

            attribute = new LDAPAttribute("documentversion", version_values);
            attrib_set.add(attribute);

            attribute = new LDAPAttribute("ou",ou_values);
            attrib_set.add(attribute);

            attribute = new LDAPAttribute("documentidentifier", identifier_values);
            attrib_set.add(attribute);

            attribute = new LDAPAttribute("documenttitle",title_values);
            attrib_set.add(attribute);

            entry = new LDAPEntry(new_dn,attrib_set);
            System.out.println(entry.toString());
```

And finally, we add our new entry!

```
            ld.add(entry);

            if (ld != null)
            {
                ld.disconnect();
            }
        }
        catch(LDAPException z)
        {
            z.printStackTrace();
        }
    }
}
```

The `searchClicker` class is called when the user clicks on the **Search for a Record** button:

```
class searchClicker extends MouseAdapter
{
    protected docManager myPanel;
    searchClicker(){this.super();}
    searchClicker(docManager panel){this.super();myPanel = panel;}

    public void mouseClicked (MouseEvent e)
    {
        try {
            String host = "localhost";
            int port = 389;
            String base = "o=airius.com";
            int scope = LDAPv2.SCOPE_SUB;
            String dn = "cn=Directory Manager";
            String pwd = "jessica98";
```

Here, we get the data from our window.

```
String titleText = myPanel.titlePanel.data_display.getText();
String authorText = myPanel.authorPanel.data_display.getText();
String locationText = myPanel.locationPanel.data_display.getText();
String versionText = myPanel.versionPanel.data_display.getText();
String publisherText = myPanel.publisherPanel.data_display.getText();
String idText = myPanel.idPanel.data_display.getText();
```

Then build our search filter:

```
StringBuffer searchFilterBuffer = new
                    StringBuffer("(&(documenttitle="+titleText+"*)");
searchFilterBuffer.append("(documentauthor="+authorText+"*)");
searchFilterBuffer.append("(documentlocation="+locationText+"*)");
searchFilterBuffer.append("(documentpublisher="+publisherText+"*)");
searchFilterBuffer.append("(documentversion="+versionText+"*)");
searchFilterBuffer.append("(documentidentifier="+idText+"*))");
String searchFilter = searchFilterBuffer.toString();

LDAPConnection ld = null;

ld = new LDAPConnection();

ld.connect(host,port,dn,pwd);
String attrs [] = {"documentauthor","documenttitle","documentlocation",
            documentpublisher","documentidentifier","documentversion"};

System.out.println("Search Filter is "+searchFilter);
```

And perform the search:

```
LDAPSearchResults res = ld.search(base,scope,searchFilter,attrs,false);

while (res.hasMoreElements())
{
    LDAPEntry findEntry = null;
    findEntry = (LDAPEntry)res.next();
```

Finally, we display the results:

```
        //will set the proper field
        new setDocValues(findEntry,"documenttitle",
                                    myPanel.titlePanel.data_display);
        new setDocValues(findEntry,"documentauthor",
                                    myPanel.authorPanel.data_display);
        new setDocValues(findEntry,"documentlocation",
                                    myPanel.locationPanel.data_display);
        new setDocValues(findEntry,"documentpublisher",
                                    myPanel.publisherPanel.data_display);
        new setDocValues(findEntry,"documentidentifier",
                                    myPanel.idPanel.data_display);
        new setDocValues(findEntry,"documentversion",
                                    myPanel.versionPanel.data_display);
    }
```

```
            if (ld != null)
            {
                ld.disconnect();
            }
        }
        catch(LDAPException z)
        {
            z.printStackTrace();
        }
    }
}
```

This class is for closing the window:

```
class WindowCloser extends WindowAdapter
{
    public void windowClosing(WindowEvent e)
    {
        Window win = e.getWindow();
        win.setVisible(false);
        win.dispose();
        System.exit(0);
    }
}

/** Add a Record to the LDAP server
 * In a real example, we would put LDAP stuff outside of this class
 */
```

And this one puts the data into the text fields that are in the display window:

```
//sets the textfields in the docManager class
class setDocValues
{
    setDocValues (LDAPEntry findEntry,String attr,JTextField data)
    {
        System.out.println("in setDocValues");
        System.out.println("looking for attr: "+attr);
        LDAPAttribute attribute = findEntry.getAttribute(attr);
        System.out.println("got attribute");
        StringBuffer buffer = new StringBuffer();
        if ( attribute == null ){
            data.setText("UNKNOWN");
        }
        else{
            Enumeration enumVals = attribute.getStringValues();
            if (enumVals == null) {
                data.setText("UNKNOWN");
            }
            else{
                System.out.println("in enumVals");
                while ( enumVals.hasMoreElements() ) {
                    buffer.append(( String )enumVals.nextElement()+"|");
                }
                data.setText(buffer.toString());
            }
        }
    }
}
```

This class, `displayPanel`, builds the actual display screen of our application:

```
class displayPanel extends JPanel
{
    public JTextField data display;
    public displayPanel(String labelText)
    {
        JPanel unitGroup = new JPanel()
        {
            public Dimension getMinimumSize()
                return getPreferredSize();
            }
            public Dimension getPreferredSize() {
                return new Dimension(300, super.getPreferredSize().height);
            }
            public Dimension getMaximumSize() {
                return getPreferredSize();
            }
        };
        unitGroup.setBackground(Color.white);
        unitGroup.setBorder(BorderFactory.createEmptyBorder(0,5,0,0));
        unitGroup.setLayout(new BoxLayout(unitGroup,BoxLayout.X_AXIS));
        JLabel label = new JLabel(labelText);
        data display = new JTextField(10);
        unitGroup.add(label);
        unitGroup.add(data display);
        setLayout(new BoxLayout(this, BoxLayout.X_AXIS));
        add(unitGroup);
        unitGroup.setAlignmentY(TOP ALIGNMENT);
    }
}
```

And that's it!

Before you can go ahead and run this example, however, you need to perform the following steps:

1. From the main console window of Directory Server, go to the Configuration tab and select Database I Schema, and from here, select the Object Classes tab:

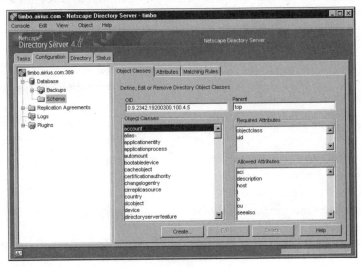

2. Modify the `document` object class so that it contains the following attributes:

- ❑ `documentidentifier` (required)
- ❑ `documentauthor` (allowed)
- ❑ `documentlocation` (allowed)
- ❑ `documentpublisher` (allowed)
- ❑ `documentversion` (allowed)
- ❑ `documenttitle` (allowed)
- ❑ `cn` (allowed)
- ❑ `ou` (allowed)

3. Go to `airius.com` and add a new `organizationalUnit (ou)`, `Documents`

Storing SQL in LDAP with JNDI

One of the most exciting things about Internet programming is the ability to do distributed computing and to share business rules (or business logic) across the various systems that make up your network.

In many environments the way business logic is implemented is with SQL queries for relational databases. Often the same queries are used over and over again, but there is no easy way to share this code from one system to another, unless you count 'cut and paste' as a code re-use mechanism. While this is probably the most popular form of code re-use, it is, needless to say, prone to errors, the biggest one of which is to forget to update all of the systems that use the query when the query needs to be changed.

With Java and the Java Naming and Directory Interface (JNDI), you can start to make this a thing of the past. You can create an object that contains a particular SQL query (or queries), store that to an LDAP server with JNDI, and then have all of the programs that need access to that query load the particular query object they need. They can then perform the query on the database.

For this example, I created a very simple Microsoft Access database, but you can use whatever database you wish, as long as it can be accessed via JDBC. Access was the handiest one for me and is likely to be the most accessible to the readers of this book.

The database has one table, called `itemTable`, which has four fields:

- ❑ `tableCounter` – our primary key, and is an `autoincrement` field
- ❑ `itemName` – the name of the item we are selling
- ❑ `itemPrice` – how much does the item cost
- ❑ `itemCount` – how much of the item do we have left

We are going to make a simple query class called `itemsToSellQuery`. This class will connect to the database and print out the items we have to sell in our simple database.

It is important to note that this class implements the `Serializable` interface, so that it can be stored using JNDI.

Here is the code for `itemToSellQuery`:

```
//This is the class we'll bind into the server
import java.io.*;
import java.sql.*;

class itemsToSellQuery implements Serializable
{
    public itemsToSellQuery() {}

    public static void main(String args[])
    {
        // Had this been real this might actually return something.
        // For our example we'll just print out some results
        doQuery();
    }

    public static void doQuery()
    {
        try
        {
            //force the driver to loaded into memory
            Class.forName("sun.jdbc.odbc.JdbcOdbcDriver");

            String url = "jdbc:odbc:ldaptest";

            Connection con  = DriverManager.getConnection(url,"","");
            Statement stmt = con.createStatement();
            ResultSet rs = stmt.executeQuery("SELECT itemTable.itemname,
                        itemTable.itemprice, itemTable.itemcount FROM itemTable;");

            while (rs.next() )
            {
                String name = rs.getString("itemname");
                String price = rs.getString("itemprice");
                String count = rs.getString("itemcount");
                System.out.println("name: "+name);
                System.out.println("price: "+price);
                System.out.println("count: "+count);
            }
        }
        catch(Exception x){
            System.err.println(x.toString());
        }
    }
}
```

The next step is to store this class in the LDAP server, which we do with the `storeQuery` class.

First, you must get an instance of the class you want to store, then you must connect to the server. Once you've done this, you can store the entry with the `bind()` method of `DirContext`.

Shown below is the full code listing for `storeQuery`:

```java
import java.util.Hashtable;
import java.util.Enumeration;

import javax.naming.*;
import javax.naming.directory.*;

import java.sql.*;
import java.util.*;
import java.io.*;

//this stores itemsToSell in LDAP
//itemDisplay retrieves itemsToSell and displays query results
public class storeQuery
{
    // initial context implementation
    public static String INITCTX = "com.sun.jndi.ldap.LdapCtxFactory";

    public static String MY_HOST = "ldap://localhost:389";
    public static String MGR_DN = "uid=kvaughan, ou=People, o=airius.com";
    public static String MGR_PW = "bribery";
    public static String MY_SEARCHBASE = "o=Airius.com";

    public static void main(String args[])
    {
        try {
            //Hashtable for environmental information
            Hashtable env = new Hashtable();

            //Specify which class to use for our JNDI provider
            env.put(Context.INITIAL_CONTEXT_FACTORY, INITCTX);
            env.put(Context.PROVIDER_URL,MY_HOST);
            env.put(Context.SECURITY_AUTHENTICATION,"simple");
            env.put(Context.SECURITY_PRINCIPAL,MGR_DN);
            env.put(Context.SECURITY_CREDENTIALS,MGR_PW);

            // Variable to store
            itemsToSellQuery query = new itemsToSellQuery();
            //Get a reference to a directory context
            DirContext ctx = new InitialDirContext(env);

            ctx.bind("cn=Sell Query,ou=Queries,o=airius.com",query);
            System.out.println("query stored");

        }
        catch(Exception e)
        {
            e.printStackTrace();
            System.exit(1);
        }
    }
}
```

Note that in order to use the code example as written above, you must first create an `organizationalUnit` entry named `ou=Queries,o=airius.com` in your directory.

Finally, to reuse this object, your other applications must bind to the server and then retrieve the object with the `DirContext lookup()` method. Note that you must cast to the correct class, as `lookup()` will return a generic Java object – remember that *all* classes in Java are derived from the `Object` class.

Here is how you could retrieve the `itemsToSellQuery` class:

```
Query = (itemsToSellQuery) ctx.lookup("cn=Sell Query,ou=Queries,o=airius.com");
```

Our last example in this section is the `itemDisplay` class, which connects to the LDAP server, retrieves the `itemsToSellQuery` object and then displays the results of the query:

```
/** itemDisplay
    This retrieves the itemsToSellQuery object from the LDAP server and then
    displays it out on the console
*/

import java.util.Enumeration;
import java.util.Hashtable;

import javax.naming.*;
import javax.naming.directory.*;

import itemsToSellQuery;
public class itemDisplay
{
    // initial context implementation
    public static String INITCTX = "com.sun.jndi.ldap.LdapCtxFactory";

    public static String MY_HOST = "ldap://localhost:389";
    public static String MGR_DN = "uid=kvaughan, ou=People, o=airius.com";
    public static String MGR_PW = "bribery";
    public static String MY_SEARCHBASE = "o=Airius.com";

    public static void main(String args[])
    {
        try {
            //Hashtable for environmental information
            Hashtable env = new Hashtable();

            //Specify which class to use for our JNDI provider
            env.put(Context.INITIAL_CONTEXT_FACTORY, INITCTX);
            env.put(Context.PROVIDER_URL,MY_HOST);
            env.put(Context.SECURITY_AUTHENTICATION,"simple");
            env.put(Context.SECURITY_PRINCIPAL,MGR_DN);
            env.put(Context.SECURITY_CREDENTIALS,MGR_PW);

            // Variable to store
            itemsToSellQuery query;
            //Get a reference to a directory context
            DirContext ctx = new InitialDirContext(env);

            query = (itemsToSellQuery)
                        ctx.lookup("cn=Sell Query,ou=Queries,o=airius.com");
```

```
            System.out.println("query retrieved\n");
            query.doQuery();
        }
        catch(Exception e)
        {
            e.printStackTrace();
            System.exit(1);
        }
    }
}
```

Here is an example screenshot of the output from this application:

Now, before you go around storing your entire collection of Java objects inside your LDAP server, keep in mind that Java objects take up considerably more space than you traditional LDAP values (names, phone numbers, etc). Some LDAP servers will be configured to handle large amounts of binary data (such as JPEG photos and Java objects) and others won't. Check with your server vendor to see what they recommend as the maximum storage size of an entry.

JNDI also provides a mechanism for storing the basic attributes for an object in LDAP and then building an object from those attributes with a `Factory` class.

While I'm not fond of JNDI as a general purpose LDAP development tool, I really love how it has made it nearly painless to store Java objects remotely. Together, LDAP and JNDI provide a secure and standardized system for developing and deploying distributed computing applications (applications that use components that are not stored locally).

Servlet Authentication with LDAP

In earlier chapters, we have covered to topic of using authentication with LDAP, but in this section, we'll look at a more 'real world' example, using Java servlets. Java servlets are designed to be the improvements upon the traditional CGI web programming model. Servlets are Java programs that can only be run inside of a web server, in a similar mechanism to the way Java applets work, except that servlets have a much more flexible security model and they don't suffer from the reliability problems that plague applets. This is because the buggiest part of the early Java API (which most applets still use) is the Abstract Windowing Toolkit for developing GUIs (sometimes referred to as the Awful Windowing Toolkit by more cynical developers). Servlets don't have GUIs, so they don't need the AWT. They are much more scalable and secure than traditional CGI, while giving you many of the benefits of Java. Java servlets are one of the areas where the hype of 'Write Once, Run Anywhere' has paid off, because server-side Java is much more stable, quicker and is able to use more functionality than your ordinary Java applet.

If you develop Java servlets you probably have, at some point, wanted to restrict access to your servlet. Using authentication over LDAP allows all of your server-side applications to share the same user database, even if they are running on different web servers. In the example that follows, we're going to look at how to use standard web authentication (BASIC authentication), which is already built in to all of the common web browsers and is the easiest one to manage. BASIC authentication is the mechanism being used whenever you go to a web site and a little gray box pops up asking for user ID and password. To get that box to pop up, you must tell the servlet to request the "Authorization" header, like this:

```
//Get Authorization header
String auth = req.getHeader("Authorization");
```

If the "Authorization" header is blank, the web server will instruct the browser that it needs this header and the web browser will pop up the box for the user to fill in.

When the boxes are filled in and the user clicks OK, the browser will return back the Authorization header, which will contain the word BASIC immediately followed by the Base64 encoded user ID and password. When decoded, the user ID and password will be separated by a colon.

Here is an example screenshot of the window asking for your user ID and password:

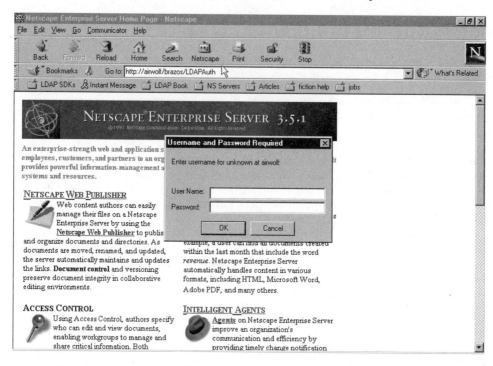

Here is a screenshot that is shown after successful authentication with our sample servlet, which we'll see at the end of this section:

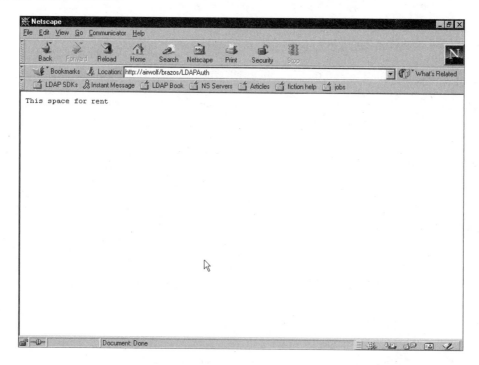

You can use any Base64 decoder you wish, but the standard JDK comes with one that you can use. Because the decoder is in the `sun.misc` package, it's officially undocumented, unsupported and may disappear at anytime, but it hasn't yet. If for some reason you don't have this decoder, there are many free ones available – there is also one in the Netscape LDAP Java SDK for you to use if you need it (it's in the `netscape.ldap.util` class).

Base64 encoding is not an encryption mechanism – it is just a scheme so that we can send information across the Internet. Usually it is used to send binary information, but it has other uses as well.

Here's how we get the user ID and password decoded:

```
sun.misc.BASE64Decoder dec = new sun.misc.BASE64Decoder();
String userpassDecoded = new String(dec.decodeBuffer(userpassEncoded));
StringTokenizer st = new StringTokenizer(userpassDecoded,":");
String uid = st.nextToken();
pwd = st.nextToken();
```

The `allowedUser()` method does all of the decoding and checking for authorization. You can actually replace all of the LDAP code in this function with your own system. Just make sure it returns a Boolean value at the end.

Shown below is the full code listing for the `LDAPAuth` example:

```
import java.io.*;
import java.util.*;
import javax.servlet.*;
import javax.servlet.http.*;

import netscape.ldap.*;

public class LDAPAuth extends HttpServlet
{
    Hashtable users = new Hashtable();

    public void init(ServletConfig config) throws ServletException
    {
        super.init(config);
    }

    public void doGet(HttpServletRequest req, HttpServletResponse res) throws
                                        ServletException, IOException
    {
        res.setContentType("text/plain");
        PrintWriter out = res.getWriter();

        //Get Authorization header
        String auth = req.getHeader("Authorization");

        // Do we allow that user
        if (!allowedUser(auth))
        {
            // Not Allowed, so report he's unauthorized
            res.sendError(res.SC_UNAUTHORIZED);
            res.setHeader("WWW-Authenticate", "BASIC realm=\"users\"");
            // Could offer to add to user list
        }
```

```
        else
        {
            //User is allowed in
            out.println("This space for rent");
        }
    }

    /* This method checks to see if the user is in the LDAP database */
    protected boolean allowedUser(String auth) throws IOException
    {
        LDAPConnection ld = new LDAPConnection();
        LDAPEntry findEntry = null;
        String dn = null;
        String pwd = null;
        String MY_HOST = "localhost";
        int MY_PORT = 389;
        String MY_SEARCHBASE = "o=airius.com";

        boolean status =false;

        try {
            if (auth == null ) return false; // no auth
            if (!auth.toUpperCase().startsWith("BASIC "))
            {
                return false; //only do BASIC
            }

            // Get encoded user and password, comes after BASIC
            String userpassEncoded = auth.substring(6);

            // Decode it, using any base 64 decoder
            sun.misc.BASE64Decoder dec = new sun.misc.BASE64Decoder();
            String userpassDecoded = new String(dec.decodeBuffer(userpassEncoded));
            StringTokenizer st = new StringTokenizer(userpassDecoded,":");
            String uid = st.nextToken();
            pwd = st.nextToken();

            String MY_FILTER = "uid=" + uid;
            ld.connect( MY_HOST, MY_PORT );
            LDAPSearchConstraints origOptions = ld.getSearchConstraints();
            LDAPSearchConstraints myOptions =
(LDAPSearchConstraints)origOptions.clone();
            myOptions.setMaxResults(0);

            // Look for an entry matching the user id passed from the browser:

            LDAPSearchResults res =
  ld.search(MY_SEARCHBASE,LDAPConnection.SCOPE_SUB,MY_FILTER,null,
            false,myOptions);

            System.out.println("getCount is "+res.getCount());
            // more than 1 user matching filter, fail.
            if (res.getCount() != 1) { return false;}

            if (res.hasMoreElements()) {
                findEntry = res.next();
                dn = findEntry.getDN();
                System.out.println("dn is "+dn);
```

```
        //prevent anonymous connections
        if ((dn == "") || (pwd == "")) { return false;}

        //now attempt to bind to server
        ld.authenticate(dn,pwd);

        //if ld.authenticate doesn't throw an exception we passed
        status = true;

        if(ld != null)
        {
            ld.disconnect();
        }
    }
}
catch(LDAPException e) {
    System.out.println(e.toString());
}
catch(Exception x) {
    x.printStackTrace();
}
return status;
}
}
```

If you want to try running this example, you will need to set your web server so that it can run the Sun standard Java servlets. (Note the Netscape Enterprise Server supports Netscape's original servlet specification, but these are not standard Java servlets). Live Software makes a package called `JRun`, which you can get at `http://www.livesoftware.com` and the Apache team has the Apache Java project at `http://java.apache.org`.

Summary

In this chapter, we have looked at a variety of tools that you will probably need to help solve the more common problems you come across as an LDAP administrator or developer.

In particular, we have seen:

- ❑ How to display common LDAP queries, such as, "Show me everyone who is a member of the Accounting department," or "Show me the list of Accounting Managers."
- ❑ How to add instant Internet accessible images via LDAP
- ❑ How to use LDAP as a Java object database including using LDAP to store SQL queries for later use in a Java application
- ❑ How to use LDAP as a document management system
- ❑ How to use LDAP as a central user database for your web authentication needs

In short, I think we have covered the full range of Internet-ready applications LDAP lets you implement with a minimum of trouble. Hopefully, the selection of examples presented in this chapter has given you some ideas and will serve as a starting point for your future LDAP development.

LDAP Glossary

Attribute: A field in an LDAP database.

cn: The common name attribute. A common name is the name that is used to refer to an entry. For a person, this would include their full name and any variation they may go by (e.g. Mark Edward Wilcox, Mark E. Wilcox, Mark "LDAP Heavyweight" Wilcox). For a non-person entry (e.g. a printer or a room), this would be set to the name an entry is commonly referred to (e.g. the "Printer in Engineering").

DAP: Directory Access Protocol.

Directory Access Protocol: A communications protocol that defines how client and servers will interact to provide a Directory Service.

Directory Information Tree: Directory service data is devised as trees. The tree has a "root", normally a value of organizational name or location or country. Then the data branches out from the root based upon certain values, which are considered branches, such as organizational name, location, country or departmental role/organizational unit. DITs are for "human" use in terms of managing directory service data.

Distinguished Name (DN): A DN is the key field of an LDAP database. A DN must be unique for each LDAP server's name space.

DIT: Directory Information Tree

Directory Service: Directory services are databases that are designed to be read from more than written to. Directory services' databases are designed to be distributed and replicated.

Directory Service Agent: Directory Service Agents provide access to a directory service client using a directory access protocol.

DSA: Directory Service Agent.

Entry: An entry is a record in the directory server. An entry is made up of a distinguished name and one or more attribute and values.

LDAP: Lightweight Directory Access Protocol

LDAP Data Interchange Format: The standard text format for transferring LDAP information. It is exchanged in UTF-8 (e.g. Unicode) format. LDIF is used to display LDAP information and can also be used to describe an LDAP database so that you can build (or modify) an LDAP database from a LDIF file.

LDIF: LDAP Data Interchange Format

Lightweight Directory Access Protocol: A TCP/IP (Internet) based protocol to provide access to a directory service through a Directory Services Agent. It was originally derived from the X.500 Directory Access Protocol designed by the International Standards Organization (ISO).

Object class: An object class is the basic building block for LDAP databases. They are defined by the attributes they can have. Each will have attributes that are required and other attributes that will be considered 'allowed'. Like any other object-oriented paradigm, object classes can be extended.

ou: The organizational unit attribute. The value of this attribute is usually either a part of the organization or a function. An example of an organizational part would be a value of the department where a person worked (e.g. Accounts). An example of a function would be the type of entry it is (e.g. People).

RDN: Relative Distinguished Name.

Relative Distinguished Name: This is the left most component of a DN (e.g. for the DN of `uid=scarter,ou=People,o=airius.com`, the RDN is `uid=scarter`). It is considered relatively unique inside the system (there should only be one entry in the system with a `uid` attribute with a value of `scarter`).

SASL: Simple Authentication and Security Layer.

Secure Socket Layer: A standard protocol for providing a secure, encrypted environment for communications.

Simple Authentication and Security Layer: A standard protocol for defining a standard mechanism to implement secure methods of communications between a client and host over an open network (like the Internet).

SSL: Secure Socket Layer.

Schema: This is a fancy word for the directory server's design. In a schema you will find the definition of the object classes (that is the attributes they contain) and the definition of the attributes (the syntax, etc). One difference between LDAP and the database formats you might be familiar with (for example, a relational database like Oracle or Microsoft's SQL Server) is that every LDAP server has a common, standard schema that you can access. This means that everyone who writes an LDAP client can expect the LDAP server to have some standard object classes and attributes.

sn: The surname attribute. This is the last name of a person.

Subschema: The name of the `objectclass` attribute that contains the schema information of the server.

Unicode: An international standard that allows for the display of the majority of known written character sets. For legacy applications it encompasses the 7-bit ASCII format. Most applications that use Unicode, use the UTF-8 encoding method, because UTF-8 can use only 1 byte to display ASCII characters and 2 bytes for all other character sets. Most other encoding schemes require 2 bytes for each character, even though ASCII characters (which still comprise the majority of applications) only require 1 byte for display.

X.500: Directory Access Protocol developed by the International Standards Organization (ISO) that uses the Open Systems Infrastructure (OSI) protocol.

B

LDAP FAQ

These FAQ will be updated regularly on my web site at http://www.mjwilcox.com and should also be posted regularly on the netscape.server.directory newsgroup.

Q: What is LDAP?

LDAP stands for **Lightweight Directory Access Protocol**, and is designed to be a standard way of providing access to directory services. LDAP was derived from X.500, the OSI Directory Access Protocol. You can find more information on LDAP in the *LDAP Roadmap and FAQ*, which you can find at http://www.kingsmountain.com/ldapRoadmap.shtml, which is maintained by Jeff Hodges.

Q: Why is it called "Lightweight"?

The protocol was given the name *Lightweight* because it was designed to not require as many computing resources as the original Directory Access Protocol (DAP), which was the protocol used to talk to X.500 servers. One way LDAP was 'lightened' was by using TCP/IP communication protocols instead of the OSI protocol DAP, because TCP/IP needs less CPU and memory to operate. A second way LDAP was 'lightened' was to make the protocol stateless. Under DAP, both the client and host had to keep track of previous operations and their current network connection to each other. With LDAP, each operation is considered separate and the client and server don't remember the previous operation. In LDAP, an operation starts with a client bind and continues until the client removes the bind.

Q: Why should I use LDAP?

LDAP is now the standard method for providing access to directory information, such as company phone numbers/e-mail addresses, application configuration information, network resources, computers and so on. It is also being used to act as a gateway to other electronic information systems, such as a meta-directory by companies like Ford and Home Depot to deploy their intranet/extranet systems. It is poised to become a standard simple database for the Internet, much like the Berkeley databases became for Unix. LDAP is a standard mechanism for communicating directory information between a client and a server. Thus, any server can become an LDAP compliant directory. There are many vendors who provide commercial LDAP servers including Netscape, Sun, Novell, Microsoft and Oracle. If you want an open source solution you can use either the original University of Michigan server or the OpenLDAP project.

Q: What is LDIF?

LDIF stands for **LDAP Data Interchange Format**. This is the *de facto* standard for displaying directory information in human readable form. LDIF is a UTF-8 (Unicode) format that is used to exchange data between the server and the client or for export between servers. It can also be used to make changes to the LDAP server when using the command line utilities, such as `ldapsearch` and `ldapmodify` that come with every LDAP SDK.

Q: What is an entry?

An LDAP **entry** is a record in the LDAP database. LDAP entries are composed of attributes and values. Each entry has a special attribute called the **distinguished name**, which is the unique name of the entry.

Q: What is a DN/distinguished name?

A distinguished name is a special attribute in a LDAP entry and is referenced with the mnemonic `dn`. The DN must be unique in the LDAP namespace. A DN is like a file path name that leads you down the Directory Information Tree. Its components must be parts of the LDAP entry. Each component of the DN is referred to as a Relative Distinguished Names (RDN). The DN is always indexed and will always be returned in any search.

An example DN: `uid=scarter, ou=People, o=airius.com`.

Q: What is a directory service?

A directory service is special database designed to provide very quick *read* access to information. Some existing directory services are Sun's NIS+ and Novell's NDS.

Q: How should I build my tree?

This is a bit like asking someone how they should paint a landscape. Summarized below are a few basic rules:

1. Design for function rather than organization.

What this means that put all of your people in a `People` branch (e.g. `ou=People`), all of your groups in a `Groups` branch. This will speed up some searches because it makes it easier to focus a search for a particular set (for example person's email address) by concentrating on a branch of the tree. Also, the function of an entry in the organization (e.g. a person) is not likely to change much over their course of their existence. If you design by structure (e.g. branching by job type such as Accounting), you'll end up having to go back and rebuild DNs all of the time because of restructuring of the organization or as people leave/change jobs.

The base of the tree should use the domain class (`dc`) as the root attribute. The `dc` should be based upon the domain name of the organization.

2. Every DN must be unique. To insure uniqueness in a global namespace, the uniqueness must start with the base of the DN (the far right hand side of the `dn` attribute).

The domain naming system has been well established and is guaranteed to be unique. So this should be the basis of your DN. For example, if your domain name is `airius.com`, then your base DN should be `dc=airius,dc=com`. You can branch out the tree by using the sub-nets that exist within your network. You may have an LDAP server that is for your mail servers with a base of `dc=mail,dc=airius,dc=com`.

3. The left most RDN should be something that is relatively unique within the organization.

Most likely this RDN will be the user ID (`uid`). If for some reason you can't use user IDs then something that is guaranteed to be unique, but will not compromise a user's privacy or security (such as a Social Security Number). Some organizations create a special 'registry' identity number that acts as a unique key. It's just a simple number that is incremented as users are added to the system.

Q: How can I use LDAP with non-LDAP aware applications?

A first step is to make the LDAP server the 'master' for user IDs, because this will encourage everyone to synchronize on a single user ID for each user in the organization, which will make the migration easier. First you add all existing users into the LDAP database. You then pre-generate a user ID for each new user that is added to the organization. When a new account is created for any non-LDAP system, the first step in the account creation process is to query the LDAP server to retrieve the user ID for the particular user.

The best way to synchronize passwords in this system is to make sure that everyone has the same user ID across all systems. The next step is to set up a secure web site using SSL, which provides for a secure mechanism for passing passwords over the network. Then use a server side program to take the users' ID and new password to call different routines (e.g. `changepw()` on Unix, change NDS password routines, etc) that can change the passwords to all viable systems.

Q: Why do I need LDAP when I have a Relational Database Management Service?

Why do you have a screwdriver when you have a hammer? Because a screwdriver is for putting in screws and a hammer is for hammering nails. LDAP and RDBMS share similarities, but each provides functionality that the other lacks.

An RDBMS is good for applications which will have as many writes as they do reads. An RDBMS is also good in applications where you need sophisticated transaction control.

LDAP is good for applications that will be read more often than written to. LDAP also makes a good choice when your database needs extend beyond the local network to an Internet or Extranet environment.

While you could use either an RDBMS or LDAP to implement an address book application (e.g. to look up e-mail addresses and phone numbers), LDAP is a better choice because more e-mail clients can query LDAP than can query an RDBMS.

Also see Steven Kile's excellent presentation on this topic:

```
http://www.stanford.edu/~hodges/talks/EMA98-DirectoryServicesRollout/Steve_Kille/index.html
```

Q: What is a schema?

A schema is the directory server's design. In a schema you will find the definition of the object classes (e.g. the attributes they contain) and the definition of the attributes (the syntax, etc). One difference between LDAP and the database formats you might be familiar with (for example, a relational database like Oracle or Access) is that every LDAP server has a common, standard schema that you can access. This means that everyone who writes an LDAP client can expect the LDAP server to have some standard object classes and attributes.

You can discover any LDAP v3 server's schema by looking for it's `cn=schema` entry.

Q: How can I access and modify the schema?

If the server is only LDAP v2 compliant, you'll have to manually change the configuration files. However, if the server is LDAP v3 compliant, then you can do it programmatically. Some SDKs have special routines for this, so check your documentation. Actually, you can do this with the command line tools or any LDAP SDK. This is because the schema is stored as a regular entry in the server, but you have to access it in a specific manner:

- ❑ You must be authenticated as the Directory Server Manager
- ❑ You also need to set the dn to "cn=schema"

If you wish to display the schema, set your base to the dn of "cn=schema", the scope to `LDAP_SCOPE_BASE` and the filter as "objectclass=*". To modify it, you can update either the object classes or `attributetypes` attributes just as if you were updating any other attribute.

Also see Mark Wilcox's article at
```
http://developer.netscape.com/viewsource/index_frame.html?content=wilcox_schema.html
```

Q: How can I get the attributes of a member of a group?

You will have to perform a search and retrieve that entry. If you set the base of the search to the DN of the member and the scope to base, you will only get the entry back. Then you can act on that entry just like any other LDAP search result.

Q: How can I list the members of a group in a "pretty" manner?

Most likely you want to print out the common name of each member. To do this you will have to cycle through each member, get their full entry and then print out their common name. Here's a Perl script, written using the PerLDAP SDK, which does this.

```perl
#!/usr/local/bin/perl
#prettygroups.pl
# Pretty Prints members of a group
#Mark Wilcox
#mark@mjwilcox.com
#December 1998
use Mozilla::LDAP::Conn;  #LDAP module
use Mozilla::LDAP::Utils; #LDAP module

#Some Variables to Set
my $ldap_host = "localhost";
my $ldap_port = 389;
my $ldap_base = "o=airius.com";

#we're doing anonymous search
my $dn = "";
my $pwd = "";

my $filter = "(objectclass=groupofuniquenames)";
#now do the search
my $ldap = new Mozilla::LDAP::Conn($ldap_host,$ldap_port,$dn,$pwd) ||
                                        die("Failed to open LDAP conenction.\n");

my @attribs = ("objectclass","uniquemember");
my $entry = $ldap->search($ldap_base, "subtree",$filter,0,@attribs);

#print out results
if (! $entry)
{
    print "$filter did not return any results";
}
else
{
    while ($entry)
    {
        print "\ndn: ",$entry->getDN(),"\n";
        #$entry->printLDIF();
        my @members = @{$entry->{uniquemember}};
        for $member (@members)
        {
            print "member is $member\n";
            #now get the entry from the server
            my $temp_ldap =
                new Mozilla::LDAP::Conn($ldap_host,$ldap_port,$dn,$pwd)
                        || die("Failed to open LDAP conenction.\n");
            my @temp_attribs = ("cn");
            my $temp_entry = $temp_ldap->search($member,"base","cn=*",0,
                                                    @temp_attribs);
            if (! $temp_entry)
            {
                print "$member not a valid entry\n";
            }
            else
            {
                print "\tpretty version is ",@{$temp_entry->{cn}},"\n";
            }
        }
        $entry = $ldap->nextEntry();
    }
}
```

Q: How can I display Unicode characters in my LDAP applications?

LDAP v3 supports Unicode via UTF-8. Unfortunately, most (Unix, Windows, Macintosh) systems do not fully support UTF-8/Unicode. In these cases, if the character is not supported (e.g. it's above the standard ASCII display), it should be displayed BASE-64 encoded, or your GUI will have a standard mechanism (e.g. Windows displays a ? or a box). Netscape and Bitstream have created a free full-UTF-8 font called Cyberstream that you can use to display UTF-8 encoded text, but only on Windows 95 and above.

Q: How can I get an Object Identifier (OID)?

An **Object Identifier** (OID) is a unique string of octet digits that are required to add an attribute or object class of your own to an LDAP server.

The best place to get an OID is from the IANA. The IANA is the Internet Assigned Numbers Authority and is responsible for managing any number system for the Internet, including IP addresses and OIDs. If you request your OID from IANA, they will assign it to the standard OID private number branch (1.3.6.1.4) and keep a registry of these numbers, guaranteeing that all OIDs from the IANA will be unique on the Internet. There are other places to get OIDs and it doesn't really matter who gives you the OID. A popular saying the OID circles is "Once you have an OID, nobody cares where it came from". This is because the only important feature that an OID has to have is to be unique.

Helpful URLs:
```
http://www.isi.edu/cgi-bin/iana/enterprise.pl
http://www.alvestrand.no/objectid/1.3.6.1.4.html
http://www.alvestrand.no/objectid/ <- Make sure you register your OID
```

Q: How do I check for password expiration?

The server will send back a set of LDAP Server Control that will tell you this information. These controls will vary from server to server, so check your server's documentation. You must also check your SDKs documentation on how to access this information.

Q: Why do I get "Authorization Credentials Denied" when I try to hook up my Netscape SuiteSpot Administration server to an LDAP server?

Make sure that you have enabled the SuiteSpot Settings and have the right user IDs and passwords in the Directory Server. Also make sure that you have correct DNS entries (fully qualified domain names or FQDN) for all of your SuiteSpot servers.

Q: Can I use LDAP with NIS?

You have several options with LDAP and NIS. You can use LDAP as your back-end database for NIS, or you can replace NIS outright with LDAP. More and more versions of Unix are shipping with native LDAP capabilities. See
```
http://developer1.netscape.com:80/viewsource/markey_ldap.html
```
for more information and how you can use LDAP/NIS and the Netscape Directory Server with the Windows NT synchronization utility to provide for a single logon for your enterprise. Sun Microsystems also has a product called Sun Directory Services that allows you to migrate from NIS to LDAP on Solaris based machines.

Q: Can I use LDAP with Windows NT?

If you want to provide users with an LDAP interface to Windows NT domains, the only product that does this is the Netscape Directory Server. In Windows 2000, Microsoft will replace NT domains with the Active Directory, which will have an LDAP interface.

Q: Can I use LDAP with Novell Directory Services?

Starting with NDS 4.1x, you can add a LDAP v2 compliant gateway. Starting in NDS 5, NDS will be able to communicate using LDAPv3 to non-NDS clients.

Q: What is Active Directory?

Active Directory is the name for Microsoft's new generation of directory services, which will underpin Windows 2000. Active Directory is intended to be an open and extensible concept, supporting whatever standards, proprietary or otherwise, are deemed appropriate. However, Active Directory is increasingly becoming synonymous with Microsoft's implementation of LDAP.

Q: What is ADSI?

ADSI stands for Active Directory Service Interfaces. These are Microsoft's SDKs for implementing and using directory services within the Active Directory umbrella. There are two distinct aspects to the SDK – clients and providers. In this context, LDAP is implemented as a provider. The client SDK consists of two sets of COM interfaces. The first set is automation-compatible, and so can be used from scripting languages. The second set is pure vtable, and so can only be used from vtable-aware languages, such as Visual Basic and Visual C++. Not all providers support the second set.

Q: Can I use ADSI in NT4?

Yes, ADSI is available under NT4, with a provider for NT domains. You won't find an operational LDAP implementation, however. But you will be able to develop applications that will be directory-service independent, and hence LDAP-enabled.

Reference Section

LDAP version 3 RFCs

```
http://www.ietf.org/rfc/rfc2251.txt
http://www.ietf.org/rfc/rfc2252.txt
```

Other RFCs, quoted in the above documents, can be found at: `http://www.ietf.org/rfc/`

You can also access the LDAP RFCs via Yahoo at:
```
http://dir.yahoo.com/Computers_and_Internet/Communications_and_Networking/
Protocols/LDAP__Lightweight_Directory_Access_Protocol_/RFCs/
```

Mark Wilcox's Website

```
http://www.mjwilcox.com
```

Here you can find out more on Project PLUMS and almost everything else you want to know about LDAP!

Netscape (General)

General: `http://home.netscape.com/`
ViewSource: `http://developer.netscape.com/viewsource/`
Mozilla: `http://www.mozilla.org/directory/`

LDAP Servers

Microsoft's Active Directory: `http://www.microsoft.com`
Netscape Directory Server: `http://home.netscape.com/directory/`
Novell NDS: `http://www.novell.com`
OpenLDAP: `http://www.openldap.com`
Sun Directory Services: `http://www.sun.com`

Netscape LDAP SDKs

http://developer.netscape.com/directory/

Perl

General: http://www.perl.com
Perl for Win32: http://www.perl.com/ports/win32/Standard/x86
Perl LDAP SDKs: http://www.perl.com/CPAN//index.html

Java/JNDI

General: http://java.sun.com/products/
JNDI Tutorial: http://java.sun.com/products/jndi/tutorial
Java Servlets: http://www.livesoftware.com and http://java.apache.org

ADSI 2.5

http://www.microsoft.com/ntserver/nts/downloads/

Other LDAP SDKs

ColdFusion: http://www.allaire.com/products
PHP: http://www.php.net/
PS Enlist: http://www.pspl.co.in/PSEnList
SSJSLDAP: http://www.mozilla.org and http://www.mjwilcox.com

LDAP FAQ

http://www.mjwilcox.com
http://www.kingsmountain.com/ldapRoadmap.shtml
http://www.stanford.edu/group/networking/directory/x500ldapfaq.html

Registering OIDs

http://www.isi.edu/cgi-bin/iana/enterprise.pl
http://www.alvestrand.no/objectid/1.3.6.1.4.html
http://www.alvestrand.no/objectid/

General Information

IANA: http://www.iana.org/
IBM AlphaWorks: http://alphaworks.ibm.com
Kerberos: http://nii.isi.edu/publications/kerberos-neuman-tso.html
PADL Software: http://www.padl.com
Python: http://www.python.org
SASL: http://www.ietf.org/rfc/rfc2222.txt
University of Michigan: http://www.umich.edu/
Verisign: http://www.verisign.com
XML: http://www.xml.com

Common LDAP Object Classes and Attributes

This appendix will present the common object classes and attributes you will encounter in your endeavors with LDAP. It is intended to be a simple reference guide.

Most of your LDAP applications will likely deal with white pages services and the various person classes. This chapter contains the complete attribute listing for each of the person object classes, as well as some of the other common object classes you will likely need.

Specifically we will cover:

- ❑ Obtaining an OID
- ❑ Accessing the server schema (LDAP entry metadata)
- ❑ Object class reference
- ❑ Attribute reference

Obtaining an Object Identifier (OID)

All object classes and attributes require an object identifier (OID). This is a unique number, that generally is represented by an octet string that looks similar to an IP address. Some servers like the Netscape Directory Server allow you have an OID that is not a number, but this technically violates the RFCs. However, there are no set rules of how to get an OID. It just needs to be unique. If you want to see how to get an OID, see Appendix B.

Programmatically Accessing LDAP Schema Information

As you develop LDAP applications and build your directory servers, you will want to access the schema of the LDAP server. Accessing the schema and even modifying the schema is fairly straightforward as long as your server supports it. Schema modification is only available to servers and clients that support version 3 of the LDAP protocol. You can actually see and modify the schema with the standard command line tools `ldapsearch` and `ldapmodify`, as long as they were built with an API that speaks LDAP v3.

To display the schema, you must authenticate yourself as the Directory Manager. The base must be set to the `cn=Schema`, the scope is set to `base` and the filter is `objectclass=*`. So, the search would look something like this:

```
ldapsearch -h localhost -D "cn=Directory Manager" -w "password" -b "cn=Schema" -s
base "objectclass=*" | more
```

You will then get a display of the LDAP server's schema which will probably make you faint. This screenshot shows an example of this output of schema information for object classes:

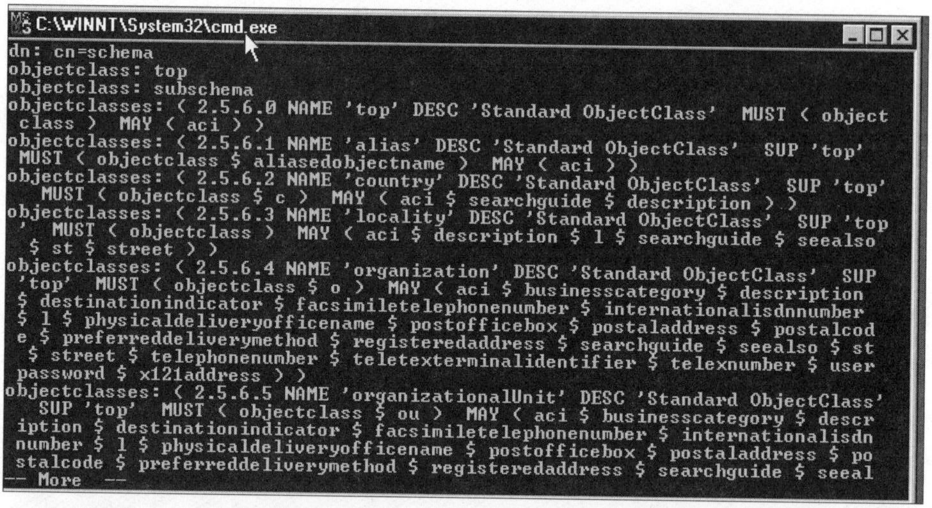

And here are the attributes:

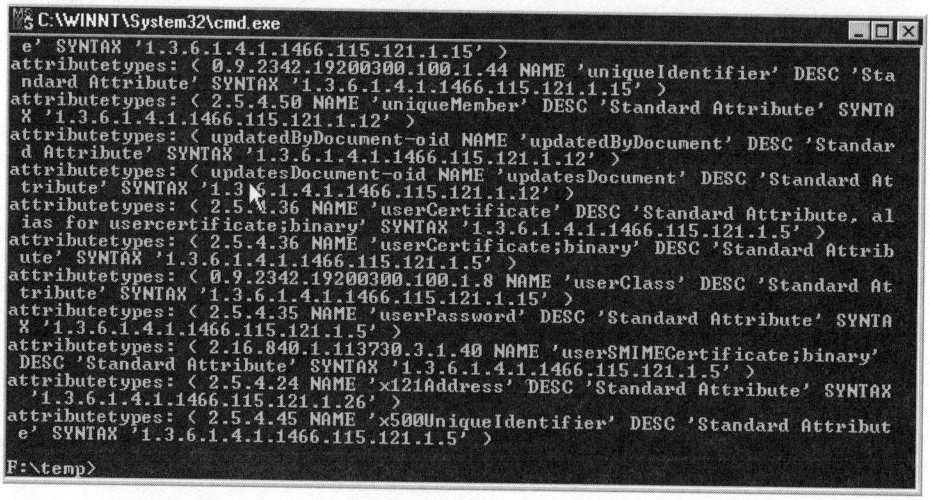

The format looks ugly, but that is to make it easier to parse. This is why you will want to use an API that handles this in a better format. Currently the Netscape Java LDAP SDK does the best job, but I expect the other LDAP SDKs to eventually add support for schema management. To modify the schema you can use the `ldapmodify` command line tool. To add or modify an object class you use the `objectclasses` attribute, and to add or modify an attribute you must use the `attributetypes` attribute. Just remember that to do this you must be bound as the Directory Manager and the DN for the entry has to be `cn=Schema`.

Accessing Schema Information with Java

The Netscape Java LDAP SDK contains three classes for dealing with the server schema. You can use this example program to add the necessary object classes and attributes to your LDAP server to support JNDI in chapters 9 and 13.

- ❏ `LDAPSchema`
- ❏ `LDAPObjectClassSchema`
- ❏ `LDAPAttributeSchema`

The `LDAPSchema` object actually retrieves the schema data and its what we use to perform the actual operations. As you can probably guess, `LDAPObjectClassSchema` deals with object classes and `LDAPAttributeSchema` deal with attribute types.

To get the schema data, you use methods of the `LDAPSchema` object. The `fetchSchemaInformation()` method initializes the object. The `getObjectClass()` and `getAttribute()` methods retrieve data about object classes and attributes.

Shown below is a coded example using the Java SDK to programmatically modify the schema:

```
import netscape.ldap.*;
import java.util.*;

public class schemaTest {

    public static void main( String[] args )
    {
        LDAPConnection ld = new LDAPConnection();
        String hostname = "localhost";
        int portnumber = LDAPv2.DEFAULT_PORT;
```

We have to authenticate to the LDAP server as the Directory Manager if we are going to modify the server's schema:

```
        String bindDN = "cn=Directory Manager";
        String bindPW = "password";

        // Construct a new LDAPSchema object to hold the schema that you want to
        // retrieve.
        LDAPSchema dirSchema = new LDAPSchema();

        try {
            ld.connect( hostname, portnumber, bindDN, bindPW );
```

We can get the schema from the server by using the `LDAPSchema` class and giving it a connected `LDAPConnection` object:

```
// Get the schema from the Directory.
dirSchema.fetchSchema( ld );
```

The `LDAPSchema` class contains methods such as `getObjectClass()` and `getAttribute()` to retrieve the schema elements. The `LDAPObjectClassSchema` class represents object class attributes and the `LDAPAttributeSchema` class represents attribute schema information.

```
// Get and print the definition of the inetOrgPerson object class.
LDAPObjectClassSchema objClass =
                            dirSchema.getObjectClass("inetOrgPerson");

if ( objClass != null )
   System.out.println( "inetOrgPerson := " + objClass.toString() );

// Get and print the definition of the userPassword attribute.
LDAPAttributeSchema attrType = dirSchema.getAttribute( "userpassword" );

if ( attrType != null )
   System.out.println( "userPassword := " + attrType.toString() );

System.out.println("-------------------------------------");
System.out.println("Adding attributes for storing JNDI Objects");
```

We add new object classes and attributes to the LDAP server in a similar way to adding new entries to the LDAP server. First, we must create a new schema type (either an object class or attribute) including adding all of the necessary information (name, OID, description, match rules, etc):

```
// Create new attributes for Java
LDAPAttributeSchema newAttrType = new LDAPAttributeSchema(
                     "javaClassName", "1.3.6.1.4.1.42.2.27.4.1.1",
                     "Fully qualified Java class or interface name",
                                 LDAPAttributeSchema.cis, true );

// Add the new attribute type to the schema.
newAttrType.add( ld );

// Add other new attribute types to the schema.
newAttrType = new LDAPAttributeSchema( "javaSerializedObject",
                              "1.3.6.1.4.1.42.2.27.4.1.2",
                              "Serialized form of a Java object ",
                              LDAPAttributeSchema.binary, true );
newAttrType.add( ld );

newAttrType = new LDAPAttributeSchema( "javaReferenceAddress",
                              "1.3.6.1.4.1.42.2.27.4.1.3",
                        "Addresses associated with a JNDI Reference ",
                                 LDAPAttributeSchema.cis, false );
newAttrType.add( ld );
```

```
newAttrType = new LDAPAttributeSchema( "javaFactory",
                                        "1.3.6.1.4.1.42.2.27.4.1.4",
                "Fully qualified Java class name of a JNDI object factory",
                                        LDAPAttributeSchema.cis, true );
newAttrType.add( ld );

newAttrType = new LDAPAttributeSchema("javaFactoryLocation",
                                        "1.3.6.1.4.1.42.2.27.4.1.5",
                                "Location of a JNDI object factory",
                                        LDAPAttributeSchema.cis, true );
newAttrType.add( ld );

System.out.println("Now Adding new objectclasses for JNDI");

// Add a new object class.
String[] requiredAttrs = new String[1];
String[] optionalAttrs = new String[1];

requiredAttrs[0] = "cn";
optionalAttrs[0] = "";

LDAPObjectClassSchema newObjClass = new LDAPObjectClassSchema(
                        "javaContainer", "1.3.6.1.4.1.42.2.27.4.2.1",
                            "top", "Container for a Java object",
                                    requiredAttrs, optionalAttrs );

// Add the new object class to the schema.
newObjClass.add( ld );

requiredAttrs[0] = "" ;
optionalAttrs = new String[2];
optionalAttrs[0] = "javaClassName";
optionalAttrs[1] = "javaSerializedObject";

// Add other new object class to the schema.
newObjClass = new LDAPObjectClassSchema( "javaObject",
                                        "1.3.6.1.4.1.42.2.27.4.2.2",
                                "top", "Serialized Java object",
                                    requiredAttrs, optionalAttrs );
newObjClass.add( ld );

requiredAttrs = new String[1];
requiredAttrs[0] = "";
optionalAttrs = new String[4];
optionalAttrs[0] = "javaClassName";
optionalAttrs[1] = "javaReferenceAddress";
optionalAttrs[2] = "javaFactory";
optionalAttrs[3]= "javaFactoryLocation";

newObjClass = new LDAPObjectClassSchema( "javaNamingReference",
                                        "1.3.6.1.4.1.42.2.27.4.2.3",
                                        "top", "JNDI reference",
                                    requiredAttrs, optionalAttrs );
newObjClass.add( ld );

// Fetch schema again from the server to verify that the changes were
// made.
dirSchema.fetchSchema( ld );
```

```
        // Get and print one of the new attribute type.
        newAttrType = dirSchema.getAttribute( "javaClassName" );
        if ( newAttrType != null )
          System.out.println( "JavaClasName := " + newAttrType.toString() );

        // Get and print the new object class.
        newObjClass = dirSchema.getObjectClass( "javaContainer" );
        if ( newObjClass != null )
          System.out.println( "javaContainer := " + newObjClass.toString() );

        ld.disconnect();
      }
      catch ( Exception e )
      {
        System.err.println( e.toString() );
        System.exit(1);
      }
      System.exit(0);
    }
}
```

Your example output will probably look something like this:

Object Classes

The information for these object classes can be found in the `slapd.oc.conf` file located in the `conf` directory of the Netscape Directory Server 4.

Object Class name	OID	Extends	Required Attributes	Allowed Attributes
Organization	2.5.6.4	superior top	o	businessCategory, description, destinationIndicator, facsimileTelephone Number, internationalISDN Number, l, physicalDelivery OfficeName, postOfficeBox, postalAddress, postalCode, preferredDelivery Method, registeredAddress, searchGuide, seeAlso, st, street, telephoneNumber, teletexTerminal Identifier, telexNumber, userPassword, x121Address
Organizational Unit	2.5.6.5	superior top	ou	businessCategory, description, destinationIndicator, facsimileTelephone Number, internationalISDN Number, l, physicalDelivery OfficeName, postOfficeBox, postalAddress, postalCode, preferredDelivery Method, registeredAddress, searchGuide, seeAlso, st, street, telephoneNumber, teletexTerminal Identifier, telexNumber, userPassword, x121Address

Object Class name	OID	Extends	Required Attributes	Allowed Attributes
Person	2.5.6.6	superior top	sn, cn	description, seeAlso, telephoneNumber, userPassword
organizational Person	2.5.6.7	superior person		destinationIndicator, facsimileTelephone Number, internationalISDN Number, l, ou, physicalDelivery OfficeName, postOfficeBox, postalAddress, postalCode, preferredDelivery Method, registeredAddress, st, street, teletexTerminal Identifier, telexNumber, title, x121Address
inetOrgPerson	2.16.840. 1.113730 .3.2.2	superior organizational Person		audio, businessCategory, carLicense, departmentNumber, displayName, employeeType, employeeNumber, givenName, homePhone, homePostalAddress, initials, jpegPhoto, labeledURI, mail, manager, mobile, pager, photo, preferredLanguage, roomNumber, secretary, uid, x500uniqueIdentifier, userCertificate, userCertificate;binary, userPKCS12, userSMimeCertificate

Attributes

The information for attributes can be found in the `slapd.at.conf` file located in the `conf` directory of the Netscape Directory Server 4.

Attribute name	Names and Aliases	OID	Value Type
abstract	abstract	abstract-oid	Case Ignore String
aliasedObjectName	aliasedObjectName	2.5.4.1	Distinguished Name
associatedName	associatedName	0.9.2342.1920030 0.100.1.38	Distinguished Name
attributeTypes	attributeTypes	2.5.21.5	Case Ignore String
audio	audio	0.9.2342.1920030 0.100.1.55	Binary Data
authorCn	authorCn documentauthor commonname	authorcn-oid	Case Ignore String
authorSn	authorSn documentauthor surname	authorsn-oid	Case Ignore String
authorityRevocation List;binary	authorityRevocationList: binary, authorityRevocationList	2.5.4.38	Binary Data
buildingName	buildingName	0.9.2342.1920030 0.100.1.48	Case Ignore String
businessCategory	businessCategory	2.5.4.15	Case Ignore String
c	c, countryName	2.5.4.6	Case Ignore String
cACertificate;binary	cACertificate;binary, cACertificate	2.5.4.37	Binary Data
certificateRevocation List;binary	certificateRevocationList; binary, certificateRevocationList	2.5.4.39	Binary Data
cn	cn, commonName	2.5.4.3	Case Ignore String
co	co, friendlycountryname	0.9.2342.1920030 0.100.1.43	Case Ignore String
createTimestamp	createTimestamp	2.5.18.1	Case Ignore String
creatorsName	creatorsName	2.5.18.3	Distinguished Name
crossCertificatePair; binary	crossCertificatePair; binary, crossCertificatePair	2.5.4.40	Binary Data
dITContentRules	dITContentRules	2.5.21.2	Case Ignore String
dITStructureRules	dITStructureRules	2.5.21.1	Case Ignore String

Table Continued on Following Page

Attribute name	Names and Aliases	OID	Value Type
dNSRecord	dNSRecord	0.9.2342.1920030 0.100.1.26	Case Ignore String
dSAQuality	dSAQuality	0.9.2342.1920030 0.100.1.49	Case Ignore String single
dc	dc, domaincomponent	0.9.2342.1920030 0.100.1.25,	Case Ignore String
deltaRevocationList; binary	deltaRevocationList; binary	2.5.4.53	Binary Data
destinationIndicator	destinationIndicator	2.5.4.27	Case Ignore String
ditRedirect	ditRedirect	0.9.2342.1920030 0.100.1.54	Distinguished Name
dn	dn, distinguishedName	2.5.4.49	Distinguished Name
dnQualifier	dnQualifier	2.5.4.46	Case Ignore String
documentAuthor	documentAuthor	0.9.2342.1920030 0.100.1.14	Distinguished Name
documentIdentifier	documentIdentifier	0.9.2342.1920030 0.100.1.11	Case Ignore String
documentLocation	documentLocation	0.9.2342.1920030 0.100.1.15	Case Ignore String
documentPublisher	documentPublisher	0.9.2342.1920030 0.100.1.56	Case Ignore String single
documentStore	documentStore	documentStore-oid	Case Ignore String
documentTitle	documentTitle	0.9.2342.1920030 0.100.1.12	Case Ignore String
documentVersion	documentVersion	0.9.2342.1920030 0.100.1.13	Case Ignore String
drink	drink	0.9.2342.1920030 0.100.1.5	Case Ignore String
facsimileTelephone Number	facsimileTelephone Number, fax	2.5.4.23	Telephone Number
givenName	givenName	2.5.4.42	Case Ignore String
homePhone	homePhone	0.9.2342.1920030 0.100.1.20	Telephone Number
homePostalAddress	homePostalAddress	0.9.2342.1920030 0.100.1.39	Case Ignore String
host	host	0.9.2342.1920030 0.100.1.9	Case Ignore String

Attribute name	Names and Aliases	OID	Value Type
info	info	0.9.2342.1920030 0.100.1.4	Case Ignore String
initials	initials	2.5.4.43	Case Ignore String
internationalIsdn Number	internationalIsdn Number	2.5.4.25	Case Exact String
janetMailbox	janetMailbox	0.9.2342.1920030 0.100.1.46	Case Ignore String
jpegPhoto	jpegPhoto	0.9.2342.1920030 0.100.1.60	Binary Data
keyWords	keyWords	keyWords-oid	Case Ignore String
knowledgeInformation	knowledgeInformation	2.5.4.2	Case Ignore String
l	l, locality, localityname	2.5.4.7	Case Ignore String
labeledUri	labeledUri, labeledurl	1.3.6.1.4.1.250.1.5 7	Case Exact String
lastModifiedBy	lastModifiedBy	0.9.2342.1920030 0.100.1.24	Distinguished Name
lastModifiedTime	lastModifiedTime	0.9.2342.1920030 0.100.1.23	Case Ignore String
ldapSyntaxes	ldapSyntaxes	1.3.6.1.4.1.1466.1 01.120.16	Case Ignore String
mail	mail, rfc822mailbox	0.9.2342.1920030 0.100.1.3	Case Ignore String
mailPreferenceOption	mailPreferenceOption	0.9.2342.1920030 0.100.1.47	Integer single
manager	manager	0.9.2342.1920030 0.100.1.10	Distinguished Name
matchingRuleUse	matchingRuleUse	2.5.21.8	Case Ignore String
matchingRules	matchingRules	2.5.21.4	Case Ignore String
member	member	2.5.4.31	Distinguished Name
mobile	mobile, mobileTelephone Number	0.9.2342.1920030 0.100.1.41	Telephone Number
modifiersName	modifiersName	2.5.18.4	Distinguished Name
modifyTimestamp	modifyTimestamp	2.5.18.2	Case Ignore String
multiLineDescription	multiLineDescription	multiLine Description-oid	Case Ignore String
nameForms	nameForms	2.5.21.7	Case Ignore String

Table Continued on Following Page

Attribute name	Names and Aliases	OID	Value Type
namingContexts	namingContexts	1.3.6.1.4.1.1466.1 01.120.5	Distinguished Name
organizationalStatus	organizationalStatus	0.9.2342.1920030 0.100.1.45	Case Ignore String
otherMailbox	otherMailbox	0.9.2342.1920030 0.100.1.22	Case Ignore String
ou	ou, organizationalUnitName	2.5.4.11	Case Ignore String
owner	owner	2.5.4.32	Distinguished Name
pager	pager, pagerTelephoneNumber	0.9.2342.1920030 0.100.1.42	Telephone Number
personalSignature	personalSignature	0.9.2342.1920030 0.100.1.53	Binary Data
personalTitle	personalTitle	0.9.2342.1920030 0.100.1.40	Case Ignore String
photo	photo	0.9.2342.1920030 0.100.1.7	Binary Data
physicalDeliveryOffice Name	physicalDeliveryOffice Name	2.5.4.19	Case Ignore String
postOfficeBox	postOfficeBox	2.5.4.18	Case Ignore String
postalAddress	postalAddress	2.5.4.16	Case Ignore String
preferredDelivery Method	preferredDelivery Method	2.5.4.28	Case Ignore String
presentationAddress	presentationAddress	2.5.4.29	Case Exact String
protocolInformation	protocolInformation	2.5.4.48	Case Ignore String
roleOccupant	roleOccupant	2.5.4.33	Distinguished Name
roomNumber	roomNumber	0.9.2342.1920030 0.100.1.6	Case Ignore String
searchGuide	searchGuide	2.5.4.14	Case Exact String
secretary	secretary	0.9.2342.1920030 0.100.1.21	Distinguished Name
seeAlso	seeAlso	2.5.4.34	Distinguished Name
serialNumber	serialNumber	2.5.4.5	Case Ignore String
singleLevelQuality	singleLevelQuality	0.9.2342.1920030 0.100.1.50	Case Ignore String single
sn	sn, surName	2.5.4.4	Case Ignore String

Attribute name	Names and Aliases	OID	Value Type
st	st, stateOrProvinceName	2.5.4.8	Case Ignore String
street	street, streetaddress	2.5.4.9	Case Ignore String
subschemaSubentry	subschemaSubentry	2.5.18.10	Distinguished Name
subtreeMaximum Quality	subtreeMaximum Quality	0.9.2342.1920030 0.100.1.52	Case Ignore String single
subtreeMinimumQuality	subtreeMinimumQuality	0.9.2342.1920030 0.100.1.51	Case Ignore String single
supportedAlgorithms; binary	supportedAlgorithms; binary	2.5.4.52	Binary Data
supportedApplication Context	supportedApplication Context	2.5.4.30	Case Ignore String
supportedControl	supportedControl	1.3.6.1.4.1.1466.1 01.120.13	Case Ignore String
supportedExtension	supportedExtension	1.3.6.1.4.1.1466.1 01.120.7	Case Ignore String
supportedLDAPVersion	supportedLDAPVersion	1.3.6.1.4.1.1466.1 01.120.15	Integer
supportedSASL Mechanisms	supportedSASL Mechanisms	1.3.6.1.4.1.1466.1 01.120.14	Case Ignore String
telephoneNumber	telephoneNumber	2.5.4.20	Telephone Number
teletexTerminal Identifier	teletexTerminal Identifier	2.5.4.22	Case Ignore String
telexNumber	telexNumber	2.5.4.21	Case Ignore String
textEncodedORAddress	textEncodedORAddress	0.9.2342.1920030 0.100.1.2	Case Ignore String
title	title	2.5.4.12	Case Ignore String
ttl	ttl, timeToLive	1.3.6.1.4.1.250.1.6 0	Case Ignore String
uid	uid	0.9.2342.1920030 0.100.1.1	Case Ignore String
uniqueIdentifier	uniqueIdentifier	0.9.2342.1920030 0.100.1.44	Case Ignore String
uniqueMember	uniqueMember	2.5.4.50	Distinguished Name
userCertificate;binary	userCertificate;binary userCertificate	2.5.4.36	Binary Data

Attribute name	Names and Aliases	OID	Value Type
userClass	userClass	0.9.2342.1920030 0.100.1.8	Case Ignore String
userPassword	userPassword	2.5.4.35	Binary Data
x121Address	x121Address	2.5.4.24	Case Exact String

Advanced LDAP: A Directory Enabled Messaging System

I really believe in LDAP. I think that LDAP is going to be one of the most important protocols to the Internet going into the next century. One of the reasons why I think LDAP is going to succeed is because there isn't an Internet protocol out there that can't benefit from LDAP. Secondly, I believe LDAP is going to succeed because it provides us with a very simple Internet-ready database system. While I realize that the first major LDAP implementations in organizations will be to centrally manage people and computing resources, once these applications are set up and you have LDAP infrastructure in place, whole other worlds are opened up.

To demonstrate this possibility, I'm going to unveil a new Internet-ready messaging system that uses LDAP for its data store. The system we'll implement here could have any type of interface you want (mail, news, etc), but we'll focus on a web-based front-end.

Note that the example presented in this appendix is still under development, so it is not yet an 'all-singing, all-dancing' application. It should, however, give you a feel for what LDAP can do.

Web Based Messaging

The World Wide Web is the fancy neon light of our Internet world, but it's the Internet's messaging systems – primarily e-mail, but also newsgroups, chat and web-based bulletin boards, etc. – that really drive the growth.

> *Messaging systems are simply applications that allow two or more people to communicate with each other.*

In the dawn of the Internet, these messaging systems were separated into their own protocols and each had their clients/servers, such as e-mail and newsgroups. The web has made it possible to remove the need for client applications. This has opened up the world of e-mail and newsgroups to an entirely new set of people, which can be seen in the popularity of systems such as Hotmail, DejaNews and Yahoo! Clubs.

I come from an educational background and studied at a major university. Like every other educational institution on the planet, we have explored distributed learning using the Internet. A key component of this environment is the ability to harness a successful collaboration environment through a common web browser.

I have a great deal of experience in this area – my first major web programming development was the overhaul of the once popular *Conference on the Web* program and this led me to LDAP. While we have chosen a unified package for our distributed learning courses and are very happy with it, I am still intrigued to know how to improve stand-alone collaboration environments.

I'm also intrigued by other uses of LDAP.

Without LDAP, your messaging systems generally fall into 2 groups:

- ❑ File-based messaging systems
- ❑ Database messaging systems

Nearly all of these systems use a CGI based approach to the development of the web interface.

File-based Messaging Systems

File-based messaging systems use the file system of the underlying operating system for their message storage and even their user-preferences storage. These types of systems are easy to develop and maintain, but they don't scale well. They also are dependent upon the file system itself for the stability of the messaging database. Finally, they are dependent upon the security of the file system and operating system to provide the security of the entire messaging system.

Database Messaging Systems

Database messaging systems are different from file-based messaging systems in that they use a database as their data source. It's the traditional view that database messaging systems are more scalable, reliable and secure than file-based messaging systems, because of advanced database technologies (such as transaction support). However, most database messaging systems such as Microsoft Exchange are proprietary (closed) systems that leave you dependent entirely upon the vendor for the communications protocol, security and reliability. I see two limitations in these types of system. One of the biggest problems with traditional database messaging systems is that they usually require a particular client to access their system (for example, Microsoft Exchange or Novell GroupWise). The second problem is that if the database gets corrupted, you can easily lose everything inside the system. The popularity of standardized Internet protocols, such as SMTP, POP3, IMAP and LDAP, has forced these proprietary systems to allow you to access their servers via standard clients. (You can now use any POP3 client to access Exchange instead of having to use Microsoft Outlook.)

The Alternative: LDAP-Based Messaging System

My idea for an LDAP-based messaging system is to have the user preferences and key elements of the messages stored in the LDAP server. I think we can probably even store the messages themselves in the system. (However, dealing with attachments is a different story). The current problem with storing a lot of information inside an LDAP server is that LDAP servers are slower at handling updates than a file-system or traditional database system. Companies and projects such Netscape and OpenLDAP are certainly working on this problem, but until is resolved, it's probably better to store the messages themselves separately from the server in a production environment.

LDAP is potentially an optimal choice for this type of application because:

- ❏ Author preferences and control can be managed in a central system
- ❏ Message security is controlled with existing LDAP access control policies
- ❏ Database system allows for scalability and transaction management
- ❏ LDAP can export to LDIF to allow for maximum portability
- ❏ System can be easily replicated and distributed for improved performance and reliability
- ❏ Message security and access control can use LDAP security, including SSL and Certificates for improved authentication control

I would like to keep the record format somewhat simple and then let individual clients decide on what to display. This way we could build different displays and add functionality as systems needed them.

One aspect of design I want to keep fairly loose in the database is message relationships. In most web-based messaging systems they follow a topic/thread/message hierarchy. Each message will have a subject (something that says what the message is about) and the first level of organization we can provide is by subject, which is also called a thread. A collection of messages organized by subjects is called a topic. This has been the traditional hierarchy of all messaging systems, it seems, since the beginning of time. However, this is not necessarily how people work, in particular compared to the way they manage messages in their physical world. As the Mozilla Grendel project states, messages are 'intertwingled'. This is a new term coined by the Mozilla team that attempts to define the complex relationships between our e-mail and newsgroup postings. What it means to us (application developers) is that it would be nice to give end-users a bit more control over how they manage their discussions. See `http://www.mozilla.org/` for more information on this concept.

In addition, I would also like to include a feature so that 'topic owners' – there has to be some basic organization in this system – could configure the interfaces for their topic areas. There needs to be basic system requirements (create new messages, reply to messages, search, and so on), but the overall layout should be under the control of the topic owner. It would also be nice if the end-user could have some control over the layout, color scheme etc. Perhaps this will be possible with something like DHTML or XML. There also needs to be a mechanism so that there can be topic owners to add and delete members and posts. At some point, there should also be a searchable index of messages.

It would be more beneficial if messages were stored in plain text for now. At some point, it would be nice to generate the headers in XML, through a friendly interface like a Java applet, and then have clients parse the XML to display them in the best way possible.

The actual development of an interface will be left to anyone who wishes to implement it. In this appendix, I will present a Java servlet based solution, but you could do a Perl-based one or even shell scripts with the command line utilities. This type of development model should pave the way so that interaction can take place in the best manner possible for the particular viewing client.

For example, the most beneficial use of the system will probably occur via a standard web browser, but people may want to be able to read messages on their Palm Pilots, their Web TVs, heck, maybe their toasters. Who knows, everything seems to be able to browse the web these days. It would be useful to be able to customize formats to these 'browsers' in a much better manner than HTML currently does – and that's what XML is designed to do.

To make it easeir to use LDAP as our data store of our messaging system, we will consider each message a complete entity, a `Message` object.

Each `Message` object will have the following:

- An author (in the form of a DN) (many)
- A subject (single)
- A message (single)
- A `messageReferral` attribute (many)
- A `notificationList` attribute (in the form of a DN to a group) (single)
- Keywords (optional)

Let's step through what each item means.

An Author

Each message must have an author who has created the message. The author should be stored in the form of a distinguished name, which allows for maximum flexibility for the developer of the messaging system. We can choose to attach a mechanism upon which we can allow for the display of fuller contact information about the author, or a faster way to group messages together by author (by choosing to display all message objects that have this author's DN attached).

If the designer of the system decides to allow for anonymous postings, then I would recommend the creation of an anonymous user entry (at least until someone can think of a better way). I'm all for the protection of privacy, but the messages need to be attached to something to make it easier to organize in the long run.

There can be more than one author in the cases where it truly was a collaborative environment.

A Subject

Each message must have a subject. That is each message must contain some text to help describe it, which should be pretty self-explanatory.

A Message

This is the meat of the entire object. Everything revolves around this component. I intend a message component to be in plain Unicode text. This could be in the form of HTML or XML or some other plain text markup language.

Perhaps in the future we may add something like `binaryMessage` or `messageURL` to handle the storage/retrieval of rich text documents (those that might be stored in a proprietary word processing format).

messageReferral

This attribute would be a DN of a message object. These would refer to other messages that this particular message refers to. This would be like a thread list in a newsgroup reader, but gives us the ability to link to more than one thread.

You could even build into the system the ability to post-link to a message. This might be particularly useful when you wish to refer to a message that occurred some time ago, like a 'see-also'.

Another use would be that you could check to see how many `messageReferrals` a particular message has pointing to, which could provide a clue to something of importance, perhaps an automatic FAQ generator.

notificationList

The `notificationList` would be a DN of a `groupofUniqeMembers` who wish to be notified when a `messageReferral` is pointed to or updated for this message. The notification could be as simple as an e-mail message or as complicated as notifying users through an ICQ chat client, such AOL Instant Messenger.

Keywords

Keywords would be words from the message to help describe it when people perform searches against the message database.

Brazos, the LDAP Messaging System

I've decided to name my messaging system concept, Brazos, after the largest river in the state of Texas, where I am from. I think in some philosophical sense, messaging systems are like rivers. How? I'm not sure. It just feels like a good analogy.

First, I'll go through the steps I took to enable Brazos on my test system – Windows NT 4/SP3 running Netscape Enterprise Server 3.6 and Netscape Directory Server 4.

First, you'll need to add some new attributes to Directory Server. If you don't remember how to modify the server's schema, see Appendix D. The new attributes are shown below:

```
attribute authorDN              authorDN-oid              dn
attribute message               message-oid               cis
attribute notificationGroupDN   notificationGroupDN-oid   dn
attribute messageRef            messageRef-oid            dn
```

Then you'll need to add the `messageClass` object class to the server:

```
objectclass messageclass
    oid messageclass-oid
    superior top
    requires
        authorDN,
        subject,
        message
    allows
        messageRef,
        notificationGroupDN,
        keywords,
        ou
```

Note that I didn't get proper OIDs for the attributes or the object class because, frankly, I didn't have time. If this project matures, I will go ahead and register a proper OID. Also, while I used Netscape Directory Server for my examples here, there shouldn't be anything that precludes using another LDAP server for this purpose.

After I added the necessary attributes and object class, I then did some DIT preparation for this system. For my test run, I decided I would put all of the messages under an `organizationalUnit` (ou) branch called `Test Topics` directly off my base root of `o=airius.com`. However, the best setup in a production system would more like be to create a brand new root called something like `o=Brazos` or `o=Messages` and branch from there. This way, we could keep the messaging system separate from our standard directory service. In this example, though, I left the base at `o=airius.com`.

If you want to try out this code, you'll need to create three groups for this setup:

- ❏ Test Topic Members
- ❏ Test Topic Managers
- ❏ Test Topic Notification

The idea behind this is that eventually only members and managers would have any privileges with respect to a particular message topic (or even on a thread-message basis). You can also pre-load a few entries into the system so that you can check out how the system works before proceeding with the component we're going to build later on. Shown below is an LDIF file containing some sample entries. This file, `myldif.ldif`, can be found with the rest of the code for this example, on the Wrox Press web site. Note that we also add an ACL, which allows any authenticated user to post a new message:

```
#this creates an organizationalUnit for us to store our messages
#this also allows only members of the directory administrators to post this ou
dn: ou=Test Topics,o=airius.com
objectclass: top
objectclass: organizationalUnit
ou: Test Topics
aci: (target="ldap:///o=airius.com") (targetattr = "*")
(version 3.0; acl "allow all Admin group";
allow (all) userdn = "ldap:///anyone";
allow(all) groupdn = "ldap:///cn=Directory Administrators,
                                    ou=Groups, o=airius.com";)
```

```
dn:subject=Sales Quota,ou=Test Topics,o=airius.com
objectclass:top
objectclass:messageClass
authorDN:uid=scarter,ou=People,o=airius.com
ou:Test Topicss
subject: Sales Quota
message: This is to let people know that we have reached our sales quota for the
quarter. We should strive to do even better next quarter
notificationGroupDN:cn=test topic notification,ou=Groups,o=airius.com

dn:subject=Growing Sales,ou=Test Topics,o=airius.com
objectclass:top
objectclass:messageClass
authorDN:uid=ahall,ou=People,o=airius.com
ou:Test Topicss
subject: Growing Sales
messageRef:subject=Sales Quota,ou=Test Topics,o=airius.com
message: I think we should go after people in Iowa. Since we primarily make corn
based products, we should go after our producers.
notificationGroupDN:cn=test topic notification,ou=Groups,o=airius.com

dn:subject=Garage Sale,ou=Test Topics,o=airius.com
objectclass:top
objectclass:messageClass
authorDN:uid=brentz,ou=People,o=airius.com
ou:Test Topicss
subject: Garage Sale
message: To raise enough money to open up an office in Des Moines, Iowa we're
having a garage sale. Meet at Sam's house Saturday morning with all of your sale
items.
notificationGroupDN:cn=test topic notification,ou=Groups,o=airius.com
```

You'll notice that I have used the `subject` attribute as the relative identifier for each message. In this test system, this was the easiest to implement. In a production system though, you would probably want to create a unique ID for each message. This is another area that is open for discussion. Remember there aren't any hard rules for this system, if you decide to try to implement it, use what you feel is right to you.

You can add the entries with a custom program, your server's import tools (if it has any) or just by saving them to a text file and using the `ldapmodify` command line utility. Here is a sample command line to add entries to your server using `ldapmodify`:

```
ldapmodify -h localhost -p 389 -d "cn=Directory Manager" -w "password" -a -f
myldif.ldif
```

After these entries are added you can test to see if they are there by using the standard `ldapsearch` command line utility:

```
C:\WINNT\System32\cmd.exe                                              _ □ ×

E:\brazos>f:

F:\temp>ldapsearch -b "o=airius.com" "subject=first*"
dn: subject=first test message,ou=Test Topic,o=airius.com
objectclass: top
objectclass: messageClass
subject: first test message
message: Blah blah
ou: Test Topic
authorDN: uid=scarter,ou=People,o=airius.com

F:\temp>ldapsearch -b "o=airius.com" "subject=Garage*"
dn: subject=Garage Sale,ou=Test Topic,o=airius.com
objectclass: top
objectclass: messageClass
authorDN: uid=brentz,ou=People,o=airius.com
authorDN: uid=scarter,ou=People,o=airius.com
ou: Test Topics
subject: Garage Sale
message: To raise enough money to open up an office in Des Moines, Iowa we're
 having a garage sale. Meet at Sam's house Saturday morning with all of your
 sale items.
notificationGroupDN: cn=test topic notification,ou=Groups,o=airius.com

F:\temp>
```

Huaco, Java Servlet Interface for Brazos

Remember how I said one of the benefits of using LDAP was that you weren't limited to what tools or clients you wished to use? We've just been using the command line tools, and here I'm going to build a web interface using the Java servlet API and the Netscape Java LDAP SDK.

> *By the way, Huaco (pronounced "Waako") is the name of the Indian tribe that had settled along the Brazos River where Waco (which is pronounced Wayko), Texas is today. I'm originally from Waco, so I decided to name this system after some parts of my hometown.*

The Huaco servlet implements the basic functionality of the system, but it does have a great deal of room to grow. (And don't complain about the look and feel – I'm a programmer not a graphics artist!)

Here are the things that Huaco does now:

❑ Lists all current messages
❑ Posts new messages
❑ Replies to messages
❑ Links replies to original messages
❑ Links authors of messages to their LDAP entries

And here are the things that I would like Huaco to do:

- ❏ More flexible security model using ACLs
- ❏ Show message hierarchy
- ❏ Group mail notification
- ❏ Custom Group notification
- ❏ Search messages
- ❏ Allow users to link messages as they please
- ❏ Convert timestamp to client local time

Huaco's code also needs to be cleaned up, but it does work – in both Netscape Communicator and Microsoft's Internet Explorer. This is most definitely a prototype. If you are interested in using this system, let me know.

To use this system, your web server must be capable of running standard Java servlets. After you have compiled this example, you must put this the `huaco.class` file into a directory where the web server will invoke it as a Java servlet. You invoke the system by just calling the servlet without any parameters like this – `http://myserver/brazos/huaco`. (You may need to specify the port number, e.g. `http://MyServer:8080/servlet/huaco`.)

This will present you with a list of messages, like this:

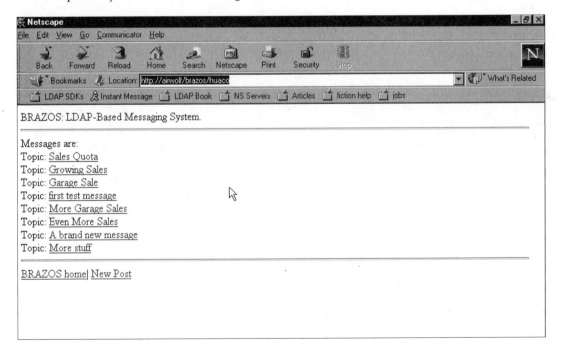

If you have only just installed the sample data from the LDIF file shown above, then you'll only see those messages here.

From here, you can select a message, which is called Topic on the menu, just by clicking on the link. I use the query string with a parameter called `subject` and the value a subject name that has been URL encoded like this:

```
http://myhost/brazos/huaco?subject=A+brand+new+message
```

Here is an example of a sample message:

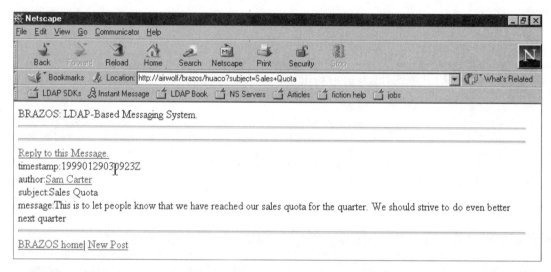

If the message is a reply to an earlier post, you will see a link to the original post:

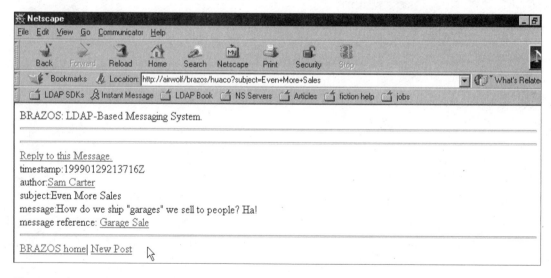

You can also post a new message with the following URL: `http://myhost/brazos/huaco?post=new`

And you would then see a screen something like this:

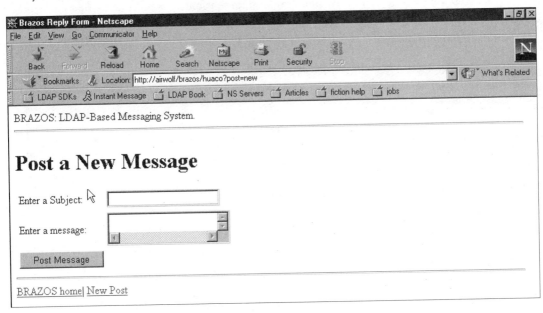

Of course, you can reply to a post with a URL like this:

```
http://myhost/brazos/huaco?reply=A+brand+new+message
```

This is what the reply screen looks like:

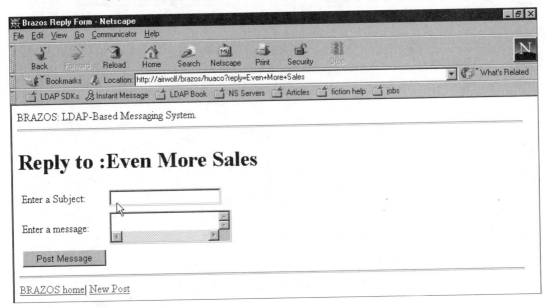

If you click on the author link in Netscape 4, then you'll see the record from the LDAP server for that person in your web browser, including any photograph if there is one:

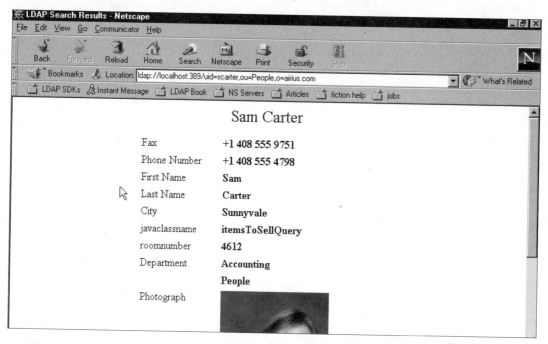

You'll get access to the record in IE 4, but it will look a bit different:

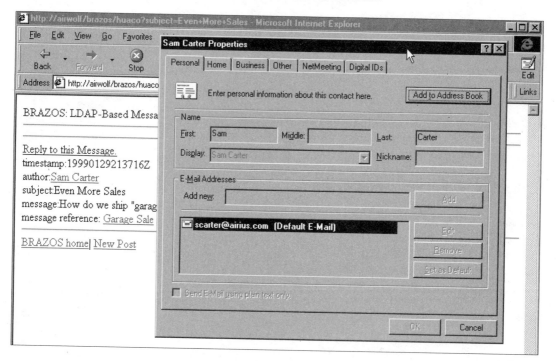

This might not be a fully formed messaging system yet, but it does prove that you can hold messages in LDAP and that it is possible to access the data from a variety of clients.

Hopefully, you have seen at least one of the benefits of using LDAP in this messaging system – that you are managing your user demographic and access control through a single interface. This interface might even be the same interface you use to manage access to the rest of your systems.

This example might have even opened your eyes to other uses for LDAP. LDAP is not designed to be a replacement for a massive RDBMS like Oracle, but it is useful for a number of different tasks. And you don't need a senior Database Adminstrator to run it.

If you find this system useful or have done other useful things with LDAP, let me know. I would be very interested in learning what other uses people have found for LDAP.

The Source Code

The remainder of this appendix will cover the source code that lies behind this system:

```
import java.io.*;
import java.util.*;
```

We need to import the packages for handling Java servlets:

```
import javax.servlet.*;
import javax.servlet.http.*;

import java.net.*;
import netscape.ldap.*;

public class huaco extends HttpServlet
{
    //LDAP variables
    LDAPConnection ld = new LDAPConnection();
    LDAPEntry findEntry = null;
    String dn = null;
    String pwd = null;
    String MY_HOST = null;
    int MY_PORT = 389;
    String MY_SEARCHBASE = null;
    private String adminMail = null ; //admin email address
    PrintWriter out;
```

Here, the LDAP variables are initialized:

```
public void init(ServletConfig config) throws ServletException
{
    super.init(config);
    //configure some parameters here
    //perhaps we could put into a props file?
    ld = new LDAPConnection();
    findEntry = null;
    dn = null;
```

```
        pwd = null;
        MY_HOST = "localhost";
        MY_PORT = 389;
        MY_SEARCHBASE = "o=airius.com";
        adminMail = "www@airius.com";
    }
```

This method is called whenever a user sends a "GET" request for the servlet:

```
public void doGet(HttpServletRequest req, HttpServletResponse res) throws
                                            ServletException, IOException
{
    res.setContentType("text/html");
    out = res.getWriter();
    //Get Authorization header
    String auth = req.getHeader("Authorization");
```

This will force the user to authenticate to the system:

```
    // Do we allow that user
    if (!allowedUser(auth))
    {
        // Not Allowed, so report he's unathorized
        res.sendError(res.SC_UNAUTHORIZED);
        res.setHeader("WWW-Authenticate", "BASIC realm=\"users\"");
        // Could offer to add to user list
        out.println("Send a message to <a href=\"mailto:"+adminMail+
          "\">"+adminMail+"</a> to request to be added to access to this group");
    }
    else {
        //User is allowed in
        //Print out a list of topic messages
        //For now we'll just print out the one we have
        //I think in "real" life, we should have a special root
        //perhaps o=messages,o=airius.com
        //bind as a user so that you can control access
        printHeader();
        String subject_values[] = req.getParameterValues("subject");
        String reply_values[] = req.getParameterValues("reply");
        String post_values[] = req.getParameterValues("post");

        if ((subject_values != null) || (reply_values != null) ||
                                            (post_values != null))
        {
            if (subject_values != null  )
            {
                for(int i=0;i< subject_values.length;i++)
                {
                    printMessage(subject_values[i]);
                }
            }
            else if (reply_values != null )
            {
                for(int x = 0;x < reply_values.length; x++)
                {
```

```
                    printReplyForm(reply_values[x]);
                }
            }
            else if (post_values != null )
            {
                if (post_values[0].equals("new") )
                {
                    postNewMessage();
                }
            }
        }
        else{
            printTopics();
        }
        printFooter();
    }
}
```

This method is called when a user sends `"POST"` to the server, which would occur when they attempt to add a new message to the system:

```
public void doPost(HttpServletRequest req, HttpServletResponse res) throws
                                                ServletException,IOException
{
    res.setContentType("text/html");
    out = res.getWriter();
    //Get Authorization header
    String auth = req.getHeader("Authorization");

    // Do we allow that user
    if (!allowedUser(auth))
    {
        // Not Allowed, so report he's unathorized
        res.sendError(res.SC_UNAUTHORIZED);
        res.setHeader("WWW-Authenticate", "BASIC realm=\"users\"");
        // Could offer to add to user list
        out.println("Send a message to <a href=\"mailto:"+adminMail+"\">"+
            adminMail+"</a> to request to be added to access to this group");
    }
    else {
        printHeader();
        String subject_values[] = req.getParameterValues("subject");
        String message_values[] = req.getParameterValues("message");
        String messageref_values[] = req.getParameterValues("messageref");

        if ((!subject_values[0].equals("")) && (!message_values[0].equals("")))
        {
            try{
                // can only have one subject and message
                //add message to server
                String msgDN = "subject="+subject_values[0]+",ou=Test Topics,
                                                o=airius.com";

                String [] objectclass = {"top","messageClass"};
                String [] subject = {subject_values[0]};
                String [] organizationalUnits = {"Test Topics"};
                String [] authors = {dn};
                String [] message = {message_values[0]};
```

```
                  //for now only deal with 1 message reference
                  String reference = "subject="+messageref_values[0]+
                                               ",ou=Test Topics,o=airius.com";
                  String [] messageDN = {reference};

                  LDAPEntry newEntry;
                  LDAPAttributeSet attrib_set = new LDAPAttributeSet();
                  LDAPAttribute attribute = new
                                   LDAPAttribute("objectclass",objectclass);
                  attrib_set.add(attribute);

                  attribute = new LDAPAttribute("subject",subject);
                  attrib_set.add(attribute);

                  attribute = new LDAPAttribute("message",message);
                  attrib_set.add(attribute);

                  attribute = new LDAPAttribute("ou",organizationalUnits);
                  attrib_set.add(attribute);

                  attribute = new LDAPAttribute("authorDN",authors);
                  attrib_set.add(attribute);

                  attribute = new LDAPAttribute("messageRef",messageDN);
                  attrib_set.add(attribute);

                  ldapFunctions ldap = new
                            ldapFunctions(MY_HOST,MY_PORT,MY_SEARCHBASE,dn,pwd);
                  ldap.connect();

                  newEntry = new LDAPEntry(msgDN,attrib_set);

                  ldap.addEntry(newEntry);
                  ldap.disconnect();
                  out.println("your message has been added.<BR>");
                  printFooter();
              }
          catch(LDAPException e)
          {
              out.println("Error occured when trying to add message: "+
                                               e.toString()+"<BR>");
              System.err.println(e.toString());
          }
      }
      else{ out.println("Message Not Complete<BR>"); }
   }
}

// Ideally printHeader and printFooter will be interfaces or will read in data
//from a  file
void printHeader()
{
   out.println("BRAZOS: LDAP-Based Messaging System.<HR>");
}
```

```
    void printFooter()
    {
        out.println("<HR><a href=\"/brazos/huaco\">BRAZOS home</a>|");
        out.println("<a href=\"/brazos/huaco?post=new\">New Post</a>");
    }

//prints out a form a user can use to add a new message
    void postNewMessage()
    {
        out.println("<HTML><HEAD><TITLE>Brazos Reply Form</TITLE></HEAD><BODY>");
        out.println("<h1>Post a New Message</h1>");
        out.println("<FORM METHOD=\"POST\" name=\"message\"
                                    action=\"http://myhost/brazos/huaco\">");
        out.println("<INPUT TYPE=\"hidden\" name=\"messageref\" value=\"\">");
        out.println("<TABLE><TR><TD>Enter a Subject:</TD><TD><INPUT type=\"TEXT\"
                                    name=\"subject\"></TD></TR>");
        out.println("<TR><TD>Enter a message:</TD><TD><TEXTAREA
                                    name=\"message\"></TEXTAREA></TD></TR>");
        out.println("<TR><TD><INPUT type=\"Submit\" value=\"Post Message\">
                                    </TD></TR></FORM></TABLE></BODY></HTML>");
    }

//prints out a single message to the screen
    void printMessage(String subject)
    {
        try{
            ldapFunctions ldap = new
                            ldapFunctions(MY_HOST,MY_PORT,MY_SEARCHBASE,dn,pwd);
            String attrs[] =
                    {"authorDN","subject","message","createtimestamp","messageRef"};

            ldap.connect();
            String filter = "(&(objectclass=messageClass)(subject="+subject+"))";
            Vector v =
        ldap.search(MY_SEARCHBASE,LDAPConnection.SCOPE_SUB,filter,attrs,false,out);

            if (v != null )
            {
                /* Loop on attributes */
                for (int i=0;i < v.size() ; i++ )
                {
                    LDAPEntry myEntry = (LDAPEntry)v.elementAt(i);
                    out.println("<HR>");

                    //print timestamp ugly but serviceable for now
                    String encodedString = URLEncoder.encode(subject);
                    out.println("<a href=\"huaco?reply="+
                                encodedString+"\">Reply to this Message.</a><BR>");
                    LDAPAttribute anAttr = myEntry.getAttribute("createtimestamp");
                    Enumeration  enumVals = anAttr.getStringValues();
                    if (enumVals != null) {
                        while ( enumVals.hasMoreElements() ) {
                            String aVal = ( String )enumVals.nextElement();
                            out.println("timestamp:"+aVal+"<BR>");
```

```
                    }
                }
            //print author
            anAttr = myEntry.getAttribute("authorDN");
            enumVals = anAttr.getStringValues();
            if (enumVals != null) {
                while ( enumVals.hasMoreElements() ) {
                    String aVal = ( String )enumVals.nextElement();
                    String authorName = getAuthorName(aVal);
                    //since IE and Netscape now support LDAP URL we can encode
                    //LDAP url may want to do something different if must
                    //support other browsers

                    out.println("author:<a href=\"ldap://"+MY_HOST+
                            ":"+MY_PORT+"/"+aVal+"\">"+authorName+"</a><BR>");
                }
            }

            //print subject
            anAttr = myEntry.getAttribute("subject");
            enumVals = anAttr.getStringValues();
            if (enumVals != null) {
                while ( enumVals.hasMoreElements() ) {
                    String aVal = ( String )enumVals.nextElement();
                    out.println("subject:"+aVal+"<BR>");
                }
            }
            //print message
            anAttr = myEntry.getAttribute("message");
            enumVals = anAttr.getStringValues();
            if (enumVals != null) {
                while ( enumVals.hasMoreElements() ) {
                    String aVal = ( String )enumVals.nextElement();
                    out.println("message:"+aVal+"<BR>");
                }
            }

            //print message referrals
            anAttr = myEntry.getAttribute("messageRef");
            if (anAttr != null )
            {
                enumVals = anAttr.getStringValues();
                if (enumVals != null) {
                    while ( enumVals.hasMoreElements() ) {
                        String aVal = ( String )enumVals.nextElement();
                        String messageRef[] = LDAPDN.explodeDN(aVal,true);
                        encodedString = URLEncoder.encode(messageRef[0]);
                        out.println("message reference: <a href=\"huaco?subject="+
                                encodedString+"\">"+messageRef[0]+"</a><br>");
                    }
                }
            }
        } //end for
    }
    else{out.println("There's no messages");}
}
catch(LDAPException e)
{
```

```java
            out.println("An Error occurred.<Br>"+e.toString());
            System.err.println(e.toString());
        }
        catch(NullPointerException n)
        {
            out.println("An error occured.<BR>"+n.toString());
            n.printStackTrace();
        }
    }

//get the author name
String getAuthorName(String dn)
{
    //      String authorName = null;
    try{
        ldapFunctions ldap = new
                             ldapFunctions(MY_HOST,MY_PORT,MY_SEARCHBASE,dn,pwd);
        String attrs[] = {"cn"};

        ldap.connect();
        Vector v = ldap.search(dn,LDAPConnection.SCOPE_BASE,
                               "objectclass=inetOrgPerson",attrs,false,out);

        if (v != null ){
            /* Loop on entries */
            for (int i=0;i < v.size() ; i++ )
            {
                LDAPEntry myEntry = (LDAPEntry)v.elementAt(i);
                LDAPAttributeSet entryAttrs = myEntry.getAttributeSet();
                /* Get an enumeration of those attribute. */
                Enumeration enumAttrs = entryAttrs.getAttributes();
                /* Loop through the enumeration to get each attribute. */
                while ( enumAttrs.hasMoreElements() ) {
                    LDAPAttribute anAttr = (LDAPAttribute)enumAttrs.nextElement();
                    String attrName = anAttr.getName();
                    Enumeration enumVals = anAttr.getStringValues();
                    if (enumVals != null) {
                        String aVal = ( String )enumVals.nextElement();
                        return aVal;
                    }
                }
            }
        }
        else{out.println("There's no messages");}
    }
    catch(LDAPException e)
    {
        out.println("An Error occurred.<Br>"+e.toString());
        System.err.println(e.toString());
    }
    catch(NullPointerException n)
    {
        out.println("An error occured.<BR>"+n.toString());
        n.printStackTrace();
    }
    return null;
}
```

```
    //print out the currently available topics
    void printTopics()
    {
       try{
          ldapFunctions ldap = new
                               ldapFunctions(MY_HOST,MY_PORT,MY_SEARCHBASE,dn,pwd);
          out.println("Messages are:<BR>");
          String attrs[] = {"subject"};

          if (ldap == null ){out.println("ldap is null!!<bR>");}
          ldap.connect();
          Vector v = ldap.search(MY_SEARCHBASE,LDAPConnection.SCOPE_SUB,
                                 "objectclass=messageClass",attrs,false,out);

          if (v != null ){
             /* Loop on entries */
             for (int i=0;i < v.size() ; i++ )
             {
                LDAPEntry myEntry = (LDAPEntry)v.elementAt(i);
                LDAPAttributeSet entryAttrs = myEntry.getAttributeSet();
                /* Get an enumeration of those attribute. */
                Enumeration enumAttrs = entryAttrs.getAttributes();
                /* Loop through the enumeration to get each attribute. */
                while ( enumAttrs.hasMoreElements() ) {
                   LDAPAttribute anAttr = (LDAPAttribute)enumAttrs.nextElement();

                   String attrName = anAttr.getName();
                   Enumeration enumVals = anAttr.getStringValues();
                   if (enumVals != null) {
                      while ( enumVals.hasMoreElements() ) {
                         String aVal = ( String )enumVals.nextElement();
                         String encodedString = URLEncoder.encode(aVal);
                         out.println("Topic: <a href=\"huaco?subject="+
                                       encodedString+"\">"+aVal+"</a><br>");
                      }
                   }
                }
             }
          }
          else{out.println("There's no messages");}
       }
       catch(LDAPException e)
       {
          out.println("An Error occurred.<Br>"+e.toString());
          System.err.println(e.toString());
       }
       catch(NullPointerException n)
       {
          out.println("An error occured.<BR>"+n.toString());
          n.printStackTrace();
       }
    }

    /** This method checks to see if the user is in the LDAP database
            */
    protected boolean allowedUser(String auth) throws IOException
    {
       boolean status =false;
```

```
      try {
         if (auth == null ) return false; // no auth
         if (!auth.toUpperCase().startsWith("BASIC "))
         {
            return false; //only do BASIC
         }

         // Get encoded user and password, comes after BASIC
         String userpassEncoded = auth.substring(6);

         // Decode it, using any base 64 decoder
         sun.misc.BASE64Decoder dec = new sun.misc.BASE64Decoder();
         String userpassDecoded = new String(dec.decodeBuffer(userpassEncoded));
         StringTokenizer st = new StringTokenizer(userpassDecoded,":");
         String uid = st.nextToken();
         pwd = st.nextToken();

         String MY_FILTER = "uid=" + uid;
         ld.connect( MY_HOST, MY_PORT );
         LDAPSearchConstraints origOptions = ld.getSearchConstraints();
         LDAPSearchConstraints myOptions =
                                 (LDAPSearchConstraints)origOptions.clone();
         myOptions.setMaxResults(0);

         LDAPSearchResults res = ld.search(MY_SEARCHBASE,LDAPConnection.SCOPE_SUB,
                                       MY_FILTER,null,false,myOptions);

         System.out.println("getCount is "+res.getCount());
         // more than 1 user matching filter, fail.
         if (res.getCount() != 1) { return false;}
         if (res.hasMoreElements()) {
            findEntry = res.next();
            dn = findEntry.getDN();
            System.out.println("dn is "+dn);
            //prevent anonymous connections
            if ((dn == "") || (pwd == "")) { return false;}
            //now attempt to bind to server
            ld.authenticate(dn,pwd);

            //if ld.authenticate doesn't throw an exception we passed
            status = true;
         }
      }
   catch(LDAPException e)
   {
      System.out.println(e.toString());
   }
   catch(Exception x)
   {
      x.printStackTrace();
   }
   return status;
}

//reply to a message
 void printReplyForm(String reply)
 {
    out.println("<HTML><HEAD><TITLE>Brazos Reply Form</TITLE></HEAD><BODY>");
    out.println("<h1>Reply to :"+reply+"</h1>");
    out.println("<FORM METHOD=\"POST\" name=\"message\"
```

```
                                    action=\"http://myhost/brazos/huaco\">");
      out.println("<INPUT TYPE=\"hidden\" name=\"messageref\"
                                          value=\""+reply+"\">");
      out.println("<TABLE><TR><TD>Enter a Subject:</TD><TD><INPUT type=\"TEXT\"
                                    name=\"subject\"></TD></TR>");
      out.println("<TR><TD>Enter a message:</TD><TD><TEXTAREA
                              name=\"message\"></TEXTAREA></TD></TR>");
      out.println("<TR><TD><INPUT type=\"Submit\" value=\"Post Message\">
                        </TD></TR></FORM></TABLE></BODY></HTML>");
   }
}
```

The final class we have seen before in Chapter 8, on the Netscape Directory SDK for Java when we built our Java GUI example. It has been modified here to make it a bit easier to deal with LDAP search results in a Java servlet (for example, the results are displayed in HTML):

```
class ldapFunctions
{
    private String ldapServer;
    private int ldapPort;
    private String bindDN;
    private String bindPassword;
    private String ldapOrgBase;
    private String ldapSearchBase;
    private LDAPConnection ld;

    public void connect() throws LDAPException
    {
        ld = null;
        ld = new LDAPConnection ();
        ld.connect(ldapServer,ldapPort);
    }

    public void disconnect() throws LDAPException
    {
        if (ld != null) {
            ld.disconnect();
        }
    }

    public void authenticate(String bindDN, String bindPassword) throws
                                                        LDAPException
    {
        ld.authenticate(bindDN,bindPassword);
    }

    public Vector search(String base,int scope,String filter,String attrs[],
                         boolean attrsOnly,PrintWriter out) throws LDAPException
    {
        /* out.println("I'm in search 1<BR> ");
        out.println("base is"+base);
        out.println("<BR> scope is "+scope);
        out.println("<br> filter is "+filter);
        out.println("<BR> attrs is ");
        for ( int x =0;x<attrs.length;x++ )
        {
            out.println("<BR> attrs["+x+"] is "+attrs[x]);
        }
        out.println("<BR> attrsOnly is "+attrsOnly);*/
```

```
        Vector v = new Vector();
        if (ld == null ) {out.println("ld is null");}
        LDAPSearchResults results = ld.search(base,scope,filter,attrs,attrsOnly);
        //out.println("got results in search 1<BR>");
        if(results != null){
            while (results.hasMoreElements()){
                System.out.println("results next element");
                v.addElement((LDAPEntry) results.next());
                System.out.println("past addElement()");
            }
            return v;
        }
        else {return null;}
    }

    public Vector search(String base, int scope, String filter, String attrs[],
                boolean attrsOnly, LDAPSearchConstraints cons) throws LDAPException
    {
        try{
            System.out.println("I'm in search 2");
            LDAPSearchResults results = null;
            Vector v = new Vector() ;
            results = ld.search(base,scope,filter,attrs,attrsOnly,cons);
            while (results.hasMoreElements()){
                v.addElement(results.next());
            }
            return v;
        }
        catch(NullPointerException ne)
        {
            return null;
        }
    }

    public Vector lfsearch(LDAPUrl url) throws LDAPException #
    {
        LDAPSearchResults results = null;
        Vector v = new Vector();
        results = ld.search(url);
        while (results.hasMoreElements()){
            v.addElement(results.next());
        }
        return v;
    }

    public Vector search(LDAPUrl url, LDAPSearchConstraints cons) throws
                                                        LDAPException
    {
        LDAPSearchResults results = null;
        Vector v = new Vector();
        results = ld.search(url,cons);
        while (results.hasMoreElements()){
            v.addElement(results.next());
        }
        return v;
    }

    public void addEntry(LDAPEntry entry) throws LDAPException {
        ld.add(entry);
    }
```

```java
public void removeEntry(String dn) throws LDAPException {
    ld.delete(dn);
}

public void setLdapServer(String ldapServer) {
    this.ldapServer = ldapServer;
}

public String getLdapSearchBase() {
    return ldapSearchBase;
}

public void setBindDN(String bindDN) {
    this.bindDN = bindDN;
}

public String getBindPassword() {
    return bindPassword;
}

public void setBindPassword(String bindPassword) {
    this.bindPassword = bindPassword;
}

public String getBindDN() {
    return bindDN;
}

public void setLdapSearchBase(String ldapSearchBase) {
    this.ldapSearchBase = ldapSearchBase;
}

public String getLdapOrgBase() {
    return ldapOrgBase;
}

public void setLdapPort(int ldapPort) {
    this.ldapPort = ldapPort;
}

public int getLdapPort() {
    return ldapPort;
}

public void setLdapOrgBase(String ldapOrgBase) {
    this.ldapOrgBase = ldapOrgBase;
}

public String getLdapServer() {
    return ldapServer;
}

public ldapFunctions() {
}

public  ldapFunctions(String ldapServer, int ldapPort, String ldapOrgBase)
{
    this.ldapServer = ldapServer;
    this.ldapPort = ldapPort;
    this.ldapOrgBase = ldapOrgBase;
}
```

```
    public ldapFunctions(String ldapServer, int ldapPort,String ldapOrgBase,
                                         String bindDN,String bindPassword)
    {
      this.ldapServer = ldapServer;
      this.ldapPort = ldapPort;
      this.ldapOrgBase = ldapOrgBase;
      this.bindDN = bindDN;
      this.bindPassword = bindPassword;
    }
}
```

Index

Index

Index

Index

Index